THE ENCYCLOPEDIA
OF FALCONRY

THE ENCYCLOPEDIA OF FALCONRY

ADRIAN WALKER

Lanham and New York

THE DERRYDALE PRESS

Published in the United States of America
by The Derrydale Press
4720 Boston Way, Lanham, Maryland 20706

Distributed by NATIONAL BOOK NETWORK, INC.

ISBN 1-56416-174-9
Copyright © 1999 Adrian Walker
First Derrydale printing 1999

∞™ The paper used in this publication meets the minimum requirements of American National Standard for Information Sciences—Permanence of Paper for Printed Library Materials, ANSI/NISO Z39.48–1992.
Manufactured in Great Britain

Acknowledgements

Acknowledgements are due to the modern writers who either have granted permission for their words to be quoted in *The Encyclopedia of Falconry* or have provided invaluable reference by the very fact that their own books have been published. Also, grateful thanks to falconers, authors, scholars and others from home and abroad who were willing to discuss falconry and related matters with me.

I would like to express my appreciation to photographer Ken Taylor for the efforts he has made on the book's behalf. I am grateful to Andy Reeve for allowing the hawks in his care to be photographed, and to Sian Goff for setting up shots. I am indebted to Beryl and Ken Yull for allowing me to use photographs they took of some of the hawks I have flown over the years. I was glad to be allowed by the Zoological Society of London to use some of Michael Lyster's photographs; thanks to them and to Michael for his personal help. Further thanks are due to: Whipsnade Wild Animal Park for permission to show Michael Rickett's picture of the steppe eagle and myself (back flap); Faris Al-Timimi for giving me language guidance in connection with falconry in the Middle East and for allowing me to reproduce his photographs; Roger Upton for granting permission to quote text from one of his books and reproduce the picture of a hawk van. The portrait of the 4th Earl of Bedford as a boy is reproduced by kind permission of the Marquess of Tavistock and the Trustees of the Bedford Estate. The photograph of James VI's 'hawking set' is reproduced courtesy of The Burrell Collection, Glasgow. The hawking scene used for the endpapers is taken from *Book of British Birds* (© Reader's Digest Assoc. Ltd, 1976).

Definitions, derivations and explanations from the *Oxford English Dictionary*, 2nd edition, 1989, are reprinted by permission of Oxford University Press. I have also used, with the Publisher's knowledge, some extracts from older written works (not necessarily on falconry) which I found in the *OED*. Copyright material from *English Hawking and Hunting in The Boke of St. Albans* by Rachel Hands, 1975, is reprinted by permission of Oxford University Press. Words and definitions from *Revised Medieval Latin Word-List from British and Irish Sources* (R. E. Latham, M.A.) are reprinted by permission of The British Academy. Acknowledgement to HarperCollins Publishers for granting permission for the use of words from *The Falcons of the World* by Tom J. Cade, and to A. & C. Black (Publishers) Ltd for permission to quote extracts from *A Manual of Falconry* by M. H. Woodford. Acknowledgement for help and ideas and thanks for permission to use words and images to: Jemima Parry-Jones, MBE; Dr Eirene Williams and Anthony Mavrogordato; Phillip Glasier; Susan M. Thornton, BSc, BVetMed, MRCVS (veterinary consultant); Prof. John E. Cooper, DTVM, FRCPath, FIBiol, FRCVS; Sally Mackenzie; John Cummins; Stanford University Press, California; the British Library; Bedfordshire Libraries (and Ruth Lambert, Library Manager, Dunstable); the British Museum; the Victoria and Albert Museum (and Andrew Spira); the Department of the Environment; the Poetry Society (London); Mr J. S. Lofthouse of Lofthouse Publications, Pontefract (copyright-holder *Falconry* by Gilbert Blaine); my sister Karen Beggs of Kee-Two Wildlife Rehabilitation Centre in British Columbia. In instances where no acknowledgements are given for the use of words or images, reasonable efforts have been made to trace copyright-holders.

My wife, Linda Walker, is owed special thanks for too many things to list.

From Schlegel and de Wulverhorst's Traité de Fauconnerie *(1844–53). A lure with a pair of wings on each side, a hawking bag viewed from front and back, and three views of a hood proper. Bottom left and right: Two views of a rufter hood.*

FOREWORD
Five Hundred Years of Kindly Speech

To take a hawk from the wild, tame her and turn her loose, hungry to hunt, is falconry in essence.

How hunting with hawks began will never be known. An implausible scenario is of one particularly ingenious man, at some moment in the distant past, becoming the originator of falconry in taking a hawk on his fist with the intention of fashioning her into as much a hunting tool as a spear or a trap. However it is conceivable that an elementary notion of falconry was born when Man began to observe the behaviour of wild birds of prey and took to robbing them when they killed, and that the transition from piracy to falconry involved much trial and error over a considerable span of time.

Among further uncertainties is when and where falconry originated. There is some agreement that the *organized* hunting of quarry with birds of prey was first developed among nomadic herdsmen in Central Asia and could date back four thousand years. Drifting slowly but resolutely from the East, falconry reached Britain in the 6th or 7th century.

While the views and experience of falconers and author-falconers from outside Britain have been considered in the compilation of this book, the focus is on the English pursuit, in particular the specialized language used in falconry between the late Middle Ages and the present day. At the dawn of printing in England, that language is already relatively ancient; out of a melting-pot of foreign and home influences, the in-house names for the hawks, the tools, the concepts and methods have acquired some stability of meaning. Were they wholly settled and had the English language behaved itself for the next five centuries, *The Encyclopedia of Falconry* might have taken the form of a simpler word-list.

As far as the printed word is concerned, the launch point for this compilation is the earliest printed English-language hawking treatise, which is arguably among the least useful to the latter-day practising or would-be falconer. It appeared in 1486 (a mere decade after the first book came off William Caxton's press at Westminster) as part of *The Boke of St Albans*, and is attributed to one Dame Juliana Berners (or, among other forms, Juliana Barnes). This mysterious lady, apparently

'In so moch that gentill men and honest persones have greete delite in haukyng...'. The first page of text from the hawking section of The Boke of St Albans, 1486.

a prioress, produced a work which in the greater part relies for its authority on earlier manuscripts. Despite its limited practical usefulness, it brings its own beguiling aura to the present century and offers, through a fog of time, tantalizing glimpses of an even more remote era in British falconry. Although clearly influential during the ensuing centuries, it is not a complete working treatise, and it assumes (as numerous subsequent treatises do) that the reader already has some knowledge of the subject. It is often anomalous and ambiguous, yet for the purposes of terminological research (therefore for the present book) it has significance as a repository for some of the 'kindly speech' of falconry at that time.

Some later English writers on hawking matters put not only their erudition into their writings, but their souls as well. Short-winged hawk specialist Edmund Bert, above all others, is the man with whom many contemporary falconers would love to share a day's hawking. It is clear from his *An Approved Treatise of Hawkes and Hawking* (1619) that Bert had humour, a peculiar mixture of humility and dogmatism, and barrow-loads of common sense. He also had a kind of fondness for the hawks he trained and flew, which is not entirely characteristic in a time of witchcrafty doctoring and an insensitivity to the suffering of animals. I have a feeling that he would have disapproved of a certain unsubtle corrective measure for a hawk which took the wrong quarry: 'Take the pray from hir angerly', says 16th century writer George Turbervile, 'and beat hir therewith about the head'. Bert advocates a gentler way of correcting a goshawk which has taken a hen at a nearby house. The member of the hawking party who is closest to the incident is to pick up both hawk and hen, hurry to the nearest pond, and 'thereinto over head and taile wash them both together three or foure times', which I trust does not mean duck them. Once detached from her illicit quarry, the hawk is encouraged to forget about the episode by being given other things to do, for which she is rewarded. A severe but reasoned way of bringing to perfection 'a Hawke that will royle and seeke for Poultry'.

Bert is a man who would join a modern hawking party and, with no more than a short pause for adjustments and a few polite words for whoever was in charge of the field, stride out into an alien countryside in the expectation of a really good time. He would be as fascinated with us and our methods as we are with him and his.

Closer to our own time is E.B. Michell. He was responsible for the treatise *The Art and Practice of Hawking*, published in 1900. The work is entertaining, colourful and informative, with (it is generally accepted) an unrivalled chapter on lark-hawking. This somewhat flamboyant writer can be forgiven for his lapses into Latin (a custom which was becoming a trifle passé in his day) and his tendency to anthropomorphize. While I can easily tolerate his word-smithery in 'Hack hawks, when taken up, should be as round as balls and as bumptious as undergraduates', I experience more than a touch of biliousness while reading 'They [old rooks] remember very well and with a fluttering heart the appearance of the little squadron of horsemen which once brought with them Lady Long-wing, who made such a dreadful example of poor papa Caw-Caw'. The man is perfectly capable of imagery which is simple but vivid and suitable for adults: take as an example 'The down-wind stoop of a peregrine is terrible'.

Michell comes across as a man determined not only to educate the novice but also to leave his mark upon the language of falconry. It is difficult to prove conclusively, but it seems to me that he coined quite a few terms which have at least attempted to elbow their way into favour.

Of all English dissertations on training the sparrowhawk, the late Jack Mavrogordato's *A Hawk for the Bush* is the most practical and complete. This modern classic, first published in 1960 and revised about a decade later, is a realistic, wise, no-nonsense treatise on how to bring that fragile little accipiter to efficiency as a hunter. In compiling his work, this writer drew on decades of experience as an austringer – or sperviter, as one who kept and flew sparrowhawks once was known. Additionally, he made the book refreshingly readable. His pages are not lacking in lighter, witty moments, which give remission from the forthright and serious nature of the book as a whole. To familiarize the raptorial trainee with humans of every description, this stratagem is suggested: '... If your household is deficient in well-trained women and children there is quite a lot to be said for the falconer getting himself up in "drag", and wearing skirts and fancy hats, instead of the dull old clothes with which the hawk is so familiar'. Of course he did not mean this ruse to be taken too literally and employed suddenly, which might well shake the delicate equilibrium of the hawk and scare her witless.

Contrasting sharply with the many worthy publications is a wealth of material which has dubious instructional value, but for the purposes of terminological research may have its uses. There are, for example, those skimpy beginner's guides, which loiter somewhere between angling and yachting in compilations, so fashionable in the 19th and early 20th centuries, of outdoor pursuits or rural sports; these are practically useless to the falconer, and dangerous to the hawk that is trained from their pages, but sometimes they unexpectedly

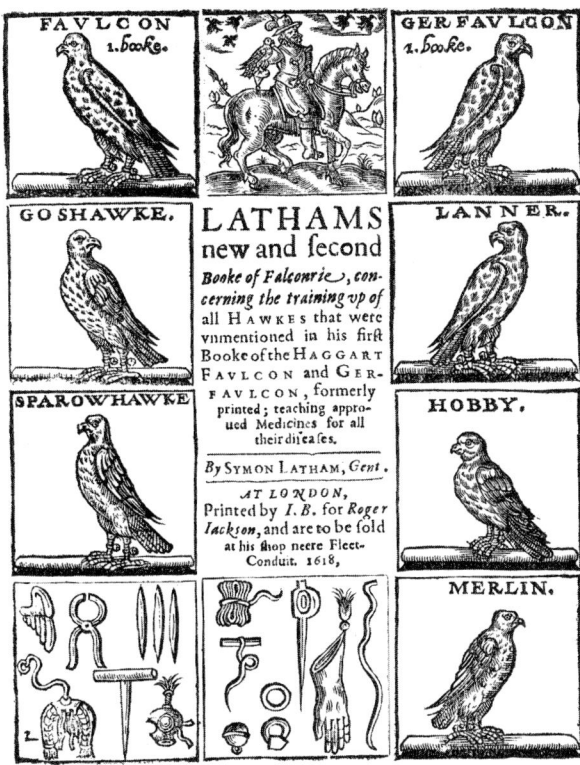

A preliminary page from Symon Latham's second treatise (1618).

yield helpful scraps of information to those of us who are interested in language. There are also fuller treatises about which the same observations might be made. One such is the famously plagiaristic hawking section of Richard Blome's *The Gentleman's Recreation* (1686), which is a good read despite its many shortcomings. After some years' work, Blome and certain advisers amassed, rehashed, 'improved' and added to information found in the earlier classic English hawking treatises. They ended up with an oddly uncoordinated product, which is perhaps unsurprising as Blome, the ultimate editor, was himself not a falconer. Nonetheless, the words of this slightly naughty layman do (and should) appear in *The Encyclopedia*.

It will be obvious to readers of this book that I have had difficulties with certain definitions and concepts; after all, one is sometimes faced with a bunch of explanations, only one (perhaps none) of which fully agrees with one's own understanding. I have spent sleepless nights wondering if I have on some occasion made an interpretation, or offered an opinion, which is dreadfully wrong. I was reassured (and slept better) when I discovered that confusion is not new. Perversely, I found it encouraging to read Symon Latham, in the early 17th century, lightly taking issue with his predecessor George Turbervile about the relative merits of the falcon gentle and the haggard peregrine, and precisely what factors define them. On the second matter, the musings of these grandees are considered in *The Encyclopedia*.

Take, then, the tabur styke: was it a kind of lure, or does a re-examination of a passage in a 15th century text cast doubt on that long-held belief? And does a tyrrit swivel, or is it a simple metal ring? One would think that defining the simply named 'lines' mentioned by the old authors would present few problems; yet I am not the first to have tied myself in knots in an attempt to discover exactly what form it (or, one could be forgiven for thinking, they) took. Other troublesome questions are tackled and investigated, and evidence is set down; but, as a careful reporter might, I have on more than one occasion left it to a knowledgeable readership to come to its own conclusions.

It seems that the idiomatic confusion that exists in the English language of falconry has come about chiefly in two ways, each a relative of the other. One is in the misinterpretation of an antecedent text whose archaic phraseology is a distraction, or whose unfamiliar type or script is easily misread. The second is in the making of a snap decision on the complete meaning of a term or phrase on a page without scrupulous consideration of the passage or chapter which embraces it. It is not unexpected to find that when a misunderstood gleaning is taken up, personalized and bequeathed to later generations to fiddle with, there comes an accumulative distortion of meaning, sense, or slant.

An example of how without due care a mistake might be made (or the point missed) is in the phrase 'funking on the bank', to be found in E.B. Michell's respected century-old treatise. It has been taken by at least one later writer as idiomatically correct when applied to a hawk which jumps indecisively on and off the side of her bath and runs round it before committing herself to the water. In fact, Michell is saying that hawks can behave like schoolboys cavorting at the waterside before finally jumping in. On reflection, though it is not the case here, there are plenty of instances where a misunderstanding has sneaked into a language and become a permanent resident.

In reading and attempting to digest any of the numerous antiquarian English-language hawking treatises, it is pardonable to pay the least attention to passages which contain obviously superannuated information. After all, nowadays one would not wish to get one's hawk drunk on strong wine in the course of an immemorial treatment for a digestive disorder, even if the recommended soft cushion would make her stupor comfortable; nor would one think of trying to obtain adder's blood to help heal her broken beak. Nor is there any point in considering the optional methods of stitching up her eyelids, known as seeling. No shame, then, in shuddering and hastily passing on. Yet every aspect of the art, every procedure in it, has some significance, and every written word has some weight; so for the present work, millions of words have been weighed, and this has yielded a harvest of some 1500 names, terms and idioms directly or indirectly associated with falconry through a half-millennium. Taken together, I believe they offer a unique, often oblique look at the falconer's and austringer's art.

Hitherto, James Edmund Harting's glossaries of terms appended to his transcript of the anonymous 16th century manuscript *A Perfect Booke for the Kepinge of Sparhawkes or Goshawkes* (1886) and his *Bibliotheca Accipitraria* (1891) have been acknowledged as the most useful and broadly correct and have been used not infrequently by authors of later works as a basis for their own glossaries. Presumptuously (especially considering I have not always agreed with his views and explanations), I feel that this revered gentleman would have approved of the present much more exhaustive collection, which appears to be the first attempt to compile a complete list of English terms used formerly and currently to particularize the intricacies of the gentle art of falconry. But development of the subject continues as our grasp of the old idioms improves and the language used in our own time adapts for the future. To further this, I invite readers to submit new entries for inclusion in any revised edition of *The Encyclopedia of Falconry*. Equally welcome will be suggestions for adjustments or corrections to entries found in the present book; it would not surprise me to find that there are differing views about (for example) the currency or obsoleteness of certain terms. I am confident that there will be a positive response to this invitation.

Contents

Introduction	xv
Abbreviations Used in the Encyclopedia	xvi
THE ENCYCLOPEDIA	1
Appendix: Diseases and Ailments	142
Source List and Further Reading	150

Illustration plate sections	Between pages
1 Plate numbers 1 to 23	16–17
2 Plate numbers 24 to 43	48–49
3 Plate numbers 44 to 59	80–81
4 Plate numbers 60 to 79	112–113

Hardly a motion could be made by the hawk, hardly a feather shaken, but a special term was applied.

> The Hon. Gerald Lascelles, *Falconry* (from *Coursing and Falconry*), 1892.

INTRODUCTION
Outline

The *Encyclopedia of Falconry* lists names, terms and idioms which are peculiar to falconry, also lay terms which have been adopted or adapted by falconers, and descriptions of concepts and practices which are directly connected to or have some connection with falconry. Added are a small number of entries which for the moment are unverified as authentic to falconry.

SPELLING

Wherever possible, quotations from written works have been taken from original texts or facsimile reprints. In these cases, any spelling and punctuation inconsistencies have been left unaltered; but in the earlier material, the long 's' has been replaced by the modern form and 'u/v' and 'i/j' have been unified and modernized to make the words gentler on the reader's eye.

HEADINGS

Headings and sub-headings in bold and sub-headings in plain signify a rough grading of occurrence in the research texts, i.e. bold most frequently met with, plain less so. An example is **HAWK, Passage**; PASSAGE-HAWK; PASSAGEHAWK; **PASSAGER**.

SOURCES AND DATES

A number in superscript with a source (Brit.–Ir.[48]), with a date (1611[23]), or after a section of text[81], refers to an entry in Source List and Further Reading. Where two dates appear, e.g. 1686 [1929], the second is that of the edition used in the compilation of this book, the first that of the original edition. Where the date of an early occurrence of a term is known, it will appear, e.g. SILE (1398).

NAMES AND GENDER

The names hawk and falcon can be problematical. It is suggested that the reader who is uncertain about defininitions in the context of falconry begins by consulting **HAWK** 1 (n.) and following entries, and **FALCON** 1 (n.) and next entry.

In the English-speaking West, it is customary when speaking generally (that is, when the sex is not a consideration) to refer to a falconer's hawk as 'she' rather than 'it'. This tradition is observed throughout *The Encyclopedia*, except where a quoted author in a verbatim passage chooses otherwise. For clarity only, therefore, the falconer or austringer is 'he', but should of course be read as 'he or she'.

LIMITATIONS

There has been no attempt to give word profiles of all the birds of prey used in falconry, past or present. Their full natural histories are outside the scope of this book; in consequence, profiles are limited to data which have some bearing on their adaptability to be used as falconers' birds, such as wild habitat, prey preferences and hunting techniques. As to the training and equipping of hawks, *The Encyclopedia* does not endeavour to be instructional; therefore descriptions of practices are purposely restricted in complexity.

Falconer, peregrine and pointer. (E.&D. Hosking; FLPA, Images of Nature).

Abbreviations Used in the Encyclopedia

adapt. = adaptation of
adj. = adjective, adjectival.
adopt. = adoption of, adopted from.
Brit.–Ir. = British-Irish, i.e. from British or Irish source.
C. = century.
c. = circa.
cf. = confer (compare).
chap.hdg = chapter heading.
fl. = flourished.
FR = recommended further reading. A superscript number (e.g. FR[65]) refers to an entry in Source List and Further Reading.
ft. = footnote.
gl. = glossary.
ibid. = from the same book or passage.
inf. = collected informally (e.g. from the spoken word).
in transl. = in translation (to English).
lay = outside falconry.
MS, MSS = manuscript, manuscripts.
n., ns = noun, nouns.
N.Am. = North America.
obs. = obsolete, or thought to be so.
occ. = occasional.
OED = The *Oxford English Dictionary*.
qu., qus = quotation, quotations.
sci. = scientific.
unc. = uncommon, in uncommon use.
unv. = unverified as authentic to falconry.
vb, vbs = verb, verbs.

A

ABATE (obs.) (From Old French *batre* = to beat, or *à* + *batre*.) Of a hawk, to make a vain attempt to fly from the fist or the perch while restrained; an obsolete form of BATE (vb).

'If that she abate, let her flee . . .' – c.1430[10].

ACCIPITER (Latin = bird of prey.) The genus which contains (among others) the short-winged hawks of traditional falconry. Typically, they inhabit forests and woodland. There are some 50 species world-wide[13], from thrush-sized sparrowhawks to the Northern European Goshawk, a female weighing up to, sometimes in excess of, 1500 grams. They might roughly be divided into two groups. Broadly, those in the sparrowhawk group are the smaller, having long legs of fragile appearance, and prey predominantly on birds, while those in the goshawk group have shorter, less slender legs, many species taking both bird and mammal prey. The females in both groups are markedly, sometimes considerably, larger than the males. The distinctive configuration of short but broad wings, somewhat rounded at the tips, and a long tail are adaptations for manoeuvrable flight through obstructed hunting-grounds.

The irides of the eye vary considerably in colour from species to species, though they tend to be pale. In the goshawk (*Accipiter gentilis*), the eye colour darkens from greyish or amber in immature birds to a fiery orange-yellow or red in maturity. The colour once had significance to falconers, especially in the East and Far East; a particular shade, it was thought, indicated certain traits or potential in a hawk.

The two hawks from this genus flown in traditional British falconry are the goshawk (*A.gentilis*) and the sparrowhawk (*A.nisus*). In recent times, some other species of short-winged hawks have been tried by Western austringers, and a few have been regularly flown.

ACCIPITER; plural **ACCIPITERS** A term sometimes used by falconers today and by contemporary ornithologists for a hawk of the genus of the same name. Short-winged hawk is the falconer's traditional term.

ACCIPITRARY (rare, unv., obs.) A keeper of hawks, a falconer, or one who catches hawks. More in TRAPS AND TRAPPING.

ACCIPITRIDAE The family which contains (among others) the genera *Accipiter*, *Buteo*, *Parabuteo*, *Aquila*, *Spizaetus* and *Hieraaetus*, from which birds for falconry have been and are drawn.

AERIE (n.); **AERY** Forms of EYRIE.

AERIE (vb, obs.) Of a hawk, to build an EYRIE.

AGES OF HAWKS See formulæ in HAWK, White.

AIRE (n. and vb, obs.) Old form of eyrie or aerie, the nest of a bird of prey. In OED, the verb aire is 'To build an aerie, to breed as a falcon'.

ALA SPURIA The ALULA. Also see BASTARD-WING.

ALPHANET (unc.) A pale North African race of the lanner falcon, taken to be *Falco biarmicus erlangeri*. Obsolete names which may indicate the same bird are Sahara lanner, Tunisian lanner, Tunician, and Punycian falcon (last three 1575[81]). Michell (1900[59]) has the unidentified Punic falcon (with the obsolete scientific name *Falco punicus*) as resembling the peregrine, but smaller.

ALULA (sci.); plural **ALULÆ** (Latin, diminutive of *ala* = wing.) The rudimentary thumb in birds, the term sometimes used by contemporary falconers. An alternative scientific (Latin) name, rarely if ever used by falconers, is *ala spuria*, which literally means false wing. Also see BASTARD-WING.

AMERICAN SAKER Uncommon and obsolete name for the prairie falcon; see FALCON, Prairie.

ANKLETS See AYLMERI under JESSES.

AQUILA (Latin = eagle.) The genus which contains the eagles sometimes referred to as true eagles; the golden eagle (*Aquila chrysaetos*) is the species which historically has been most widely trained as a falconer's bird. Although used formerly and currently only to a limited extent in Western falconry, there has been a long tradition of hunting medium-sized and larger ground-quarry with golden eagles in parts of Central Asia.

ARM (obs.) The leg of a hawk, including the tarsus which correctly is part of the FOOT.

ARM A BIRD (obs.) To put JESSES and a BELL or bells onto a hawk.

ARM-BRACE A support for the arm while carrying such as a large eagle on the fist; the simplest form is a stick pushed through the belt and used as a lever to share the load between the fist and the free hand. A rest and arm-sling have been used by Oriental falconers to help bear the weight of a heavy bird. Also see CRUTCH.

ASBORNO A famous name in hawk bell manufacture. See BELL (n.).

ASPERE HAWK; ASPERE-HAWK; ASPARE HAWK Obsolete forms of SPARROWHAWK.

AUSTRINGER (Adopt. Old French *austruchier*, *ostruchier*. Old French *hostur*, *ostour* = the goshawk; Modern French *autour*. Also spelt OSTRINGER, earlier OSTREGIER, OSTREGER, OSTRAGER, others; all obs.) One who keeps, trains and hunts with short-winged hawks, or (formerly) one who keeps and flies goshawks specifically:

> 'Now be cause I speke of Ostregeris: ye shall understonde that thay be calde Ostregeris that kepe Goshawkys. or Tercellis. and tho that kepe Sperhawkys and muskettys ben called Sperviteris. and keperis of all other hawkys ben callidde Faukeneris.' – 1486[5].

Here, 'Goshawkys. or Tercellis.' means female or tiercel (male) goshawks. See SPERVITER. Most commonly today, the term falconer is applied to one who keeps, trains and flies any long-, short- or broad-winged hawk, or eagle, although austringer survives (in lesser use) as one who keeps and hunts with short-winged or sometimes broad-winged hawks.

AYERYE See c.1520 qu. in EYRIE.

AYLMER, Major Guy The deviser of an alternative to traditional JESSES.

AYLMERI Under JESSES.

AYLMERI, 'False' Under JESSES.

AYRE Obsolete form of EYRIE.

AYRER See EYERER.

B

BACK Under DOGS IN HAWKING.

BAG The total number of quarry taken in a given period.

BAG, Hawking; FALCONER'S BAG; FALCONER (obs.) (Also FALCONERE, FAULKNER; both obs.) A multi-pocketed game and equipment bag, referred to in old texts as bag, pouch or sometimes purse. Western European art of the Middle Ages and later seems only to show in detail (in still lifes and portraits) bags used by the privileged classes. These are often roughly trapezoid in outline, of high quality, and sometimes richly decorated. A c.1670 example (for reference, not on display) in the Victorian and Albert Museum, London, is leather with silk embroidery. Today, the hawking bag is usually workmanlike and made of leather, or canvas, or sometimes waterproof materials such as polyester. Now, as formerly, it is hung at waist level on a shoulder-strap or from a belt loop. It is worn on the right side by right-handed falconers (the shoulder-strap over the left shoulder), as it is customary in the West to have the hawk on the left fist. It has compartments or pockets at front and back and is hung on a swivel so that it can be turned, enabling either side to be reached quickly.

A mid-19th century French language treatise[74] notes that one pocket of the bag is designed to hold a meat box; but according to Salvin & Brodrick (1855[73]), to the falconer's equipment

> '... should be added a small semicircular tin box or pouch for carrying the meat in for feeding the Hawks, which is strapped round the waist ...'.

Similarly, in traditional Japanese falconry, a small wooden food box (*egôshi*) is attached to the falconer's belt; the falconer taps it to call his hawk

A hawking bag, said to be Elizabethan, on a frame of silver-gilt and enamel.

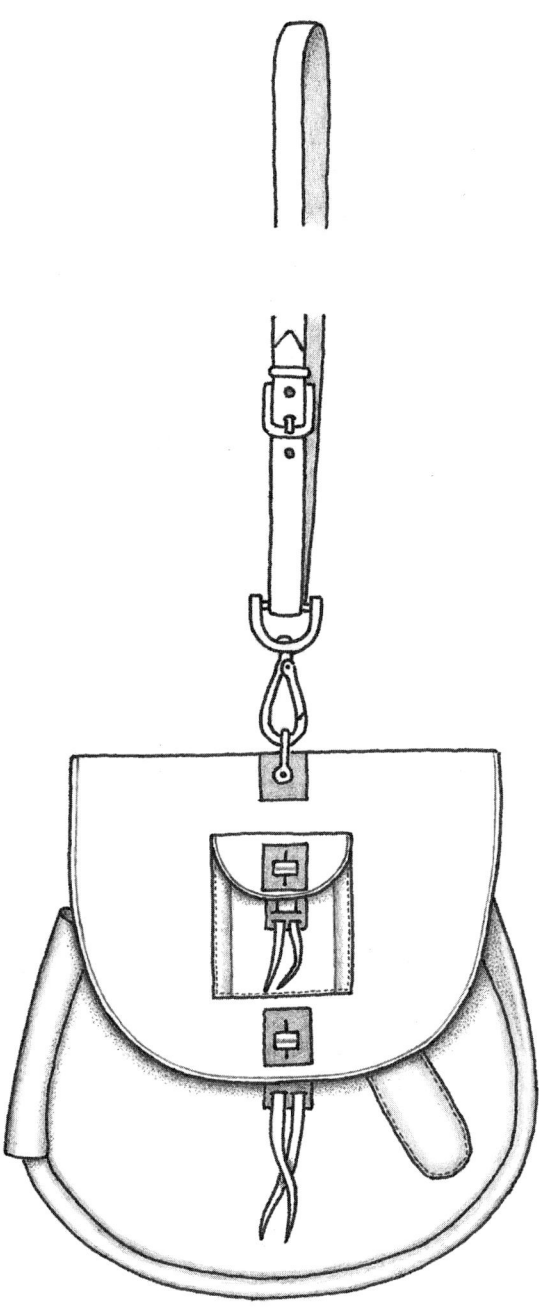

A pattern of modern hawking bag incorporating pockets front and back for game, hawk meat, lure and small items of furniture. The swivel between bag and shoulder-strap allows the bag to be turned.

which has learned to associate the sound with food[45]. In Western falconry, tapping the fist (or to 'knok the fyste' – c.1575[38]) with the free hand when calling a hawk is sometimes used to bring about the same result. Boxes for meat are no longer employed. Most modern bags have a waterproof meat pocket to prevent leakage of blood and meat juices; this is usually removable for cleaning.

In the 13th century, Emperor Frederick[35] describes a large meat pouch carried by a mounted falconer; it was hung from the cantle (at the rearward end of the saddle) and contained such as a live pigeon or chicken on which to feed a hawk if needed. The term lure-bag ([?]recent) may occasionally equate to hawking bag; otherwise it describes a bag or pouch (worn at the waist) of sufficient size to carry only the lure.

BAG, Falconer's   See preceding entry.

BAGGED QUARRY; BAGGED GAME See QUARRY, Bagged.

BAIT   Obsolete spelling of BATE.

BAL-CHATRI   Under TRAPS AND TRAPPING.

BANDS   Alternative to BARS.

BARAK   Under TRAPS AND TRAPPING.

BARBARY FALCON; BARBERIE FALCON See FALCON, Barbary.

BARE FACED (1615[49], obs.) (Also BARE-FACED (1615[49], obs.), BARE-FACED and BARE-

FASTE (both 1619[6], obs.).) Of a hawk, not wearing a hood. Alternatively, sometimes, bare-headed or bareheaded (both obsolete). Today, unhooded is correct. More in HOODS AND HOODING.

BARE-HEADED; BAREHEADED Alternatives to BARE FACED.

BARRED; BARRING See next entry.

BARS; BANDS The breast feathers of, for example, the adult European goshawk are said to be barred or to have bars or barring, replacing the vertical drop-like streaks of the immature bird. The darker transverse stripes on the tails of some hawks are referred to as bars or (perhaps most commonly today) bands. Berners[5], writing on short-winged hawks in the 15th century, says:

> 'And ther gooth blacke barris overwarde [across] the tayle. and thos same barris shall telle yow when she is full summed. or full fermyd.'

This passage suggests that the dark bands be counted as a crude method of determining whether a new feather is full-grown. More in ENTER-PENNED; also see FULL-SUMMED.

BASE GAME See GAME, Base.

BASTARD-WING The group of feathers at a bird's WRIST, supported by a small structure (the ALULA) analogous to the pollex or inner digit of the fore limb in mammals, and in Man the thumb. Darwin (1859[27]) says:

> 'The "bastard-wing" may safely be considered as a rudimentary digit.'

The bastard-wing has aerodynamic implications for flight.

BATE (vb) (From Old French *batre* = to beat. Obs. spellings: BATTE (1615), BAIT. Obs. form: ABATE.) Of a hawk when fearful, startled, upset, or impatient to be off: to attempt to fly from the fist or the perch while restrained.

> '*Batting*, or to batte is when a Hawk fluttereth with her wings either from the pearch or the mans fist, stryving as it were to flie away, or get liberty.' – 1615 gl.[49]

This writer also uses the extant spelling. To bate off is correct ('she bated off twenty times in ten minutes' – 1900[59]; here, the fist is inferred). She might also bate off the fist, bate off the perch, or BATE AT, towards, or away from something. A particular hawk might be said to be prone to bating. Bating may be used adjectivally in 'a bating hawk'; a bater is a hawk which bates often or excessively. See plate 47.

BATE (n.) The action of a hawk in bating: a bate, more than one bate, 'many bates' (1619[6]).

BATE AT Of a hawk, to attempt to fly at (quarry, lure, food, or the falconer's fist) while restrained by her leash. She might also bate towards something (for example daylight or an open door while tethered on her perch in the mews). To bate away from is to attempt to escape from (something she is afraid of) while restrained.

BATE AWAY FROM See preceding entry.

BATE OFF See BATE (vb).

BATER A hawk which bates often or excessively. See BATE (vb).

BATE TOWARDS See BATE AT.

BATH A wide shallow portable receptacle is used for hawks, today often custom-made in fibreglass. Formerly, materials such as iron, earthenware or wood were usual. Also see qu. in FEATHER, Pinched.

BATHING

> '*Bathing* is when you set your Hawke to the water, to wash or bath her selfe, either abroad or in the house.' – 1615 gl.[49]

A trained hawk will usually bathe regularly if water is offered to her. She takes her bath while loose in mews or pen, or from her perch in the weathering ground. Bathing is essential in helping her keep her feathers in good condition and is said to help broadcast OIL throughout her plumage; see PREEN GLAND. There are numerous reports of trained hawks which, if not offered a bath in the morning before being taken to the field, will seek a puddle or shallow stream to bathe in soon after they are turned loose. Bert (1619[6]) writes of taking his hawk to a brook two or three days after she had been peppered, and allowing her to bathe while restrained by her leash. See PEPPER (Appendix).

BATTE Obsolete spelling of BATE (vb).

BATTING Obsolete spelling of bating; see BATE (vb).

BAWREL (obs.); **BAWRET** (obs.) An unidentified kind of hawk, or the female and male respectively of an unidentified hawk. Blome (1686 [1929][9]), who is not infrequently unreliable, notes of the bawrel:

'This *Hawk* for Largeness and Shape, is somewhat like the *Lanner*, but hath a longer *Body* and *Sails**. She is generally a fast goer aforehead, and a good *Field-Hawk*; and in Enclosures will kill a *Pheasant*, but being a Longwinged *Hawk* is unfit for the *Coverts*.'

*Wings. This information appears to have been read and adapted by the compiler of a later dictionary; the entry reads:

'Bawrel, a kind [of] Hawk, that for Size and Shape, is somewhat like the Lanner, but has a longer Body and Sails.' – 1706[67].

A suggestion is that bawrel may be a corruption of boreal (= northern), therefore perhaps bawrel is GYRFALCON and bawret is jerkin (the male); see annotation to 'Theys haukes belong to an Emproure' under NAMES 3. In Cox (1677[25]), in a list of long-winged hawks (which includes 'The Gerfaulcon and Jerkin') are the phonetically similar bockerel and bockeret; these are also unidentified, as are boccarell and boccaret (1672 – OED).

BAWTERE See annotation to 'Theys haukes belong to an Emproure' under NAMES 3.

BAY-WINGED HAWK Lay name for the Harris' hawk; see HAWK, Harris'.

BEACH (unc., obs.) (Spelt 'beache' (1575[81]).) To give (a hawk) a small amount of food. Example of use, see 1575 qu. in BECHINS.

BEACHING (unc., obs.) A small amount of food. See 1575 qu. in BECHINS.

BEAK; **BEKE** (obs.) Formerly, the upper part of a hawk's beak:

'The Beke of the hawke is the upper parte that is croked [crooked].' – 1486[5].

The phrase 'clap' and 'beak', denoting the lower and upper parts respectively, occasionally occurs in old texts; Stonehenge (1856 gl.[76]) has 'chap' and 'beak'. The beaks of hawks are of a shape evolved for tearing the flesh of prey. The notching on each cutting edge (tomium) of the upper part in falcons is known as a TOOTH, notch or, formerly, nook. This configuration is thought to provide the means for breaking the spinal cord of prey. In other hawks, in the absence of a tooth, a 'lobe' or downward curving cutting edge is sometimes present; this is known as a festoon. More in TOOTH.

BEAK-OPENING See HOODS AND HOODING.

BEAM-FEATHERS; **BEAM FEATHERS** See FEATHERS, Primary.

BEAMS See FEATHERS, Primary.

BEAR FULL GORGE See FULL-GORGED.

BEAT 1 Of quarry, to out-manoeuvre or out-fly a hawk.

BEAT 2 Of the falconer or other members of the hawking party, to walk a tract of land in order to put up quarry. One who beats is sometimes known as a beater; he might use a beating stick to thrash undergrowth.

BEATER A member of the hawking party who walks a tract of land, thrashing undergrowth or other cover or scouring woods, to flush quarry.

BEATING STICK A stick for beating undergrowth to put quarry out to hawks.

BEAVY Obsolete spelling of BEVY.

BECHINS (French *beccades* in '*Donner à tirer*, permettre au faucon de prendre quelques beccades . . .' – 1868[29]. In transl.: 'To give tiring, to allow the hawk to take bechins . . .'. Modern French *becquée* = beakful, titbit, *bec* = beak.) Morsels, beakfuls, titbits of food used to reward a hawk. To give a hawk a few bechins is to allow her to take a few beakfuls of meat. Turbervile (1575[81]) uses the uncommon and obsolete form 'beaching' to mean a small amount of food; his verb 'beache' (unc., obs.) means to give such an amount (to a hawk). He notes:

'If she [sparrowhawk] have nothing above [in her crop], give hir some little beaching, and beache hir oftentimes before companie, hooding and unhooding hir.'

BECK, Fly to the See FLY TO THE VIEW.

BEKE Obsolete spelling of BEAK.

BEKE, Fly to the See FLY TO THE VIEW.

BELL (n.); **HAWK BELL**; **HAWK-BELL**; **HAWK'S BELL** (obs.) The ringing of the bell betrays the whereabouts of a hawk when she is out of sight in the field, perhaps on a kill, or when she is lost. When she is on her perch and the falconer is within earshot, the character of its ringing can indicate if her movements are normal or she is in difficulty. Among the materials used in bell-making have been brass, nickel and silver, also the alloy Monel (or monel). Instead of a swinging tongue or clapper, the bell has inside a loose irregular-shaped piece of glass or metal which rolls and bounces.

A leg-bell is attached to a TARSUS or one to

each tarsus with a small leather strap known as a BEWIT. A tail-bell is secured to the base of one deck (or central tail-) feather (see FEATHERS, Deck) or to the bases of both deck feathers and lies on the upper side of the TRAIN (plate 36). A method of tail-belling recorded in the 13th century by Emperor Frederick[35] is to pierce the [bases or barrels of the] deck feathers and so attach the bell; this writer was opposed to tail-belling as apparently the train was dragged down by the weight of the bell he used. In Mavrogordato's English treatise (1973[58]) on training sparrowhawks, the method of tail-belling is basically the same, using waxed thread and a lightweight bell.

In traditional Japanese falconry, the bell lies on a flat plate of shell or bone which, while acting as a sounding-board, prevents it from falling down between the tail-feathers; a small leather strap is attached to the barrel of each of the deck feathers, led through holes in the plate and fastened to the two loops of the bell[45].

An accepted Western method of attachment is similar, although the bell has a single loop; a leather strap is passed through the loop and two holes in the plate (often now a flat piece of plastic) and the ends glued and bound to the barrels of the deck feathers. There have been (and are) other methods. A tail-bell is generally thought to outlast and ring better than a leg-bell. Added benefits are, when used on falcons, freeing the rather short tarsus of one piece of furniture and, in the case of short-winged hawks, taking advantage of their frequent habit of shaking the tail from side to side when not in flight, which sounds the bell. A neck-bell is worn on a strap round the hawk's neck. This method of belling has chiefly been used in India; it has been tried and employed in the modern pursuit in North America, but has not caught on in Britain. In the East, the bell would sometimes be mounted on the HALSBAND. Berners (1486[5]) recommends that when a hawk is wearing two bells, one should ring a semitone lower than the other to produce a discordant sound. This is said by some to carry well and be less readily confused with wild bird-calls. Falconers are choosy about a bell's ring, as different sounds suit different ears. Certain modern North American bells are highly thought of: Asborno is a famous name. However, there are modern bells made currently in Britain and elsewhere which compete with American bells for excellence. In the 15th century, according to Berners:

> '... For Goshawkes somtyme Bellis of Melen were calde the best. and thay be full goode for thay comunely be sownden with silver and solde ther after. Bot ther be now used of Duchelande bellys: of a towne calde durdright. and thay be passing goode....'.

'Melen' is Milan, famous at that time for exporting high-quality bells for hawks[26]. Hands[37] suggests that the phrase 'sownden with silver and solde ther after' probably means 'soldered with silver, and priced accordingly'. 'Duchelande bellys' is Dutch bells, and 'durdright' is Dordrecht in south-

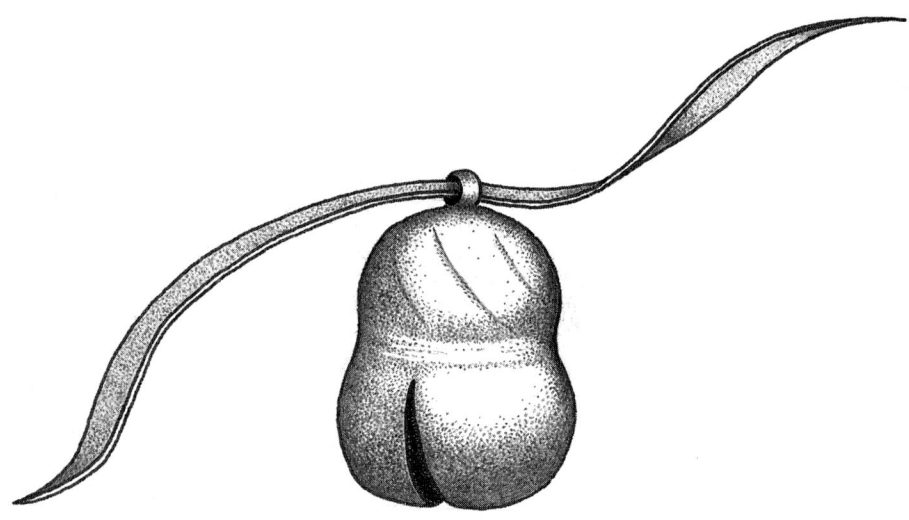

Lahore or Indian bell.

western Netherlands. Dutch bells have seen wide use in the West until recent times. James Harting says:

> 'The Dutch bells, to be obtained of Mr K. Mollen, Valkenswaard, by Eindhoven, Holland, are very good; but the Indian bells are most prized by modern falconers, on account of their superior tone and lightness.' – 1898[40]

Indian (otherwise Lahore, sometimes Pakistani) bells, unlike the spherical Dutch pattern, are elongated and waisted; they have a long history of use in the West.

Turbervile (1575[81]) writes of obsolete 'luring bells', worn by a falcon newly flying loose, stooping well to the LURE, and yet to be entered at quarry:

[Middle English passage from The Boke of St Albans, in blackletter type: 'Of hawkys Bellys.' followed by commentary on hawks' bells.]

'Of hawkys Bellys': comments on hawks' bells from the hawking section of The Boke of St Albans *(1486).*

> 'When your hawke will come, and stoupe to the lewre roundly and without ramagenes, then if she be a haggard, you must put hir on a payre of great lewring bels, and the like shall you do also to a soarehawke. And so much the greater ought your bells to be, by how much more you see your hawke gyddyheaded, or like to rake out at checke. For it can be no hurt to clogge hir w^t great bells at ye first, until hir conditions be knowen & well perceyved.'

The suggestion in this passage is that the hawk (haggard or sore hawk, each wild-caught, and with experience of hunting for herself), should be temporarily hampered by heavy bells until her behaviour and inclinations are known; 'rake out at checke' means fly off and chase quarry the falconer has not chosen for her. Michell (1900[59]) writes:

> 'A merlin which is flying ringing§ larks does not wear bells, for it is impossible to get any which are sufficiently light, and at the same time loud enough to be of any use.'

This is an opinion not universally agreed with. Today, it would be thought irresponsible to fly any hawk without a means of tracking her.

§'Ringing' here refers to the skylark's upward flight.

BELL (vb) To equip (a hawk) with a bell or bells; the procedure is known as belling. To tail-bell a hawk is to attach a single bell to one or both of her central tail-feathers, known as deck feathers or decks; the procedure is known as tail-belling. See preceding entry.

BELL, Neck See BELL (n.).

BELLED; TAIL-BELLED Wearing a bell or bells, or a tail-bell. More in BELL (n.).

BELLING; TAIL-BELLING The procedure of equipping a hawk with a bell or bells, or a tail-bell. More in BELL (n.).

BELLS, Dutch Hawk bells, spherical in shape, with a long history of use in Western falconry. More in BELL (n.).

BELLS, Hack (Also written HACK-BELLS (1898[40]).) Bells worn by a hawk at hack; their ringing betrays her whereabouts. More in HACK BELLS under HACKING.

BELLS, Indian See next entry.

BELLS, Lahore Famous bells for hawks (otherwise called Indian bells, sometimes Pakistani bells) historically made in Lahore. Elongated, waisted and light in weight, they have a long history of use in Western falconry. See BELL (n.).

BELLS, Luring (unc., obs.) Large, heavy bells put on a hawk in the early days of flying her loose. See 1575 qu. in BELL (n.).

BELLS, Pakistani See BELLS, Lahore.

BEME FEATHER OF THE TAIL See FEATHERS, Deck.

BEME FEATHERS OF THE WING See FEATHERS, Primary.

BERKUTE (Other spellings. Russian бéркут = golden eagle.) The golden eagle, taken to be subspecies *Aquila chrysaetos daphanea*, flown at medium and larger ground-quarry (deer and wolves) in Central Asia.

BERRY Variant of burrow; see BURY.

BERY; BEERY Obsolete variants of burrow; see BURY.

BEVY; BEAVY (obs.) A company of quails.
 '*Beavy of Quails*, are a brood of young *Quails*.' – 1677 gl.[25]

BEWET Obsolete spelling of BEWIT.

BEWIT (Apparently diminutive of Old French *beue* = a collar or fetter. Also BEWET (1575[81]), plural 'bewettis' (1486[5]), 'bewets' and 'bewettes' (1575[81]), BUETT (c.1600[63]), others; all obs.) A narrow supple leather strap for attaching a bell to a hawk's TARSUS; the leg-bell is always fitted above the jess (see JESSES). There are two types: one is secured by passing the free ends in a particular order through holes punched in the leather; the second, a button bewit, has at one end a rolled 'knot' known as a BUTTON, and a slit or 'buttonhole' at the other:
 'Bewits, in Falconry, denote pieces of leather, to which a hawk's bells are fastened, and buttoned to his legs.' – 1753[21].

The Harting glossary of 1886 appended to *A Perfect Booke*[38], has:
 'BEWITS . . . thin strips of leather by which the bells are fastened to the legs, and (in the case of a Goshawk) to the tail.'

A traditional way of attaching the bell (in this case of Dutch pattern) to the hawk, with the bewit in a simple loop round the tarsus. (From a late 19th century drawing).

The application of the term bewit to the leather strap used in tail-belling is uncommon, although no alternative appears to exist. In the modern pursuit, a bewit may also be used for attaching a radio transmitter to a hawk's tarsus; more in TELEMETRY.

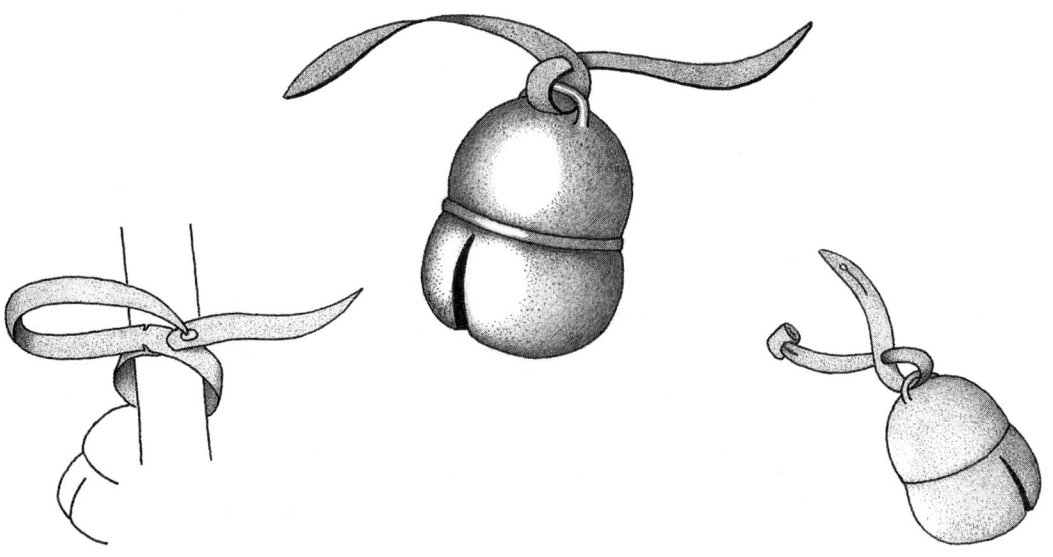

Top: The traditional pattern of bewit, arranged so that the bell's metal loop is kept away from the hawk's tarsus. Lower left: Once knotted on and pulled tight, the free ends are trimmed short. Lower right: A button bewit.

BEWIT, Button A type of BEWIT.

BIND See BIND TO.

BIND THE TAIL; TIE THE TAIL See TAIL, Bind (or Tie) the.

BIND TO Of a hawk in an attack, to grip (quarry) with the feet. As a rule, the short-winged hawks, buteos and eagles take quarry by binding to it the moment they strike it. Falcons may also do so; the larger species, travelling at great speed in a stoop, may first strike the quarry with the hind talons to disable it or knock it down. Turbervile (1575[81]) has 'bind with'; this is relatively uncommon and probably obsolete. Bind may also be used by itself:

'BIND . . . to fasten on the quarry in the air.' – 1891 gl.[39]

'. . . If, after getting above it [quarry], she [falcon] makes two or three stoops at it before binding, what better?' – 19th century Persian, in transl.[68].

Currently, bind and bind to are correct when applied to seizing quarry either in the air or on the ground.

BIND WITH Alternative to BIND TO.

BIRD-LIME; LIME Under TRAPS AND TRAPPING.

BIRD OF PREY Orders *Falconiformes* and *Strigiformes*. Order *Falconiformes* is subdivided into families, and further into genera, some of which contain species of diurnal birds of prey used historically and currently in falconry. Family *Accipitridae* includes genera *Accipiter*, *Buteo*, *Parabuteo*, *Aquila*, *Spizaetus* and *Hieraaetus* (true or short-winged hawks, broad-winged hawks or buzzards, the Harris' hawk, true eagles, and certain so-called hawk-eagles); family *Falconidae* includes genus *Falco* (falcons). Hawks from a small number of other genera have been tried or seen occasional use as falconers' birds.

Order *Strigiformes* is separated into two families: *Strigidae* (typical owls, including genus *Bubo*) and *Tytonidae* (barn owls). The term bird of prey is not often used by falconers who, when speaking or writing generally, usually prefer 'hawk' when referring to any of their long-, short- or broad-winged hawks. Raptor is a semi-scientific term which embraces all the birds of prey; it is used by scientists and ornithologists and occasionally by contemporary falconers for their hawks. Raptor suggests predatory behaviour: Latin *raptor* means one who seizes or drags away, a robber, etc.

BLACKCOCK See next entry.

BLACKGAME; BLACK GAME; HEATH GAME Black grouse (*Lyrurus tetrix*), occasional quarry in British game-hawking. Among English vernacular names for the male are blackcock, heath-cock (1902[42]) and occasionally moor-cock (which is also an alternative name for the male red grouse). The female is greyhen. Hett (1902[42]) has heath fowl as a group-name for red or black grouse. Pack is the usual term for a gathering or family of grouse.

BLACK SPARROWHAWK See SPARROWHAWK, Black.

BLOCK (n.); **BLOCK PERCH; BLOCK-PERCH** Under PERCHES.

BLOCK (vb) (Origin obscure.) Of a hawk in the field, to perch in a tree or on some elevated vantage point. Note: In a 19th century French-language treatise[74], 'bloquer' means the same, while 'prendre motte' (take stand) is to alight on the ground. More in STAND, Take.

BLOCK (or **RE-BLOCK**) **A HOOD** See HOOD-BLOCK 1 under HOODS AND HOODING.

BLOOD, In (obs.) An old hunting phrase, sometimes found in a falconry context, meaning full of life, vigorous; 'out of blood' (obsolete), meaning not vigorous, also occurs. Turbervile (1575[81]) describes a hawk as being 'well in bloude, and well quarried', meaning (in effect) hunting vigorously and successfully. Also see QUARRIED.

BLOOD, In the Of feathers, still developing and supplied with blood. The obsolete phrase 'in the quill' appears to be in effect the same. The uncommon and unverified 'out of the blood' describes a feather which is hard down, that is, fully grown and hard, the blood supply having stopped.

BLOOD, Out of See BLOOD, In.

BLOOD, Out of the See BLOOD, In the.

BLOOM A dusting from disintegrating POWDER-DOWN, sometimes visible on the outer surface of a hawk's plumage.

BLUE HAWK See HAWK, Blue.

BOB 1. Said of a hawk when she ducks her head to avoid being hooded. If she does this excessively, she might be described as being HOOD-SHY.
2. Of a falcon, to execute a characteristic rapid

up-and-down movement of the head, denoting intense interest in something she has seen; bobbing often immediately precedes flight. Phillott (1908 ft.⁶⁸) notes:
> 'When the Spring stirs in their [sakers'] blood and the migration restlessness is on them, they will sometimes when unhooded look up skywards, and call. One sign of their becoming *mast** is bobbing before rousing.'

*Perhaps excited, or similar: compare must or musth (from Persian *mast* = intoxicated) = a state of frenzy associated with the breeding season in certain male animals. Note: The obsolete verb 'coly' is a falconer's idiom, according to Berners (1486⁵), and may refer to a hawk's head movements; it occurs in 'yowre hawke colyeth and not beckyth'. Compare obsolete lay verb colly, which means (of a bird) to turn the head from side to side; 'beckyth' may be the same as becks, meaning (in an obsolete lay sense) nods the head.

BOBBED; BOBBED WITH THE HOOD Under HOODS AND HOODING.

BOCCAREL; BOCCARET See BAWREL.

BOCKEREL; BOCKERET See BAWREL.

BOLT 1 (obs.) (Perhaps adopt. bolt = (in one sense) to move off suddenly, to dart away.) Of a short-winged hawk, to fly quarry straight from the fist. Obsolete 'fly at bolt' appears to be the same.

BOLT 2 Of a man, to flush (a rabbit) from the bury with a ferret; of a ferret, to flush a rabbit. Also, of the rabbit, to flee the bury.

BOLT, Fly at See BOLT 1.

BONELLI'S EAGLE See HAWK-EAGLES.

BOOSE; BOOZE Obsolete spellings of BOWSE.

BOUGH, Take a See STAND, Take.

BOUSE Spelling of BOWSE.

BOUZE; BOWZE Obsolete spellings of BOWSE.

BOWER (obs.); **BOWESS** (1486, obs.); **BOWET** (unc., obs.) (From bough + -er, -ess, -et; it is conceivable that suffix -ess signifies (or originally signified) the female specifically.) A young short-winged hawk when she first leaves the eyrie and clambers onto boughs.
> 'And when they bene unclosed and begynneth to feder any thyng of lengthe Anoon be kynde they will draw somwatt out of the nest: and draw to bowis. and come agayn to ther nest And then thay be clepit Bowessis.' – 1486⁵. This might be paraphrased: 'When they are hatched and their feathers grown to a good length, they will naturally climb onto boughs, and then return to the nest; at this stage, they are called bowesses.'

There is a marked similarity between this and the following passages, suggesting a common source.
> 'When they [eyasses] begynne to feder ... they woll drawe them oute of here neste, and clambre over bowes, and come agayn to here neste, and then beth clepid bowers.' – 1460¹⁰.

Bowet is taken to be the same, but may be a misspelling:
> '*Bowet*, is when a young *Hawk* draws any thing out of her Nest, and covets to clamber on the bowes.' – 1677 gl.²⁵

BOWESS See preceding entry.

BOWET See BOWER.

BOWISER (obs.) Apparently the same as or similar to BRANCHER (n.) in the traditional understanding, that is, a young short-winged hawk able to hop or make experimental flights from branch to branch, but perhaps not leaving the nest-tree. In *A Perfect Booke* (c.1575³⁸), the
> 'Bowiser is sone mande [soon manned], and redy to be trayned to anythinge you lyst [choose].'

Harting, in his 1886 glossary appended to this text³⁸, notes:
> 'BOWISER ... a young hawk able to fly from bough to bough.'

BOWNET See TRAPS AND TRAPPING.

BOW-PERCH; BOW PERCH See PERCHES.

BOWSE (now unc.); **BOUSE** (now unc.) (Middle English bousen, apparently from Middle Dutch *bûsen*. Obs. spellings: BOWZE, BOUZE, BOOSE, BOOZE; also BROWSE (unc.).) Of a hawk, to drink, sometimes to drink excessively. A healthy hawk drinks little, relying largely on moisture in her food, although falconers make sure that water (primarily for bathing) is on offer regularly. A sick hawk or one suffering stress from travelling might drink more than usual, as might one whilst moulting or during hot weather. Two comments on bowsing are:
> '... She may bathe when she will, and bowze, as naturally they are enclined to do, and it doth them singular great pleasure, for bowzing may oftentimes preserve them from sicknesse ...' – 1575⁸¹;

> '*Bousing* is when a Hawke drinketh often, and seemes to be continually thirsty.' – 1615 gl.⁴⁹

BOWSER ([?]obs.); **BOUSER** ([?]obs.) A hawk which drinks (perhaps excessively).

BOX, Meat or **Food** See BAG, Hawking.

BRACES Alternative name for HOOD-BRACES, found under HOODS AND HOODING.

BRAIL (n.) (Taken to be related to Medieval Latin (Brit.–Ir.[48]) *braellum*, *braiellum*, etc. = a breech-girdle, belt. Obs. spelling: BRAYLE.) A narrow strip of soft leather to tie up a hawk's wing and prevent it from being opened; a device to discourage her from bating. The closed wing is inserted at the WRIST into a slit cut lengthwise in the strip. A complete procedural description is given by Harting (1898[40]):

> 'If a hawk during the process of training is troublesome to carry, and frequently bates off the fist, a "brail" should be put on the right wing, that is, the wing nearest the falconer as the bird sits on his left hand. This is a narrow strip of soft leather (about half the width of a jess), having a slit in it about a third of the way down long enough to admit the shoulder [meaning the wrist] of the wing, which being inserted, the longer end is brought down and under the closed wing, and then tied to the shorter end in a bow on the back. This plan effectually prevents a bird from extending its wing, and so "bating off," and for this reason is often adopted when hawks are carried on a cadge in the field, or when travelling. But as a rule only Peregrines and Jerfalcons are thus treated.'

Although obsolete in this rôle, the brail is currently used occasionally to immobilize an injured wing.

A mid-19th century source[76] describes a double brail which immobilizes both wings; this arrangement is uncommon.

BRAIL (vb) To immobilize (a hawk or her wing) using a BRAIL (n.), after which both the hawk and her wing are said to be brailed.

BRAILED Of a hawk or her wing, fitted with a BRAIL (n.). It would be correct to say 'a brailed hawk' and 'a brailed wing', as well as 'the hawk (or her wing) is brailed'.

BRAILS See FEATHERS, Brail.

BRANCHER (n.) (Obs. spellings: BRAUNCHER, BRAWNCHER.) Historically, a young short-winged hawk which is able to hop or make experimental flights from branch to branch, perhaps venturing from tree to tree, but has not yet left the immediate vicinity of the eyrie. The term has survived into modern usage, but is now applied to both short- and broad-winged hawks.

There is disagreement on a definition in some older texts, as can be seen from the following extracts.

> 'And after saynt Margaretis day* thay will flie fro tree to tree. And then thay bene calde Brawncheris.' – 1486[5].

*Taken to be 20th July. Turbervile (1575[81]) writes:
> 'The brancher, is she that followeth the old Hawke, from braunch to braunch, and tree to tree, whiche is also tearmed a ramage Hawke.'

In the Cox glossary (1677[25]),
> '*Brancher*, is a young *Hawk* newly taken out of the *Nest*.'

In another case, a brancher is:
> 'A young hawk which can hop but not fly.' – 1856 gl.[76]

A Perfect Booke (c.1575[38]) suggests that the brancher has begun to hunt, and therefore equates to the sore-hawk of some later writers:
> 'Brauncher is harde to be mande [manned] & then best because she hathe bene fed always by her dame & prayd for herselfe.'

The Harting glossary of 1886, appended to this treatise, simplifies the definition:
> 'BRAUNCHER ... a young hawk that has lately left the nest.'
>
> 'When it has left the nest it becomes a "brancher:" a "soar-hawk," or "soarage," when it has begun to prey for itself.' – 1852[16].

See HAWK, Ramage, and HAWK, Sore, also note in NAMES 1.

BRANCHER (adj.) Sometimes met with today in such as 'brancher redtail' (inf.).

BRANCH OR STAND (unv., obs.) An uncommon term found in the Cox glossary (1677[25]). There appears to be a connection with take stand (STAND, Take), take a bough (under STAND, Take) and DRAW AFTER. The entry reads:
> '*Branch or Stand*, is to make the *Hawk* leap from Tree to Tree till the Dog springs the *Partridge*.'

BRAYLE 1 Obsolete spelling of BRAIL (n.).

BRAYLE 2 (unv., obs.) Uncommonly, a hawk's VENT or that region. In one instance, it is the vent (or that region) of a short-winged hawk specifically; see 1611 qu. in FEATHERS, Brail. For comparison, a French-language treatise (1853[74]) has a similar region in a hawk as *brayer*:
> 'La région du bas-ventre est désignée sous le nom de brayer.'

BRAYLES Obsolete spelling of brails; see FEATHERS, Brail.

BREAK See next entry.

BREAK INTO; BREAK (obs.); BREAK IN UPON

(obs.) Of a hawk, to begin to feed on (a kill), first breaking or tearing the skin.

> 'If she has killed a rook or other bird, as often happens, she should be allowed to break well into it before being taken up.' – 1898[40].
> '... When she beginneth to breake it and to take bloude ...' – 1575[81].
> '... You must contrive so that the hawk, instead of breaking in upon that unsavoury morsel*, shall proceed by mistake to begin her meal upon a pigeon ...' – 1900[59].

*In this case, a rook kill; hawks are not over-fond of the flavour of rook.

BREAK IN UPON   See preceding entry.

BREAK TO THE HOOD   Under HOODS AND HOODING.

BREASTBONE   The sternum, which (or the outer rim of which) falconers sometimes refer to as the keel in their hawks. A falconer will regularly palpate the area around the breastbone to ascertain how well-fleshed and -muscled she is; the pectoral muscles which power the wings for flight lie in this region.

BREAST-FEATHERS   See FEATHERS, Breast.

BRING BACK UP   Of a falconer, to increase the flesh (on a thin hawk) by good and plentiful feeding.

BROADWING; BROAD-WING   See HAWK, Broad-winged.

BROAD-WINGED HAWK   See HAWK, Broad-winged.

BROOK-HAWKING; HAWKING AT THE BROOK   Under HAWKING, Categories of.

BROW   The ridge above the eye, pronounced in some species of hawk. More technically, it is the supra-orbital ridge, a term rarely used by falconers.

BROWSE   Uncommon and obsolete form of BOWSE.

BUBO   A genus of large owls. See EAGLE OWL.

BUETT   Obsolete spelling of BEWIT.

BURROW   See next entry.

BURY; BERRY (now unc. or obs.)**; BERY** (1486, obs.)**; BEERY** (1519, obs.) (Variants of burrow.) A rabbit's burrow. Not in a falconry context:

> 'I have nede of a feret, to let into this beery to styrt out the conies.' – 1519[44],

and:
> 'Musk-Rats who live in holes and Berries like Rabbits.' – 1685[15].

The Berners (1486[5]) list of collective terms includes 'a Bery of Conyes'.

BUSSARD   Obsolete spelling of BUZZARD.

BUTCHER BIRD, Warder   See SHRIKE.

BUTEO   (Latin = a kind of hawk.) The genus which contains (among others) the red-tailed hawk (*Buteo jamaicensis*), the ferruginous hawk (*B. regalis*) and the common buzzard (*B. buteo*), all of which are used in contemporary falconry. The genus contains 25 species[13] in the Old and New Worlds. Their rather long, broad wings and broad tail are adaptations for soaring. In general, their wild hunting techniques lack the dash and style coveted by austringers. Of the three species mentioned here, only the red-tailed hawk has been fully accepted as an austringer's bird. Buteo (plural buteos) has been adopted by some modern falconers as a general name for a hawk (otherwise buzzard) of the genus *Buteo*.

BUTEO; plural BUTEOS   A term used by some modern falconers as a general name for a hawk (otherwise buzzard) of the genus of the same name.

BUTTON   A particular kind of 'knot' at one end of a narrow strip of leather. It is made by rolling or folding the leather two or three times at one end, punching a hole through the fold, then threading the entire strip through the hole and pulling it tight. It is assumed that this method was used by Turbervile (1575[81]) for his

> '... Lease [leash] made with a button at the end.'

When a hide LEASH is threaded all the way through one ring of the SWIVEL, the button abuts the ring and acts as a stop; the free end of the leash might then, for example, be tied to the perch. On field and mews JESSES used with aylmeri, the buttons abut the eyelets of the anklets; the free ends of the jesses might then be attached to one ring of the swivel. A button BEWIT has a button at one end and a slit or 'button-hole' at the other. On HOOD-BRACES (under HOODS AND HOODING), buttons provide grip for fingers and teeth when a hood is struck (that is, loosened before removal).

BUZZARD   (Old French *busart*. An obs. English spelling is 'bussard' (1618[50], 1619[6]).) In the Old World, a hawk of the genus *Buteo*; an example is the common buzzard (*Buteo buteo*), native to

Britain and used in contemporary British falconry. In North America, the indigenous birds in this genus are invariably 'hawks' in their common names (for example ferruginous hawk), 'buzzard' being reserved for those native to the Old World. In Britain, falconers sometimes replace 'hawk' with 'buzzard' in the names of the North American buteos used in falconry (for example ferruginous buzzard). In North America, buzzard is an archaic vernacular name for the native vultures.

BUZZARD, Common *Buteo buteo* A broad-winged hawk which habitually soars, its races distributed throughout the Palearctic regions from the Azores and Cape Verde through to Japan. The nominate Eurasian *Buteo buteo buteo* is resident in Britain. It breeds in woodland and feeds on small mammals up to the size of rabbits, some slow-moving birds, reptiles and amphibians, and larger insects. Carrion also features in its diet. Until recent times, it was described in such terms as 'cowardly, slothful and degenerate', therefore useless as an austringer's bird. The view that it is unsuitable for falconry survives to some extent, unjustly in the view of some austringers. It is flown from the fist straight at quarry, or out of trees. Full-grown rabbits are taken with females, occasionally pheasant; other quarries have been grey squirrels and moorhens. Today it is looked on as suitable for a beginner, being physically sturdy, often temperamentally steady, and relatively easily manned, trained and entered at quarry; it is therefore judged ideal for the novice who aspires to flying a red-tailed hawk or a goshawk. (Plate 3).

BUZZARD, Ferruginous See HAWK, Ferruginous.

BUZZARD, Red-tailed See HAWK, Red-tailed.

C

CADGE (Cf. archaic vb cadge = to go about as a pedlar, street-seller, etc. An obs. form appears to be CAGE: '... You shall seldome or never buy a Hawke from the Cage that is not lowsie ...' – 1575[81]. Also STAGE (obs.).) A portable perch in various designs for transporting hawks to or in the field and (formerly) to offer them for sale. Latham (1615 gl.[49]) notes:

> '*Cadge*, is taken for that on which Faulconers carry many *Hawkes*, together when they bring them to sell.'
> '*Cadge*, is that circular piece of Wood on which *Hawks* are carried when they are exposed to sale.' – 1677 gl.[25]

FIELD CADGE; CADGE PROPER (obs.; 'proper' signifying ordinary, usual). This pattern has a long history of use in Western falconry for the transportation of falcons, tethered short and hooded to avoid crabbing (grabbing one another; more in CRAB). It is of sufficient size to accommodate a number of birds. It is little used in the contemporary pursuit where a hawking outing is, as a rule, a small-scale affair employing fewer birds than formerly. It is four rails arranged in a rectangle, padded on the top

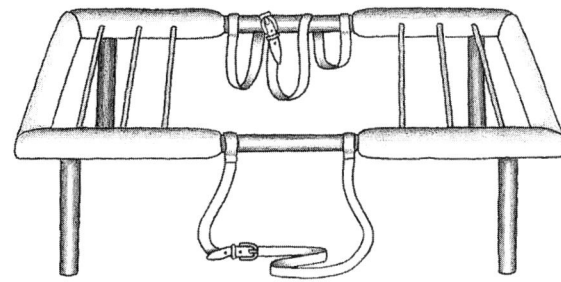

Field cadge or cadge proper.

where the birds perch. It has four short fixed legs; or

> 'At each corner of the frame is a small jointed leg, which can be hooked up when the cadge is being carried, and let down when it is to be deposited on the ground.' – 1900[59].

The carrier (cadger, cadge boy, cadge man; all these terms are obsolete) stands in the centre of the frame, supporting it with shoulder-straps (crossed) and steadying it with his hands (plate 46). Oval, D-shaped and circular versions also existed, although it is not known how commonly they were employed in the field.

BOX CADGE. Used to some extent today, it is an unlidded box-shape with some or all of the edges padded for perching. On it, hawks might be tethered by their leashes through holes in the sides using the cadge knot, described in SCREEN PERCH (under PERCHES); there are other arrangements. When together on a box cadge, hawks ideally are hooded. This pattern is used primarily for the transportation of hawks in a vehicle.

> 'A little sawdust is put in the box, to the depth of an inch or two, to catch the "mutes" from the birds which are tied on with their trains towards the centre, and the cadge is complete.' – 1898[40].

SPRING BOX CADGE (obs.). A modification of the box cadge; a design which apparently did not catch on. The box is set on springs to reduce jarring during travelling.

POLE CADGE. A long padded pole with short legs at each end, held in the centre whilst being carried. This type of cadge is not used today in the West. Michell[59], at the turn of the 19th and 20th centuries, claims (incorrectly) to have invented it.

CADGE KNOT. The knot for tying a hawk's leash to the cadge. It is made in the same way as the screen perch knot; see SCREEN PERCH under PERCHES. Alternatively, the falconer's knot (KNOT, Falconer's) might be used.

CADGE BOY   See CADGER.

CADGE MAN   See CADGER.

CADGE PROPER   See CADGE.

CADGER (obs.); **CADGE BOY** (obs.); **CADGE MAN** (obs.) One who carries hawks on a CADGE.

CAGE   See CADGE.

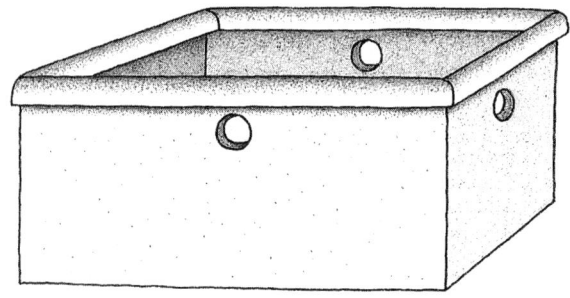

Box cadge.

CALL   1 Of a falconer, to summon (a hawk) by whatever means. It may imply summoning her with calls or whistles (she is taught to respond to voice, whistles or both in her training), or by showing her the lure with or without an audible signal. It may also imply summoning her either to the fist or the lure. Bert (1619[6]) writes thus of a goshawk in training:

> 'I never call her* above eight or tenne yards, untill I finde that shee is bolde enough and not fearefull, and that she be farre in love with my voyce, which I never faile to give her, even from the beginning of her feeding, untill shee is flying, and that is lowde enough, as if I were to call her thirty or forty score, although I call her but ten yardes.'

*Here, the fist is implied. The fuller idioms 'call to the lure' and 'call to the fist' are also correct. Formerly and currently, the idiom 'to call off a hawk' is correct, and such phrases as (of the hawk) 'called off to the lure' (1898[40]) are met with occasionally. To call off a hawk (the procedure known as calling off) is usually, of an austringer, to call a short- or broad-winged hawk from such as a post or a companion's fist to the lure or to his own fist as part of her training, or for exercise. Michell (1900[59]) writes:

> 'As for the short-winged hawks, and for such others as will not keep on the wing willingly without going to perch, they must be exercised chiefly by the device known as calling off . . . where two men go out, and, standing at a distance from one another, alternately bring the hawk across the intervening space by showing the lure or the outstretched fist*. If two men are not available the hawk may be deposited on a railing, gate, or post, and the falconer may walk away . . .'.

But elsewhere in the text, this writer uses the term in the context of flying a falcon at game:

> 'If your [unpromising, inexperienced game-] hawk will not mount properly, but potters about in a useless way at a mean height . . . You may call her off half a mile or so from the lee side of an open moor, and, as she come across it up-wind, let beaters from each side try to drive grouse inwards towards her line of flight. If you can once enable her to take a grouse there are hopes of her yet.'

In scattered instances in other texts, the term is used to mean to encourage a hawk (not by any specific means) to leave her perch and fly quarry. In certain circumstances, the uncommon 'lure off' might be used. Harting (1898[40]) writes:

> 'If . . . [a lost hawk] has taken stand in some tree, she may be lured off, down wind, with a live pigeon in a string.'

The terms 'call back', meaning to recall (a hawk) with the voice or by whistling and (or) by swinging the lure, and 'call in', meaning to summon (her) to the fist or lure, sometimes occur formerly and currently. Also see WHISTLE (vb), and WHISTLE OFF.

*Today, flying a hawk back and forth between two people is sometimes known as flying her fist to fist (inf.).

CALL 2 (obs.) According to Berners (1486[5]): of a wild hawk, apparently to court, or to vocalize whilst courting:

'And in the tyme of their love they call. and not kauke.'

Also see CAWKING TIME.

CALL BACK See CALL 1.

CALL IN See CALL 1.

CALLING-CRANES (obs.) A creance, that is, the line on which a hawk in training is called. More in CREANCE; also see CALL 1.

CALLING OFF See CALL 1.

CALL OFF See CALL 1.

CALL OUT OF THE HOOD See FLY OUT OF THE HOOD.

CALLS Used by the falconer to encourage, CALL or call off a hawk, having familiarized her with them as signals during her training, or to startle quarry into flight. The form a call should take is specified by some English-language writers. Unless otherwise stated, all those in the following list are probably obsolete:

'Huff', 'huff. huff. huff' – 1486[5]; to flush quarry.

'Wó, hó, hó' – 1575[81]; a call of encouragement to the hawk while she is feeding on the lure.

'Howe, howe, howe' – 1618[50]; to flush quarry and to encourage the hawk.

'Yo-hohup, yohup, yohop', 'Helover-helaw-helaw-helope', 'Hooha, ha ha ha', 'Whoop', and 'Up-ho' – 1855[73].

Also met with:

'Hello', perhaps related to 'halloo' used in other forms of hunting. Somewhat similar is:

'Lo birde, lo, Hey lo birde, hey lo' – 1575[81]; to call a hawk to the lure.

'Hey gar, gar, gar' – 1575[81]; to encourage a falcon waiting on (see WAIT ON) to stoop when quarry has been flushed.

'Whyloe, whyloe' – 1575[81]; to call back a falcon.

'Towe, Towe' or 'Stowe, Stowe' – 1575[81]; to call a hawk to the fist.

'Howit, Howit' – 1575[81]; to encourage a hawk when quarry is sprung.

'Ware Hawke ware' – 1575[81]; apparently to warn dogs away from a hawk feeding on a kill.

'Hoo, ha, ha!'; according to Michell (1900[59]), to encourage a falcon to stoop from her PITCH. This and 'Hey, gar, gar, gar!', the writer notes, were still often used in his day.

'Who-whoop'; according to Michell (1900[59]), the falconer's death-cry when (in this case) his falcon has bound to her rook quarry.

Heard today (and sometimes referred to as 'the shout'):

'Hoy', 'hey' and 'ho'; often to encourage a falcon to stoop.

In the 13th century, Emperor Frederick[35], who used the voice to flush quarry as well as to call his birds, commented that the inhabitants of Britain called their falcons to the lure by swinging it conspicuously high rather than with a vocal summons. Although the 'Anglians' explained that this simply was their custom, the Emperor surmised that they did not wish a falcon to mistake a shout to flush quarry for a summons to the lure.

The probably obsolete verb to cherk (variants chirk, chyrke or chuck), when used of a falconer, is to make a chirruping sound with the lips as an encouragement to a hawk to feed or as a friendly and calming signal. Turbervile (1575[81]) says:

'... Chyrke wyth your voyce, and use those other soundes which Falconers do to their Hawkes ...'.

On approaching a hawk on a kill, the Berners (1486[5]) recommendation is:

'... Whiles yowre hawke plumith [plumes, plucks] cumme softely towarde hir. alway nere and nere. and if she leve plumyng. and loke upon yow. stonde styll and cherke hir. and whistyll hir. tyll she plume ayen [again]. and thus serve hir tyll ye be right nere hir.'

Latham (1618[50]) recommends

'... using your voice in whistling or chirping unto her ...'.

Also see MARK!

CALL TO THE FIST or -LURE See CALL 1.

CANCELEER (vb, obs.) (Cf. Modern French *chanceler* = to falter, waver, etc. Among other English spellings: CANCELLEER, CANCELLIER, CANCELIER, CHANCELEER; all obs.) Particularly of a stooping falcon, to make one or more abrupt turns or adjustments in her flight. According to Worlidge (1675[85]), it is:

'When a ... Hawk, in her stooping, turns two or three times on the Wing, to recover herself before she seizes.'

CANCELEER (n., obs.) The action of a hawk in canceleering; see preceding entry.

CANVAS (obs.); **CANVASS** (obs.) (Probably from Latin *cannabis* = hemp (a material for, among other things, net-making).) To ensnare (a hawk) in a net.

CARPUS (sci.); **CARPAL JOINT** (sci.) The outer major joint of the wing, corresponding to the human wrist. To falconers, it is perhaps most commonly known as the wrist.

CARRIAGE The carrying on the fist of a hawk during the process of manning. More in CARRY 1 (vb).

CARRIER A hawk which carries. See CARRY 2 (vb).

CARRY 1 (vb) Broadly, of a falconer, to hold (a hawk) on the fist and walk about with her. Historically the term is principally applied to walking about with an unmanned or not fully manned hawk, often for several hours at a stretch during the day, as part of the process of manning; see MAN. This is used as an opportunity for careful and gradual introduction to strange sights and activity, and for such as

'... frequent unhooding and rehooding and occasional turnings of the hand to induce the hawk to shift her position.' – 1908 ft.[68]

Today, shorter periods of carriage during manning are looked on as sufficient, indeed more effective, certainly more humane. It is often recommended that, in order to settle a trained short-winged hawk, she should be carried briefly before she is flown. OED has 'carry' as a noun (17th century, obsolete), meaning 'Manner of carrying [a hawk]'. An example of use might be 'a bad carry', suggesting that the hawk is awkward to carry on the fist, or unmanageable (perhaps frequently bating) whilst being carried.

CARRY 2 (vb) Often found by itself: of a hawk, to obey a natural instinct to fly away with a kill to where she might feed on it alone and unopposed. Also met with in such phrases as 'cary hir game', this found in Berners (1486[5]). To avoid a hawk carrying in the field, Berners suggests:

'... Softe and layserly [leisurely, without haste]: fall oppon yowre kneys. and prevely [covertly] while she plumyth [plumes, plucks]. sett yowre honde and be sure of the gesse.... and if ye doo the contrary: she wyll for feere cary hir game. or let it go quyke. and that is bot losse to yow and yowre hawke also.'

For a hawk at hack, food is often tied to the hack board to discourage her from forming the habit of carrying; see HACKING. In manning (see MAN) and the earlier stages of training, the falconer has ideally made himself unthreatening to his hawk in all circumstances. In the training ground he may thwart her instinct to carry not only by using a lure of a certain weight and (or) by holding on to the lure-line, but also by accustoming her to remaining on the lure without anxiety while he makes in to pick her up. In the second part of Bert's treatise (1619[6]), 'Wherein the Austringer is taught to reclaime his Hawke from any ill-condition', is a method of discouraging her from carrying a kill into a tree or, should she try, to bring her to the ground where she can be picked up:

'... Take a leather in all poynts fashioned like a bewet, put it about her hinder tallent [hind talon], and then button it to her bewet, whereon her bell hangeth, and it will so holde up her tallent that shee cannot at all gripe with it, then shee cannot sit upon a bough, holde a Partridge, and feede.' The strap should not be too restrictive '... lest it should hinder her trussing a Partridge ...'.

There appear to be few records in English-language hawking literature of this device having been used. As yet, no English name has been found for it.

CARRY (n.) See CARRY 1 (vb).

CARRY-FIST (obs.) (Also CARVIST (1677, unc., obs.) and MURZALET (unc., obs.).) A hawk taken from the wild early in the year. She is presumed to be a bird of the previous year rather than one of greater age. Because of the season she is taken, she is said to need very frequent CARRIAGE to tame her. Turbervile (1575[81]) writes:

'The fourth speach and tearme that is bestowed on them (as my Italian Author* doth call them) is, that they are tearmed *Marzaroli***, and so are they called from January, February, Marche, April, untill the middest of May. I have no proper englishe phrase for them, but they are very tedious and paynefull, and the reason is, for that they must be kept on the fiste al that space§.'

*The source in question appears to be the writings of 'one Francesco Sforzino Vycentino, an Italyan Gentleman Falconer', whose opinions (among those of other foreign writers) Turbervile regularly expresses.

**The English equivalent (or near equivalent) is 'murzalets'; both terms presumed to be from Italian *marzo* = March, a reference to the time of year the hawks might be taken; compare Turbervile's 'March Hawks' in LANTINER.

§It is assumed that the core point here is (or

2: *Young male Barbary falcon. From a lithograph by William Brodrick (1873).*

1: *Blyth's hawk-eagle.*

3: *Wild common buzzard still-hunting.* (John Hawkins)

4: *The famous escapee from London Zoo in the 1960s, 'Goldie' the golden eagle.*
(M. Lyster / © Z.S.L.)

5: *Goshawk (immature).*
(John Hawkins)

6: **Opposite**: *Greenland falcons. Lithograph, from a painting by J. Wolf (1820–1899).*

7: **Left**: *Young hobby with a full crop and the vestiges of nestling down visible on her crown.* (John Hawkins)

8: *Female lanner falcon.* (B.E. & K.L. Yull)

10: *Young female merlin from Salvin and Brodrick's* Falconry in the British Isles.

9: Opposite: *Young female lanner. From a lithograph by William Brodrick (1873).*

12: *The wild peregrine's eyrie.* (John Hawkins)

11: Opposite: *Male merlins (adult and young) on the screen perch; from Salvin and Brodrick's* Falconry in the British Isles.

13-15: *Three lithographs of peregrines from Salvin and Brodrick's* Falconry in the British Isles, *1873 edition. Left to right: Young falcon at hack, first year tiercel and old tiercel on the cadge.*

16: *Male prairie falcon.* (M. Lyster / © Z.S.L.)

17: *Untrained male red-tailed hawk, nervous and tight-feathered.* (B.E. & K.L. Yull)

18: *Female saker on Arabian-style perch.* (K. Taylor)

19: *Male sparrowhawk, or musket.* (John Hawkins)

20: *The sparrowhawk's eyrie.* (John Hawkins)

21: *Young female sparrowhawk. From a lithograph by William Brodrick (1873). Note bow perch with screen.*

22: *Adult male sparrowhawk. From a lithograph by William Brodrick (1873).*

23: *Chromolithograph frontispiece from James Edmund Harting's* A Handbook of British Birds, *1901.*

should be) that hawks taken between January and mid-May require more manning than a young hawk taken the previous year.

Cox (1677[25]), in his glossary, uses the uncommon 'carvist', phonetically similar to carry-fist, in a sketchy definition:

> '*Carvist*; a *Hawk* may be so called at the beginning of the year, and signifies as much as to carry on the Fist.'

CARVIST   Form of CARRY-FIST.

CAST   1 (vb) To take hold of and immobilize (a hawk) in a particular way. This is usually carried out by a companion while the hawk is on the falconer's fist; she may be taken from behind or from the front. The ideal method is to grasp her in one deft movement with both hands, firmly but gently gripping her body and at the same time confining her closed wings:

> 'To cast a *Hawke*, is to take her in your hands before the pinions of her wings*, and hold her from bating or striving, when you administer any thing unto her.' – 1615 gl.[49]

*In effect, forward of her primary feathers. She is then said to be or have been cast. While cast, procedures such as jessing (see JESSES) or coping (see COPE) may be carried out. She might be pressed gently breast downwards on a cushion during such as IMPING and TAIL-BELLING. A cloth (sometimes formerly a silk handkerchief, perhaps a tea-towel today) between hands and hawk is recommended, or soft gloves to be worn, to help avoid rumpling, damaging, or removing OIL from feathers.

CAST   2 (vb) To disgorge indigestible material (fur, bone and feathers) which in a healthy hawk is formed into a compact, sweet-smelling pellet known as a casting. To cast through the hood is to cast while hooded.

CAST   3 (vb) See 1486 qu. and notes in CAST OFF.

CAST, A   Two, as in 'a cast of hawks':

> 'I sent ... to my lo^d Carew a caste of marlyns and a goshawk.' – 1613[12]
>
> '...I had in charge at the least two cast of River-Hawks*.' – 1618[50]

*Falcons primarily for flying at duck.

> 'CAST ... a "cast of hawks," *i.e.*, two; not necessarily a pair.' – 1891 gl.[39]

The Berners list of collective terms, 'The Companys of beestys and fowlys' (1486[5]), includes 'a cast of haukis of ye tour.ii' and 'a lece of thessame haukis.iii'. See HAWK OF THE TOWER; for 'lece', see LEASH, A. Two hawks flown together are said to be flown in a cast. To fly double is, to fly in a cast; to fly single is, to fly alone; both idioms are obsolete and so far unverified as authentic.

There has been a long tradition in Britain and Europe of flying the larger falcons in a cast at quarry such as herons and kites, and of flying merlins in a cast at skylarks. The naturally sociable Harris' hawk, recently adopted as an austringer's bird, is the only broad-winged hawk suited to this practice. Short-winged hawks are never flown together, their highly aggressive nature making them a danger to each other.

The purpose of flying hawks in a cast is in certain cases (and to some degree) to compensate for the difference in size and strength between a single hawk and a larger quarry; it is also to give the hawks a tactical advantage over elusive and difficult quarry, whatever its size. To illustrate the tactics of two merlins pursuing a skylark, Lascelles (1892[47]) writes:

> 'It is a common thing to lose sight of the lark in the clouds, even on a clear day, and not unfrequently both the hawks flying with him will also disappear fairly overhead in the air. Presently the two larger specks reappear, and then in front of them you may see the smaller dot, falling like a bullet from the clouds into a fence below, with the little falcons stooping right and left at him till he is taken just as he gains his sanctuary.'

Michell (1900[59]) uses the terms 'double flight' and 'single flight' for flights with merlins at larks, employing (respectively) a cast and a single hawk; these terms are obsolete and unverified as authentic.

CAST, Fly in a   See preceding entry.

CAST A FEATHER   See FEATHER, Drop a.

CASTING   1 A disgorged pellet, containing in a healthy hawk indigestible material. The formation, constituents, texture, smell and appearance of a casting may give the falconer an indication of a hawk's health.

CASTING   2; **CASTINGS** Indigestible materials or roughage (fur, bone and feathers) with a hawk's food, which she will later disgorge. Also applied to natural materials (feathers, once called plumage in this context, or fur) added by the falconer to a hawk's meat to ensure that a good pellet (to falconers, correctly a casting) is produced. Stuff such as wool or tow (1856[76]) or thrums (short pieces of waste coarse yarn) were once given as a substitute for natural materials. Mentioned in a 15th century text is new blanket cloth cut into pieces ('pelettis of an inche longe', 'pellettis of cloth'[5]) pushed into a holes made in morsels of meat; the meat and cloth were, in this case, moistened in water before being fed to the hawk every third day. Turbervile (1575[81]) specifies 'knottes of hempe, or the shaving of a Hasell [hazel] wande'.

> '... My castings that I give, are Thrums, gotten of the Weaver, I get them washed, but not with Sope, I cut the threads an inch long or lesse ...' – 1619[6].
>
> '*Casting*, is any thing that you give your Hawk to clense her gorge with, whether it be flannell, thrummes, feathers, or such like.' – 1615 gl.[49];

in the text, this last writer suggests

> '... Adding unto the inke [neck] of a dove as much cleane washt flannell in quantitie, as may make her a reasonable casting [pellet].'
>
> 'A medecyne for to make an hawke to cast that is a comberyd with castyng with in her body. Take the Juce of Salandyne. and wete a morcell of flesh therin. the mowntenaunce of a Note. and yeve that morcell to the hawke. and that shall make hir for to cast hir olde casttyng. and the hawke shall be safe.' – 1486[5].

This might be paraphrased: 'A medicine for a hawk that is unable to cast. Take the juice of celandine and wet in it a morsel of flesh the size of a nut and give the morsel to the hawk; that shall make her cast, and then she shall be safe.'

CASTING, A (obs.) A quantity or sufficiency of casting (roughage in the form of feathers or other indigestible material) given to a hawk.

> 'In the morning, take care that your hawk eats no feathers with her meat, but in the evening give her a "casting" of feathers.' – 1908 in transl.[68]

CASTINGS See CASTING 2.

CAST OFF; THROW OFF To encourage (a hawk) to fly from the fist with a forward movement of the hand. A sketchy passage in Berners (1486[5]) suggests that 'cast (a hawk)' and 'cast (a hawk) to quarry' were at that time idiomatically correct; the heading is '... Caste yowre hawke', the text as follows:

> 'And if yowr hawke [goshawk] reward to any fowle by countenance for to flee ther to ye shall say cast the hawke ther to. and not lett fli ther to.' This might tentatively be paraphrased: 'If your hawk notices quarry and shows a readiness to fly it, you shall say cast the hawk to it, and not let her fly to it.'

Michell (1900[59]) has 'the throw-off' as the falconer's act of casting off a hawk; this is uncommon and obsolete.

CASTREL Obsolete form of KESTREL.

CAST THE CROP See CROP, Cast the.

CAST (THE) GORGE See CROP, Cast the.

CAST THE HOOD See HOODS AND HOODING.

CAST THROUGH THE HOOD See CAST 2 (vb).

CAST TO QUARRY See 1486 qu. in CAST OFF.

CAST TO THE PERCH (obs.) According to Berners[5] in the 15th century:

> '... Ye shall say cast yowre hawke to the perch. and not set youre hawke uppon the perch.'

CATCH (obs.) According to Bert (1619[6]), quarry caught by a hawk; such a kill (it appears) might be used in the training of a different hawk:

> '... You must call her [goshawk] to a catch or lewer ... Let her please her selfe upon the catch, offer not to meddle with it, but let her freely and peaceably injoy it ...'.

CATCH-DUCK (unc., obs.) Used by Latham (1618[50]) to describe a goshawk for flying at duck:

> '... An excellent catch-Ducke shee will make.'

CAWK; CAUK See next entry.

CAWKING TIME (obs.); **CAWKING-TIME** (obs.) (Cf. obs. lay vb cawk = '... to call as some birds.' – OED; also cf. obs. lay vb cauk = 'to tread, to copulate as birds. Hence cauking.' – OED.) The term occurs in some earlier texts on falconry as the time when wild hawks pair or court. But in Berners (1486[5]), to call (not 'kauke') appears to mean to court, or to vocalize whilst courting:

> 'And in the tyme of their love they call. and not kauke. And we shall say that they trede*.'

*Otherwise TREAD or copulate. In Cox (1677 gl.[25]),

> '*Cawking time*, is Treading time.'

CEASE Spelling of SEIZE.

CERCELL Spelling of SARCEL.

CERE (Latin *cera* = wax. Medieval Latin (Brit.–Ir.[48]) *cera* = wax: part of a falcon. Obs. spellings: SEAR(E), SERE.) The naked, wax-like skin at the base of a hawk's beak into which the nostrils (see NARES) are pierced. This definition (with the spelling sere) is given by Berners[5] in the 15th century:

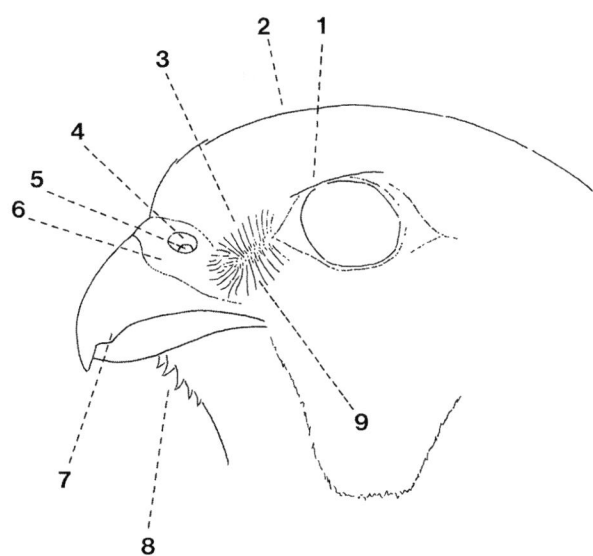

Some obsolete and surviving names for parts of a hawk's head, in this case a falcon's. 1: Brow. 2: Crown. 3: Lore. 4: Nare. 5: Frelon (pronounced in falcons). 6: Cere. 7: Nook (falcons). 8: Barb feathers. 9: Crine feathers.

'The yolow [yellow (skin)] be twene ye Beke & ye yeghen [eyes] is calde ye Sere.'

Also (ibid.):

'Knawe ye: that the skynne a bowte yowre hawkys legges & his fete. is calde: the Seris of hir legges and hir fete. whether thay be watery hewed or of waxy colowre yolowe.'

In the same text, the obsolete adjectival ensered (meaning skinned) occurs in 'a faire enserid legge'; fair perhaps means of pleasing appearance rather than pale, therefore describes a leg of the desired yellow colour. Cox (1677[25]) refers to 'the Sear of the Foot'.

CESSEL   Perhaps the same as SARCEL.

CHANCELEER   Form of CANCELEER (vb).

CHAP   (obs.) (Cf. lay chop = jaw, and chaps = lower part of the face.) The lower part of a hawk's beak (1856 gl.[76]). Either half of the bill of a bird (OED).

CHASE, Stern; STERN FLIGHT; TAIL-CHASE A chase from behind, as opposed to a stoop from above; a hawk's level-flight pursuit of quarry.

CHECK   1 (vb); **CHECK** (ns); **FLY AT CHECK** Note: It will be seen from the following sub-entries that, in the context of falconry, CHECK nouns appear to owe their origin to the verb.

CHECK 1 (vb). Suggestive of a hesitation by a hawk, or a change of mind. By itself, it means to change from one quarry to another (usually of inferior kind) during a flight. (Note: The unverified and obsolete 'make out' may have a similar or connected meaning, or may be related to RAKE AWAY.) Fuller idioms, such as to check at (for example a pigeon) are sometimes met with, implying that the hawk abandons the intended flight to fly at another quarry. Latham (1615 gl.[49]) writes:

'*Checke* or to kill, Checke is when Crowes, Rookes, Pies [magpies], or other birds comming in the view of the Hawke, shee forsaketh her naturall flight to flie at them.'

FLY AT CHECK. 'At check' is adverbial (compare 'at heel' in 'walk at heel'). The idiom means (of a hawk) to change from one quarry to another during a flight; this definition, though little used, is correct today. Although the term has come to mean changing from the original to any other (perhaps easier) quarry, 'check' suggests base game, that is, quarry of an inferior kind. Blaine (1936 [1970][8]) uses the idiom in the context of a falcon in rook-hawking leaving the intended quarry and turning off downwind after other rooks. Very occasionally, to fly at check is simply and literally to fly at base game; this application is probably obsolete and perhaps not strictly accurate.

CHECK 1 (n.). A hesitation by a hawk in the pursuit of one quarry because she has seen another, or a change of focus and direction leading to her abandoning the original quarry to pursue another. In OED, check (n.) is (in one sense) 'A false stoop, when a hawk forsakes her quarry for baser game'; more in STOOP, False.

CHECK 2 (n., now unc. or obs.). Quarry (usually of an inferior kind) which induces a hawk to abandon the intended flight. Also see GAME, Base.

'If your hawke go out to anye checke, and kill a Doove or a Crow, or anye other checke and feed upon it ... hood hir up, and flee not with hir in two or three dayes after ...' – 1575[81].

The same writer uses the phrase 'rake out after a checke'; fuller qu. in RAKE AWAY. See FLY ON HEAD.

CHECK   2 (vb) See FIST, Check at the.

CHECK, Fly at   See CHECK 1 (vb).

CHECK AT   See CHECK 1 (vb).

CHECK AT THE FIST   See FIST, Check at the.

CHERK   (probably obs.) (Also CHIRK, CHYRKE and CHUCK (all obs.).) Of a falconer, to chirrup with his lips; more in CALLS.

CHESSES   Obsolete form of JESSES.

CHICKEN HAWK   (vernacular, obs.) In Britain, the GOSHAWK, the name apparently referring to the wild hawk's predation upon domestic poultry.

CHIN-STRAP   See HOODS AND HOODING.

CHIRK; CHYRKE Spellings of CHERK.

CHIRP   Of a falconer, to chirrup with his lips; more in CALLS.

CHOP   See CUT DOWN 1.

CHUCK   Form of CHERK.

CLAP   (obs.) The lower part of a hawk's beak.
  'The neder parte of hir beke is calde the clape of the hawke.' – 1486[5].
Also, beak is an obsolete name for the upper part only.

CLAWS   See FOOT (n.).

CLEAN   (obs.) The state in a hawk after enseaming; see ENSEAM.

CLEAN, Make   (obs.); **CLEANSE** (obs.) Of a falconer, to cleanse (a hawk) internally, the central purpose of enseaming; to ENSEAM (a hawk).

CLEANSE   See preceding entry.

CLEES; CLEYS   Obsolete forms of CLAWS, found under FOOT (n.).

CLITCH   Form of CLUTCH.

CLOKE   (obs.) To claw, to scratch, not necessarily of a hawk, but compare CLOKES under FOOT (n.).

CLOKES   See FOOT (n.).

CLOSER   See FOOT (n.).

CLUTCH   (obs.); **CLITCH** (obs.) Of a hawk in an attack, to grip (quarry) with her feet. But Berners (1486[5]), writing on short-winged hawks, has STRAIN as idiomatically correct:
  '. . . She streynith and not Clithith nor Cratchith.'
'Clithith' appears to be an error for clitchith (clitches); the obsolete lay verb cratch means scratch. BIND TO is the current idiom.

CLUTCHES   See FOOT (n.).

COAPE   Obsolete spelling of COPE.

COAT   (obs.) A hawk's feathers, or her plumage in its entirety. For examples of use, see qus in MAIL (n.), INTERMEWED, and HAWK, White.

COLY   See BOB.

COME   By itself: of a hawk, to respond when called (to the fist or the lure). It is sometimes used to mean (of a hawk in training):
  'To begin to obey the falconer' – 1855[73].
Harting in his 1891 glossary[39] has:
  'COME TO . . . to begin obeying the falconer';
were this to read 'COME, TO', idiom and definition would be compatible. Formerly and currently, 'come to' is met with most frequently in the fuller idioms 'come to the lure' and 'come to the fist', applied to a hawk at any stage.
  '. . . She commeth by all the company [past the whole hawking party] merrily to the fist . . .' – 1619[6].

COME TO THE FIST   or -**LURE** See preceding entry.

COMMER   (unc., obs.) (Form of 'comer'.) To Latham (1618[50]), a hawk that comes promptly and reliably to the fist is 'a certain and bold commer', and 'an ill commer' is to Bert (1619[6]) one which does not.

CONDITION   A hawk's physical state.

CONDITION, Hard   See next entry.

CONDITION, High or low   A hawk's physical state, with particular regard to how well-fleshed she is and how that relates to her keenness to hunt and her performance in the field:
  'Some hawks fly best when they are in high condition, and others when they are somewhat lower.' – 1826[75].
By itself, the word high (obsolete spellings hie, hey, heye and hye) means well-fleshed, sometimes overweight, or 'in good condition' (1891[39]). Too high means over-fat, therefore not KEEN. On the reasons for unresponsiveness in a hawk when called, Turbervile (1575[81]) writes:
  '. . . Eyther hath she over gorged hir selfe, or otherwise she is to hye and too full of fleshe.'
By itself, low means underweight, or almost so, and lacking in energy; too low means underweight. 'Hard condition' is used by Phillott (1908 ft.[68]) to mean strong through exercise.
  With the same meaning as 'well-fleshed', Berners (1486[5]) uses 'high estate':
  '. . . Sum put hawkys in mew* at high estate. and sum when thay be right low. and sum whan thay be full§.

'When she is once well entred kepe her heye': facsimile page from the anonymous 16th century manuscript *A Perfect Booke for Kepinge of Sparhawkes or Goshawkes.*

and sum when they be Empty§ and lene. and sume when thay be myserabull lene.'

*In the MEWS to moult. §Taken to mean (respectively) well-fed or with a full crop, and unfed and hungry.

Until recent times, the actual or measured weight of a hawk was not a consideration, while in the modern pursuit the WEIGHING MACHINE is judged to be indispensable. Formerly, condition was determined by observation; flesh and muscle in the region of the KEEL and elsewhere was gauged by palpation, and MUTES, general appearance and behaviour were closely watched. Today in the West, these procedures remain crucial; the weighing machine is employed as an additional aid:

'A weighing machine is a wonderful aid to correct conditioning of a trained hawk, but it is not an end in itself and needs to be used in conjunction with a falconer's understanding of how his hawk is behaving and reacting.... In many ways the real skills of falconry lie in the understanding and management of "condition".' – 1987[84].

Also see WEIGHT, Flying.

CONDITIONING   Regulation by the falconer of a hawk's physical state.

CONY; CONEY   English name (now uncommon) for the wild rabbit. Once, rabbit was applied to the young only.

COOK'S BIRD   (obs.) (Cf. obs. *cuisinier*, a French alternative name for the goshawk.) A former English name for the GOSHAWK, signifying a good provider of game for the pot.

COOL   (obs.) Of meat, not rich, less rich, bland; the opposite is HOT.

COOPER'S HAWK   See HAWK, Cooper's.

COPE; COAPE (1614, obs.) (Cf. French *couper* = to cut, pare away, etc.) To trim, cut back, or pare and re-shape overgrown talons or beak. It is correct to say 'cope a hawk' and 'cope her talons and (or) beak'. The procedure is known as coping.

The shape of a wild hawk's beak is maintained through wear from the bones of her prey and by 'stropping' on abrasive surfaces (see FEAK); perching on rock or rough bark keeps talons at a nice length and sharpness.

'If you break or rive her pounce, or but coape it so short that she bleed ... yet it will indanger her life.' – 1614[57].

The hypothetical 'coped hawk' has so far not been met with, but 'coped' is the state in a hawk, or of her talons and (or) beak, after coping. Writing of a goshawk, Bert (1619[6]) recommends:

'... Let her be short coped, so I would advise all short-winged hawkes to be used, for the safty of thy owne hands ...'.

There is as yet no satisfactory explanation for the use of the verb 'feate' in Turbervile's 'You must also feate hir beake & cope hir reasonably' (1575[81]); it has been taken as a form of feak, which in the common understanding means (of a hawk) to clean her beak by 'stropping' it on some surface. Conceivably, it may be an adoption of the obsolete lay verb 'feat', meaning to equip or make fit, therefore here, by implication, to trim and shape.

COPED   See preceding entry.

COPHOOD   (obs.) (Cf. cop = the crest on a bird's head.) A hood, or an unidentified type of hood.

COPING   See COPE.

COPING-IRONS   (obs.) Implements for coping a hawk's talons and beak, presumed to be either clippers or collectively clippers and files, and perhaps a knife:

'*Coping-Irons*, are used in coping or paring the *Hawks* Beak, Pounces, or Talons, when over-grown.' – 1677 gl.[25]

Clippers, small files of different shapes, emery-boards, and sometimes a sharp knife are used today. See COPE.

COURAGE (obs.); **CURRAGE** (1486, obs.) A desirable attribute in a hawk, which encapsulates such as bravery, vigour and strength of body and spirit.

> 'Iff ye will that yowre hawke flye in the morowtide. fede hir the nyght before with hoote [hot,(?)freshly killed] mete. and wash thessame meete in ureyne [urine] and wryng owt the water clene. and that shall make hir to have lyst [list, inclination, desire] and currage to flie i[n] the morow in the best maner.' – 1486[5].

COVER; COVERT Bushes, thickets, copses, woods or other vegetation in which a hawk's quarry might seek refuge.

COVERT See preceding entry.

COVERT, Fly to the See FLY TO THE COVERT.

COVERTS See FEATHERS, Covert.

COVEY A collected family or number of partridges, and sometimes a gathering or family of grouse. Pack is the more usual term for grouse.

COWRING (unv., obs.) (Form of 'cowering'.) Taken to be an authentic falconry term by the compiler of an 18th century encyclopedia of arts and sciences; it is defined thus:

> 'Cowring, in falconry, the quivering of young hawks, who shake their wings, in sign of obedience to the old ones.' – 1728–51[20].

For this, a source such as Latham (1615[49]) was doubtless used; Latham explains that the wild adult tiercel, on approaching the falcon, shows his subjection by

> '. . . bowing down his body and head to his foot, by calling and cowring with his wings, as the young ones doe unto their dam, whom they dare not displease . . .'.

CRAB (Apparently the same as Dutch *krabben* = to scratch or claw.) Usually by itself: of a hawk, to attack or grab another with her feet, or (of hawks) to fight. Less commonly, a hawk might crab *with* another:

> 'There are some Falcons whiche will not flee with other Hawkes, but draw backward, and stirre not: some other will crabbe with every Hawke, and flee of purpose to crabbe with them . . .' – 1575[81].

The action is

> 'CRABBING, *i.e.*, grabbing; said of hawks when two are flown together, and one seizes the other on the quarry by mistake.' – 1891 gl.[39]

Turbervile (1575[81]) notes that when hawks are on perches,

> '. . . You sette your stones [stone perches] one so farre from another, that when your hawkes bate, they maye not reach one another for crabbing.'

CRABBING See preceding entry.

CRAB WITH See CRAB.

CRANES Obsolete form of CREANCE.

CRANES, In (obs.) The same as 'on a creance'; see CREANCE.

CRAW (obs.); **CROW** (obs.) A hawk's CROP.

CREANCE (Apparently from Latin *credo* = to trust, put faith in. 'So F. [French] créance, a string to retain a bird *de peu de créance*, i.e. whose indications cannot yet be well trusted' (OED). Alternatively, implicative of the falconer putting his trust in the creance as a safe restraint for his hawk. Obs. spellings and forms: CREAUNCE (1486[5]); in Turbervile (1575[81]), CRIANCE, CRYANCE, CRYAUNCE, and the extant spelling; in Latham (1615[49]), CREYANCE, CRIANCE, CRYANCE, and the extant spelling; in Bert (1619[6]), CRANES and CALLING-CRANES.) A long, light, high breaking-strain line on which a hawk in training is called or flown before she can be trusted loose. The weight or gauge is chosen according to the size and power of the hawk. In Britain it was once made of packthread (1615[49]), a stout thread or twine; Harting (1898[40]) claims that 'a plaited fishing line is best'. Elsewhere, it has been of other materials; examples are horsehair in the East[72], silk in the Far East[45]. In the modern pursuit it is of braided Terylene; it is tied to the SWIVEL or to the SWIVEL-SLITS of the jesses with the falconer's knot and wound onto a stick when not in use. In Latham (1615 gl.[49]), it is tied in an unknown way to the leash:

> '*Creance* is a fine small long line of strong and even twound [evenly twined] Packthreed, which is fastened to the Hawks leash, when she is first lured.'

Currently, a hawk is said to be on a (sometimes on the) creance when flown while restrained by a creance; obsolete equivalents are 'in the creyance' (1615[49]), 'in cranes' (1619[6]), also creanced (uncommon and no longer in use). Another obsolete variation is in:

> 'After a while she will be flown to it [the lure] in a creance, that is, a line attached to the end of the leash, or, better still, to the swivel from which the leash has been detached.' – 1900[59].

Another use for the creance has been for bagged or captive quarry; after a short-winged hawk has been enseamed (see ENSEAM) and trained and is ready for hunting, the Berners (1486[5]) recommendation is to

> '... Let sum felow of yowris preveli [covertly] take the partrich owte of yowre bagge. and ty it by the legge: with a creaunce. and cast it up as high as he can. and as soon as the hawke seith hir she will flie ther to. ...'.

On entering a young goshawk, which has flown but not taken a partridge, Bert (1619[6]) notes:

> '... Having a browne Chicken in my bagge, the necke I pull in sunder, but breake no skinne, and tyed to my Lewers [lure] or Cranes [creance] ... I throw it out fluttering, and thereupon please her as well as if she had killed a Partridge ...'.

The creance is also used for winding up a hawk, a method of ensnaring a nervous bird by entangling her legs; more in WINDING UP under TRAPS AND TRAPPING.

CREANCE, Dragged Sometimes used with a hawk whose training is almost complete but which cannot altogether be trusted loose. The CREANCE, not held by the falconer, is dragged along the ground behind the hawk in flight, slowing her somewhat and allowing the falconer to regain hold of it should she be disobedient.

CREANCED (unc., obs.) Of a hawk, on a CREANCE.

CREAUNCE Obsolete spelling of CREANCE.

CREEP, Fly at (or **to**) **the**, and **Killed at the** See FLY AT (or TO) THE CREEP.

CREPE Form of creep, in 'slayn at the Crepe' (1486[5]); see FLY AT (or TO) THE CREEP.

CREYANCE Obsolete spelling of CREANCE.

CRIANCE Obsolete spelling of CREANCE.

CRINELS (obs.); **CRINETS** (obs.); **CRINITES** (obs.) The crine feathers; see FEATHERS, Crine.

CRINES The crine feathers; see FEATHERS, Crine.

CRIVETS (unv., obs.) Apparently an error for crinets; see FEATHERS, Crine.

CROP (Obs. alternatives: GORGE, GOORGE (1486[5]), CRAW, CROW, apparently CROUPE (1486[5]).) The sac above the sternum (breastbone) of birds of prey excluding owls, serving as the first receptacle for food before it is passed to the stomach. More in CROP, Put over the.

CROP, A The contents of the crop, that is, the meat in a hawk's crop after a meal, or the amount of food allowed to her, or obliquely, a meal; hence such as a small crop, a half crop, a full crop, all used currently. This, from a magazine article written by falconer F.H. Salvin, reprinted in Harting (1898[40]), would not be considered archaic today:

> 'I always feed my Gos in the evening, giving her half or three-quarters of a crop, and a full crop on Saturdays ...'.

Such as a half crop −, half a crop −, or a crop of beef or rabbit are also correct currently. Also see GORGE, A.

CROP, Cast the; **CAST THE GORGE** (obs.) Of a hawk, to be sick; to throw up the undigested contents of the CROP, an indication of possible illness. See INFLAMMATION OF THE CROP (Appendix).

CROP, Put away the See next entry.

CROP, Put over the To expel the crop (often in portions) into the stomach with a writhing movement of head and neck; crop here means the contents of the CROP (anatomical). When a hawk has put over (or less commonly put away) her crop, the crop is empty. Similarly, in Latham (1615[49]):

> '... Every night after shee hath put away her supper, give her halfe a dozen small stones* with the stumpe of a wing ...'.

*See RANGLE. The same author also writes of a hawk having

> '... put away her supper from forth her gorge ...'.

For guidance as to a hawk's state of health, Bert (1619[6]) watches

> '... how she putteth over her meate, how shee doth indue* it ...'.

*Digest; see ENDUE. Put over is also used by itself:
'A hawk, if carried, puts over more quickly than if resting on the perch.' – 1908 ft.[68]
'An hawke puttithover [putteth over] when she remevith the mete from hir goorge in to hir bowillis. And thus ye shall knawe it whan she puttithover she traversith withe hir bodi. and speciali with the necke: as a Crane dooth or an other bridde.' – 1486[5];
the same writer also uses the current form (put over).

CROP, Spoil the (unc., obs.) According to Harting (1898[40]), to harm or adversely affect a hawk's digestion. One way of doing so, this author writes, is to give her TIRING after a big meal:

> '... for at that time the less exercise the better ...'.

CROSSING FLIGHT See FLIGHT, Crossing.

CROUP (1486[5]) Apparently an obsolete form of CROP.

CROWN   The uppermost part of a hawk's head.

CRUTCH   (obs.) An alternative to the fist when carrying a heavy bird: a T-perch (a pole with a cross-piece at one end). This pattern is known to have been used by mounted falconers in Kirghizstan, Central Asia, for bearing the weight of an eagle (see BERKUTE). The bird perches on the horizontal section while the foot of the pole is fitted into a socket in the saddle. Contemporary author Beebe[4] (N.Am.) writes of carrying an eagle in training on, and flying her to, a T-perch, but not while on horseback.

CRUTCH-PERCH   See T-PERCH under PERCHES.

CRYANCE; CRYAUNCE   Obsolete spellings of CREANCE.

CRYNETS   (obs.) The crine feathers; see FEATHERS, Crine.

CURRAGE   See COURAGE.

CUT   See next entry.

CUT DOWN   1; CUT (occ.); CHOP (probably recent; inf.) Usually of a falcon, to hit (flying quarry) with a disabling or mortal blow using the hind talons, and not BIND TO it:

> 'The statement that a peregrine cutting down a grouse or partridge without binding kills it "stone-dead" in the air, is doubtless occasionally true.' – 1900[59].

CUT DOWN   2 (probably recent; inf.) To reduce (a hawk's) weight so as to make (her) KEEN. A falconer might cut her down or cut down her weight, or she might have her weight cut down; after which she might be said to have been or (occasionally) to be cut down.

D

DARING   (obs.); DORRING (obs.) (Cf. lay verb dare = 'To daze, paralyse, or render helpless, with the sight of something; to dazzle and fascinate.' – OED. The 'lark lure' (a mechanical device incorporating a revolving blade set with small mirrors) was to fascinate and attract skylarks to within reach of Man's nets or guns.) The long obsolete practice of catching skylarks for human consumption. One method, only tenuously connected to falconry, involves putting up a falcon, often a hobby, the threat from which keeps the larks on the ground where they feel safest; they are then trapped with nets. Elyot (1531[31]) witnessed 'daring larks with a hobby' and made a written record. A scene in a picture by Flemish painter Stradanus (1525–1603) shows a variation on the foregoing method (plate 45). A hooded hawk on the fist is being encouraged by the falconer to beat her wings, no doubt by rocking or raising and lowering the fist to upset her balance. At the sight of the hawk, the (unidentified) small wild birds remain on the ground to be taken by an assistant with a noose on the end of a long pole. An identical method is described in a 19th century Persian treatise on falconry (1908, in transl.[68]); the captured larks were used afterwards as live lures at which to ENTER merlins. The writer incorrectly claims to have invented the method.

Note: One whose occupation was catching larks was usually known as a lark-catcher, although White[83] has larker. Both are lay terms and obsolete. This observation was made in 1881[55]:

> 'A lark-catcher will catch and slaughter ignominiously in a single night more skylarks than a falconer can hope to catch with one hawk in a year.'

DEAD GROUND   Ground, out of sight or over the horizon, onto which a hawk or the quarry might go.

DECK   (unc., obs.) Of a hawk, to fan the tail and spread the wings, indicating ill temper. Compare MANTLE (vb 3).

DECK-FEATHERS   See FEATHERS, Deck.

DECKS   See FEATHERS, Deck.

DECOY   If the term is used in the context of trapping, it is often a captive hawk or owl employed to attract the attention of a wild hawk and draw her towards the trap. Sometimes formerly, an eagle owl was used by British falconers as a decoy to attract quarry such as rooks and kites to within range of their hawks. More in EAGLE OWL.

DEGOUTED (obs.); **ENGOUTED** (obs.) (Degouted: Old French *deguter* = to spot or sprinkle with drops. Engouted: perhaps formed on en- = (in one sense) put on + gout = (in one sense) a drop-like spot of colour. Cf. Latin *guttatus* = splashed or spotted.) Of a hawk's feathers, marked with spots. A passage in Berners (1486[5]) gives evidence of the antique preoccupation with differing feather colourations and their perceived significance:

'And communely every goshawke and every tercellis braylis* bene bysprenged with blake speckes. like Armyns. . . . Bot and a spare hawke be so Ermyned uppon the brayles. or a Musket. oder ye shall say she is Degouted to the uttermost brayle. and much it betokynis hardenes.' This might be paraphrased: 'Commonly, every female and tiercel goshawk's brails are besprinkled with black specks like ermines. . . . When either a sparrowhawk or a musket is so ermined upon the brails, you shall say she is degouted to the last brail, and this indicates hardiness in her.'

Of a hobby:

'Hir brayle feathers* are engouted twixte red and blacke.' – 1575[81].

*See FEATHERS, Brail. Haglures (so far unverified as authentic to the English language of falconry) is an obsolete term for spots on feathers. But similar *aiglures* and *égalures*, which are markings or spots on a hawk's wings and back, occur in a mid-19th century French-language treatise on falconry[74].

DEPLUME (obs.) Of a hawk, to pluck feathers from a kill. More in PLUME 1 (vb).

DESERT FALCON See FALCON, Desert.

DEVOICE (modern) Of a veterinary surgeon, to perform a surgical operation to silence a SCREAMER.

DHO-GAZA; DO-GAZA; DO-GUZ See TRAPS AND TRAPPING.

DISCLOSE See next entry.

DISCLOSED (obs.) Of a young hawk, hatched, just hatched, or hatching.

'Now to speke of hawkys. first thay been Egges. and afterwarde they bene disclosed hawkys. . . .' – 1486[5]; also (ibid.), 'unclosed' (obs.).

'*Disclosed*, is when young *Hawkes* are newly hatch'd, and as it were disclosed from their shels.' – 1615 gl.[49]

To Cox (1677 gl.[25]),

'*Disclosed*, is when the young just peep through the shell.'

There is a verb to disclose, meaning either (of a brooding hawk) to hatch (an egg), or (of a young hawk) to hatch; both have been little used by falconers and are obsolete.

DOG, Lie to the See next entry.

DOGS IN HAWKING Historically in the West, the rôle of dogs in hawking is, in simple terms, to locate quarry in the field and flush it. A subsidiary duty may be to follow the flight and guard the hawk on a kill. In certain categories of the pursuit, such as long-obsolete heron-hawking, dogs were employed to follow the falcons and assist at the kill. It is usually difficult precisely to identify breeds of dogs in the older texts. In Italy in the 13th century, Emperor Frederick[35] used dogs of the greyhound type in heron- and crane-hawking to follow the flight and assist the hawk in subduing the quarry, even killing it. In some instances, English-language author-falconers of the 16th and 17th centuries, in their treatises on hunting with short-winged hawks, write of using spaniels, sometimes in teams, for working cover and flushing. These are undoubtedly springer spaniels, a breed deliberately developed in England in Romano-British times for springing game and perhaps used in falconry from the dawn of the pursuit in Britain more than 1,000 years ago. Like the springer, the pointer pre-dates the gun and has a long history of use in hawking. The setter was bred from spaniel stock for the gun but has since been adopted as a hawking dog. Today, springers,

On point. (Archibald Thorburn; courtesy the Tryon and Swann Gallery).

pointers and setters are still used by falconers and austringers, but there is general agreement that a number of other breeds can be taught to point, work cover, and flush satisfactorily.

POINT (vb). Of a dog, to indicate the presence and location of quarry by standing rigidly and staring towards it.
COME ON TO POINT. To begin to point.
ON POINT. Pointing.
A POINT. The term suggests both the place where quarry lies and the response of the dog in pointing. A falcon might wait on 'at a great pitch over a point' (1892[47]). A dog might find a point, or stay on a point.
STEADY (or **STAUNCH**, ? obs.) **ON A POINT.** Steadily pointing.
SOLID POINT. A point which, by the dog's demeanour, suggests to the falconer the likely presence of the right quarry.
STAUNCH POINT (? obs.). A solid point.
HARD POINT (unv.). A solid point. Other combination terms with the same meaning are met with, such as sure point and firm point.
HOLD (THE) POINT. To remain steadfastly pointing.
FALSE POINT (n.). A point where the desired quarry is not present, perhaps having already gone from the spot and left its scent, or a point at the wrong quarry. In Woodford (1987[84]), it is noted that skylarks may have a game scent, which would induce a dog to point. False point sometimes occurs as a verb.
LIE TO THE POINT; LIE TO THE DOG. Of quarry located by the dog or which is pointed by him, to lie or remain in cover until flushed.
HONOUR THE POINT. See BACK (below).
STEAL THE POINT. See BACK (below).
BACK. To point in response to seeing another dog pointing. To honour the point is for the backing dog to remain behind the pointing dog and not steal the point by coming alongside or past him.
SET (form of sit). Of a setter, to indicate where quarry lies by crouching or sitting and pointing his muzzle towards it.
RUN. Of a falconer, to work (a dog or dogs) in the field, encouraging (him or them) to locate quarry by scent.
GO IN. Of a dog on the falconer's command, to make towards the spot where quarry lies or has put in to cover, in order to flush it.
RUN IN. Of a dog, to go in to the flush ahead of the falconer's command to do so.

WORK. Of a dog, to seek quarry by scent; also in combinations such as work the ground and work cover. Also, of a falconer, to run (a dog or dogs) in the field.
FLY OVER DOGS. Perhaps particularly (but not exclusively) of a falconer game-hawking, to fly (a hawk) with dogs.
HAWK OVER DOGS (1900[59]). The same as the preceding.

The following will be found in their alphabetical places in *The Encyclopedia*:
FLUSH ('reflush' under same heading)
FLUSH, The ('the reflush' under same heading)
RETRIEVE
RETRIEVE, The

DORRING   Form of DARING.

DOWN; FULLY DOWN. Of a feather, full-grown, met with in such as 'her deck feathers are not yet down' or '– fully down'.

DOWN, In the   Said of a young hawk in her first feathering or down.

DOWNCOME, At the   (obs.) In effect, by stooping and striking. A falcon might 'kill it [quarry] at the downecome' (1618[49]); fuller qu. in MARK, Fly to.

DOWNY   North American falconers' name for a young hawk still in her first feathering or down.

D-PERCH   Under PERCHES.

DRAW   1 (obs.) Of a hawk, to fly at (quarry) in a manner which is not fully understood. Berners (1486[5]) suggests that the verb was misused in her day; unfortunately, neither the misuse nor the correct usage are fully elucidated in the text:

> 'Som folke mysuse this terme draw. and say that thayr hauke will draw to the Ryver. And that terme draw is propurli assigned to that hawke that will slee* a Roke or a Crow or a Ravyn: upon a londe§ sittyng. and then it most be sayd that sich an hawke will draw weell to a Rooke.'

*Slay; also see TAKE.

§'Londe' is an obsolete spelling of land; the implication appears to be that 'draw' is misused when applied to a hawk flying waterfowl.

DRAW   2 (obs.) Of wild hawks, according to Berners (1486[5]), to nest-build:

> 'And we shall say that hawkys doon draw when they bere tymberyng to their nestes. and nott they beld ne make [build or make] ther nestes.'

DRAW   3 See DRAW AFTER.

DRAW 4 See MEW, Draw from the.

DRAW AFTER (probably obs.) Of a short-winged hawk, to follow (the austringer or his dogs), flying from perch to perch, in anticipation of quarry being flushed; or of the austringer, to encourage (her) to follow in the same way. Applied to a goshawk:

'. . . If in the wood-land you shall sometime make her draw after you, and serve her with the Spaniels, it will doe her good . . .' – 1619[6];

and (ibid.):

'I must herein suppose that shee will draw after the dogges, or otherwise after her keeper . . .'.

'. . . By your softest voice or whistle draw her along after you . . .' – 1618[50].

By itself, 'draw' may in one obsolete sense mean to draw after. Also see FOLLOW.

DRAWER See note in TABUR STYKE.

DRAW FROM THE MEW See MEW, Draw from the.

DRAWING See MEW, Draw from the.

DRAW (or **TAKE**) **OUT OF MEW** See MEW, Draw from the.

DROP A FEATHER See FEATHER, Drop a.

DROPPING See 1615 qu. in MUTE.

DRUM See TABOR, and TABUR STYKE.

DUCK-HAWK See HAWK, Duck.

DUTCH METHOD (of trapping hawks) See TRAPS AND TRAPPING.

E

EAGER (Obsolete spellings: EGAR (c.1575), EAGRE (1575[81]), EEGRE (1486[5]).) Hungry, keen. Of a short-winged hawk during her reclamation:

'. . . When she will come* redely, let her fast w^t a q[uar]ter gorge** at the most from morninge to vii a clok at nyght, and then call her loose abrode ii or iii tymes before you sup her; for at that tyme she muste be kept veary egar in this sorte for ii dayes, leste she gett the toye of checking§ wch if she take not then, she will never have it.' – c.1575[38].

*'To the fist' is implied here.

**A small meal; more in GORGE, A.

§This is taken to mean 'lest she gets the notion of shying from the fist'.

Another example of use of eager in GLEETOUS.

EAGLE (Middle English egle; Latin *aquila*.) The eagles with a history of use as falconers' birds are chiefly the golden eagle (*Aquila chrysaetos*) and certain so-called HAWK-EAGLES. See EAGLE, Golden.

EAGLE, Bonelli's See HAWK-EAGLES.

EAGLE, Golden *Aquila chrysaetos* ('Golden' relates to the tawny feathers at the crown and nape which are particularly conspicuous in sunlight.) One of the so-called true eagles. Although too heavy to carry easily on the fist without some kind of CRUTCH or an ARM-BRACE, the golden eagle has been used in falconry in various parts of the world, but rarely in the West, and then only where the terrain is suitably open and hilly. Those in Britain who have flown it have taken rabbits and hares and apparently foxes and small deer. It has been flown at medium and large ground-quarry in Central Asia, where its use as a falconer's bird has a long history. (Plates 4 and 70).

There are scattered references in older English hawking literature of true eagles being used in European falconry. Species are often difficult to identify, but it seems that, among others, the Imperial eagle (*Aquila heliaca*, formerly *A.imperialis*) of Europe and Asia and the steppe eagle (a Eurasian race of *A.rapax*) have been used experimentally or to a limited extent.

EAGLE, True An eagle of the genus *Aquila*, one being the golden eagle (*A.chrysaetos*).

EAGLE OWL *Bubo bubo* (Also GREAT OWL (obs.).) Once used by English falconers as a decoy to attract quarry such as rooks (Plate 59). Jessed as a hawk, it might be tethered on a high perch, presently luring rooks which would mob it and be too preoccupied to observe the presence of falconer and falcon:

'Recently the Old Hawking Club [dissolved 1926] employed an eagle owl for this purpose. He lived for several years at the Zoo in Regent's Park [London Zoo], pending his annual outing to the Wiltshire downs during the rook-hawking season.' – 1936 [1970][8].

In kite-hawking, Lascelles (1892[47]) describes a method of luring the quarry to within reach of the falconer's birds:

'As soon as the bird [kite] was descried soaring in mid air, generally at a height so great that it could hardly be distinguished, a live owl was let fly by the falconers, to whose legs was attached a fox's brush. This both impeded the owl's flight ... and also presented to the kite the spectacle of a bird of prey, such as could easily be robbed, carrying off some quarry.'

Sebright (1826[75]), in his notes on this method, describes the decoy as a 'great owl', which is probably the European race of the Eurasian eagle owl (*Bubo bubo bubo*). An Eastern practice of luring wild hawks into nets using an eagle owl is described in DHO-GAZA (under TRAPS AND TRAPPING).

Owls have no tradition of use as falconer's birds, although the European eagle owl has occasionally been trained and flown at quarry in modern times, as has its relative the American great-horned owl (*Bubo virginianus*). On training owls, FR[65].

EAGLET A young eagle. The term seems rarely to be used by falconers.

EAR-COVERTS See FEATHERS, Covert.

EGG YOLK Traditionally, a nutritious supplement given to a hawk during the moult or when she is in low condition. Raw egg has been recommended (1856[76]), added to meat, when FRET MARKS on feathers are noticed. A remedy for a hawk 'that hath loost her corrage*' is, according to Berners (1486[5]), 'Oyle of spayne [oil of Spain, olive oil]', clear wine, and the yolk of an egg with her beef.

*Vigour of body and spirit; more in COURAGE.

EIAS; EIASSE Obsolete spellings of EYASS.

EIRY Obsolete spelling of EYRIE.

EMARGINATION A reduction in breadth in primary feathers towards the tip (see FEATHERS, Primary); the narrowing of the feathers often creates slots at the wing-tip, giving a hand-like appearance when the wing is spread. Such feathers are said to be emarginated or notched. The posterior or trailing portion of the vane is often sharply emarginated in the outer primaries of raptors which habitually soar. Emargination has aerodynamic implications.

EMBOWELLED (obs.) Said of a hawk when her crop is empty and her bowels stiff, when the process of digestion is not yet complete:

'And if her goorge be wide* and the bowell any thyng stiffid. ye shall say she is embowellid and hath not fully endewed**. and as long as ye may fele§ any thyng in hir bowellis it is perlous [parlous, perilous] to gyve her any mete.' – 1486[5].

*This phrase means 'if her crop is empty'.
**Digested her food; see ENDUE.
§With the fingers.

EMMEW (unv., obs.); **IMMEW** (unv., obs.) Apparently to put (a hawk) into the mews.

EMPTY (obs.) Of a hawk, having had no food; having no food in her CROP and (or) PANNEL; or obliquely, hungry or very hungry. For an example of use, see fourth 1575 qu. in FRET MARKS.

ENDEW Spelling of ENDUE.

ENDUE (obs.); ENDEW (obs.); INDEW (1619[6], obs.) (From Latin *induco* = to draw into, induct.) To digest food. The Latham glossary entry (1615[49]) is:

'*Endew*, is when a *Hawke* digesteth her meat, not only putting it over from her gorge*, but also cleansing her pannell**.'

*See CROP, Put over the.
**This phrase it taken to mean (in effect) muting, that is, expelling droppings. In the text, this writer's phrase 'perfectly endured' appears to mean (of the hawk's meal) completely digested.

ENEAW; ENEWE Spellings of ENEW.

ENEW (obs.) (Formed on en- = (in the sense of) to put into + Old French *ewe* (Modern French *eau*) = water. Alternative spellings: ENEWE and ENNEW (both 1486[5]), ENNUE, ENEAW (1612), INEW, INEAWE (1612), also ENMEW; this last may be a misspelling, or is confused with emmew which apparently means to put (a hawk) into the mews; all obs.) Originally, of a hawk, to drive (quarry, specifically waterfowl) into the water. In this 15th century example of its use, there may be a tautology:

'And if it happyn as it dooth oftimes the fowle for fere of yowre hawke woll spryng and fall ayen [again] in to the Ryver. or the hawke sees hir. and so lie styll and dare not arise. ye shall say then yowre hawke hath enneweD the fowle in to the Ryver....' – 1486[5].

With the spelling enew, the OED definitions are

'Of a hawk: To drive (a fowl) into the water' and 'Of a fowl: To plunge in the water'. The term later came to mean to drive (quarry) into cover or put (it) in. The Harting glossary (1891[39]) has:
'ENEW, or INEW ... the same as PUT IN ...';
this application is also obsolete.

ENGOUTED   See DEGOUTED.

ENMEW   Perhaps a misspelling of ENEW.

ENNEW; ENNUE   Spellings of ENEW.

ENOIL HERSELF   See OIL HERSELF.

ENSAYME   (vb and n.) See next entry.

ENSEAM   (obs.) (Old French *ensaimer*. Cf. obs. lay English seam = fat, grease. Alternative spellings: INSEAM, ENSAYME.) Of a falconer, to prepare and tone up a hawk's digestive system in a holistic way, a practice which was once considered indispensable in the readying of a hawk for hunting. The process (termed enseaming) had several elements which usually included administering RANGLE and purges and the feeding of washed meat (see MEAT, Washed). Together these were believed to 'cleanse' an unreclaimed or newly moulted hawk of internal fat, in particular that which lines the stomach, or of 'grease, fat, and glut' as an early 17th century writer puts it[23]. She would thereby be 'made clean' internally. Enseaming is looked on by some today as a lost art in the perfecting of a hawk's inner physical health and digestion.

The less intricate modern method of a hawk's preparation (with judicious dieting and exercise) appears to be anticipated in the chapter on enseaming in *A Perfect Booke* (c.1575[38]):
> 'Ensayming is to take her gresynes and foulnes [greasiness and foulness] awaye wch is done by continuall cleane fedinge, castinge, tyringe, water & callinge, wherby she maye come by breth and wynde at will before in no wyse you maye enter her.'

Yet later in this text is a 'scouringe' (purge) which the anonymous author notes is good for speeding up the process of enseaming. Uncommonly, to enseam can mean (of the hawk herself) to become free of internal fat and other 'impure substances' as a result of the above regimen. According to Berners (1486[5]), 'ensayme' is also the internal fat itself:
> 'Ensayme of an hawke is the grece. ...'.

ENSEAMED (obs.); **INSEAMED** (obs.)   A hawk's state after the process of enseaming has been completed; see preceding entry. A hawk might be or have been enseamed, and may be referred to as an enseamed hawk. The opposite (that is, fat, or not in flying condition, or yet to be enseamed) is seamed, but this idiom is so far unverified as authentic.

ENSEAMING   See ENSEAM.

ENSERED   See CERE.

ENSILE; ENSILED   See SEEL.

ENTER   By itself: of a falconer, to initiate (a newly trained hawk) in taking wild quarry; to fly (her) at wild quarry, the result being her first kill. The idiom (by itself) has sometimes been applied when the hawk is given bagged (or captive) quarry for her first kill; this is thought to be incorrect, a consensus being that strictly speaking she is not 'entered' unless her first kill is wild. However, with the bagged quarry specified, constructions such as 'enter her at a bagged partridge' are acceptable.

The fuller 'enter (her) at quarry' or (say) '– at duck' are correct when that quarry is wild. Once she has taken her first wild quarry, she is said to be entered or to have been entered, and the point when she takes it has occasionally been referred to as her entering.

Of a recently trained hawk, Turbervile (1575[81]) uses the obsolete phrase 'well entred and quarred' (well entered and quarried), which means (in effect) hunting successfully; more in QUARRIED.

To introduce a previously entered hawk to a quarry new to her is to enter her, but the quarry is always specified: 'Hares being scarce, I entered her at pheasant'. The verb enter means to introduce in the idioms 'enter (a hawk) to the lure' and '– to the hood'. Obsolete 'enter to the field' and '– to the covert' are used by Latham (1618[50]) to mean (respectively) to introduce (a hawk) to hunting in open country and in countryside featuring thickets, copses or woods.

ENTER AT QUARRY   See preceding entry.

ENTERED; ENTERING (n.) See ENTER.

ENTERMEWED; ENTERMURED   See INTERMEWED.

ENTERMEWER   See INTERMEWER.

ENTERPEN   See next entry.

ENTERPENNED (obs.); **ENTIRPENNED** (1486, obs.) (Form of inter- = (in one sense) between + penned = feathered.) There have been conflicting definitions of this term. It may describe a hawk whose moult is not finished, her growing feathers being not yet fully down, or whose moult has finished (that is, the same as INTERMEWED), or, less plausibly, whose wing-feathers have become somehow entangled, perhaps round her leg. The confusion may be due to differing interpretations of a perplexing passage in Berners (1486[5]), which says:

> 'Say an hawke hath a long wyng. a faire long tayll with. vi barris [bars, bands] owt. and stondith uppon the.vii. This hawke is entirpenned That is to say when the federis of the wynges bene bitwen the body and the thighis.'

Elsewhere in this text, the number of bands visible on new tail-feathers is suggested as a guide to how well grown they are, although seven dark bands exceeds the number found on the tail-feathers of goshawks and sparrowhawks with which the treatise deals. Of course, a way of arriving at a different total is to count both the dark and light bands. Here, 'stondith' (meaning stands) is less likely to be connected with physically standing (with a foot, hence perhaps the 'entangling' explanation) than with the expectation of another band to appear. The words 'the feathers of the wings are between the body and the thighs' might suggest the length of the hawk's primary feathers, or their growth so far.

An 18th century definition of the verb 'enterpen' is as follows:

> 'A Hawk enterpenneth, that is, she hath her Feathers wrapt up, snarled or intangled.' – 1736[2].

In this case, if the passage were to be judged in isolation, it might be tempting to conclude that wrapped, snarled and entangled relate to developing feathers which are still furled in their protective sheaths.

ENTER TO THE FIELD or **COVERT** See ENTER.

ENTER TO THE HOOD See HOODS AND HOODING.

ENTER TO THE LURE Under LURE (n. and vb).

ENTERVIEW (unc., obs.); **INTERVIEW** (unc., obs.) (View may be a corruption of mew, in which case the term is taken to be formed on French *entre-* = between + French *muer* = to moult; otherwise, second element from French *voir* = to see, significance uncertain.) A hawk in her second year, between her first and second moults (compare INTERMEWER), and perhaps the period itself. See 1677 qu. in HAWK, White.

ERIE Obsolete spelling of EYRIE.

ESCAPED HAWKS Under TRAPS AND TRAPPING.

EYAS Alternative spelling of EYASS.

EYASS; EYAS (Once NYAS; also NIAS(E), NIAISE, NYESS (1852), NIARD, others; all obs. Perhaps influenced by Middle English ey = egg, or mutated into 'an eyas' from 'a nyas'; Latin *nidus* = nest. Cf. Old English nædre = an adder. The Berners (1486[5]) etymology is:

> 'An hawke is calde an Eyes of hir Eyghen. for an hauke that is broght up under a Bussard or a Puttocke: as mony be: hath wateri Eyghen. For whan thay be disclosed and kepit in ferme tyll thay be full summyd. ye shall knawe theym by theyr wateri Eyghen. And also hir looke will not be so quycke as a Brawncheris is. and so be cause the best knawlege is by the Eygh. they be calde Eyeses.' This might be paraphrased: 'A hawk is called an eyass because of her eyes, for a hawk that is reared under a buzzard*, as many are, has watery eyes**. When they are hatched and kept confined§ until they are full summed, you shall know them by their watery eyes. Also, her look will not be so lively as a brancher's [see BRANCHER (n.)]. Therefore, the best knowledge suggests that they are called eyasses because of the eye.'

*It is unconfirmed that this suggests Man's intervention in placing eggs under buzzards; puttock (or puddock) is an English provincial name for the common buzzard (*Buteo buteo*), also an English vernacular name for the kite or for any hawk.

**Taken to mean pallid in colour as if diluted with water.

§The phrase 'in ferme' is taken to mean in confinement, although whether the place in question is a cage or the mews is not known; more in FERME, In.

Obs. spellings: EYES (1486), EYESS (1891[39]), EYESSE (1575), EIAS (1615[49]), EIASSE, others.)
A nestling hawk, unable to fly; a young wild hawk taken from the eyrie for the purposes of falconry. Whilst aware that in his day eyass was equally applicable to a short-winged hawk, Turbervile (1575[81]) notes that

> 'The firste name and terme that they bestowe on a Falcon, is an Eyesse, and this name dothe laste as long as she is in the eyrie, & for that she is taken from the eyrie.'

Today, an eyass is also a captive-bred nestling, and both the wild-caught and captive-bred birds will be termed intermewed eyasses when they have moulted for the first time in captivity. The term is

Young hawk by Archibald Thorburn

also used adjectivally in such as eyass sparrow-hawk, eyass musket. It is met with in further combinations such as intermewed eyass musket.

Touching on an eyass short-winged hawk's vices and tameness as a hunting bird, the anonymous author of *A Perfect Booke* (c.1575[38]) notes:

'Nyas is worst for diverse causis, but yet are redye of cominge and will never be lost.'

A young hawk which is incompletely trained may sometimes be termed an eyass; this application is not strictly correct. Also see JASS.

EYE (c.1430[10], obs.) (Apparently mutated into 'an eye' from 'a nye' (the latter now only dialect). Also NIDE (archaic).) A brood of pheasants.

EYE-PIECES; EYEPIECES Under HOODS AND HOODING.

EYER (obs.) (Cf. Medieval Latin (Brit.–Ir.[48]) *eyero* = to nest.) Of hawks, to nest, nest-build, or breed.

'And we shall say that hawkis doon Eyer. and not brede. in the woodes.' – 1486[5].

Writing of the wild peregrine, Latham (1615[49]) may intend the verb 'eyrees' to mean nests or nest-builds, in:

'. . . Shee for the most part Eyrees and breeds on the tops of high rocks in the cold aire . . .'.

EYERER; EYRER (both 1486[5] and obs.) (Cf. Medieval Latin (Brit.–Ir.[48]) *eyrerius* = a nesting bird. Obs. adjectival ayrer, meaning breeding, may exist in combinations such as 'ayrer falcon'.) A breeding or brooding hawk.

EYES; EYESS Obsolete spellings of EYASS.

EYREE See EYER, and EYRIE.

EYRER See EYERER.

EYRIE; AERIE (Thought to be from Latin *area* = an open place or space, and not connected with Middle English ey = egg. Numerous obs. English spellings and forms, such as AERY, AYRE (c.1575[38]), EYREE (1575[81]), AIRE, ERIE, EIRY (last three 1615[49]).) To falconers (often), the wild nest, nest ledge or breeding place of any diurnal bird of prey. To the layman, the nest or nesting place of an open-spaces bird of prey such as the golden eagle or peregrine.

'Eyrie or ayrie, among falconers the place or nest where hawks sit and hatch and feed their young.' – 1757[30].

In his treatise on falconry, Latham (1615 gl.[49]) has:

'*Erie* is the nest or place where a *Hawke* buildeth and bringeth up her young ones, whether in woods, rockes, or any other places.'

In a modified sense:

'An Ayerye of goosse hawks.' – c.1520 (OED);

compare Medieval Latin (Brit.–Ir.[48]) *heyrius* = eyrie or brood, depending on context.

FALCO (Latin = falcon.) The genus which contains (among others) the falcons of traditional falconry. It consists of some 35 species[13] which vary from thrush-sized birds weighing less than 100 grams to the largest, the gyrfalcon, a female weighing up to 2000 grams. The wings of falcons are long and markedly tapered towards the tip when spread. Tail lengths vary from short to rather long. The legs are generally short, and the feet powerful in those species used in falconry. Many species have a darkly-marked moustachial stripe tapering downwards from the eye; the irides of the eye are almost invariably dark. Each cutting edge (sci. tomium) of the upper part of the beak is sharply notched; this configuration is known to falconers as a TOOTH or notch, formerly nook.

The females are larger than the males, sometimes markedly so. Historically, the falcons used most widely in Western falconry are the gyrfalcon (*Falco rusticolus*), peregrine falcon (*F.peregrinus*), saker falcon (*F.cherrug*), lanner falcon (*F.biarmicus*), and merlin (*F.columbarius*). The Indian lugger falcon (*F.jugger*) has not been flown widely in the West but has a history of use by native falconers on the Indian subcontinent. The American prairie falcon (*F.mexicanus*) has been added to the list of falconers' birds in recent years and is highly thought of.

FALCON 1 (n.) (Numerous obs. spellings.) A diurnal bird of prey of the genus *Falco*, often referred to by falconers as a long-winged hawk or longwing. The term 'true falcon' occasionally occurs in older literature, often referring to the peregrine falcon in particular. Formerly, the 'noble' falcons were the gyrfalcon and the peregrine, saker and lanner falcons, the most highly esteemed of the long-winged hawks used in traditional Western falconry. In the wild, falcons are largely of open countryside, therefore flown in that environment by falconers. In the most basic of terms, a falcon is put up to WAIT ON until quarry is sprung beneath her by falconer, beaters or dogs; or she is flown from the fist in the case of lark-hawking with merlins; or she is flown out of the hood in such as rook-hawking and (formerly) heron-hawking; see FLY OUT OF THE HOOD. She is not usually called to the fist in the manner of a short-winged hawk, but to the lure, hence the old name 'hawk of the lure'.

FALCON 2 (n.) Traditionally and currently, the name for the female peregrine when the subject is this species in particular, distinguishing her from the tiercel (the male). Sometimes formerly (less widely today), it is applied to the females of other long-winged hawks in falconry, but not usually the merlin and hobby, however:

> 'FALCON, the female Peregrine *par excellence*, but applied generally to the females of all long-winged hawks.' – 1891 gl.[39]

Formerly, when the intention was to indicate that a hawk (other than a peregrine) was female, or when referring to a female hawk, to give the species name was often considered sufficient; hence gyrfalcon, saker or goshawk (or their variants) would indicate either female or species, depending on context.

There are other interpretations of the term 'falcon'; it has been, although not commonly,

> '. . . The female of any hawk as opposed to the male, when used by falconers.' – 1892 gl.[47];

and in the Salvin & Brodrick glossary (1855[73]) it is

> 'The female Peregrine and Goshawk "par excellence;" also the general term for the long-winged Hawks.'

FALCON (vb, unc., obs.) To hunt with falcons.

FALCON, Barbary *Falco pelegrinoides* (This entry presupposes that, despite some uncertainty, the Barbary falcon is not a subspecies of peregrine falcon, and that this hawk and the red-naped shaheen should be regarded as a distinct species. See SHAHEEN.)
Alternative names:
  TARTARET (obs.; Tartar- = (?)of supposed Tartar origin + diminutive -et.)
  TARTARET FALCON (obs.)
  BARBERIE FALCON (1575[81], obs.)
A smallish peregrine-like falcon of North Africa, used as a falconer's bird. Falcons (females) have been used with success in Britain to fly at partridge, the tiercels at small quarry such as starlings (*Sturnus vulgaris*).

> 'That falcon which is called the Tartaret or Barbary Falcon, whome they doe chiefly use in Barbary*.' – 1575[81].

*Former name for lands along the north coast of Africa. (Plate 2).

FALCON, Desert The saker falcon. Desert falcons is sometimes used as a group-name for saker, lanner, lugger and prairie falcons.

FALCON, Greenland See GYRFALCON.

FALCON, Iceland See GYRFALCON.

FALCON, Labrador See GYRFALCON.

FALCON, Laggar See FALCON, Lugger.

FALCON, Lanner *Falco biarmicus* (French *lanier*; Old French *lanier* = cowardly. Significance uncertain but perhaps explained by the antique application of 'lanner' to a variety of hawks, some considered ignoble or uncourageous in the context of falconry.) Alternative names and forms:
  LANNER. In recent and current use, shortening denoting the species; formerly, sometimes the female in particular.
  LANER(E) (obs.). The species or the female in particular.
  LANARE (obs.). In Berners (1486[5]), the female:
  > 'Ther is a Lanare and a Lanrell*. And theys belong to a Squyer.'

*Taken to be a misspelling of lanrett, an old spelling of lanneret.
>LANNARD (unc., obs.)
>LANNERET. The male.
>LANRETT (obs.). The male.
>KITCHEN HAWK (obs.). This sobriquet appears to be connected to the taking of game for the pot; compare COOK'S BIRD.

The lanner falcon is widespread through much of Africa; it is also found in parts of the Middle East and Mediterranean Europe. Historically in Western falconry, the lanner has long been present as a falconer's bird, although somewhat overshadowed by the preferred peregrine falcon. It has been flown in recent times by British falconers at birds such as rooks and moorhens, and game birds to some extent; it is however little used in falconry in Britain today. Turbervile[81] writes in the 16th century:
>'With this hawke may you flye the ryver . . .', that is, fly her at waterfowl; he also notes that in France, falconers '. . . use to flee with a caste or leashe of Laners [two or three together] to the brooke . . .'.

Considering that latter-day falconers in Zimbabwe have spoken highly of the lanner as a small bird hawk or game-hawk, it is doubtless suitable for wider use outside Africa. Temperamentally steady and easily tamed, it is regarded as suitable for the falconer of modest experience who plans to progress to a peregrine. (Plates 8, 9, 36 and 74).

FALCON, Lugger *Falco jugger* (Hindi *laggar*.)
Alternative spellings and forms:
>LUGGER. Shortening denoting the species.
>LAGGAR (occasionally LUGGAR, LUGGUR) FALCON
>JUGGER, perhaps JUGGER FALCON (both unc. and obs.)

The lugger is found in India and some bordering and neighbouring countries including Pakistan and Afghanistan to the west and Myanmar to the east. The wild hawk preys on small- to medium-sized birds, small mammals, lizards and insects. It has not seen extensive use in the West, although it is reckoned to be capable of taking similar quarry to the lanner. It has a history of use by native falconers on the Indian subcontinent.

FALCON, Norway See GYRFALCON.

FALCON, Peregrine *Falco peregrinus* (Latin *peregrinus* = coming from foreign parts, stranger, foreigner, a reference to migratory habits.) Traditionally and currently, the female is referred to as

Peregrine falcon. (Derek Middleton; FLPA, Images of Nature).

the falcon, the male the tiercel; more in FALCON 2 (n.), and TIERCEL.
Alternative names and forms:
>PEREGRINE. Current shortening denoting the species.
>FALCON PEREGRINE (obs. Also spelt 'fawken peregryne' (1486[5]); others). The peregrine falcon (species), the form probably taken directly from Latin *Falco peregrinus* used by Albertus Magnus c.1250; the modern French is *faucon pèlerin*.
>'Fawcons pelegrynes, that have stande and rested longe on the perche hath grete desyre to flye abrode.' – 1525[11].
>DUCK HAWK; DUCK-HAWK. An English provincial and North American vernacular name for the peregrine falcon (species).
>PIGEON HAWK; PIGEON-HAWK. Former vernacular English name.
>FALCON GENTLE, FALCON-GENTLE or GENTLE FALCON (all obs.). Correctly, the female peregrine, although they may occasionally occur as equating to peregrine falcon (species). See notes and qus in FALCON GENTLE.
>GENTLE (obs.). The female peregrine in particular, or very occasionally the peregrine falcon (species).

TIERCEL (or **TERCEL**) **GENTLE** (obs.). The male.
TERCEL- or (**TARCEL-**) **GENTLE** (obs.). The male.
TASSEL GENTLE (1677[53], obs.). The male.
SLIGHT (or **SLEIGHT**) **FALCON** (obs.). The peregrine falcon (species) or the female in particular. According to the Wood & Fyfe glossary[35], the slight falcon is 'The female peregrine falcon, caught in early autumn, after leaving the nest, but before migration.' More in FALCON, Slight.
SLIGHT TERCEL (obs.). The male. According to the Wood & Fyfe glossary[35], it is
  'The male peregrine falcon caught before migration.'

The peregrine falcon is virtually cosmopolitan, occurring in perhaps more than 20 subspecies world-wide, most commonly in open country. The wild peregrine is a supremely efficient aerial hunter, the larger races taking avian prey up to the size of geese. Typical hunting tactics involve stooping at flying prey from above and either killing or disabling it with one blow from the hind talons, or repeatedly stooping and striking to exhaust it before knocking it down or binding to it. In falconry, it is rarely flown at fur; it is (and traditionally has been) flown at a wide variety of flying quarry, reflecting the broad range of prey it takes in the wild. It is the most versatile of all the falcons, flown by British falconers at (among others) grouse, blackgame and ptarmigan, gulls, rooks and duck, and at magpies with tiercels. Formerly in Western falconry, it was flown in a cast at herons and kites. (Plates 12, 13–15, 60–62 and 71).

FALCON, Prairie *Falco mexicanus* Alternative names:
  PRAIRIE The species; a popular shortening.
  AMERICAN SAKER (unc., obs.). This is almost certainly an exclusively lay term; it occurs in a late 19th century English dictionary: 'A . . . falcon of western North America, Falco polyagrus or F.mexicanus, is known as the *American saker*.' – 1891[19].

A falcon of the arid and semi-arid plains and steppes of western and central North America, south to Mexico. Somewhat less robust in appearance than the peregrine, it preys chiefly on small- to medium-sized birds and some mammals. American falconers think highly of it, considering it second in quality only to the peregrine. Although admired by British falconers, it is flown in Britain less extensively than the peregrine, but at similar quarry. (Plate 16).

FALCON, Saker *Falco cherrug* (From Arabic *saqr*; this name is used today by Arabs when speaking generally about birds of prey (except vultures and eagles).) Alternative names and forms:
SAKER. Shortening denoting the species, or (formerly) the female in particular.
SAGER (c.1400, obs.).
SACRE (obs.). The species or the female in particular. 'Ther is a Sacre and a Sacret [male]. And theis be for a knyght.' – 1486[5].
DESERT FALCON. The saker falcon (species). Saker, lanner, lugger and prairie falcons are sometimes known collectively as desert falcons.
SAKRET. The male.
SACRET (obs.). The male.
SAKERET (obs.). The male.
SACKERET (obs.). The male.

Found in Central Europe and Asia east to Manchuria, the saker is the second-largest of the world's falcons, the gyrfalcon being the largest. Its wild prey includes small mammals, sometimes reptiles, even large insects, and birds from sparrow-size to duck. In falconry, it is perhaps most strongly associated with the highly-organised hawking culture in the Middle East and with flights at houbara (Macqueen's) bustard, *Chlamydotis undulata*. Phillott (1908[68]) notes that in his day passage sakers were flown at bustard in India, usually out of the hood; they were also trained to wait on when flown in districts full of ravines, out of which quarry had to be flushed. He mentions that sakers were trained for kites and hares there. In certain Eastern cultures, the larger species of falcon were flown, usually in a cast, at unnaturally large ground-quarry in cooperation with hounds; an example is the use of sakers in Persia to fly gazelles. In the 13th century, Emperor Frederick[35] wrote at length of the merits of the falcons he had experience of flying in Italy; he broadly assigns sakers to the heron, noting that they exhibit their most beautiful flights in heron-hawking. There are scattered records in older English literature of the saker having been flown in Britain at a variety of avian quarry and hares. It has been flown in recent times in Britain at rooks, crows, grouse and pheasant, but not extensively. (Plate 18).

FALCON, Slight (obs.); SLEIGHT FALCON (1575, obs.) (The etymology of 'slight' in this context is uncertain. A suggestion has been that this and German *schlicht* (meaning simple, plain) have a common origin; significance not known.) Usually the peregrine falcon (species) or the female peregrine in particular. In the Wood & Fyfe glossary[35], it is the female peregrine falcon caught in early autumn before migration; similarly (ibid.) the slight tercel is the male peregrine caught at the same time. Turbervile (1575[81]) seems to suggest that adjectival 'ramage' and 'sleight' are interchangeable when referring to falcons, that is, either may be applied to wild birds in their first year and 'praying for themselves'; fuller qu. in HAWK, Ramage. OED equates slight falcon with falcon gentle, the latter correctly being the female peregrine.

FALCON, Sultan See SHAHEEN.

FALCON, Tartaret See FALCON, Barbary.

FALCON, True See FALCON 1 (n.)

FALCONER 1 (Many obs. spellings, including FAULKNER (1386), FAUKENER (1486), FAWKNER (c.1575), FAWCONER (1581), FAULCONER (1677).)

Historically, one who keeps, trains and flies hawks, or falcons specifically. Today, falconer is correct for one who keeps and hunts with long-, short- or broad-winged hawks, or eagles, although austringer survives in lesser use as one who keeps and hunts with short-winged hawks, sometimes broad-winged hawks. The term is also an official designation, as in Hereditary Grand Falconer, and in:

> 'The Emperor of China in his sporting excursions ... is usually attended by his grand falconer.' – 1797 [1847][7].

Other titles such as 'master falconer' and 'assistant falconer' occur in some older English texts.

German falconer of the 16th century, from an engraving by an unknown artist.

Falconer and falcon impeccably turned out. Note the flat woven leash, a modern successor to the traditional hide version. (A. Walker).

FALCONER 2 (obs.) (Alternative spellings: FALCONERE, FAULKNER; both obs. French *fauconnière*[74].) A game and equipment bag carried by a falconer. See BAG, Hawking.

FALCONER, Hereditary Grand In England since the 17th century, the royal appointment 'Hereditary Grand Falconer of England' has been held by the Dukes of St Albans. It has been a sinecure since the 19th century. Also see plate 44.

FALCON GENTLE (obs.); **FALCON-GENTLE** (obs.) (French *faucon gentil*. Gentle in this context is taken to mean noble [of excellent breed or spirit (OED)]; it is also spelt gentil, gentile, etc.) The term applies only to the peregrine falcon. Correctly, it is the female peregrine, although it may occasionally occur as equating to peregrine falcon (species); tiercel gentle (in numerous spellings and forms) is the male. 'Gentle' undoubtedly relates to the hawk's superior qualities, particularly in hunting. Turbervile (1575[81]) broadens this a little, with female being implicit:

> 'There are seaven kindes of Falcons*, and among them all for hir noblesse & hardy courage, & with all the francknesse of hir mettell, I may, & do meane to place the Falcon Gentle in chiefe. This Falcon is called the Falcon Gentle, for hir gentle and curteous condition and fashions. In hart and courage she is valiant, ventrous, strong . . .'.

Latham (1615[49]) attempted to look beyond the eulogies in Turbervile's words for a better definition of falcon gentle and came to the conclusion that in fact his predecessor considered the hawk should be so named only during her first year:

> 'And whereas hee [Turbervile] theresheweth a difference between them, in calling the one a Faulcon gentle, and the other a Haggard faulcon: I take it, his meaning was, that eyther the eias, or the ramage hawke, of the same and one kinde, should bee the faulcon gentle, and the *Haggard faulcon*, that was taken wilde, having prayed for her selfe.'

It is worth noting that in the 1605 d'Arcussia list of French terms for wild hawks caught in different seasons, *gentil* is given for a hawk taken between June and August. For more, see NAMES 2.

An obsolete alternative English form is in:
> 'The frequent agitation of the wings in flying shews the Hawk to be a Gentile Falcon.' – 1678[71].

By itself, gentle (also obsolete) sometimes occurs as the female peregrine in particular and very occasionally as the peregrine falcon (species). It is clear that historically in Western falconry certain races of peregrine have been held in higher esteem than others, i.e. region of origin has long been a consideration in choosing this hawk. In the old list of 'the naamys of all maner of hawkys & to whom they belong'[5] (in NAMES 3) are mentioned what appear to be three kinds of peregrine. In apparent descending order of merit, they are 'a Fawken gentill. and a Tercell gentill', 'a Fawken of the rock', and 'a Fawken peregryne'; the distinctions are obscure. Also see FALCONS, Noble.

*The further six falcons for falconry which Turbervile acknowledges are 'the Haggart Falcon, whiche is otherwise tearmed the Peregrine Falcon', 'The Barberie, or Tartaret Falcon', 'The Gerfalcon', 'The Sacre', 'The Laner', and 'The Tunician'.

FALCON HERONER   See HERONER.

FALCONIDAE   The family of birds of prey which contains the genus *Falco*.

FALCONIFORMES   Order *Falconiformes* is subdivided into families, and further into genera, some of which contain species of diurnal birds of prey used historically and currently in falconry. More in BIRD OF PREY.

FALCON OF THE ROCK   See NAMES 3.

FALCON PEREGRINE ('Fawken peregryne' – 1486[5], 'Fawcons pelegrynes' – 1525[11].) See FALCON, Peregrine.

FALCONRY AND HAWKING Traditionally and strictly in Britain, falconry has been the inclusive pursuit of keeping, training and hunting with falcons, while hawking has been the act of hunting with either short-winged hawks or falcons; it should be noted however that more than one antiquarian English-language treatise has 'hawking or falconry' in its title or subtitle. Although there exists a verb (of Man) to falcon, it has been little used and is obsolete. The phrases (of Man with any kind of hawk) to go hawking and to fly a hawk are favoured currently; to hawk, meaning (of Man) to hunt with a long- or short-winged hawk, and to hawk at, meaning (of Man) to fly a hawk at (quarry), have fallen into disuse. It is doubtful if the verb to hawk, when applied to the hawk herself, has ever been part of the English falconer's or austringer's language, although it exists as a lay term. It seems that there has never been an English term for the complete pursuit of keeping, training and hunting with short-winged hawks specifically. The term hawking has long been used in combinations such as heron-hawking, kite-hawking and lark-hawking, categories of the

A 16th century heron-hawking party. The horsewoman is Queen Elizabeth I. From The Booke of Faulconrie or Hauking *by George Turbervile (1575).*

A hawking scene from the title page of George Turbervile's 1575 treatise.

pursuit which use falcons, as well as in such as rabbit- and hare-hawking, which historically usually use the goshawk. Commonly today in the English-speaking West, falconry and hawking have a simplified interrelationship: falconry encompasses keeping, training, and hunting with raptors, be they falcons, short-winged hawks, buteos or eagles, while hawking is the hunting itself with any of these birds.

FALCONS, Noble (obs.) The term (used in the English written word mainly before the 17th century) embraces the gyrfalcon and the peregrine, saker, and lanner falcons, regarded as the 'aristocracy' of the long-winged hawks and perceived as giving the finest flights at quarry. Furthermore, the falcons and the short-winged hawks were divided into two groups: respectively the noble and ignoble hawks.

In the 13th century, Emperor Frederick (in transl.[35]) specifies two kinds of peregrine: the peregrine falcon and the true noble falcon, apparently respectively northerly and southerly races of the same species.

FALL ([?]obs.) Of a hawk, to alight on the ground. It is used by itself and in the austringer's term 'fall at mark'; see MARK, Fall at. Also, to fall is (of avian quarry) to alight on the ground, often with the intention of evading the hawk.

FALL, The (obs.) During a chase, the action or moment of avian quarry alighting on the ground, often with the intention of evading the hawk. Bert (1619[6]) writes of a particular tiercel goshawk's tactic in taking a pheasant; the hawk

'... would most assuredly have him by the head at the fall, when the Pheasant would lye stretched out at length and never stirre feather.'

FALL AT MARK See MARK, Fall at.

FANNING; WING-FANNING; WINNOWING Of a hawk, exercising on the perch by beating her wings. Falcons do this often, and the true eagles sometimes.

FAULCONER Obsolete spelling of FALCONER 1.

FAULKNER 1; FAUKENER; FAWKNER;

38 FAULKNER

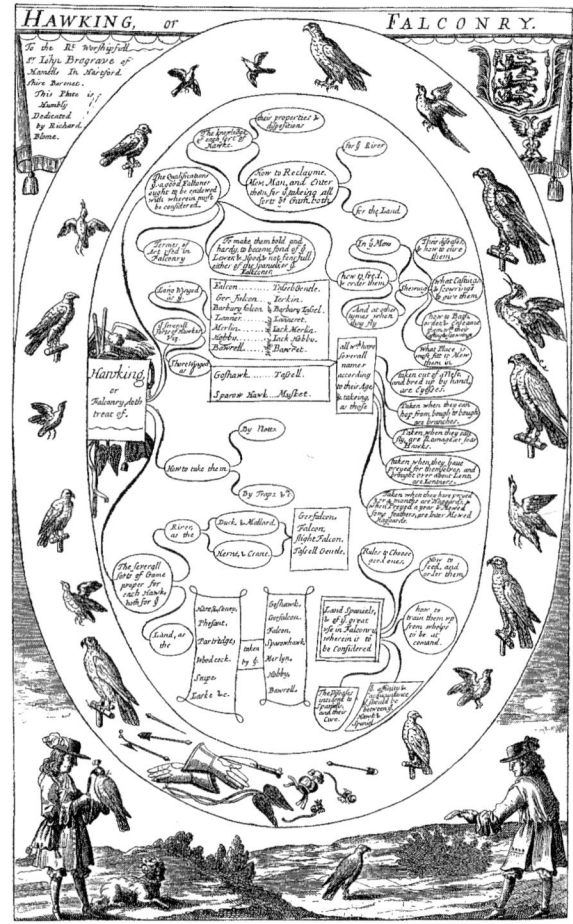

Various aspects of falconry. The instruments on either side of the hood, gloves, lure and bells are instruments for cautery. From Richard Blome's The Gentleman's Recreation *(1686).*

FAWCONER Obsolete spellings of FALCONER 1.

FAULKNER 2 Spelling of FALCONER 2.

FAULT BARS See FRET MARKS.

FEAK (Obs. alternatives: FREAK, SEW (by itself) and SEW THE BEAK (both rendered from Berners[5]), SNYTE THE BEAK and SNYDE THE BEAK (both rendered from Berners[5]), perhaps SMITE THE BEAK, perhaps SWEEP.) Of a hawk after feeding, to wipe her beak clean on the perch or the falconer's glove with a stropping motion. In one instance it is (of a falconer) to clean the hawk's beak, presumably with his fingers:

'I . . . gently pulled her off the pelf*, feaked and hooded her . . .' – 1852[16].

*What remains of the kill; more in PILL (n.). In the Berners list (1486[5]) of 'The kyndeli termis that belong to hawkis',

'The fawrith [fourth] is an hawke snytith. or sewith hir beke. and not wipith hir beke.'

And (ibid.):

'She bekyth when she sewith: that is to say she wypith hir beke.'

Although 'bekyth' has been interpreted as synonymous with feaks (taken to be from beke, an old spelling of beak), it is probable that the last part of this extract only relates to 'sewith'; therefore the meaning of 'bekyth' remains uncertain, but conceivably may be the same as becks, which means (in an obsolete sense) nods the head.

The verb feate (which has been taken to be a form of feak) is considered in COPE.

FEAT(E) See 1575 qu. and notes in COPE.

FEATHER In the context of hunting with hawks, feathered quarry.

FEATHER, Beam ('Beme feder of the tayle' – 1486[5].) See FEATHERS, Deck.

FEATHER, Covert See FEATHERS, Deck.

FEATHER, Drop a (Also CAST or SHED A FEATHER.) Of a hawk, to moult a feather. The feather itself might be dropped, cast or shed.

FEATHER, Fly at See FLY AT FEATHER.

FEATHER, Parts of a There appear to be no terms for the components of a feather which are unique to falconry. Traditional names are:

QUILL. Usually applied to the hollow base or barrel (sci. calamus) of a major feather.

SHAFT is usually the flexible pith-filled section of the mid-rib (sci. rachis) outward of the barrel, but may be used for the whole of the feather's mid-rib from base to tip.

WEB (later also **VANE**) is the main soft surface-area on either side of the feather's mid-rib.

PITH (occ.). The soft inner core of a feather's shaft.

FEATHER, Pinched (probably recent or modern) Of a developing feather, 'pinched' or constricted at the base. Such a feather is weak and will fall (or perhaps be knocked) out, or 'pinch out'. The condition is called pinching off by Cooper (1985[22]). A 19th century Persian writer (in transl.[68]), discussing management during the moult, says:

'Now, were you to substitute a copper or an earthen basin [for the recommended clay-lined tank], there would be a danger that while splashing about in the water, the moulting hawk might strike the half-grown wing- or tail-quills that are full of blood against the hard substance of the basin, and that the injury might cause the blood to dry up in the quills, which would thereby become "strangled," and would eventually drop out.'

FEATHER, Sarcel   See SARCEL.

FEATHER, Sore   (unc., obs.) An immature feather, that is, a feather of a first-year hawk before her first moult:

'... That kind of feather is called the Sore feather.' – 1575[81].

FEATHER PERFECT   Describes a hawk which has no damaged feathers. Aside of broken major feathers adversely affecting a hawk's performance, the good overall condition of her plumage is a point of pride to a falconer.

FEATHER PLUCKING   In a hawk, the action of pulling out her own feathers with her beak; a form of self-mutilation due to dietary deficiency or boredom. Compare AGGRESTEYNE (Appendix).

FEATHERS, Back   A hawk's upper body feathers.

'The federis upon the backe halfe be called the backe federis.' – 1486[5].

FEATHERS, Barb; GARB FEATHERS (occ., obs.) (Barb from Latin *barba* = beard; garb is perhaps a misspelling.) The small feathers under a hawk's lower beak.

'The federis under the beke be calde the barbe federis.' – 1486[5].

FEATHERS, Beam   (now occ.); BEAMS (now occ.) Alternative names for the primary feathers; more in FEATHERS, Primary.

FEATHERS, Blood; FEATHERS IN THE BLOOD   Developing feathers supplied with blood.

FEATHERS, Brail; BRAILS (Perhaps from Latin *bracæ* or *braccæ* = trousers, breeches, pantaloons. Obsolete spellings: BRAYLE FEATHERS, BRAYLES.) The soft pendant feathers under a hawk's tail, around the area of her VENT.

'... An hawke hath long smale white federis. hangyng undeer the tayll: from hir bowell downe warde. and the same federis ye shall call the brayles or the brayle federis.' – 1486[5].

The same writer also uses the form 'braylfederys'. The compiler of a French and English Dictionary (1611[23]) has:

'*Brayeul*: The parts, or feathers, about a hawkes fundament, called by our Faulconers the brayle* in a short-wingd, and the pannel in a long-wingd, hauke.'

*Taken in this instance to be the VENT, or that region, an uncommon application. More in BRAYLE 2; also see PANNEL.

FEATHERS, Brayle   See preceding entry.

FEATHERS, Breast; MAILS (obsolescent); MAIL (1891 gl.[39], obs.) (Also written BREAST-FEATHERS.) The feathers of a hawk's breast. The usual current term (breast feathers) was used in the 15th century by Berners[5] ('brest federys'). Mail (spelt 'maill' and 'mayll') also occurs in the same text; more in MAIL (n.).

FEATHERS, Contour   The feathers which are external and visible and determine the contours of a grown bird's body. A term not commonly used by falconers.

FEATHERS, Covert; COVERTS   General terms for the minor feathers covering the lower parts of the major feathers of a hawk's wings and tail. Usual current names which specify different groups are: primary coverts and secondary coverts (covering the lower parts of the primary and secondary feathers), also known collectively as wing-coverts (on the upper surface of the wing) and under wing-coverts, and upper and under tail-coverts.

'Ther bene also federis that cloos upon the sarcellis*. and thossame be calde the covertis or the covert federis. and so all the federis be calde that bene next over the long beme federis**. and the fagg federis§ upon the wynges.' – 1486[5].

*See SARCEL.
** See FEATHERS, Primary.
§See FEATHERS, Secondary. Turbervile (1575[81]) uses 'covert feathers' for the two central feathers of the tail; more in FEATHERS, Deck. Ear-coverts are the small feathers covering the external end of the auditory canal.

FEATHERS, Crine; CRINES (Latin *crinis* = the hair; French *crin* = horsehair, bristles, etc. Obs. forms: CRINELS, CRYNETS and CRINETS ('Crynettis' and 'Crinettis' – 1486[5]), CRINITES. CRIVETS in the Blome glossary (1686 [1929][9]) appears to be an error.) The short hair-like feathers which grow between a hawk's eye and upper beak; this region is known as the LORE. The same region might be described as being 'around the CERE'; Berners (1486[5]) notes:

'Ther be oon an hawke long smale blake federis: like

heris abowte the sere & thossame: be calde Crinettis of y^e hawke.'

The lay equivalent is usually 'bristles'.

FEATHERS, Deck; DECK-FEATHERS; DECKS (Dutch *dekvederen*[74] (Dutch *dek* = cover, covering; Dutch *veder* = feather); French *couvertures* or *couvertes* (1853[74]). In English texts, 'deck feathers' begins to see broader acceptance in the 19th century.) The two central feathers of a hawk's tail. If a hawk is tail-belled, it is to one or both of these that the bell is attached. In a normal moult, the deck feathers are the first tail-feathers to be dropped. The 'Beme feder of the tayle' (obsolete) is described by Berners (1486[5]) thus:

> 'An hawke hath.xii.federis uppon his tayle. and oon pricipall feder of thessame is in the myddis. and in maner all that oder bene covertid under thessame feder. and that is called the Beme feder of the tayle.'

It is, therefore, the upper, most-visible of the two deck feathers when the tail is folded. The 'covert feathers' of Turbervile (1575[81]) equate to the deck feathers:

> 'In fleeing with a Goshawke, it happeneth oftentymes that fleeing in the Snowe, and killing their pray upon the grounde, they fill their Belles with Snowe, so that the Falconer cannot tell where to finde them. At suche tymes then, fasten a Bell upon the two covert feathers of your Hawkes Stearne or Trayne, and that aloft neare to hir rumpe. For so doe the Falconers of *Dalmatia* [region of Eastern Adriatic] use at all times of the yeare to flee with their Hawkes.'

Also, Turbervile uses 'covert feather' for the 'principall feather' of the tail, which appears to be the same as the 'Beme feder of the tayle' of Berners. According to the Wood & Fyfe translation from Medieval Latin[35], the cover feathers or tail covers of 13th century Emperor Frederick equate to the deck feathers, and the covered feathers the remaining tail-feathers; these terms have not been met with elsewhere, therefore for the time being are not considered to be part of the English language of falconry.

Also see TRAIN 1 (n.).

FEATHERS, Down In grown hawks, the soft feathers hidden beneath the contour feathers (FEATHERS, Contour), providing insulation.

FEATHERS, Fagg See FEATHERS, Secondary.

FEATHERS, Flag; FLAGS See FEATHERS, Secondary.

FEATHERS, Garb See FEATHERS, Barb.

FEATHERS, Pendant (obs.) In Berners (1486[5]):

> '. . . The federis that bene at the Joynte: at the hawkes kne thay stonde hangyng and sharppe at thendes [the ends]. thos be calde the pendaunte federis.'.

These are taken to be the group of soft feathers, more or less visible, which hang about the upper leg. They are sometimes known collectively as the flag, but the authenticity of this as a falconer's term is as yet unverified.

FEATHERS, Primary; PRIMARIES (Also BEAM FEATHERS or BEAM-FEATHERS (now occ.), and BEAMS (now occ.). Beam taken in the sense of central in importance or strength, as in the beam of a plough. Also FLIGHT-FEATHERS (occ.) and FLIGHTS (unc.), although these are usually applied to the primary and secondary feathers collectively. Occasionally PENS or PENNES (both obs.). Also PRINCIPAL FEATHERS and PRINCIPALLES (both 1575[81] and obs.), and PRINCIPAL-FEATHERS and PRINCIPALS (both obs.). Also termed manual feathers or manuals, but usually not by falconers.) The outer ten major feathers of the wing. It is not unusual among falconers to count (or number) them 1 to 10, beginning at the wing-tip. Of the primaries in a normal moult, number 10 left and right are dropped first in short-winged hawks, number 7 left and right in falcons; primary number 1 on each wing (the SARCEL) is moulted last in both cases. Also see LONG-OPEN. In Berners (1486[5]), the obsolete term 'beme federis of the Wyng' equates to the primary feathers. For the 'Beme feder of the tayle' of this writer, see FEATHERS, Deck.

FEATHERS, Principal (obs.); **PRINCIPALS** (obs.) (Also written PRINCIPAL-FEATHERS (obs.).) Often, the primary feathers (FEATHERS, Primary); but in the Cox glossary (1677[25]),

> '*Principal-feathers*, are the two longest Feathers in the *Hawk*'s Wings.'

Harting (1891 gl.[39]) has:

> 'PRINCIPALS, the two longest feathers in the wing of a hawk.'

According to another writer, the principals are:

> 'The first two feathers.' – 1856 gl.[76],

taken to mean the first (outer) feather in both wings (see SARCEL).

FEATHERS, Reform the (obs.) Of a hawk, to rearrange her feathers with her beak. This somewhat confused guidance comes from Berners (1486[5]):

> 'And sum tyme yowre hawke cowntenansis as she piked hir. and yet she proynith not. and then ye most say she Reformith hir federis and not piketh hir fed-

eris.' This might be paraphrased: 'Sometimes your hawk makes as if to pick herself, and yet she does not preen, and then you must say she reforms her feathers and not picks her feathers.'

See also PICK, and PREEN.

FEATHERS, Secondary; SECONDARIES; FLAG FEATHERS (occ.) (Also FLAGS (occ.). Also FLAGG FEATHERS (1486, obs.) and FAGG FEATHERS (1486, unc., obs.). Flag perhaps from Latin *flaccus* = flabby, flaccid, these being less stiff than the neighbouring primary feathers; but cf. lay vb fag = (in one sense) to droop. Also termed cubital feathers or cubitals, but usually not by falconers.) The next group of wing-feathers inward of the primaries (see FEATHERS, Primary). Under the heading 'Flagg or faggis federys', Berners (1486[5]) writes:

'The federis at the wynges next the body be calde the flagg or the fagg federis.'

FEATHERS, Tail-   See TRAIN 1 (n.).

FEATHERS IN THE BLOOD; BLOOD FEATHERS Developing feathers supplied with blood.

FED UP   Said of a hawk when she has had her full ration of food, and sometimes while being fed ad lib. during a rest from flying. Compare FULL-GORGED.

FEED   In a list of 'The kyndeli termis that belong to hawkis' in Berners (1486[5]):

'The thride [third] is feede yowre hawke. and not gyve hir meete.'

FEEDING STOCK   (obs.) (Spelt 'fedyng stokke' (1486).)
According to Berners (1486[5]), a 'food board' for the mews. 'Stokke' is taken to be the same as stock, a log or block of wood; the hawk's food would be tied to it. The pertinent passage notes:

'It behovyth that yowre hawke have a fedyng stokke in hir mewe. and a longe stryng tyed therto: to fastyn hir mete with for ellis she will cary it a bowte the hous. and soyle it with dust.'

Also see note in HACK BOARD under HACKING.

FEED ON THE FIST   Of a hawk, to take a meal on the fist; of a falconer, to give (a hawk) a meal on the fist.

FEED THROUGH THE HOOD   Of a hawk on the fist, to feed with the hood on. Of a falconer, to feed (her) while she is hooded, the traditional method of encouraging a newly caught hawk (blind to frightening, distracting sights) to begin feeding. This is now not widely practised beyond perhaps the first day or two, as the hawk soon learns to associate hooding with food and develops the habit of picking hopefully and blindly at the glove. In former times, the hawk-trapper's rufter hood (see HOODS AND HOODING) was made with a wide beak-opening so that a newly caught hawk could feed comfortably through it. It is possible that the term 'feed (or tire) through the hood' owes its origin to old manuscript or printed passages such as these following. In *A Perfect Booke* (c.1575[38]), the anonymous writer sets down a ruse for entering a hawk to the hood:

'Theare is a prety slaight [clever trick] to let her tyre* through the hode and so nymbly whiles her beake is through to strike it on gently & never fayle.'

*TIRE, or simply feed. The procedure is better explained by Bert (1619[6]) in his discourse on making a HOOD-SHY hawk hood well; after many experiments,

'... I thoght of feeding a hawke through the hoode, cutting the hole for her beake very wide, it is but the marring of a hoode. I would have the hole so wide, as when I did holde it by the tassell§, she should very easily (when it was layd upon the meate) feede through it. I would continue feeding her so three or foure dayes, never offering in all that time to put it on.... When I found her thus securely feeding, and her head in the hoode, I would then gently and lightly raise my right hand, a very small motion will serve, and so leave the hood upon her head...'.

§The tuft of small feathers topping some varieties of hood, otherwise known as a plume; it is gripped between the fingers when hooding and unhooding a hawk. To pull through the hood is (of the hawk) to feed through the hood.

FEED UP   Of a falconer, to give (a hawk) her full ration of food for the day, for example when the day's hunting is finished, or as a memorable reward after a successful flight. For a sparrowhawk newly entered at bagged quarry, Turbervile (1575[81]) advises:

'... When she killeth, feede hir up alwayes...'.

She is then said to be fed up. It can also be to feed (a hawk) fully in preparation for resting or moulting her. When used of the hawk, it is to take a full meal, perhaps most commonly with the food in question named: she might feed up on her kill, or on partridge, rabbit, etc. Compare GORGE (vb).

FERME   (obs.) (Form of firm, in the sense of solid.) According to Berners (1486[5]): of a hawk, having her feathers full-grown:

'And when she waxith nygh ferme . . .'.
More in FULL-SUMMED.

FERME, In (obs.) (Cf. Medieval Latin (Brit.–Ir.[48]) *firma* = a cage for young hawks, and French *enfermer* = to shut in.) Taken to mean in confinement, in:

'. . . Whan thay [hawks] be disclosed [hatched] and kepit in ferme tyll thay be full summyd. . . .' – 1486[5]; fuller qu. in EYASS.

FERRETING Under HAWKING, Categories of.

FERRUGINOUS HAWK; FERRUGINOUS BUZZARD See HAWK, Ferruginous.

FESTOON The 'lobe' or downward-curving cutting edge (sci. tomium), more or less pronounced, on either side of the upper beak in some raptors. A term not authentic to falconry, but see TOOTH.

FETCH Of a hawk, to reach or catch up with (quarry):

'. . . Gulliver had fetched his quarry and put in two stoops . . .' – 1900[59].

The idiom may also mean (of the hawk) to reach the quarry, turn it, or shepherd it into a new position.

FIELD, The 1 The hawking party, among which might be beaters and markers.

FIELD, The 2 The environment in which hawking takes place. One might, for example, locate one's hawk in the field by the sound of her bell.

FIELD, The 3 (obs.) Open country, as in FLY TO THE FIELD.

FIELD, Fly (to) the See FLY TO THE FIELD.

FIELD, Make to the See MAKE.

FIELD-BLOCK; FIELD BLOCK See BLOCK under PERCHES.

FIELD-HAWK; FIELD HAWK See HAWK, Field.

FIELD-ROOM (unc., obs.) Open space; sufficient space for a hawk to fly in unimpeded.

FIST The gloved hand on which a hawk is carried. In the West, it is the left hand unless a left-handed falconer chooses otherwise. Wrist has occasionally been used as an alternative term in the context of falconry, but not by modern falconers; otherwise, it has been a much-used lay or poetic name for the hand which carries a hawk. From Emperor Frederick[35] in the 13th century comes the suggestion that a hawk should be carried on the left, sometimes on the right fist, depending on the

Goshawk by Archibald Thorburn

direction of the wind: for the comfort of a carried hawk, the wind should always be at her head.

FIST, Check at the Of a hawk, to refuse to come to the fist; to shy from or show suspicion or fear of the fist. In *A Perfect Booke* (c.1575[38]), the verb check is used by itself, 'at the fist' being implied: of a short-winged hawk during her reclamation,

'Feede her always upon yo[r] fyste, and never take her from the pearche w[t]ought some bit of meate in yo[r] hande . . . until she hathe flowne longe. This will make her love the fyste, well cominge & never check and loke for meate no where elles.'

FIST, Come to the See COME.

FIST, Jump to the Of a hawk, to jump a short distance from a perch, or from the ground, to the fist. Encouraging a hawk to do this (using food as a reward) is an important phase in the earlier stages of training. Also met with is 'spring to the fist'; this is uncommon and obsolete. Also a falconer might jump a hawk to the fist (inf.).

FIST, Knock the (obs.) (Spelt 'knok the fyste' (c.1575[38]).)

Of a falconer when calling a hawk to the fist, to attract her attention by patting the glove with his free hand. Today, a falconer might 'tap the fist'; the idiom (not the practice) is uncommon. More in BAG, Hawking.

FIST, Spring to the See FIST, Jump to the.

FIST, Tap the See FIST, Knock the.

FIST-BOUND Applied to short-winged hawks and others flown from and called to the fist: obsessively preoccupied with the fist, ignoring quarry and taking every opportunity to come to the fist in the expectation of a reward of food.

FLAG See FEATHERS, Pendant.

FLAGS See FEATHERS, Secondary.

FLESH, Full of; -, Low in See next entry.

FLESH, Raised in (obs.)
  '*Raised in flesh*, is when a *Hawke* growes fat, or prospereth in flesh.' – 1615 gl.[49]
Turbervile (1575[81]) uses the obsolete idioms 'hie and full of fleshe' and (for a lean hawk) 'low in fleshe'.

FLICK (probably recent) Of a hawk while feeding, to toss away torn-off beakfuls of meat, sometimes indicating loss of appetite through ill-health.

FLIGHT A chase after quarry by a hawk. It is correct to say a flight at a rook if the quarry is to be specified, and such as a ringing flight or a waiting-on flight for different styles. Also see SLIP (n.).

FLIGHT, Crossing (1891 gl.[39]) The flight of a wild bird unconnected with the chase which crosses between the hawk and her quarry, perhaps causing her to be distracted and check; see CHECK 1 (vb).

FLIGHT, Great See first 1575 qu. in MOUNT, At the.

FLIGHT, Ringing The circling flight of a falcon as she mounts to her PITCH or as she upwardly pursues her quarry. See RING UP.

FLIGHT, Single; -, Double See CAST, A.

FLIGHT, Stern A chase from behind, as opposed to a stoop from above; a hawk's level-flight pursuit of quarry. Other idioms with the same meaning are stern chase and tail-chase.

FLIGHT, Waiting-on See WAIT ON.

FLIGHT-FEATHERS; FLIGHTS Usually, collectively the major feathers (primary and secondary) of the wing, perhaps occasionally the primaries in particular. See FEATHERS, Primary.

FLIGHTS See FEATHERS, Primary.

FLUSH Of a falconer, his dogs, or other members of the field, to put (quarry) out of cover, or to drive or startle (it) into flight. Less commonly the quarry might be said to flush, meaning to take wing or rise quickly. To reflush quarry is to flush it for a second time during a chase; compare RETRIEVE.

FLUSH, The The act (by the falconer, his dogs, or other members of the field) of putting quarry out of cover, or driving or startling it into flight. The reflush is the second flushing of quarry during a chase; compare RETRIEVE, The.

FLY Of a falconer, to hunt with (a hawk). Of a hawk, to hunt or chase (quarry), not necessarily with a successful outcome. A falconer might fly his peregrine; a goshawk might fly a hare in good style; a hawk might be flown; a pheasant might be flown by a goshawk.

FLY AT Of a falconer, to hunt (quarry) with a hawk. Of a hawk, to hunt or chase (quarry), not necessarily successfully. An austringer might fly his goshawk mainly at rabbits; a sparrowhawk might be given her first experience of flying at blackbirds; a merlin might be flown at larks. Obsolete 'fly to', with the same meaning, is met with occasionally.

FLY AT BOLT (obs.) Of a short-winged hawk, to fly (quarry) straight from the fist. To bolt appears to be the same; more in BOLT 1.

FLY AT CHECK In the common understanding: of a hawk, to change from one quarry to another during a flight. More in CHECK 1 (vb).

FLY AT FEATHER; FLY AT PLUME (obs.) Used rather in the general sense than for any one occasion: of a falconer, to fly (a hawk) at birds; of a hawk, to fly at birds. Also a hawk might be flown at feather.

FLY AT FUR Used rather in the general sense than for any one occasion: of a falconer, to fly (a hawk) at rabbits and hares or other furred animals; of a hawk, to fly at these quarries. Also a hawk might be flown at fur.

FLY AT HACK Under HACKING.

FLY AT MARK See MARK, Fly at.

FLY AT PITCH ([?]obs.) Of a falcon, to WAIT ON at the height from which she will stoop. More in PITCH (n.).

FLY AT PLUME See FLY AT FEATHER.

FLY AT (or **TO**) **THE CREEP** (obs.) Of a short-winged hawk, to fly quarry from the fist following a cautious approach to a likely spot by the austringer:

> 'And yowre hawke fleeth at or to the Creepe when ye have yowre hawke on yowre fyst and crepe softely to the Ryver or to the pit. and stelith softeli to the brynke therof. and then cry huff. and bi that meane Nym [take] a fowle.' – 1486[5].

Also (ibid.), 'slayn at the Crepe' means (of quarry) killed under the same circumstances.

FLY DOUBLE (unv., obs.) Of hawks, to fly in a cast. More in CAST, A.

FLY FIST TO FIST (modern, inf.) Of a falconer and a companion, to fly (a hawk) back and forth between their fists for exercise or as part of her training. More in CALL 1.

FLY FREE See FLY LOOSE.

FLY FROM THE FIST Of a falconer, to hunt (with a hawk) where the flight at quarry begins at the fist. It is most commonly applied in hunting with short-winged hawks, but also in some other categories such as lark-hawking with a merlin. Sometimes it is, of the hawk herself, to fly (quarry) straight from the fist. In categories of hawking where the larger falcons are flown from the fist and out of the hood at quarry such as rooks, the idiom is FLY OUT OF THE HOOD.

FLY GROSS (unv., obs.) Perhaps both (of a hawk) to fly at larger avian quarries such as herons, and (of a falconer) to fly a hawk at the same. Compare 'great flight' in 1575 qu. in MOUNT, At the.

FLY IN A CAST See CAST, A.

FLYING WEIGHT See WEIGHT, Flying.

FLY LOOSE; **FLY FREE** Of a falconer, to discard the creance and fly (a hawk) unrestrained, perhaps for the first time.

FLY ON HEAD (now unc. or obs.) Of a hawk during a flight: to miss the intended quarry and pursue another; also see CHECK 1 (vb). To Cox (1677 gl.[25]):

> '*Fly on head*, is missing her *Quarry*, and betaking her self to the next Check, as Crows, &c.'

Harting (1891 gl.[39]) simplifies it thus:

> '. . . To miss the quarry and check.'

Compare FLY OUT ON HEAD under HOLD IN THE HEAD.

FLY OUT OF THE HOOD Traditionally, in categories of the pursuit such as heron- and rook-hawking: of a falconer, to fly (one of the larger species of falcon) from the fist but keeping (her) hooded until quarry rises or comes into view. When the falconer judges the time is right, he unhoods her and casts her off. Note: Before the wide use of the hood in Western falconry, it is probable that to prevent the hawk from bating at movements in the field, it was customary to distract her attention by feeding her TIRING on the fist; there is some evidence that, alternatively or additionally, the falconer shielded her with his body or clothing until he was ready to cast her off.

Historically it has been less common to fly hawks other than falcons out of the hood, but Latham (1618[50]) uses the term 'flye from forth the Hood' in the context of flying partridge with a goshawk:

> '. . . Use her to flye from forth the Hood, [because] often bating at Partridge sprung to other *Hawkes*, discomforts and discourages her, so that when her turne is to flye, her edge is off, and her courage* is lost.'

*See COURAGE. In *A Perfect Booke* (c.1575[38]) is the uncommon idiom 'call out of the hood'. This is taken to mean: of the austringer, to summon (a short-winged hawk during her reclamation) from the fist of a companion, who unhoods her at the call. The suggestion is that this has advantages later on:

> '. . . When she is flyinge use to call her ought of ye hode & that will make her flye as sone as it is ofe wch is a singuler poynt.'

Note: Although historically the hood has been little used in Japanese hawking, it is known that to some extent goshawks were flown out of the hood at certain avian quarries[45].

FLY OUT ON HEAD See HOLD IN THE HEAD.

FLY OVER DOGS Under DOGS IN HAWKING.

FLY SINGLE (unv., obs.) Of a hawk, to fly alone, that is, not in a cast. More in CAST, A.

FLY TAIL TO TAIL (obs.) Of a hawk, to refuse to chase (quarry) with commitment or to give up a flight; or to chase (quarry) but refuse to catch (it). Compare TURN TAIL, and REFUSE.

FLY THE FIELD See FLY TO THE FIELD.

FLY THE RIVER See FLY TO THE RIVER.

FLY THROUGH THE MOULT To hunt (with a hawk) during the period of her annual moult as an alternative to resting her for the summer season. Also, she might be flown through the moult. More in MOULT A HAWK.

FLY TO See FLY AT.

FLY TO MARK See MARK, Fly to.

FLY TO THE BECK See FLY TO THE VIEW.

FLY TO THE BROOK (obs.) Of a falconer and his hawk, or of the hawk herself, to hunt waterfowl at the river. See BROOK-HAWKING under HAWKING, Categories of.

FLY TO THE COVERT (obs.) Of a falconer, to fly (a hawk) in countryside featuring cover such as thickets, copses or woods: for example a goshawk at pheasant.

FLY TO THE FIELD (obs.); **FLY THE FIELD** (obs.) Of a falconer, to fly (a hawk) in open country, for example a goshawk at partridge (1618[50]). Turbervile (1575[81]) writes of hawks 'which are good to flee the field'.

FLY TO THE LURE See LURE-SWINGING under LURE (n. and vb).

FLY TO THE MARK See MARK, Fly to the.

FLY TO THE QUERRE (obs.) (Medieval English querre is a form of quarry.) This idiom may literally mean (of a hawk) to fly at quarry, but in Berners (1486[5]) it appears to have a special significance:

> 'And yowre hawke fleeth to the querre. when ther be in a stobull tyme Sordes of mallardes in the felde. and when she espith theym and commyth coverte her selfe. and flie prevyli under hedges or law bi the grownde. and nym oon of hem. or thay rise then ye shall say that the fowle was slayn at the querre.' This might be paraphrased: 'Your hawk "flies to the querre" when there is, in stubble time, gatherings of mallards in the field; when she sees them and approaches hidden, flying furtively along hedges or low to the ground and takes one of them before they rise, then you shall say that the fowl was "slain at the querre".'

FLY TO THE RIVER (obs.) FLY THE RIVER (obs.) Of a falconer and his hawk, or of the hawk herself, to hunt waterfowl at the river.

> 'An hawke [short-winged] fleeth to the Ryver dyversis ways....' – 1486[5];

fuller qu. in FLY TO THE VIEW.

> 'With this hawke [lanner] may you flye the ryver...' – 1575[81].

FLY TO THE TOLL See next entry.

FLY TO THE VIEW; -TO THE BECK; -TO THE TOLL (all obs.) (Tentatively rendered into modern form from the following 15th C. extracts.) A Berners passage (1486[5]) contains these three idioms which are obviously related:

> 'An hawke fleeth to the Ryver dyversis ways. and slethe [kills] the fowle dyver[s]li. That is to say she flieth to the vew or to the beke. or to the toll. & all is bot oon. as ye shall knawe here after.'

Concerning entering a goshawk at waterfowl, this writer states:

> 'A Goshawke or a tercell [female or male goshawk] that shall flee to the vew. to the toll. or the beke. in this maner she is taught. ye most fynde a fowle in the Rever. or in a pitte preveli [covertly]. and theen sett youre hauke a grete space of. uppon a mooll hill or on the grownde. and crepe softeli towarde the fowle: from yowre hawke streght way. and when ye come almost ther as the fowle lyeth. looke backewarde towarde the hawke. and with yowre hande or with yowre tabur styke*: becke yowre hawke. to come to you. and when she is on the wyng. and comyth low bi the grounde. and is almost at yow. then smyte youre tabur [tabor, drum]. and cry. huff. huff. huff and make the fowle to spryng. and with that noyse the fowle wil rise and the hawke wyll nym [take] it.'

It is reasonably clear that to fly to the view is (of a short-winged hawk) to fly quarry the austringer has sighted or located, then flushes when she is in flight. To fly to the beck appears to be the same, but the austringer has called her off by beckoning her silently. It is apparent from the above passage that to fly to the toll has a similar meaning; there may be a connection with the old verb toll, which means (in a lay sense) to decoy or attract (wild animals) for the purpose of capture.

*See TABOR, and TABUR STYKE.

FOLLOW (recent); **FOLLOW ON** (recent) Chiefly of the goshawk, but also broad-winged hawks, and the Harris' hawk *par excellence*: to accompany the austringer walking in the field, taking stand until he overtakes her then flying ahead and finding a new perch, in anticipation of quarry being sprung. Compare DRAW AFTER. To follow (inf.) is also (of the hawk) simply to pursue the austringer when he walks away.

FOLLOW ON See preceding entry.

FOOD See MEAT, Hawk.

FOOD BOX; MEAT BOX See BAG, Hawking.

FOOT (n.) That with which a hawk takes quarry

or prey; for anatomical accuracy, it comprises the toes and the long bone above (the tarsus). The arrangement of toes is three forward and one aft.

TALONS. Obs. forms: TALLANTES, TALLENTS. Invariably to falconers today, the sharp horny nails arming the toes of birds of prey; perhaps originally those of a falcon specifically. But writing on short-winged hawks, Berners (1486[5]) notes:

> '**Talons**. Fyrst the grete Clees [great claws] behynde. that strenyth [strain, grip] the bake of the hande. ye shall call hom Talons.'

A hawk's (or specifically a falcon's) foot was once sometimes referred to as the hand. Turbervile (1575[81]) writes of coping (trimming) 'hir tallantes, hir powlse, and hir petie single'; powlse has not been met with elsewhere; it may be an error for pounce (see below). Clearly this writer means to implicate nails on different toes.

CLAWS (obs.). Other obsolete forms CLEES, CLEYS. The nails of a hawk, traditionally those of a short-winged hawk.

TOE. Currently, any digit on a hawk's foot.

CLUTCHES (occ., obs.). Collectively, the toes (armed with nails) of a hawk. The obsolete verb clutch or clitch is, of a hawk in an attack, to grip (quarry) with the feet; the current idiom is BIND TO.

CLOKES (occ., obs.). The same as clutches (above). Compare obsolete verb cloke, which means to claw or scratch, but not necessarily of a hawk.

POUNCES (obs.). '...The claws of a hawk.' – 1891 gl.[39], that is, the nails. Turbervile (1575[81]) says a sparrowhawk should have 'sharpe pounces, small and blacke'; although here apparently referring to all the nails, he also writes of coping a hawk's 'pownc"es and talons', which may be the fore and hind nails respectively. In the same text is a chapter headed 'Of the breaking of a Pounce, or Cley [claw] of your Hawke'. In Berners (1486[5]), it is uncertain whether the pounces are particular toes or nails, such as the two inner fore, or all of them:

> '**Pownces**. The Clees with i [within] the fote ye shall call of right her Pownces.'

HAND (unc., obs.) The foot of a hawk, or the foot of a falcon specifically. Compare French 'la main du faucon, le pied de l'autour' (19th C.[74]), that is, hand of a falcon, foot of the goshawk.

STRETCHER (obs.) A hawk's toe.

SINGLE (obs.); SENGLE (obs). A hawk's toe. To Holme (1688[43]), 'The Singles, or Petty Singles, are the Toes of the Hawk'. OED (using 'claw' to mean toe and nail in combination) has single as:

> 'The middle or outer claw on the foot of a hawk or falcon', and it is 'Chiefly in *pl.*[ural], the middle claws being called the *long singles*, and the outer the *petty singles*. In early use the singles were distinguished from pounce and talon; later writers sometimes use the word vaguely to denote all the claws.'

LONG SINGLE or LONG SENGLE (both obs.) A hawk's middle fore toe. Although somewhat ambiguous, the Berners definition seems to agree:

> '**Longe Sengles**. Bott certaynly the Clees that are upon the medyll stretcheris [middle toes] ye shall call the loong Sengles.'

KEY (obs.); **CLOSER** (obs.). A hawk's middle fore toe, (?)perhaps that of a short-winged hawk:

> '**The key or Closer**. Understond ye also that the longe Senclees [singles; note form] be calde the key of the fote. or the Closer. For what thyng som ever it be y^t [that] yowre hawke strenyth [grips]: open that Sengle. and all the fote is oppen. for the strength ther of fortyfieth all the fote.' – 1486[5].

PETTY SINGLE or PETTY SENGLE (both obs.). A hawk's toe, or the outer fore toe:

> '**Pety Sengles**. And the uttermest [outermost] Clees ye shall call the Pety Sengles.' – 1486[5].

SERES OF THE LEGS AND FEET (obs.). The skin of a hawk's legs and feet; more in CERE.

TARSUS (sci.); plural **TARSI**. The term used by falconers today to some extent: the long bone above the toes, otherwise referred to as leg but which correctly is part of the foot; to it, a jess is attached. Obsolete stalk is the same.

STALK (obs.). The tarsus of a hawk, the part of the 'leg' to which a jess is attached; correctly, the long bone of the foot above the toes. The 'Tokens of a good hawke' in *A Perfect Booke* (c.1575[38]) are:

> 'Large: heade slender: beake thick and greate like a parot: seare fayre: nares wyde: stalke short and bygg: foote large, wyde, and full of strengeth: mail thick: wynges large w^t narow fethers: heye of fleshe and ever disposed to feede egerly.'

FOOT (vb) 1. Of a hawk, to strike at, take and subdue (quarry) with her feet. A good footer is a hawk which is naturally dextrous with her feet when taking quarry; the opposite might be a poor or clumsy footer.

> '... With eyesses it is rather the exception to be really good footers, whereas with haggards and many red passage hawks it is almost the rule.' – 1900[59].

In the case of eyass sparrowhawks:

> 'When they beginne to waxe full somed*, give them Sparrowes, and other small birdes whole, that they may learne to plume, foote, and tyre ...' – 1575[81].

*See FULL-SUMMED.

2. Of a hawk, to strike aggressively or defensively at, and grip the falconer's hand with her foot; this appears to be a recent application. Footy (probably recent) means prone to this behaviour.

FOOTER, A good A hawk which uses her feet well in taking quarry; more in FOOT (vb 1).

FOOTING In a hawk, the action of using her feet to take and subdue quarry. The quality is often specified (good footing, poor footing, etc.); more in FOOT (vb 1).

FOOTY (probably recent) Of a hawk, prone to striking at the falconer's hand with her foot.

FORK-TAILED KITE Obsolete name for the red kite (*Milvus milvus*). See KITE, Royal.

FORM The overground lair and nesting place of a hare.

FORMED Of a hare, at rest in the form.

FREAK Obsolete alternative to FEAK.

FRELON (rare, obs.) (Correct in French falconry in the 19th C.[74].)
The small bony tubercle inside the nare of some hawks. In the case of falcons, frelons are thought to act as 'baffles', controlling or restricting airflow through the NARES during a stoop. Turbervile (1575[81]) refers to

> '... y^t little stert* y^t groweth up in the midle of the nares ...'.

*Obsolete lay stert (or start) is an outgrowth of some kind.

FRET MARKS; HUNGER TRACES; HUNGER STREAKS; HUNGER-STREAKS; TAINTS (1575[81], obs.) (Fret (vb) = (in an obs. sense) to become eaten away or worn. Also FAULT BARS (unc.). Also TAYNTS ('tayntys', singular 'Taynt' and 'taynte'; all 1486[5] and obs.); cf. taint (n.) = (in one sense) a blemish or stain. Also SHOCK-MARKS (unc.).) Semi-transparent lines of imperfection across the vane of a feather, sometimes with a corresponding malformation of the shaft

Fret marks, in this case on tail-feathers; the result is a loss of sections of vane.

which may fracture at that point. The cause is some severe shock or stress to a hawk of any age while new feathers are developing. The traditional thinking has been that the shock is due to a shortage of food:

> 'Ye may also knawe an Eyes [eyass]. bi the palenese of the seres of her legges[.] of the sere [cere] over the beke. And also by the tayntys that be upon her tayll and her wengys wiche tayntys com for lacke of fedyng. when thay be Eyes.' – 1486[5];

and (ibid.):

A quasi-armorial cut from Symon Latham's second book of 1618. The collected furniture occurs in almost identical form in other treatises. Despite its crude depiction, most items can be recognised or guessed at. Clockwise from top left: leash, glove, varvels, bell, wing probably for stroking, coping-irons, imping needles, T-perch, lure, hood, and creance. The remaining two items are so far unidentified. The varvels appear to be of tube type. Affixed to one is a flat shield for the owner's crest; there is a c.1600 example of this pattern in the Victoria and Albert Museum.

'A Taynt is a thyng that gooth overwarte [overthwart, across] the federis of the wynges. and of the tayll lyke as and it were eetyn with wormys. and it begynyth first to brede at the body. in the penne and that same penne sh[a]ll frete asonder. and falle a way thurrow thessame taynte and then is the hawke disparagid for all that yere.'

Although 'fret marks' appears to be a recently-adopted term, it is worth noting the Berners words 'that same penne sh[a]ll frete asonder' in the foregoing passage.

In the 16th century, Turbervile[81] asserts that there are three kinds of the condition he calls 'the Teynte'. One, which he notes is contagious, is

'... when theyr principalles or long feathers [both = primaries] beginne to droppe off, by meanes whereof many Hawkes are marred and cast awaye, without knowledge howe to helpe it.'

The second results from poor husbandry and feeding, and

'... fretteth the principals of a Hawke to the verie Quill ... Sometymes both in the mew and out of the mewe it happeneth that by feeding them with filthie and lothsome fleshe, they become full of filth both within and without, whereof breedeth suche a sort of Wormes, as doe utterlye frette asunder and marre their feathers.'

'The thirde kinde of Teynte is knowne in Hawkes by the ryving of their principal feathers throughout alongst the upper side of the webbe of them. And that happeneth commonly for want of cleane feeding, and due attendance.'

Writing of the care of newly taken eyasses, the same writer uses taint as a verb (uncommon and obsolete) in:

'And when yee feede them, give them tender flesh, and after that, lette them not stand emptie any more too long for hindering their feathers, and tainting them.'

FRILL (n., unc., obs.) In a hawk, the ruffling of her feathers when she is trembling with cold. This idiom is unverified as authentic to falconry.

FRILL (vb, unc., obs.) Of a hawk, to tremble with cold. This idiom is unverified as authentic to falconry.

FULL FERME(D)   See FULL-SUMMED.

FULL-GORGED (obs.); **FULL GOORGED** (1486[5], obs.) Said of a hawk when she has had a full meal or when she has a full crop. Compare FED UP. In OED, the obsolete 'to bear full gorge' is to be full fed.

FULL-SUMMED (Summed: Old French *som(m)é* = completed. Also written FULL SUMMED. Obsolete spellings: 'full sommyd' (1486[5]), 'full sommed' and 'full somed' (both 1575[81]), 'full sumd' (c.1575[38]).) Said of an EYASS: having her first true feathers (after the downy stage) fully grown. Said of a hawk at a later stage: having her feathers full-grown after the moult. Full-summed (used today to some extent) and HARD DOWN (adopted later and currently in

24: Ornate leather furniture embroidered with silk and metal thread belonging to King James I of England (VI of Scotland), 1566–1625: hawking bag (centre), hood proper (top), lure (left) and glove. The bag is made in self-contained halves, designed to hang back-to-back at the waist. The lure would be completed by tying on wings. (Glasgow Museums: The Burrell Collection)

25-26: Putting a falcon on her block (right). How to put a falcon on the high perch and tether her (below); the knot is made in the same way as the screen perch knot in recent and modern times. From an early 14th century French copy of Emperor Frederick II of Hohenstaufen's 13th century treatise. (Courtesy Sotheby's)

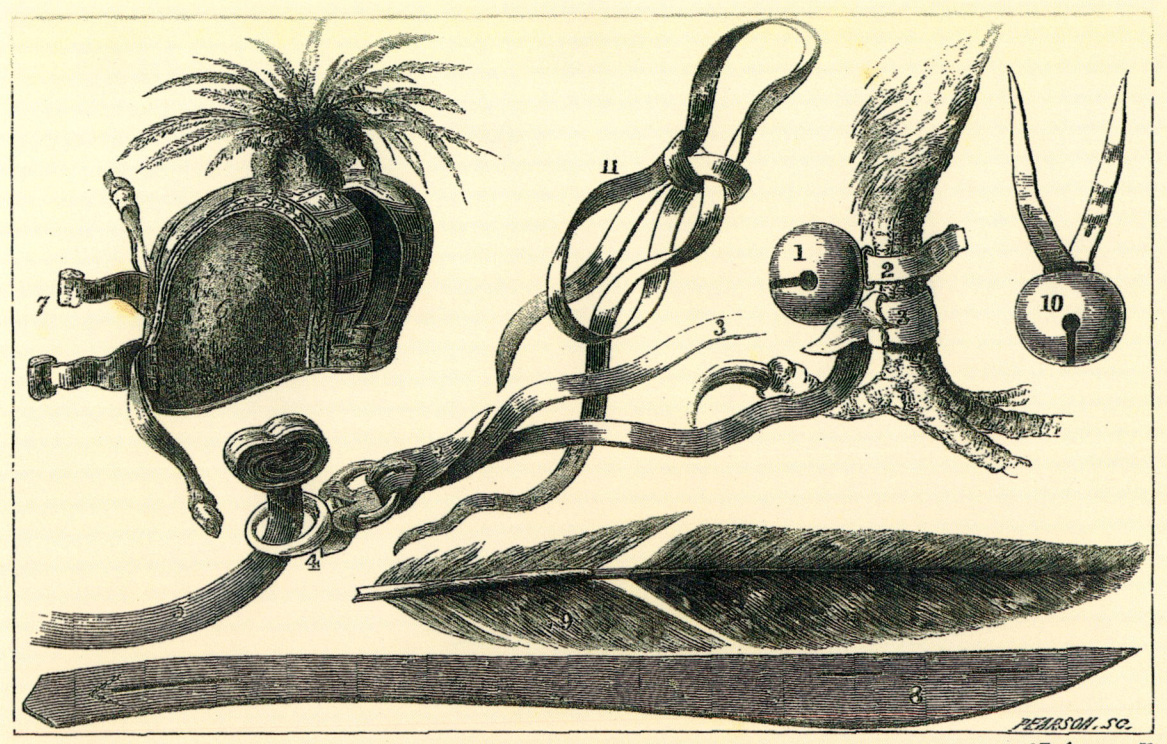

Explanation of the Plate.

[*To face page 50.*

1. The bell.
2. The bewit, by which it is attached to the leg.
3. 3. 3. The jesses, though the whole length of one only is given.
4. The swivel attached to the jesses.
5. The leash passing through the swivel.
6. A hood.
7. The hood's braces or ties.
8. A jess, the swivel-slit sewn at the end to prevent its tearing out.
9. A feather, with the imping needle inserted ready to push up.
10. A bell, showing the holes in the bewit through which the ends of the bewit pass.
11. The falconer's knot, which is always used for fastening hawks to the block or perch.

27: Opposite above: Furniture (including a Dutch pattern hood) and procedures from Freeman and Salvin's Falconry, Its Claims, History, and Practice, *1859.*

28: Opposite below: *The hawk van.*

29: *Putting on the hood.* (B.E. & K.L. Yull)

30-32: *Sian Goff drawing the hood, using fingers and teeth. The bird is a female saker.* (K. Taylor)

33-34: *Two views of the Arab hood.* (Faris Al-Timimi)

35: *Falcons wearing Arab furniture. Arabian perches like these are sometimes seen in use in the West.* (Faris Al-Timimi)

36: *Adult female lanner falcon wearing a tail-bell.* (M. Lyster / © Z.S.L.)

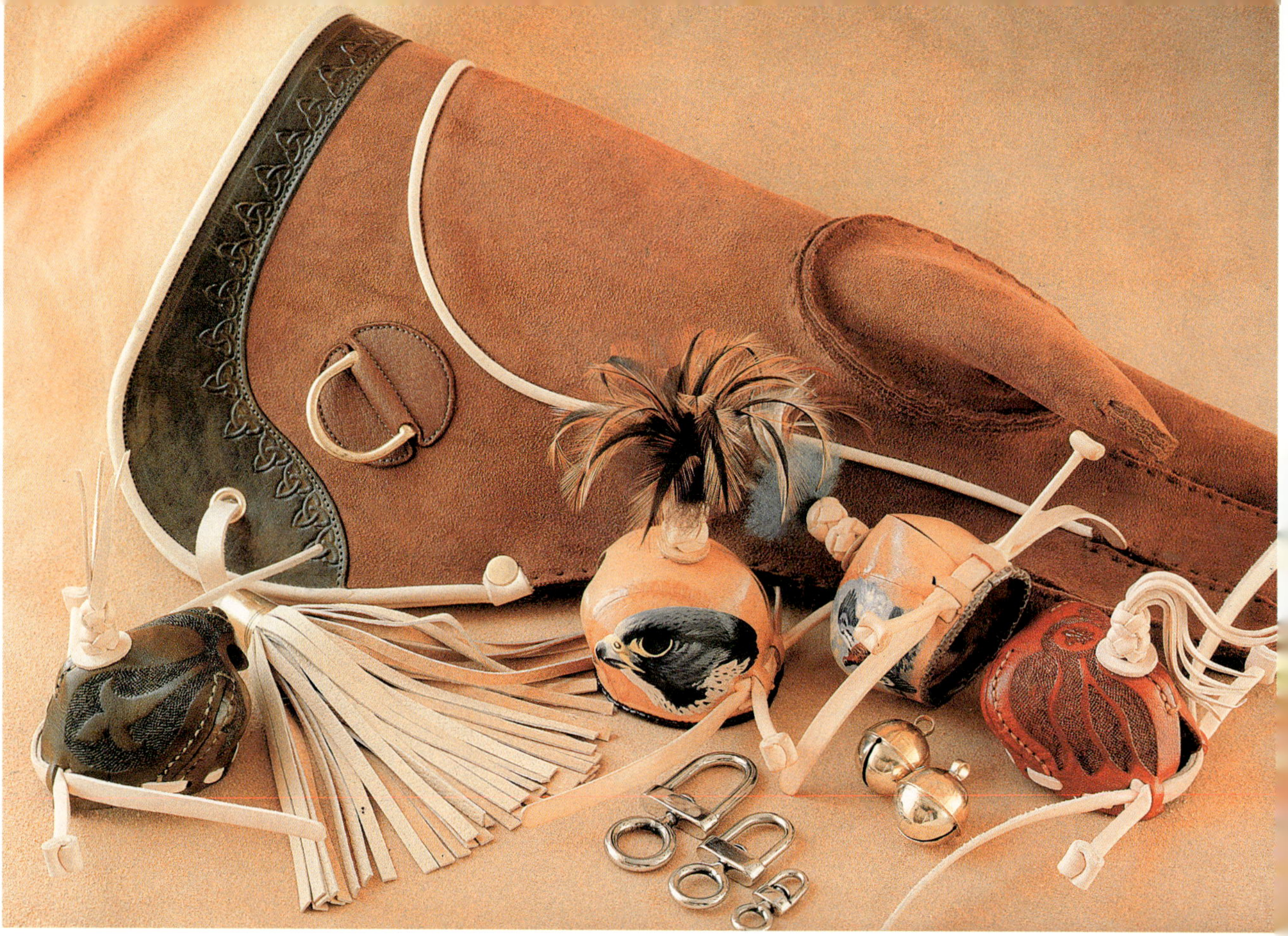

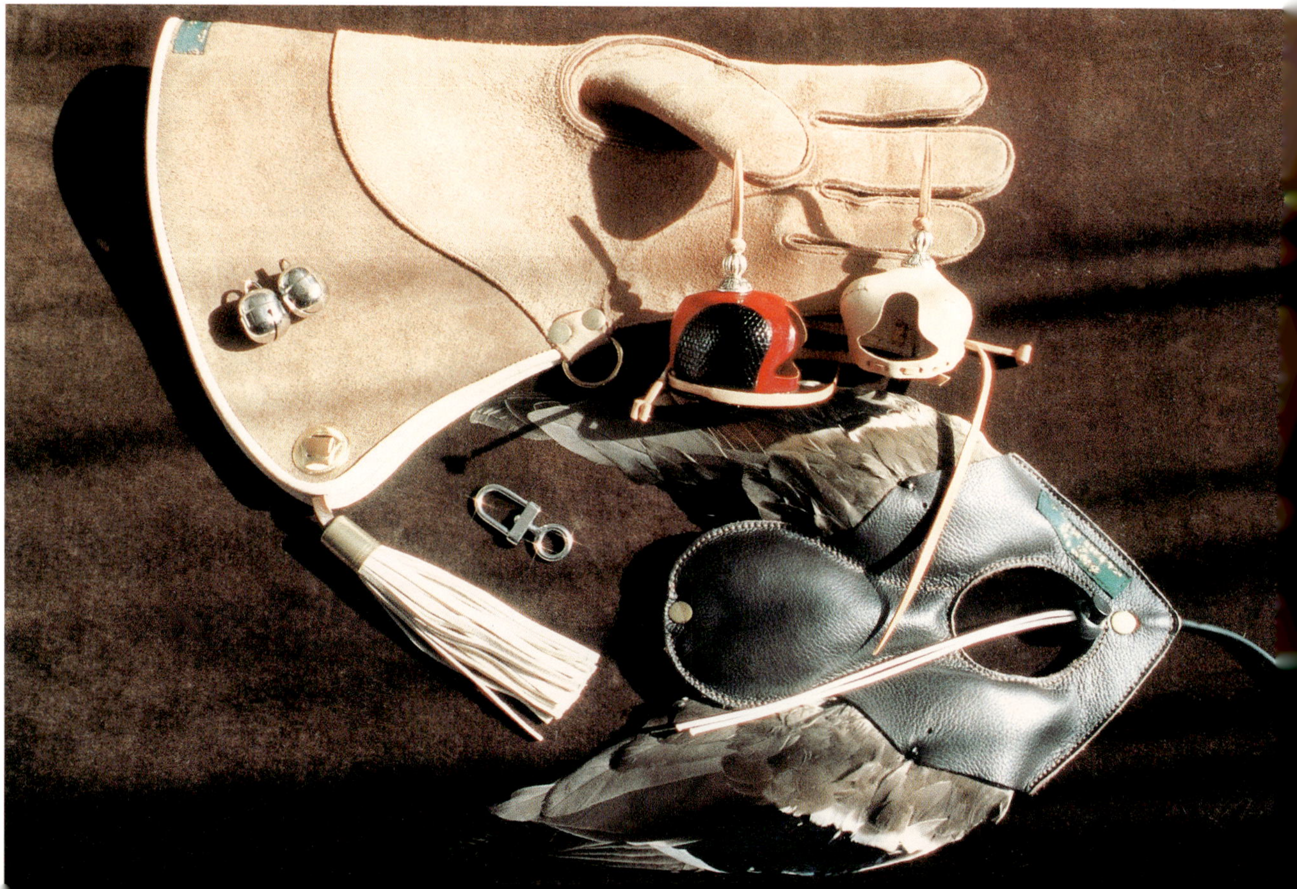

37-40: *Modern falconry furniture by Ben Long of Denbigh. Opposite above and below: Gloves, hoods, swivels, bells and lure. Below left: Anglo-Indian hood. Below right: Dutch-style hood.*

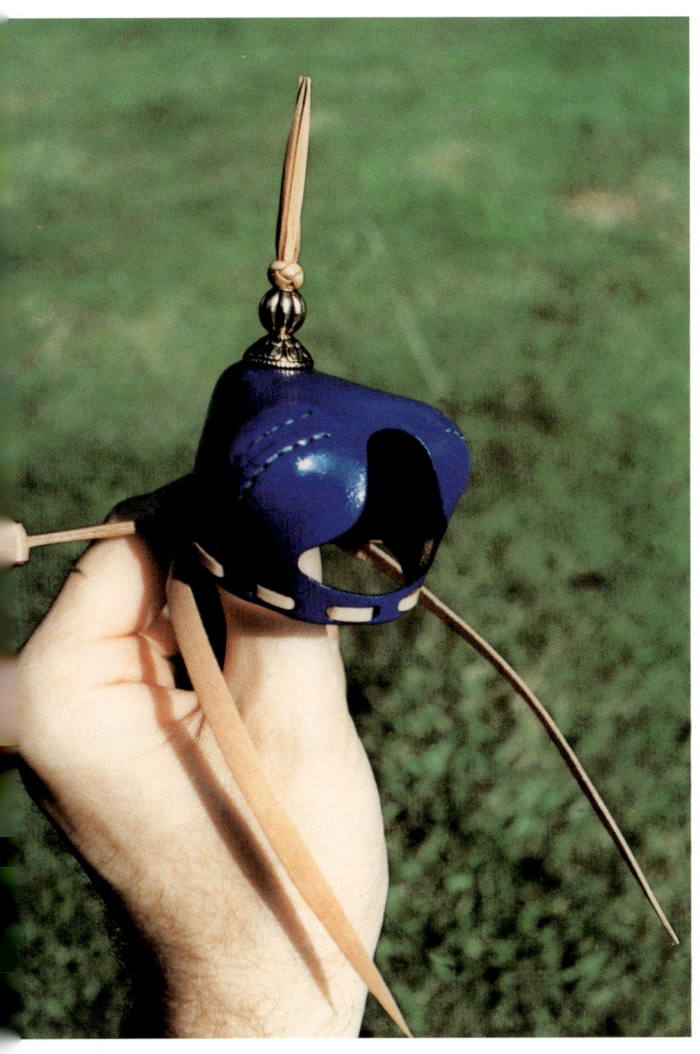

41: *Contemporary weathering ground.* (K. Taylor)

42: *Old-style mechanical scales, converted for weighing hawks.* (K. Taylor)

43: *Telemetry. In this case, the receiver is mounted on folding antenna (shown collapsed). The transmitter is on the left.* (K. Taylor)

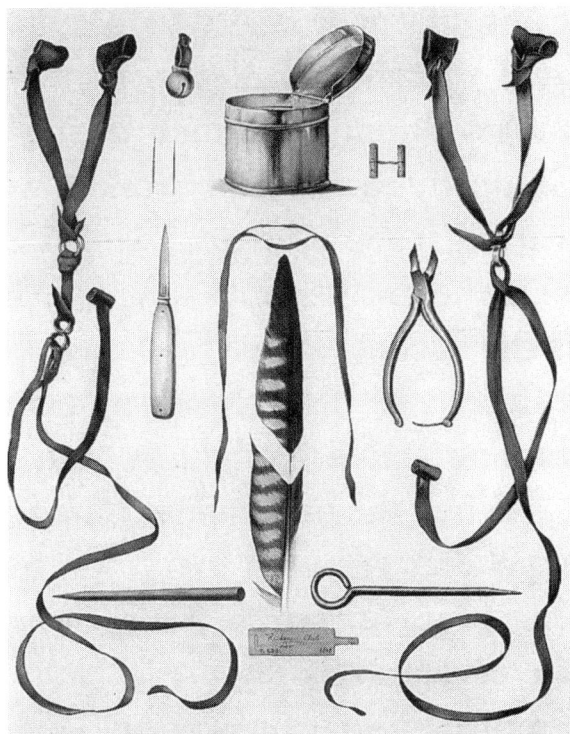

Items of furniture and accoutrements shown in Schlegel and de Wulverhorst's mid-19th century Traité de Fauconnerie. *Left: All joined in order are traditional jesses, short leash, swivel and leash, intended for a goshawk. The brass rings or varvels between jesses and short leash are knotted on and would in this case be removed before a flight, whereas the long-used flat or tubular patterns would not. Right: Jesses, swivel and leash intended for a falcon. Top centre: A meat box; to its right, a sheath for the beak of a heron taken alive, and to its left, a pair of imping needles. Centre: An imped feather, showing the inserted needle; the leather slip is a brail. Below: The brass plaque is for identifying a heron, released after being taken by hawks. The knife and clippers are for coping. The two awl-like tools are (left) for opening the slits in jesses during fitting and (right) for knotting bewits.*

use) are in effect synonymous, the only distinction being in their literal meanings: the first signifies that the hawk's moult is completed, the second that all her feathers are fully grown and hard. Berners (1486[5]) has the obsolete 'full fermyd' (meaning full firmed, full hardened), 'full ferme' and 'ferme', all equating to full-summed. Turberville (1575[81]) uses full-summed when referring to the development of the feathers themselves in:

'. . . If shee bee well mewed, and have all hir feathers full sommed . . .'.

Summed (probably obsolete) is synonymous with full-summed; in OED, summed can be (of a hawk) 'having the feathers full-grown', and is 'said also of the plumage'.

'*Summ'd* is when a *Hawke* hath all her feathers, and is fit either to be taken from the Crie [error for erie = eyrie] or Mew.' – 1615 gl.[49]

A hawk which has not completed her moult is said to be unsummed (probably obsolete):

'*Unsumm'd* is when a *Hawkes* feathers are not come forth, or els not com'd home to their full length.' – 1615 gl.[49]

Also see PENNED, Hard.

FUR In the context of hunting with hawks, furred quarry such as rabbits and hares.

FUR, Fly at See FLY AT FUR.

FURNITURE The equipment and accoutrements used in the care, training and flying of hawks (plates 24, 27 and 37–40). Although traditionally certain items are made by the falconer (FR Glasier[36], Ford [33], Beebe and Webster[3]), today a full range is available from suppliers.

GAME A collective term for certain wild birds and animals pursued in hunting. To falconers, it may be strictly defined as birds of the grouse kind, partridges and quails, the pheasant and some other gallinaceous birds. It may be broadened to include waterfowl and others. It may sometimes be applied to rabbits and hares by falconers, but they favour fur or sometimes ground-game; the hunting of these animals with hawks is not game-hawking (usually in Britain flying the larger falcons at birds of the grouse kind and partridge) but rabbit- and hare-hawking. Less commonly, game is any quarry flown at with a hawk.

GAME, Bagged See QUARRY, Bagged.

GAME, Base (obs.); **CHECK** (now unc. or obs.) (Base = inferior or lowly in this context; cf. 'base vermine, such as Rats' (1680).) Historically, quarry considered to be of lesser quality, such as rooks, crows or doves; quarry of lesser quality which might induce a hawk to abandon the intended flight. More in CHECK 1 (vb).

GAME-BIRDS To falconers, usually the various grouse, partridges and quails, the pheasant and other gallinaceous birds.

GAME-HAWK A falcon (usually) for GAME-HAWKING, found under HAWKING, Categories of.

GAME-HAWKING Under HAWKING, Categories of.

GARDEN A HAWK (unc., obs.) To WEATHER a hawk. Compare this from Schlegel's French-language treatise (1853[74]):

> 'Jardiner les oiseaux, c'est les exposer au soleil ou à l'air.' In translation: 'To "garden" birds is to expose them to sun or air.'

An 18th century English dictionary definition is:

> 'To put her on a Turf of Grass to chear her.' – 1706[67].

GATE See PITCH (n.).

GENTLE (n.) See FALCON GENTLE.

GENTLE (adj., obs.) Tame.

GENTLE, Make (obs.); **GENTLE** (vb, obs. and rare) Of a falconer, to tame (a hawk).

GENTLE FALCON See FALCON GENTLE.

GER Shortening of gerfalcon; see GYRFALCON.

GERFALCON Obsolete spelling of GYRFALCON.

GESSE; GESSES Obsolete spellings of jess and JESSES.

GESTS Obsolete form of JESSES.

GET BACK UP (modern, inf.) Of a bating hawk, to recover the fist. More in REBATE TO THE FIST.

GET GOING (modern, inf.) To prepare (a hawk) for hunting after a period of idleness.

GET IN See MAKE IN.

GIERFALCON Obsolete spelling of GYRFALCON.

GILL; JILL The female ferret. See FERRETING under HAWKING, Categories of.

GLEAM (n., [?]obs.) (Cf. 'gleim, any sticky substance, as bird-lime or glue; also rheum or phlegm' – OED; rheum = (in one sense) a bodily secretion or discharge. Perhaps also SLIME (obs.).) The substance (a small amount of bile or mucus) thrown up by a hawk after she has cast (disgorged a pellet). To produce this substance is to gleam (the verb perhaps still in minor use).

> 'And when shee hath caste, then hoode hir agayne, gyving hir nothing to feede on, untill she gleame after hir casting.' – 1575[81].

GLEAM (vb) See preceding entry.

GLEET (obs.) (Old French *glette* = slime, filth. Alternative forms: GLET(T) (1486, obs.), GLITTE (obs.), GLUT (obs.). Perhaps also SLIME (obs.).) Bile or mucus. In Berners (1486[5]), it occurs in 'foule glet' and 'the glett y^t she hath engenderid' in a passage on 'sekenes that haukis have i[n] their Entrellis'.

GLEETOUS (obs.) Apparently bilious. Berners (1486[5]) describes a sick hawk as 'very eegre and gleetous of the seekenes'; this appears to mean 'very hungry, and bilious from her illness'. In OED, glittous is 'Of a hawk: Affected with phlegm'; phlegm is taken to be bile or mucus.

GLET(T) Form of GLEET.

GLITTE Form of GLEET.

GLITTOUS See GLEETOUS.

GLOVE, Hawking The gloved hand is known as the fist. The glove is made of leather and traditionally is usually of gauntlet type, easy-fitting at the wrist so that it may be put on and removed easily. In the West it is worn on the left hand (unless a left-handed falconer chooses otherwise) as a secure foothold for a hawk and to protect the hand from sharp talons. The original primary purpose of the customary tassel on the lower edge of the wristguard (gauntlet) appears to be to hold onto when the glove was removed and waved by the falconer or whirled round his head to attract the attention of a hawk in flight; this practice is archaic. Today, the gauntlet is usually slit from forearm to wrist (formerly sometimes slit and gusseted), often with a tasselled loop of leather (known as a tassel) through eyelets. Sometimes incorporating a pierced wooden ball which may be tucked under the belt, the tassel is now chiefly for hanging up the glove. Sometimes modern gloves have a sewn-in metal ring or leather loop to which the free end of the hawk's leash might be tied as a security measure. A short glove is now often used with smaller hawks; occasionally, one covering only thumb and first two fingers is worn with such as merlins and small accipiters. A single thickness glove is suitable for small hawks, reinforced with one overlay of leather or more on wrist, thumb and first two fingers for birds of greater size and power. For extra protection, a falconer might wear a second fingerless glove on top of the existing glove. There is also a reinforced gauntlet type which reaches to the elbow for use with large eagles. An Arabian-style gauntlet mitten with thumb and two large fingers is sometimes seen in the West. Genuine buckskin is generally reckoned to be the most suitable material for glove-making, strong yet supple enough for the hand to sense the movements of the hawk. From Emperor Frederick[35] in the 13th century comes the suggestion that a glove be covered with fur to keep a hawk's feet warm in winter weather.

The Arab mangala, not used by Western falconers but mentioned in some English-language treatises, is an alternative to the glove; it is a tube shaped wrist and hand protector or 'cuff' of padded canvas or carpet.

In some Eastern cultures, the fist is the right hand, and sometimes no glove is worn. A soft glove may be worn on the throwing hand when THROWING A HAWK.

GLUT 1 (obs.) (Cf. Latin *glutio* = to swallow, gulp down.) Bile or mucus, or GLEET.

GLUT 2 (unc., obs.)
'The lower intestines [of a hawk]' – 1856 gl.[76]

GO IN 1 See MAKE IN.

GO IN 2 Under DOGS IN HAWKING.

GOLDEN EAGLE See EAGLE, Golden.

GOORGE Spelling of GORGE (vb and n.).

GOOSE HAWK See HAWK, Goose.

GORGE (vb, obs.); GOORGE (1486, obs.) Of a hawk, to feed until her crop is full, when she is said to be full-gorged (obsolete).
'She goorgith when she filleth hir goorge with meete.' – 1486[5].
Also a hawk might have 'over gorged hir selfe' (1575[81], obs.). According to the Lascelles glossary (1892[47]), to gorge is (of a falconer)
'To give a hawk as much as she will eat.'
This is also obsolete. Also see FEED UP.

GORGE (n., obs.); GOORGE (1486[5], obs.) The

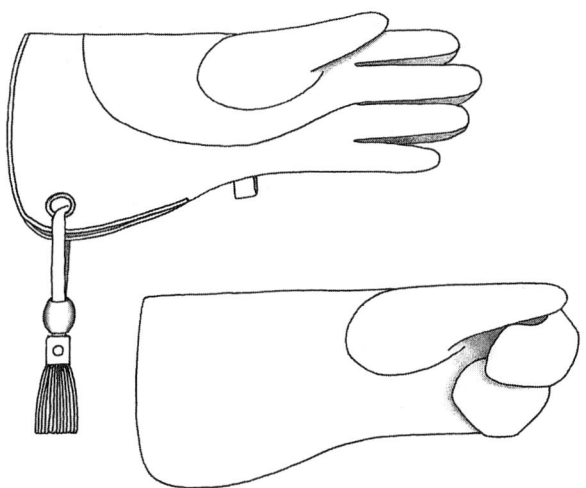

Top: One pattern of modern hawking glove with, in this case, traditional tassel and a sewn-in loop for attaching the hawk's leash. It has one leather overlay. Bottom: Arabian-style gauntlet mitten.

CROP. To Latham (1615 gl.[49]), 'gorge' (for a hawk) is idiomatically correct:

> '*Gorge*, is that part of the *Hawke* which first receiveth the meat, and is called the Craw or crop in other fowles.'

Crop (when applied to hawks) began generally to supersede gorge in the 19th century.

GORGE, A (obs.) By itself, usually a substantial or full meal.

> 'Eagles and all short-winged hawks should have a gorge, that is to say, as much as they choose to eat, about three times in a fortnight . . .' – 1900[59].

Otherwise, it is a meal when its size is indicated, such as in 'a full gorge' and in:

> '. . . Let her fast w^t a q[uar]ter gorge at the most . . .' – c.1575[38];
> 'Bot of all fleshes after she is mewed. a resenable goorge of an hoote haare [hot* hare] is beest. . . .' – 1486[5];
> 'That the diseases whiche Hawkes have in their heads, do commonly come of giving them too great gorges, and of foule feeding: the meane to knowe it.' – 1575 chap.hdg[81];
> 'I have already forewarned you, to be circumspect in her diet, that it may be of light and coole** meate, and small gorges thereof.' – 1615[49].

*(?)Freshly-killed.

**Not rich. A hot gorge (obs.) is a meal of freshly-killed food given to or taken by a hawk. A live gorge (unv., obs.) may be the same, or may mean a meal taken by a hawk from her kill in the field.

GORGE, A full See preceding entry.

GORGE, A hot See GORGE, A.

GORGE, A Live See GORGE, A.

GORGE, Cast the (obs.); **CAST GORGE** (obs.) Of a hawk, to be sick; to throw up the undigested contents of the crop, an indication of possible illness. The current idiom is cast the crop. See INFLAMMATION OF THE CROP (Appendix).

GOS; plural **GOSSES** Popular shortening of GOSHAWK. What appears to be an early written occurrence is in 1889 by F.H.Salvin in Harting (1898[40]).

GOSHAWK (Northern) *Accipiter gentilis* (Old English gos = goose + Old English hafoc = hawk. A goose is not usual prey for a wild goshawk; it is therefore uncertain why the goshawk was so named. It seems possible that the name came about through a misunderstanding, especially considering that goshawk has also been an English vernacular name for both the wild common buzzard

American goshawk with grey squirrel kill. (L. Lee Rue; FLPA, Images of Nature).

(*Buteo buteo*), a hawk incapable of taking geese, and peregrine falcon which will take geese on occasions. Historically in Western falconry, geese have generally (but not invariably) been considered overlarge to hunt with goshawks. Elsewhere, notably in Japan, goshawks have been flown at unnaturally large quarries, including geese[45].)

Formerly, 'goshawk' was usually reserved for the female, while 'tiercel' (and its variants) was customary for the male: 'He [in this case a male eyass goshawk] is termed a Tyerclet' (1575[81]). Perhaps most commonly from the late 19th century to the present day, when the subject is goshawks specifically, she is 'the female' while he is often 'the tiercel'; in other contexts, she is usually 'female goshawk' while he may be either 'tiercel –' or 'male goshawk'. Note: An uncommon and obsolete definition of 'falcon' has been:

> 'The female Peregrine and Goshawk "par excellence . . ."' – 1855 gl.[73]

American goshawk. (R. Austing; FLPA, Images of Nature).

Alternative names and forms:
GOS-HAWK or **GOSS-HAWK** (both obs.)
GOOSE HAWK (chiefly vernacular, obs.)
GOS; plural **GOSSES**. Popular shortening.
COOK'S BIRD (obs.). The goshawk, indicating a hawk which is a good provider of game for the pot. Compare the obsolete French sobriquet *cuisinier*, adopted, according to Schlegel (1853[74]), either because a goshawk brought profit to the kitchen or because it was once customary to keep her in the kitchen.
CHICKEN HAWK (vernacular, obs.) In Britain, the goshawk, the name apparently referring to the wild hawk's predation upon domestic poultry.
PARTRIDGE-HAWK. Former English vernacular name. In North America, a vernacular name for the American goshawk.
PIGEON HAWK; **PIGEON-HAWK**. Former vernacular English name.

The northern goshawk is found throughout much of the northern hemisphere. The nominate subspecies *Accipiter gentilis gentilis*, largely of Europe, and the somewhat dissimilar and smaller *A.g.atricapillus* of North America, are both used as austringers' birds. The European goshawk, with a long tradition of use in falconry in Britain, had become extinct as a wild breeding species in the British Isles by the turn of the 19th and 20th centuries. Losses of austringers' birds, fortified by re-introductions, have led to its current status of quite rare breeding resident. Historically, races of *A.gentilis* feature strongly as hunting birds in a number of Eastern and Far Eastern cultures. In traditional Japanese falconry, the goshawk has enjoyed a status equal to that of the peregrine falcon in Europe. Its versatility as a wild hunter is legendary, as is its fiercely persistent predatory behaviour. Highly manoeuvrable, it takes both bird and mammal species in swift chases in woodland as well as prey in fair flight in the open. As an austringer's bird, it is flown from the fist straight at quarry, or out of trees. Western austringers fly goshawks at ground-quarry to the size of rabbits, sometimes hares with the female, some game-birds, and waterfowl usually no larger than duck. (Plates 5 and 63–64).

A goshawk, just about recognisable, from George Turbervile's 1575 treatise.

GOSHAWKS There are numerous species of so-called goshawks throughout the world. Broadly, they are larger than the sparrowhawks, their tarsi and toes proportionately shorter and thicker; their prey is as a rule less exclusively birds taken in flight. Historically, only *Accipiter gentilis* has had any significant use as an austringer's bird. Of the northern goshawks, the nominate European (*Accipiter gentilis gentilis*) has long been used in European falconry. Other races feature in the traditional falconry of the East and Far East. Of New World goshawks, *A.g.atricapillus* is flown by North American falconers and should be regarded, according to some, as a separate species.

GO UNDER (probably modern, inf.) Occasionally heard today: of a hawk, to become (sometimes rapidly) dangerously underweight through having been cut down too severely; see CUT DOWN 2.

GRATE, Mew at the Under MOULT A HAWK.

GREASE (obs.) In a hawk, internal fat, particularly that which may be lining the stomach, understood to be removed by enseaming; see ENSEAM.

GREASE FOR LEATHER Today, falconers commonly use modern saddlery dressings for keeping the leather of jesses, hide leashes and bewits fed and supple; but one home recipe is:
 '1 oz (28 g) beeswax
 2½ oz (71 g) white wax (good quality candles)
 5 oz (142 g) liquid paraffin.' – 1987[84].
Another, from the previous century, is:
 'Mutton suet is as good as anything for this purpose, though some Falconers mix a little wax and oil with the fat.' – 1855[73].

GREAT-HORNED OWL *Bubo virginianus*. See EAGLE OWL.

GREAT OWL Obsolete name for the EAGLE OWL (*Bubo bubo*).

GREENLAND FALCON; **GREENLANDER** See GYRFALCON.

GREYHEN See BLACKGAME.

GRINS; **GRINES** See URINES under TRAPS AND TRAPPING.

GROSS, Fly See FLY GROSS.

GROUND-GAME Broadly, ground-dwelling game; to falconers, particularly rabbits and hares. Ground-quarry is to falconers any ground-dwelling quarry hunted with hawks.

GROUND-QUARRY See preceding entry.

GROUSE, Black See BLACKGAME.

GROUSE, Red *Lagopus scoticus*, the main species flown at in British grouse-hawking, the secondary species being the black grouse. Among English vernacular names for the red grouse are moor-cock (male; also an occasional vernacular name for the blackcock), occasionally moorhen (female), moor-bird (either sex) and, as group-names, moor-fowl and moor-game. Pack is the usual term for a gathering or family of grouse.

GROUSE-HAWKING See GAME-HAWKING under HAWKING, Categories of.

GURGIPING See next entry.

GURGITING (obs.) (Latin *ingurgito* = to gorge, guzzle. The Blome glossary (1686 [1929][9]) has GURGIPING; this may be a misspelling.) Of a hawk, choking on an overlarge mouthful.

 '*Gurgiting*, is when a *Hawke* is stuft or sufforated*

Male white phase gyrfalcon on mallard kill. (John Watkins; FLPA, Images of Nature).

with any thing, be it meat or otherwise.' – 1615 gl.[49]
*Taken to be a form or misspelling of suffocated. In one instance, a gurgiting (obs.) is a substantial meal:

> 'When she strikes it [quarry] down, she is allowed a "gurgiting".' – 1852[16].

GURGITING, A See preceding entry.

GYR Popular shortening of GYRFALCON.

GYRFALCON *Falco rusticolus* (Etymology disputed; according to OED, the ultimate source of the first element (gyr-) is now said to be Old High German *gîr* = vulture; significance unclear. The usual suggestion has been that gyr- is from Latin *gyrus* = a circle, circuit, suggestive of circling flight.)

In the older texts, 'gyrfalcon' (and its variants) is often reserved for the female; 'jerkin' (or variant) is customary for the male.

Alternative names and forms:
GYR FALCON; **GYR-FALCON** (both archaic)
GERFALCON. An alternative spelling used into the 20th century but now invariably replaced by gyrfalcon.
GERFAWKEN (obs.). In this case, the female:
   'Ther is a Gerfawken. a Tercell of a gerfauken. And theys belong to a kyng.' – 1486[5].
Note: 'Tiercel' has been (and is) used for the males of various hawks in falconry (notwithstanding many having their own traditional names), usually (as here) in combination with the species name. More in TIERCEL.
JERFALCON (obs.).
GIERFALCON (obs.).
GREENLAND FALCON ('white' phase); **GREENLANDER**[59].
ICELAND FALCON ('grey' phase); **ICELANDER**[59].
NORWAY FALCON ('black' phase); **NORWEGIAN**[59].
LABRADOR FALCON. According to Michell (1900[59]), a dark 'species of the ger family, found, as its name imports, in Labrador'.
GER. Obsolete shortening.
GYR. Recent and current shortening.
JER. Obsolete shortening.
JERKYN (1575[81], obs.). The male.
GYRKIN (obs.). The male.

The wild gyrfalcon is found in Greenland, Iceland, and Arctic regions of Europe, Asia, and North America. It is an irregular winter visitor to northern Britain, vagrant further south. The prey of the wild falcon includes Arctic game-birds, sea birds, waterfowl up to the size of geese, and hares. It is the largest of the world's falcons. Beebe[4] believes that in level or climbing pursuit of prey, it is capable of higher sustained speed than any other raptor. A wild gyr is said most commonly to strike avian prey in level pursuit rather than by mounting, stooping and striking as the peregrine habitually does, although this last tactic is sometimes used.

A traditional conclusion has been that the gyrfalcon occurs in three main colour-phases, referred to as 'black', 'grey', and 'white', classified as Norway, Iceland, and Greenland falcons respectively;

> 'In fact, the different plumage types grade imperceptibly into one another, with every kind of intermediate condition represented in different individuals.' – 1982[17].

The older authorities assumed these were two or three distinct species, but a recent view is that the gyr is

> '. . . a monotypic species, with much individual variation, white individuals occurring chiefly in the northern part of the range, darker birds further south.' – 1968[13].

The gyr was once flown by Western falconers at cranes, storks, herons and kites, categories of falconry which involved the much-admired high ringing flights. It has since been flown at a wide variety of quarry, largely avian (such as game-birds, waterfowl, gulls and rooks), but also occasionally at hares and rabbits. The gyr, an embodiment of power and stunning good looks, was once much favoured as a gift to illustrious personages who may or may not have practised falconry, although traditionally and historically in a number of cultures it has been greatly prized by those of high station who flew hawks. (Plates 6 and 67).

GYRKIN Obsolete spelling of jerkin, the male GYRFALCON.

H

HACK (vb and ns) For these and combination terms which include 'hack', see HACKING.

HACKED See next entry.

HACKING (The verb hack is of uncertain origin. It is perhaps related to the verb hatch (to produce young from eggs), or is a blend of this and heck = (in one lay sense) a rack for holding fodder; see HACK BOARD (below).) A controlled method of raising young hawks as wild with the aim of benefiting them physically and behaviourally when used in falconry. Birds may be reared from the nestling stage to flight in a building overlooking suitable tracts of land, or in a man-made eyrie. Food is provided covertly by the falconer. The hawks master flight skills and develop some muscular strength naturally. They return regularly to the nest-site to feed and will roost nearby. They are trapped here before they have killed for the first time or when they have only recently taken wild prey. The Michell (1900[59]) term 'hacking to the board' refers to the practice of providing hawks with food on a hack board; the food is usually secured to this, discouraging a hawk from forming the habit of carrying, that is, obeying a natural instinct to fly away with a kill to where she might feed on it alone. In an alternative method, a hawk may be made to the lure or trained to come to the fist before being given liberty. Whilst at hack she is called at regular intervals to feed upon one or the other. Michell calls these 'hacking to the lure' (for falcons) and 'hacking to the fist' (for short-winged hawks).

Associated terms:

HACK (vb). Of a falconer, to keep (hawks) at hack.

FLY AT HACK (unc.). The same as the above.

HACK 1 (n.). The complete programme (or the period) of hacking hawks. It might be a full or long hack or a short hack.

HACK 2 (n.) See HACK BOARD (below).

A HACK. A group-name for hawks together at hack; it might be a hack of peregrines.

AT HACK. Describes hawks which are being hacked.

HACK BACK. To release or re-introduce (a hawk) to the wild, employing the procedures of hacking. Once, as a matter of course, an unwanted hawk was disposed of by hacking her back. Young wild orphans and recuperated injured wild hawks are hacked or hacked back by rehabilitation experts.

HACK BELLS; also written HACK-BELLS (1898[40]). Bells worn by a hawk at hack; their ringing betrays her whereabouts. Once, heavy bells were used, additionally serving to slow her down and discourage her from hunting. In Salvin & Brodrick (1855[73]), it is recommended that
  '... large bells, or leaden weights, covered with soft wash-leather, should be fastened to their legs ...',
and Sebright (1826[75]) mentions
  'Small leaden bells ...'.
Michell (1900[59]) notes that
  'Sometimes hawks' bells are even loaded with lead.'

HACK JESSES (inf.). Jesses which have no slits at the free ends, therefore unlikely to become HOOKED UP during a hawk's hack.

HACK BOARD; HACK-BOARD; HACK (obs.); FOOD-BOARD ([?]modern N.Am. only[66]). The board on which the food for hawks at hack is laid or, usually, fastened. At the end of their hack, the hawks are trapped here or close by and taken up for training. Note: Turbervile (1575[81]) uses 'hacke' (obs.) for the board on which food is passed into the mews for a moulting hawk; compare FEEDING STOCK.

HACK HOUSE. A building from where hawks are hacked.

HACK HAWK; TACKLER (1686 [1929] gl.[9]; unv., obs.). A hawk at hack.

HACKED. Describes a hawk whose training has been preceded by hacking. 'Lure-hacked' is used by Michell (1900[59]) to mean (in this case, of a merlin) having been hacked to the lure, that is, regularly called to and fed on the lure during her hack.

UNHACKED. Describes a hawk whose training has not been preceded by hacking, or one which has not yet been hacked.

WELL-HACKED. Describes a hawk which has been successfully hacked, that is, one which has fully benefited from having been at hack.

HACKING TO THE BOARD; – TO THE FIST; – TO THE LURE See preceding entry.

HAGGARD (n.); **HAWGARD** (1615[49], obs.) (Cf. French *hagard* = haggard, wild-looking, or (of a hawk) wild.) A wild hawk in full adult plumage, or after she has moulted at least once in the wild state. An intermewed haggard is a wild-caught hawk which has moulted at least once in the wild and at least once in captivity; more in INTERMEWED. Traditionally the haggard is usually considered less malleable in training than the passage hawk (strictly a peregrine trapped on her first southward migration) or sore hawk (a hawk of the first year, before her first moult) and is described in such terms as obstinate, independent and set in her ways due to her long experience of living wild. However Latham (1615[49]) states his firm preference for the haggard when discussing the relative virtues of falcons at different stages of their development. Used adjectivally (in combinations such as haggard sparrowhawk) the term indicates that the hawk is in her second year at youngest, having moulted at least once in the wild. To Cotgrave (1611[23]), it loosely describes (in this case) a falcon

> '... that preyed for her selfe long before she was taken.'

Of the peregrine (implicitly female), Turbervile (1575[81]) notes:

> 'The seconde [after the falcon gentle in a list] is the Haggart Falcon, whiche is otherwise tearmed the Peregrine* Falcon.'

*'Peregrine' is strongly adjectival here, meaning in effect (according to this writer) from distant or unknown parts, or wanderer, or (oddly) suggestive of 'beautie and excellencie'. More in FALCON, Peregrine.

HAGGARD (adj.) See preceding entry.

HAGGART (adj.) See HAGGARD (n.).

HAGLURES (unv., obs.) (French *aiglures*, *églures* (1853[74]).) Spots on feathers. More in DEGOUTED.

HALSBAND (German); **JANGAOLI** (Indian) (German *Halsband* = collar.) Of Eastern origin, an aid to launching a short-winged hawk from the fist, in the form of a neckband and line somewhat resembling a dog's collar and leash. The hawk is held steady in a semi-prone position by drawing down on the line and gripping it between finger and thumb of the fist; she is thrown with a rapid forward motion, the grip on the line being released at the last moment. It is described by Michell (1900[59]) as

> '... a *halschband*, or linen collar, which serves to steady the flight.'

Writing on hawks and falconry in India, Radcliffe (1871[70]) notes:

> 'Eastern falconers ... use a sort of collar, made of light leather or plaited silk, worn on the hawk's neck, a cord attached to the collar being held between the finger and thumb; it is called the "halshband," and is supposed in the case of short-winged hawks to give the hawk an advantage when thrown at a bird off the fist, keeping her head straight during the violent motion of the hand. ... These halshbands were very often handsomely jewelled, and of fine workmanship.'

It is reported by Cox (1985[24]) that the so-spelt jangoli or Hals-band is still used by contemporary austringers in Pakistan; the materials he mentions are plaited silk or cotton, and leather. It is, he writes, made in one piece, the loop for the hawk's neck formed by threading one end through a slit in the other; a bell is sometimes attached, presumably at the hawk's throat. It is not infrequently depicted in Persian art, and a traditional Persian story of a king's lost hawk mentions a jewelled halsband[68]. Persian falconer Taymer Mirza (fl. mid-19th century, his treatise in transl. 1908[68]) advises that a halsband should not be used in scrubby, bushy country where it may become snagged and perhaps hang the hawk. Although often mentioned in recent and contemporary English-language treatises, the halsband has not seen wide use in the West.

HAND 1 Under FOOT (n.).

HAND 2 Perhaps only rarely if ever applied by falconers to their hawks: the outer (or distal) segment of the wing.

HAND-FOWL See QUARRY, Bagged.

HAND-LURING See LURE-SWINGING under LURE (n. and vb).

HANDSAW See HERN.

HANG ON See WAIT ON.

HARD Of a SLIP, or a falcon's stoop, strong, fast, committed. Latham (1618[50]), in a description of a flight by a goshawk, uses it thus:

> '... And at my comming in to the reterive*, the *Spaniels* sprung one [partridge] to her, the which shee flew very hard and killed ...'.

*The second springing of quarry; more in RETRIEVE, The. Also a falconer is said to stoop a falcon hard, that is, exercise her rigorously to the swung lure.

HARD DOWN (recent); **HARD-DOWN** (recent) Said of an EYASS: having her first true feathers (after the downy stage) fully grown and hard. Said of a hawk at a later stage: having her feathers full-grown and hard after the moult. Also occasionally said of any or all of the grown feathers. Also see PENNED, Hard, and FULL-SUMMED.

HARD PENNED See PENNED, Hard.

HARE- and RABBIT-HAWKING See HAWKING, Categories of.

HARES and RABBITS
 HARE (Genus *Lepus*). Jack, sometimes buck (male); doe (female); leveret (young). Customarily, hares are the largest mammal species taken in traditional and modern Western falconry. Both the brown hare (*L.europaeus*) and blue hare (*L.timidus*, also known as Scottish, mountain, and hill hare) are flown at to some extent by British austringers. The black-tailed and white-tailed jackrabbit, or jack, are two species of *Lepus* hunted in North America.
 RABBIT (European, genus *Oryctolagus*). Buck (male); doe (female); rabbit (young, formerly, the species being cony). Rabbits are widely hunted by British austringers. The slightly smaller cottontail (Genus *Sylvilagus*) is, in austringers' terms, the American equivalent.

HARRIS' HAWK; HARRIS See HAWK, Harris'.

HAWGARD Obsolete spelling of HAGGARD (n.).

HAWK 1 (n.) (Old English hafoc.) A general name, often used by falconers, for a bird of prey used in falconry, but almost invariably only embracing the long-, short- and (since their relatively recent introduction) broad-winged hawks. Rarely, any bird of prey used in falconry, which would add eagles and certain hawk-eagles to this list.

Hare in her form by G. E. Lodge

HAWK 2 (n., lay) To the well-informed layman, a hawk of the genus *Accipiter*. The term in this sense is rarely used by falconers, who traditionally refer to a bird of this group as a short-winged hawk or shortwing, and sometimes accipiter today, the synonymous 'true hawk' being met with sporadically in hawking literature.

HAWK 3 (n., obs.) When a distinction between the sexes is necessary, the female in particular, but so far only found applied to the goshawk.
 'That the Tarsell [male] is more prone to these ill conditions then the hawke, and how to reclaime him that will seeke out for a Dove-house; with which fault I never knew Goshawke tainted.' – 1619 chap.hdg[6].
Note that in this passage goshawk is also used for the female.

HAWK 4 (n.) In North America, 'hawk' is used in the common names of native raptors of the genus *Buteo* (for example red-tailed hawk) as well as for those in the genus *Accipiter*, such as Cooper's hawk. British falconers perhaps favour 'hawk' in the common names of North American buteos used in falconry, but 'buzzard' is sometimes substituted; an example is ferruginous buzzard.

HAWK (vb, obs.) Of a falconer, to hunt with a trained hawk. Bert (1619[6]) uses the term in:
 '... Goe hawke in the Woodland, and make choyse to fly at such Partridges as will flye to a woode ...'.
As an old but surviving lay term, it means (of a wild bird of prey) to hunt on the wing. More in FALCONRY AND HAWKING.

-HAWK The final element in combination terms for hawks employed in different categories of hawking, preceded by the quarry flown at.

HAWK, Aspare; ASPERE HAWK; ASPERE-HAWK Obsolete forms of SPARROWHAWK.

HAWK, Bay-winged Lay name for the Harris' hawk; see HAWK, Harris'.

HAWK, Blue (obs.) Specifically the peregrine falcon in full adult plumage, the term referring to her blue-grey upper colouration. A red hawk is a hawk (not specifically the peregrine) of the first year, before her first moult, named for her reddish-brown plumage.

HAWK, Broad-winged; BROADWING; BROAD-WING (all recent) To falconers, a hawk of the genera *Buteo* or *Parabuteo*; the terms relate to the breadth rather than the length of the wing, although the wings are rather long. Four broad-winged hawks have been introduced into the modern pursuit: the red-tailed hawk, the ferruginous hawk, the common buzzard, and the Harris' hawk.

HAWK, Chicken (vernacular, obs.) In Britain, the goshawk, the name apparently referring to the wild hawk's predation upon domestic poultry.

HAWK, Cooper's *Accipiter cooperii* (Named for American zoologist W.Cooper, 1798–1864.) The Cooper's hawk's breeding range is southern Canada and the United States south to north-western Mexico. It is a typical woodland dwelling short-winged hawk, although it will hunt over more open tracts of land. It is roughly intermediate in size between the European sparrowhawk and the goshawk. Although some mammal species are taken, it preys for preference on birds such as the native blackbird and meadowlark; a female may on occasion take some game-birds and duck. Its hunting technique is usually based on surprise, often involving a swift dash from a perch in cover. It has a short history of use in falconry but is now occasionally used by British and more widely by North American austringers. Like a goshawk, it is flown from the fist straight at quarry or out of trees. The female will take part-grown rabbits and some game-birds, the male smaller quarry.

HAWK, Duck; DUCK-HAWK An English provincial and North American vernacular name for the peregrine falcon. Otherwise, a falconer's hawk (usually long-winged) for flying duck.

HAWK, Ensiled See SEEL.

HAWK, Ferruginous *Buteo regalis* (Ferruginous = of the colour of iron rust, denoting the partial rufous colouration of adult birds.) Alternative name:
   FERRUGINOUS BUZZARD (sometimes in Britain) The largest of the North American broad-winged hawks, with no history of use as an austringer's bird before the mid-20th century. It is found in the inland west, frequenting plains and prairie, and preys on ground squirrels, prairie dogs, jackrabbits and prairie hares, small rodents, small- to medium-sized birds including game-birds (although rarely in flight), and occasionally snakes. American austringers, flying it from the fist, out of trees or off poles, take rabbits and hares with it. Although used little in Britain, it is thought potentially suitable to be flown there at rabbits and hares either with long slips or from the soar in open hilly country.

HAWK, Field (1618[50], obs.); **FIELD-HAWK** (1686 [1929][9], obs.) A hawk for flying in open country as opposed to 'to the covert', that is, in country which may feature thickets, copses or woods.

HAWK, Goose (chiefly vernacular, obs.) The GOSHAWK.
   '... An Ayerye of goosse hawks.' – c.1520 (OED).

HAWK, Hack; TACKLER (unv., obs.) A hawk at hack. See HACKING.

HAWK, Harris' or **Harris's** *Parabuteo unicinctus* (Named in the common form for Edward Harris by US naturalist and artist John James Audubon (1785–1851); Audubon was accompanied by Harris on his Missouri River trip in 1843.) Other names:
   HARRIS; plural **HARRISES**. Popular shortening.
   BAY-WINGED HAWK. Lay.
The genus *Parabuteo* contains one species. The Harris' hawk is a broad-winged hawk found in

Cooper's hawk. (E.&.D. Hosking; FLPA, Images of Nature).

Ferruginous hawk in flight. (W.S. Clark; FLPA, Images of Nature).

south-western United States, south through to Chile, in sparsely wooded or more open, often arid, areas. Its usual prey is birds of various sizes, rabbits and rodents. As its scientific (generic) name implies, it is not a true hawk nor a buteo, though it is regarded as being close to the latter. Despite having only a brief history of use in falconry, the Harris' hawk has achieved a unique niche in the modern pursuit. It has been found to be easily tamed and entered at quarry and is therefore considered to be an ideal first bird; furthermore, it is a capable and versatile hunter which may be flown with enjoyment by an experienced austringer. More agile than the buteos, it is flown from the fist straight at quarry, out of trees or off poles, and is sometimes used by British austringers to fly ground-quarry from the soar in open hilly country. It will take quarry up to the size of rabbits, sometimes hares, occasionally pheasant. It is known that wild Harrises cooperate in the hunt, therefore, as austringers' birds, they may successfully be flown in a cast. (Plates 56, 76 and 79).

HAWK, Kitchen Obsolete name for the lanner falcon; see FALCON, Lanner.

HAWK, Lady's See MERLIN.

HAWK, Lenten; **LENT-HAWK** See LANTINER.

HAWK, Long-winged; LONGWINGED HAWK (1686, unc.); **LONGWING** To falconers, a hawk of the genus *Falco*; a falcon. The terms refer to her long, narrowish, tapering wings and differentiate her from the short-winged hawk. Historically in the West, the most widely flown of this group have been the gyrfalcon, the peregrine, saker and lanner falcons, and the merlin. The method of slipping and the style of flight vary depending on the hawk used and the quarry flown at. All are flown in open country and all are called back to the lure after an unsuccessful flight, hence the synonymous 'hawk of the lure' (obsolete).

HAWK, Made See MAKE.

HAWK, Make (now unc.) (Also written MAKE-HAWK (now unc.); possibly QUARRY HAWK (obs.); MAKE-FALCON (unv., obs.) An experienced falcon flown in a cast with one of less experience, to encourage and educate (or help MAKE) the latter. Note: historically in the West, only falcons have been flown in a cast; today, the sociable Harris' hawk may be flown in this way.

> 'A *Make-hawke* is an old staunche flying Hawke, which being inur'd to her flight, wil easily instruct a younger Hawk to be waining in her pray.' – 1615 gl.[49]

> '... The beginner, when it sees the "make-hawk" pursuing a rook, will be tempted to join in the flight and share in the kill.' – 1987[84].

> 'Two falconers go forth together, one carrying the initiate and the other the expert hunter. The make-falcon is now loosed, and when it is seen that she is giving chase to a crane and it cannot escape ... then the young falcon also is slipped, so that she may be present at the capture of the crane or at least see it seized as a crane should be caught.' – 13th century, in transl.[35]

See CAST, A.

HAWK, March   See LANTINER.

HAWK, Mewed   (probably obs.) A hawk which has completed her moult, or a hawk in her second year, having moulted once. In this Berners (1486[5]) passage, it appears to be the latter:

> 'And iff yowre hawke shall flie to the partrich. looke that ye Ensayme her or she flie. whether she be Brawncher or Eyes Or mewed hawke.' This might be paraphrased: 'If your hawk is to be flown at partridge, make sure you enseam her before she flies, whether she is a brancher, an eyass or a mewed hawk.'

See ENSEAM, BRANCHER (n.), and EYASS.

HAWK, Moulted   A hawk which has completed her moult, or one in her second year, having moulted once; more in MOULTS.

HAWK, Noble; -Ignoble   See under FALCONS, Noble.

HAWK, Passage; PASSAGE-HAWK; PASSAGEHAWK; PASSAGER (Less common, with 'passage' strongly adjectival, are: passage falcon (1898), passage tiercel, passage peregrine, etc.) A wild hawk, strictly the peregrine, still in immature plumage, trapped whilst on passage or more specifically on her first southward migration. Sometimes passage hawk is used loosely for a wild hawk (usually the peregrine) which has left the eyrie, is hunting for herself, and is yet to moult. In Salvin & Brodrick (1855[73]):

> 'The term Passage Hawk is always applied, *par excellence*, by Falconers to the migrating Peregrine, although other Hawks, under similar circumstances, might come under the same denomination.'

Elsewhere in this text, it is another term for a HAGGARD taken upon migration. The obsolete combination 'passenger soare-Falcon' (1615[49]) is a passage hawk, 'soare' apparently emphasizing that she is in her 'red' or immature plumage. An intermewed passage hawk, or intermewed passager, is a passage hawk which has moulted at least once in captivity.

Traditionally (and usually), the passage hawk (strictly the peregrine) and sore hawk (see HAWK, Sore) are considered more desirable as falconers' birds than the HAGGARD, being malleable in training and at the same time practised in flight skills and hunting; and:

> 'Just as a passage falcon is superior to an eyess, having been on the wing for some time, and having learnt to catch and kill prey for herself, so is a haggard Sparrow-hawk to be preferred to an eyess, being as easily trained, knowing her business from the start, and giving less trouble in feeding.' – 1898[40].

Also see 1900 qu. and note in WILD-CAUGHT.

HAWK, Pigeon; PIGEON-HAWK   Former vernacular name in England for the goshawk, sparrowhawk, peregrine falcon and merlin. In North America, a vernacular name for the merlin.

HAWK, Pole   (obs.) A live hawk tethered to a pole, used by trappers as a decoy to attract the attention of hawks on passage. See DUTCH METHOD under TRAPS AND TRAPPING.

HAWK, Quarry   (unv.) A possible synonym for make hawk; see HAWK, Make.

HAWK, Ramage (obs.); **RAMAGE-HAWK** (obs.); **RAMAGE** (obs.); **RAMAGER** (obs.) (Archaic English ramage = branches of trees; Latin *ramus* = a branch. Medieval Latin (Brit.–Ir.[48]) *ramagius* = [of a hawk] 'ramage', snared after leaving nest. Obs. adj. ramage = (of hawks) wild in the sense of untame, and in an obsolete lay sense = (of animals) wild, shy, untamed. Ramage occurs adjectivally in specific combinations such as ramage falcon, ramage goshawk, etc.; these are also obs.) In the common understanding, a young wild hawk which is either about to leave or has left the vicinity of the eyrie. The literal and perhaps original definition appears to be a hawk which is able to fly from branch to branch, perhaps tree to tree; hence (in the case of short-winged hawks) a blurring of distinction between ramage hawk and brancher; see BRANCHER (n.). Under the heading

'Of the names of a Falcon, according to hir age and taking', Turbervile (1575[81]) writes:

> 'The seconde name [after eyass] is a ramage Falcon, and so she is called when she hath departed and left the eyrie, that name doth laste, and she is called ramage hawke, May, June, Julie, and August.'

And (ibid.),

> 'There are three sortes of Falcons. viz. *Niasses, Sorehawkes,* and *Hawkes,* taken praying for themselves at large, whiche our Falconers call ramage or sleight* Falcons.'

*See FALCON, Slight.

HAWK, Ramish (obs.); **RAMMISH HAWK** (obs.); **RAMISH** (obs.); **RAMMISH** (obs.) Forms of ramage hawk and ramage (see preceding entry). Bert (1619[6]) writes:

> 'There is small difference* betweene the *Haggart* and the *Rammish* [goshawk], onely the *Rammish* Hawke hath had lesse time (by preying for her selfe then the other) to know her owne strength and worth . . .'.

*To this might be added 'potentially as hunting birds', although Bert notes that in the rammish hawk is his 'especiall delight'. Also see RAMISH (adj.).

HAWK, Red (now unc.); **RED-HAWK** (now unc. or obs.) (Red relates to reddish-brown immature plumage, as does sore, formerly sometimes spelt soar.) A hawk of the first year, before her first moult,

> '... *i.e.* in the 'red' or immature plumage (sometimes also termed a 'soar' hawk).' – 1892 gl.[47]
> 'RED-HAWK ... the modern term for a "Sore-hawk" ...' – 1891 gl.[39]

Note: It is possible that red hawk originally applied to the peregrine exclusively, but it is met with applied to other hawks at this stage of their development. Compare HAWK, Sore.

HAWK, Red-tailed *Buteo jamaicensis* ('Red-tailed' refers to the distinctive reddish tail of adults in some races.) Alternative names:

RED-TAIL
REDTAIL
RED-TAILED BUZZARD (sometimes in Britain)

A broad-winged hawk with races from Alaska south to Central America, the Bahamas and West Indies. It is a highly versatile predator, taking a broad range of bird and mammal species and other prey. As an austringer's bird, it is usually flown from the fist straight at quarry, or out of trees or off poles, but under the right conditions it may be encouraged to seek height and take certain quarries from the soar. The most suitable quarries for a red-tail in Britain include rabbits, hares, grey squirrels, pheasant, moorhens and duck. From the middle of the 20th century in North American falconry, it has enjoyed a steady increase in use; it is now said to be the most widely flown hawk on the continent. It is temperamentally steady, therefore relatively easy to man, train and enter, and is bigger, considerably stronger and more resolute a hunter than its relative, the Eurasian common buzzard. (Plates 17 and 55).

HAWK, Rick- See RICK-HAWK.

HAWK, River- See RIVER-HAWK

HAWK, Round winged See HAWK, Short-winged.

HAWK, Seeled See SEEL.

HAWK, Sharp-shinned *Accipiter striatus* (Named in the common form for the distinctive shape (in section) of the hawk's leg.) Alternative names:

SHARP-SHIN
SHARPIE or SHARPY

Smaller than the European sparrowhawk, this tiny accipiter of the sparrowhawk type is from the Americas, frequenting woodland and sparsely wooded tracts of land. Its wild prey consists almost exclusively of small birds, often taken on the wing after a short dash. *A.s.velox* is flown by North American austringers; usually only the female is

Sharp-shinned hawk. (R. Austing; FLPA, Images of Nature).

used, flown or thrown at sparrows and other small birds, sometimes at doves and quail. See THROWING A HAWK.

HAWK, Short-winged; **SHORTWING**; **SHORT-WING** To falconers, a hawk of the genus *Accipiter*. The terms refer to her short, broad, round-ended wings and differentiate her from the long-winged hawk. Turbervile (1575[81]) uses 'round winged hawks' for birds in this group; this is uncommon and obsolete. The synonymous 'true hawk' is met with sporadically in hawking literature. In the wild, short-winged hawks are largely of forest, woodland and tracts of land close to woodland fringes. An austringer may hunt with a short-winged hawk in open or less open countryside depending on the quarry he is flying her at. Traditionally she is flown from the fist straight at quarry (sometimes, in the case of the smaller species, thrown), or out of trees, and is usually called back to the fist after an unsuccessful flight rather than to the lure, hence the obsolete name 'hawk of the fist'. Historically and currently in falconry, the most important and highly-esteemed of the group is the goshawk.

HAWK, Small-bird Obsolete, perhaps exclusively lay name for the SPARROWHAWK. Otherwise (occasionally; written 'small bird hawk') a hawk for taking small avian quarry.

HAWK, Sore (now unc.); SOARAGE (obs.) (Cf. sorrel = a horse of reddish-brown colour; French *saure* = (of horses) sorrel. Other forms: SOREHAWK (probably obs.), SOREHAWK (probably obs.), SOAR-HAWK (obs.), SOARHAWK (unc., obs.), others.) In the common understanding, a wild hawk in her immature (or 'red') plumage, also known as a red hawk; a hawk of the first year, hunting for herself. This is not always precisely agreed upon, as can be seen from the following extracts.

> '*Sore-hawke*, is from the first taking of her from the eiry, till shee have mewed her feathers.' – 1615 gl.[49]
> 'When it has left the nest it becomes a "brancher:" a "soar-hawk," or "soarage," when it has begun to prey for itself.' – 1852[16].

Similarly, a soar-hawk is
> 'A young hawk able to take game.' – 1856 gl.[76]

A time scale is sometimes specified for the term; Michell (1900[59]) states (without quoting sources) that
> 'The period during which she [peregrine] could properly be called a soar-hawk lasted, according to some eminent writers, from June 15th to September 15th, when the migrating time begins, and she came to be more properly spoken of as a passage-hawk . . .'.

But Turbervile (1575[81]) believes that
> '. . . They [young falcons] are called sore Hawkes, from the ende of August, to the laste of September, October, and November.'

Then (ibid.), writing of the sparrowhawk:
> 'The Sore Hawke, is she that hath flien, and prayed for hir, and is taken before the mewe.' The last part of this definition might be paraphrased: '. . . and is trapped before her first moult.'

This writer holds the uncommon belief that
> 'They are called Soarehawkes, bicause when they [sparrowhawks] have forsaken the woodde, and beginne to pray for themselves, they flee up aloft upon pleasure, which with us Falconers is called soring.'

Another use for soarage, see SORE AGE.

HAWK, Tree- See TREE-HAWK

HAWK, True (occ.) A hawk of the genus *Accipiter*.

HAWK, White (obs.) (The significance of the adj. white remains uncertain. That it is a reference to the paler adult plumage is possible.) A hawk in her third year.
> 'The *Age* of a *Hawk*: The first year, a *soarage*. The second year, an *Enterview*. The third year, a *White Hawk*. The fourth year, *a Hawk of the first Coat*.' – 1677[25].

There are variations on this, for example: first year, red hawk; second year, mewed hawk; third year, white hawk; fourth year, hawk of the first coat. And:
> 'HAWK OF THE FIRST COAT. A falconer's term for a Hawk of the fourth year, when it has attained its full growth and perfection. A Hawk of the fifth year was moreover called "a hawk of the second coat," and so on.' – 1913[79].

These formulæ are obsolete.

HAWK AT (obs.) Of a falconer, to fly a hawk at (quarry); of a hawk, to fly at (quarry). More in FALCONRY AND HAWKING.

HAWK-BELL; **HAWK BELL**; **HAWK'S BELL** See BELL (n.)

HAWK-BOOK (unc.) A falconer's diary, the term used by Michell (1900[59]).

HAWK-EAGLES An informal group-name for certain eagles (not all of the same genus), some of which have outward characteristics of the true hawks (genus *Accipiter*), chiefly in the combination of long tail and short wings, adaptations for manoeuvrable flight in woodland.

Hodgson's hawk-eagle. (E.&.D. Hosking; FLPA, Images of Nature).

Bonelli's eagle. (H. Schrempp; FLPA, Images of Nature).

Genus *Spizaetus*: Small to fairly large somewhat accipiter-like tropical forest eagles of the Old and New Worlds. There are records of Hodgson's (feather-toed[13] or mountain[13], *S.nipalensis*), changeable or crested (*S.cirrhatus*; plate 75), Blyth's (or mountain[13], *S.alboniger*; plate 1), ornate (*S.ornatus*), and Wallace's (*S.nanus*) hawk-eagles having been used in falconry, although there is limited history of their use in the West. Suitable quarry is such as rabbits, hares and pheasant. They are flown in a similar fashion to the goshawk. Hawk-eagles have a long history of use in traditional Japanese falconry, although in former times they were considered less 'noble' than the exalted goshawk. *S.nipalensis* has seen use there (formerly and in recent times) usually as a hare-hawk, sometimes for duck, but trained birds have also taken martens, racoon dogs and foxes[45]. **Genus *Hieraaetus*:** Small to medium-sized eagles of usually wooded regions in Europe and Asia, Africa and Australia. Those with some history of use are the African hawk-eagle (*H.fasciatus spilogaster*) and Bonelli's eagle of southern Eurasia (*Hieraaetus fasciatus fasciatus*). Both may be flown from the fist straight at quarry, or out of trees. Harting (1898[40]) writes of seeing the Bonelli's eagle flown in France at rabbits bolted by ferrets. The African hawk-eagle is highly thought of as a falconer's bird, although it has little (and only recent) history of use in British falconry. In modern times, it has been flown in southern Africa at game-birds and, sometimes at night with artificial light, at hares and the nocturnal hopping rodent, the springhare (*Pedetes capensis*)[41].

HAWKER 1 (unc., obs.) A lure of unknown design.

HAWKER 2 (unv., obs.) (Old English *hafocere*.) One who engages in hawking; one who keeps, tends and trains hawks; a falconer. This is perhaps an exclusively lay term.

HAWKERY (1850, OED; unv., unc., obs.) A place where hawks are kept (OED).

HAWK HOUSE; HAWK-HOUSE A building in which hawks are kept. More in MEWS.

HAWKING See FALCONRY AND HAWKING.

-HAWKING The second element in combination terms for different categories in hunting with hawks, preceded by the quarry flown at. Also see BROOK-HAWKING in next entry.

HAWKING, Categories of
  BROOK-HAWKING; HAWKING AT THE BROOK Obsolete terms for hawking along rivers for waterfowl, chiefly duck. The pursuit in medieval times (as portrayed in European art of the period) involved the use of beaters, sometimes drummers, and dogs to flush quarry from cover such as reed-beds. In the 13th century, Emperor Frederick[35] was using peregrines, put up to wait on while duck were flushed beneath them. Today, duck, as a rule flushed from

ponds, are hunted with a falcon waiting on or flown out of the hood. Historically in the West, the goshawk has long been used for hunting duck, and this continues today.

FERRETING The use of ferrets to bolt rabbits from the warren for hawks to take; the history of the pursuit is uncertain. The most suitable hawk in this category is the goshawk, although others, such as the red-tailed hawk and Harris' hawk, have been used in recent times with success. In the late 19th century, Harting[40] writes of seeing the Bonelli's eagle flown in France at rabbits bolted by ferrets.

FERRET (*Putorius furo*. Latin *putor* = a foul smell, malodorousness; Latin *fur* = a thief). Hob (male), gill or less commonly jill (female). The ferret is described as domesticated, sometimes semi-wild (or -tame); its ancestor is the polecat (*Mustela putorius*; Latin *mustela* = a weasel). What are thought to be the earliest written references begin more than 2000 years ago in Greece. It is possible that the ferret was used there for destroying rodents. It has since been widely used coped (its mouth tied or sewn up to prevent it laying up, that is, remaining in the bury after killing and feeding on a rabbit), muzzled or unmuzzled to flush rabbits from the warren to be caught in nets. Albino animals are invariably used in hawking, the colouration known as 'polecat' (hence polecat-ferret) being too reminiscent of quarries the hawk may have been flown at.

GAME-HAWKING Usually applied in Britain to flying the larger falcons at birds of the grouse kind and partridge. However, the term has been broadened and applied by some (perhaps particularly in North America) to flying any hawk at GAME. The term is not applied to the hunting of hares and rabbits, although these are sometimes referred to as game, sometimes groundgame. Sub-divisions of game-hawking may be renamed according to the quarry flown at (such as grouse-hawking and partridge-hawking). In Britain the supreme classic of game-hawking is generally considered to be flying a falcon over dogs at red grouse (*Lagopus scoticus*), when a falcon (or game-hawk) is put up and waits on until game is flushed.

HARE- and RABBIT-HAWKING The hunting of hares (plates 63–64) and rabbits in the open, traditionally in the West with the goshawk, and in recent and modern times with certain of the eagles, hawk-eagles, buteos, and the Harris' hawk, also to a limited extent (at rabbits) with the Cooper's hawk and the black sparrowhawk. Alternatively, rabbits might be flushed from the warren with ferrets for hawks to take. In the West, hare- and rabbit-hawking with falcons have not been widely pursued, although there are records of such as gyrfalcons being used singly and in a cast for flights at hares. There are anecdotal accounts of peregrines taking hares, such as when

'. . . A particularly fine, high-mounting grouse-falcon, called "Parachute," was waiting on at a great pitch over a point, which turned out to be at a blue hare instead of a grouse. To the surprise of all, the moment the hare moved the falcon came down like a flash, and striking it behind the ears rolled it over and over.' – 1892[47].

HERON-HAWKING The discontinued practice of flying a cast (two) or leash (three) of the larger species of falcon at the common heron (*Ardea cinerea*). Peregrines or gyrfalcons were usually used, sometimes sakers, flown out of the hood. In Britain and Europe it was considered to be the supreme classic of hawking and greatly admired for the dramatic high ringing flights of quarry and falcons, its popularity affirmed by eulogistic accounts in old texts. Heroner is the old term for a falcon used in heron-hawking; otherwise it is heron-hawk. (Plates 51 and 66).

KITE-HAWKING The discontinued practice of flying falcons at the red kite (*Milvus milvus*), considered in Britain and Europe to be one of the classics of hawking and esteemed for the impressive mounting flights of hawks in pursuit of a particularly difficult and elusive quarry. Historically, usually a cast or leash of gyrfalcons (sometimes peregrines, occasionally sakers) was used, flown out of the hood. For notes on the use of an owl as a decoy in kite-hawking, see EAGLE OWL.

LAMPING The occasional pursuit of hunting rabbits or hares with a short- or broad-winged hawk after dark, using a beam of bright light. In Zimbabwe in recent years, the African hawk-eagle has been flown at hares and springhares (*Pedetes capensis*) using this method (1983[41]).

LARK-HAWKING Traditionally in Britain and Europe, flying merlins, singly or in a cast, at the skylark (*Alauda arvensis*). It is much-admired for the ringing flights where quarry and pursuing falcon or falcons mount sometimes to great heights. It has been described as 'heron-hawking in miniature'. It has been common practice not to hood merlins and to fly them straight from the fist when the quarry rises. See 1892 qu. in CAST, A.

MAGPIE-HAWKING In Britain, flying falcons out of the hood, often tiercel peregrines in a cast, at the magpie (*Pica pica*).

> 'Two tiercels should be flown together, as the magpie shifts so rapidly from the stoop, and avails himself so cleverly of every possible covert that might protect him, that a single hawk has not much chance with him, and the whole beauty of the flight consists in the pretty double stooping in which the one tiercel takes up the chance that the other has missed.' – 1892[47].

ROOK-HAWKING In Britain, flying a falcon (one of the larger species, often a peregrine) out of the hood at rooks (*Corvus frugilegus*) either rising from open ground or on passage to or from their feeding grounds. Falconers often will not fly their rook-hawks deliberately at the carrion crow (*C.corone*) because of its strength as an opponent in the air and its stabbing beak on the ground. Jackdaws (*C.monedula*, usually referred to as choughs ['choffs' – c.1575[38]] in old English texts), are extremely agile fliers, often outwitting and outflying a falcon, and are not often taken. (Plates 60–62).

SEAGULL-HAWKING Flying the larger species of falcon (especially peregrines, traditionally often in a cast) out of the hood at gulls. In Britain, the protected common gull (*Larus canus*) and black-headed gull (*L.ridibundus*) are looked on as the species offering the best flights.

HAWKING, Go See FALCONRY AND HAWKING.

HAWKING AT THE BROOK See BROOK-HAWKING under HAWKING, Categories of.

HAWKING BAG See BAG, Hawking.

HAWKING GLOVE See GLOVE, Hawking.

HAWKING JACKET See JACKET, Hawking.

HAWKING POLE See POLE, Hawking.

HAWK MEAT; HAWK'S MEAT; HAWK FOOD See MEAT, Hawk.

HAWK OF THE FIRST COAT (obs.) A hawk in her fourth year. See 1677 qu. in HAWK, White.

HAWK OF THE FIST (obs.); BIRD OF THE FIST (obs.) A short-winged hawk, the names signifying that she is customarily called to the fist and not to the lure as is a falcon. And:

> 'They fly from thence [the fist] instead of swooping from the air.' – 1852[16].

HAWK OF THE LURE (obs.); BIRD OF THE LURE (obs.) A falcon, the names signifying that she is customarily called to the lure and not to the fist as is a short-winged hawk.

HAWK OF THE MOUNTEE (obs.) Used in the plural by Michell (1900[59]) to mean long-winged game- or duck-hawks. More in MOUNTY.

HAWK OF THE SOAR (obs.) A falcon which in hunting mounts and waits circling at a height for quarry to be flushed beneath her. The verb soar can mean WAIT ON in the context of falconry, but this application is obsolete; more in SOAR (vb 2).

HAWK OF THE TOWER (obs.) (Tower from Latin *turris*. Cf. lay vb tower = to mount to a great height, rise aloft.) A falcon, apparently signifying that in hunting she characteristically seeks height; see RING UP and WAIT ON. Berners (1486[5]) has 'haukis of yͤ tour'; and in her 'naamys of all maner of hawkys & to whom they belong' is 'hawkes of the towre', which evidently embraces all the falcons named in the list (see NAMES 3). Turbervile (1575[81]) has 'Towre Hawkes', which are falcons.

HAWK OVER DOGS See under DOGS IN HAWKING.

HAWK VAN; HAWK-VAN A wheeled vehicle, once horse-drawn (plate 28), sometimes hand-drawn, for transporting a number of hawks to the field and housing them there. Of the horse-drawn type as used in England by the Old Hawking Club in the 19th century, Michell (1900[59]) writes:

> 'A still greater luxury for the field [after the cadge], especially in rook-hawking, is the hawk-van, which is a sort of omnibus, fitted with screen perches, and hung on very easy springs. In it are conveyed the hawks which are not for the time being in use, and also spare lures and other furniture and properties, not forgetting the luncheon basket.'

HEAD To falconers, a unit in counting quarry taken. With a number (e.g. 9 head), the total of quarry taken in a given period.

HEAD TOWARDS, Having her See HOLD IN THE HEAD.

HEARNOR; HEARNNOR Forms of HERONER.

HEARONER   Form of HERONER.

HEATH-COCK; HEATH FOWL; HEATH GAME   See BLACKGAME.

HERN   An obsolete and often poetic form of heron. Latham in his treatise (1615[49]) spells it 'hearne'; Turbervile (1575[81]) has 'hearon'. Heronshaw, heronshew, heronsew and others (all obsolete) are strictly the young heron but are also used to mean heron (species). 'Handsaw', as in 'When the wind is southerly, I know a hawk from a handsaw' (William Shakespeare, *Hamlet*), is taken to be a corruption of heronshaw.

HERNSHAW; HERONSHAW   (Other similar spellings.) See preceding entry.

HERON, Common   *Ardea cinerea*, the quarry in heron-hawking. Also see HERN.

HERONER (obs.); FALCON HERONER (obs.).   (French *héronnier, faucon héronnier*; Medieval Latin (Brit.–Ir.[48]) *falco heironarius*.) A falcon for heron-hawking. Turbervile (1575[81]) has 'hearoner' (and 'hearon' for heron). Latham (1615[49]) has 'hearnnor' and 'hearnor' (and 'hearne' for heron). Later, usually 'heron-hawk'. See HERON-HAWKING under HAWKING, Categories of.

HERON-HAWK   (obs.) A falcon for HERON-HAWKING (under HAWKING, Categories of).

HERON-HAWKING   See HAWKING, Categories of.

HEY(E)   See CONDITION, High or low.

HIE   See CONDITION, High or low.

HIERAAETUS   (Greek *hierax* = a hawk or falcon + Greek *aetos* = an eagle.) The genus of eagles from which the Bonelli's eagle and African hawk-eagle have been drawn for use in falconry. See HAWK-EAGLES.

HIGH   See CONDITION, High or low.

HOB   The male ferret. See FERRETING under HAWKING, Categories of.

HOBBY (European)   *Falco subbuteo* (Old French *hobé* or *hobet*. Perhaps derived from Old French *hober* = to move or bestir oneself. Significance uncertain, but conceivably a reference to the hawk's hunting technique of dashing into a flock of small birds to take one out.) Alternative names and forms:
   HOBY (1486[5], obs.)
   HOBBIE (1618[50], obs.)
   HOBBY-HAWK (probably exclusively lay.)
   ROBIN. The male.
   JACK HOBBY (1686 [1929][9]; unc., obs.). The male.

A small migratory falcon which nests in Britain, hunting small birds and insects on the wing. Although there is no history of its serious use in Western falconry, there are numerous accounts in older English hawking literature of hobbies having been kept, manned, flown free, and stooped to the lure, when they were said to display admirable style. Few details have been found about their successful entering at quarry, although a verb 'to hobby' exists, meaning (of a falconer) to hunt with a hobby; more in next entry. In the early 17th century, Latham[50] writes briefly about the nurture of an eyass 'hobbie' for use in lark-hawking. Harting (1898[40]) notes that

> '... With all his splendid powers of flight, the Hobby, like the Kestrel, is a lazy and unpersevering bird. He seems to want pluck, and after ringing up in good style after a mounting lark, and looking as if he was sure to kill, he will give up the chase and turn idly away down wind as if it were beneath his dignity to take more trouble.'

The hobby may have once been thought suitable for beginners, hence perhaps 'Ther is an Hoby. And that hauke is for a yong man' in the old list of 'the naamys of all maner of hawkys & to whom they belong' (1486[5]); fuller list in NAMES 3. A traditional use for the hobby was in DARING (larks). (Plates 7, 49 and 68).

HOBBY   (vb, obs.) To hawk with a hobby (OED). As a verb, it is so far unverified as authentic to falconry. The hobby (*Falco subbuteo*) has almost no history of use as a falconer's bird but was once used in DARING (larks); the verb hobby may therefore be only strictly applicable in the context of daring.

HOBBY-HAWK   The HOBBY, probably exclusively lay.

HOLD IN THE HEAD   (obs.); HOLD IN (obs.) Of a falcon waiting on, to remain at her PITCH, not drift off, and concentrate on the flight arranged by falconer. Turbervile (1575[81]), writing on flying a falcon at the river, says:

> '... Your hawke will learne to give over a fowle that rakes out [flies a great distance away from where it has been put up], and hearing the keeper lewre, shee will learne the better to holde in the heade, and to make backe againe to the Ryver.'

Cox (1677[25]), in his glossary, has the obsolete term

'lean', which appears to have the same meaning:
> '*Lean*, is when the *Hawk* holds in to you.'

Note: The obsolete and unverified 'lean out' may be the same as RAKE AWAY. Turbervile uses four further obsolete idioms, all with a connection to a falcon waiting on:

FLY OUT ON HEAD ('flee out on heade') is taken to mean to fly wide of a good position for a flight, perhaps through missing the intended quarry and checking, that is, pursuing a different quarry. Compare FLY ON HEAD.

TURN HEAD ('turne heade') is taken to mean to respond to the falconer's calling and luring, watch, and make ready for the flight.

PUT IN HER HEAD is apparently the same as the above. When 'her head is in' she is watching, well placed, and prepared for the flight.

INWARDS is taken to mean in effect (of the hawk) having a thorough understanding of the falconer and his ways. Turbervile writes:
> 'Wherefore above all things, the high fleeing Hawke should be made inwards, and (as we tearme it) fond of the lewre, bycause it is no lesse prayse worthy in a high fleeing Falcon to make in and turne head at ye second or third tosse of the lewre . . .'.

Note: 'Inward' has occasionally been met with elsewhere meaning (of the hawk) cooperative or 'at one with the falconer' or similar; it is probably obsolete.

HAVING HER HEAD TOWARDS (now unc.) is, of a falcon waiting on, having her head facing (the falconer or the quarry) and in effect being in the correct position for a stoop. The idiom is used in this passage describing bagged lapwings (*Vanellus vanellus*) outmanoeuvring a falcon:
> 'They [lapwings] made rings underneath her as she was ringing up, keeping in exactly that position where she could never get her head towards them at all.' – 1900[59].

> '. . . The falconer . . . will be careful not to flush them [partridges] until he sees that the hawk is well placed, and with her head towards them, so that she may see them the moment they rise.' – 1898[40].

HOLD OUT   Of a hawk, to persist in the chase. Turbervile (1575[81]) recommends that goshawks should be flown in the first year 'to the field' (in open country) and not 'to the covert' (in enclosed, scrubby or wooded country), '. . . for so will they learne to holde out, (and not to turne tayle) in the middest of their flight.'

HOOD   (vb and n.) See HOODS AND HOODING. For some idioms and combination terms which include 'hood', see under the same heading.

HOOD, Call out of the   See FLY OUT OF THE HOOD.

HOOD, Cast through the   To disgorge a pellet while hooded; more in CAST 2 (vb).

HOOD, Feed through the   See FEED THROUGH THE HOOD.

HOOD, Fly out of the   See FLY OUT OF THE HOOD.

HOOD, Pull through the   See FEED THROUGH THE HOOD.

HOOD, Tire through the   See FEED THROUGH THE HOOD.

HOODED   See HOODS AND HOODING.

HOODED OFF AT   Flown out of the hood at (quarry).
> '. . . Proved hawks* may be hooded off at rooks at a distance of a quarter of a mile . . .' – 1936 [1970][8].

*Hawks in this instance means falcons. More in FLY OUT OF THE HOOD.

HOODER, A good   See HOODS AND HOODING.

HOODING   See HOODS AND HOODING.

HOOD OFF   (vb); **HOOD-OFF** To unhood and slip (a hawk).

HOOD-OFF, The   (n., unc.) The act of a falconer unhooding and slipping a hawk.

HOODS AND HOODING   The hood is a head covering for a hawk, customarily made entirely of leather or of leather with some additional materials. The main components of the multi-piece traditional types are stitched together; some modern North American hoods, referred to as seamless, have glued joints rather than sewn seams. The hood, when on, envelops the head, leaving only the beak and nares (nostrils) exposed. If well-made and well-fitting, it excludes all light, which has the effect of keeping a hawk still and calm. It is used most commonly with the larger falcons, but not exclusively. It is considered by some falconers to be an advantage to have any hawk good to the hood (used to being hooded) if only for stressful procedures such as imping, coping, and examination or treatment. If a hawk is to be kept good to the hood, a falconer may hood her whenever he picks her up, whether or not it is otherwise necessary to do so. For the falconer, hooding is a means whereby he can choose what he wishes his hawk not to see, such as sights or activity which would upset her or cause her to bate. Hooded in the field, she will not bate whenever any wildlife moves or attempt to leave the fist when another hawk is being flown. A falcon, when flown out of the hood, is hooded until slipped; see FLY OUT OF THE HOOD. Falcons together on the CADGE are hooded both to keep them still and to prevent crabbing (them attacking each other). When hoods were first employed in European falconry is uncertain. The assumption has been that knights returning home from the Crusades introduced them to the West, having seen them in use by Arab falconers. In the 13th century, Emperor Frederick (in transl.[35]) recorded his observation of the hood's use by Arabs:

> 'The falcon's hood is a discovery of Oriental peoples, the Arabs having, as far as we know, first introduced it into active practice. We ourselves, when we sailed across the seas, saw it used by them and made a study of their manner of manipulating this head covering.'

He notes that 'the Arabian chiefs' not only presented him with various kinds of falcons but also sent home with him falconers whose practice of hooding he adopted. The hood he used is not precisely enough described in his treatise to be certain of its design, but it seems that it was snug fitting and held on the hawk's head by friction. Attached to the back was a long narrow slip of soft leather. Once the falcon on the fist was hooded, the slip could be led along the bird's back and allowed to hang down between the tail and the wing furthest from the falconer and there gripped by the gloved hand; should the falcon cast her hood (remove it herself), it would be saved from falling to the ground. When she had become good to the hood, the slip dangled by her neck. Illustrations in the Emperor's treatise show hoods not in use hanging by their slips from the perch. As part of his continuing efforts to put his own stamp on every procedure in falconry, he modified his hoods by perforating the part which covers the bird's crown, for the purposes of ventilation. This seems to be in conflict with the principle that, to be fully effective, the hood should exclude all light.

HOODING. The procedure or art of putting a hood on a hawk. (Plates 29 and 30–32).
HOOD (vb). To put a hood on (a hawk). 'Hood up' is a less common alternative:
> '... When she has become keen and ready for a flight, she may be hooded up, and, after sitting quiet for a time, may be carried to the field.' – 1898[40].

HOOD UP. See preceding.
HOODED. Wearing a hood.
UNHOOD. Of a falconer, to take the hood off (a hawk). When not wearing a hood, a hawk is said to be unhooded or to have been unhooded; alternatively, she is bare faced or bare-headed (these last two obsolete).
DRAW OR STRIKE THE HOOD. Hood-braces (or braces) are two narrow slips of leather built in to certain patterns of hood. They are the means by which a hood is tightened once it is on a hawk's head and slackened before it is removed. To draw the hood is to tighten it; this is done by pulling (with finger and thumb and teeth) two of the four ends of the hood-braces. To strike, less commonly 'unstrike' (1615[49], obs.), the hood is to loosen it, done by pulling the other two (buttoned) ends using finger and thumb and teeth. The braces themselves are sometimes said to be drawn or struck, but this is not thought to be strictly correct. Turbervile (1575[81]) does not use conventional idioms when he writes:
> 'Then w[ith] your teeth drawing the strings, unhoode hir softly ...';

neither does Michell (1900[59]):
> '... The hood is braced up or slackened, as the case may be.'

Carrying his hawk on the fist in the field, a falconer may strike the hood in readiness for removing it in one swift movement at an appropriate moment; more in FLY OUT OF THE HOOD.
ENTER TO THE HOOD. To introduce (a hawk) to the hood; to begin hooding (a hawk).
MAKE TO THE HOOD (now unc. or obs.); **BREAK TO THE HOOD** (1892[47], obs.). To accustom (a hawk) to accepting and wearing the hood over the longer period.
MADE TO THE HOOD (now unc. or obs.). Said of a hawk when her hooding lessons are satisfactorily concluded.
GOOD TO THE HOOD. Describes a hawk which hoods well or is thoroughly used to being hooded, calmly accepting hooding as part of her routine. A falconer might hood a falcon whenever he picks her up to keep her good to the hood. Michell (1900[59]) has 'good at the hood'; this is uncommon and not used currently.
GOOD AT THE HOOD. See preceding entry.

STAND TO THE HOOD. To accept the hood calmly and well. If the hawk will not stand to the hood, she is said to be hood-shy (see below).

A GOOD HOODER. A hawk which hoods well and (rarely) a falconer who is skilled at hooding a hawk.

HOOD-SHY. Disliking, fearing or resenting being hooded through having been spoiled during her hooding lessons by the falconer's clumsiness or incompetence. When hood-shy, a hawk will duck, dodge, bate, and even vocalise angrily at the approach of the hood. If she will not stand to the hood, corrective measures may be tried:

> 'In case it [the hawk] is very rebellious the brail* may be used, or it may be rendered more tractable by drenching it with cold water, and then taking advantage of its wet state to hood and unhood it frequently.' – 1855[73].

*See BRAIL (n.). 'A hood-shy hawk' and 'she is hood-shy' are both correct. 'Hood-shyness' is used by Michell (1900[59]) and is sometimes met with currently.

BOBBED WITH THE HOOD (obs.); **BOBBED** (1619[6], obs.). (Cf. lay vb bob = to deceive, cheat, or to strike with a light blow). Precise meaning uncertain, but it appears to mean in effect hood-shy (see preceding). It seems that a hawk 'that hath bin bobbed with the hood' (1618[50]) has been subjected to a hasty, rough, or inappropriate method of hooding (such as by 'sleight of hand' rather than with a more sensitive approach) and is hood-shy as a result.

SPOILED TO THE HOOD (rare). In effect hood-shy (see above), said of a hawk which has been subjected to an inappropriate method of hooding.

CAST THE HOOD. Of a hawk, to remove her hood, often by hooking a talon on an eyepiece or the plume.

HOODS. There are a number of different designs, some of them hybrids of traditional styles.

RUFTER HOOD; RUFTER-HOOD (French *chaperon de rust*; German *Rüsthaube*, Dutch *reushuif*[74]. Harting, in two glossaries[38]/[39], has 'rufter-hood', but in his 1898 treatise[40] has 'ruster hood'. This writer perhaps thought that the f was an incorrect transliteration of the similar long s. Other forms: RUFTER and, less commonly, RUFTERHOOD). An obsolete design, once used widely by hawk-trappers as a temporary hood for a newly caught hawk. Of simple

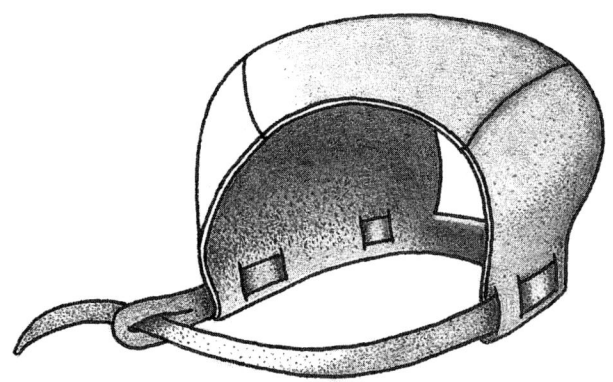

Rufter hood.

construction, it is usually depicted or described as opening wide behind for easy fitting, with a simple tie or throatlash-cum-brace with which to close it at the back. However, pictorial evidence suggests that it may occasionally have been built with no means of opening and closing it. It has a large beak-opening so that the hooded hawk can gape sufficiently wide when she casts ('... to have speciall rufter hoods to cast easilie through, either plummage, bones, or stones ...' – 1615[49]) and can easily feed with it on.

> '*Rufter-hood* is the first hood which a *Hawke* weareth, being large, wide, and open behind.' – 1615 gl.[49]

According to Stonehenge (1856[76]) it is

'... of cloth* or pliable leather ...',

and is

'... made in two pieces**, having a neat seam down the centre, and, like the hood-proper, has a hole for the beak, and also a slit at the back for a brace.'

*Although there may have been cloth rufter hoods, no evidence has been found that they were usual.

**Illustrations from various sources show that rufters may have been made in one, two or three pieces.

A hawk is sometimes able to cast her hood by hooking a talon on an eye-piece or the plume; a rufter hood has neither, therefore it is less easy for her to remove. Although primarily the hood of hawk-trappers, the rufter was once used to some extent by falconers (probably because of its 'easy' fit) mainly during the process of making her to the hood. Of a recently taken hawk:

> '... Having a greate and easie rufterhoode,

you muste hoode and unhoode hir oftentymes seeled§ as shee is ...' – 1575[81].

§Her eyelids closed by stitching; see SEEL.

HOOD PROPER; HOOD-PROPER ('proper' signifying ordinary, usual). A hood other than the rufter hood, that is, one for continued rather than temporary use.

DUTCH HOOD. A three-piece 'blocked' hood, that is, assembled and soaked in water then moulded, shaped and allowed to dry and stiffen on a hood-block. The leather is often gold-tooled, and the hood has distinctive side panels (known as eye-pieces or eyepieces) covered in such as green or red baize, 'Billiard cloth or cloth from a huntsman's pink coat ...' (1987[84]), or velvet (1855[73]). The function of the cloth, when drawn into the seams between the three leather pieces during assembly, is to make the joints light proof.

> 'As regards the colour of the eyepiece, *red* is preferable to *green*, as being more easily seen at a distance if dropped on the grass.' – 1898[40].

It has hood-braces which open and close it at the back. Customarily, it is topped with a plume of small feathers and coloured wools often bound with fine wire. It is the hood of choice to many contemporary Western falconers. Note: The name 'Dutch hood' appears to owe its origin to the fact that this hood was distributed throughout Europe from centres of manufacture in Holland, in particular the village of Valkenswaard, once the hub in Europe of hawk-trapping and associated activities. Very occasionally, this type is referred to as the European hood and is thought to be a medieval European adaptation of the Arab pattern. (Plate 40).

Indian hood.

SYRIAN HOOD. Similar to the Dutch, but instead of being open at the back when it is struck, the space is filled with a piece of soft leather, the hood-braces passing through slits cut in it. Advantages over the Dutch are said to be (a) the braces will not trap the feathers of the hawk's nape when it is drawn and (b) it is more likely remain securely on the hawk.

ARAB (ARABIAN, BAHRAINI) HOOD. A one-piece hood, less substantial and heavy than the Dutch pattern and traditionally not built on a hood-block. Unlike the Dutch, it is not open at the back; when it is drawn, the hood-braces cause the leather at the back to gather into pleats, concertina-like. It is often topped with a Turk's head knot. It is the hood of choice to some contemporary falconers. (Plates 33–34).

INDIAN HOOD. A one-piece lightweight hood, now rarely if ever seen in the West. It does not open and close, having a single brace-cum-throatlash threaded through slits around the base, the two free ends fastened together at the back to secure it on the hawk. It is topped with a Turk's head knot.

> 'The Indian hoods are excellent, easily made, and most comfortable to the hawk. In fact, they are perfection so long as the hawk is on hand [on the fist]; but hawks can readily get them off if left hooded by themselves ...' – 1892[47].

ANGLO-INDIAN HOOD. A modification of the Indian, opening at the back and with Dutch-style hood-braces added. It is widely used today

Back view of Dutch hood.

in the West, being easy to make or, if bought, relatively inexpensive. (Plate 39).

PERSIAN HOOD.
'The hood used in Persia and in the regions around *Basrah* and *Baghdad* is quite unlike the Indian hood. It is, in fact, little else than a bag of soft leather with two straps at the back to tighten it.' – 1908 ft.[68]

AFGHAN HOOD. A simple one-piece hood with no hood-braces.

SPRING-CLOSING HOOD. A recent design developed in North America. It is of leather with springy wires built in. Instead of having hood-braces, an external wire loop loosens the hood when squeezed with the fingers; when pressure is released, the hood tightens automatically.

SEAMLESS HOOD. A hood with glued joints rather than sewn seams.

COPHOOD (obs. Cf. cop = the crest on a bird's head). A hood, or an unidentified type of hood.

Components of the hood:

EYE-PIECES; EYEPIECES. The two pieces forming the sides of the three-piece Dutch hood.

BEAK-OPENING. The opening in a hood through which a hawk's beak and nares protrude.

CHIN-STRAP. The part of a hood which passes underneath the hawk's beak, forming the lower edge of the beak-opening.

THROATLASH. A slip of leather threaded through slits at the base of some patterns of hood.

HOOD-BRACES; BRACES. Small leather straps incorporated into some hoods. When the hood is drawn or struck, the braces (and therefore the hood itself) are tightened or loosened.

PLUME; also **TASSEL** (obs. Spelt 'tassell' – 1575[81], 1619[6]). The decorative tuft of small feathers and coloured wools, often bound with fine wire, on the top of some varieties of hood. It is gripped between the fingers when hooding and unhooding a hawk.

TURK'S HEAD KNOT. An ornamental knot resembling a turban which tops some varieties of hood.

Related terms:

HOOD-BLOCK 1. A wooden block carved into the shape of a hawk's head. On it, some varieties of hoods are 'blocked' into shape, the leather having been soaked first. To re-block a hood is to soak a hood which has lost its shape and re-shape it by allowing it to dry on the hood-block. Compare lay verb block, meaning (in one sense) to shape (a hat) on a block.

HOOD-BLOCK 2. A block of wood carved roughly into the shape of a hawk's head, worn on the falconer's belt. The hood, when not in use, is put onto it, braces tightened.

HOOD PATTERN. A template used as a guide for shape and size when cutting the leather for a hood or parts of a hood.

HOOD-SHY Of a hawk, disliking, fearing or resenting being hooded. More in preceding entry.

HOOKED UP (inf.) Of a hawk, caught by the JESSES on such as a twig in a tree, or a thorn in a hedge. Sometimes said of the jesses themselves.

HORN, Hunting Particularly in grander medieval and Tudor hawking expeditions, blown to encourage hawks in the field. There is evidence that it saw some use in the ensuing centuries; as late as the turn of the 19th and 20th centuries, Michell[59] writes:

'There can be no doubt that a shout of some kind, or a blast on the horn, if you prefer it, has an inspiriting effect on hawks . . .'.

HORSES Historically in many cultures where it has developed, hawking with falcons has been pursued both mounted and unmounted. Where the landscape has been open and uninterrupted such as on plains, moorland and deserts, where the

A method of mounting a horse from the left with a hawk on the fist. A modern rendering of an unfinished drawing in the Vatican codex of Emperor Frederick II of Hohenstaufen's 13th century treatise De Arte Venandi cum Avibus.

flight may be a long one, it has been essential to ride. The mounted falconer would carry his hawk in the field, cast her off, follow her flight, and swing the lure, and only dismount to pick her up off a kill. There appear to be no English falconers' terms (nor many procedures) relating to horses which differ from the expressly equestrian. One notable procedure with a specific connection to falconry is a mode of mounting a horse from the left side whilst holding a hawk on the fist, described in the 13th century by Emperor Frederick[35]. It is recommended that the hawk be transferred to the right hand so that the falconer can grasp the pommel of the saddle in his left and the cantle (at the saddle's rearward end) with his right, raising up right hand and hawk as he throws his right leg over the horse's back. The simpler method, probably more widely practised, has been to mount the horse from the right, keeping the hawk on the left fist. Riding whilst hawking was taken so much for granted by the authors of the older treatises that it was usually only referred to in passing. In the British pursuit, in scattered instances, a few details may be found, such as in this from Harting (1898[40]):

> 'The best kind of horse for hawking is a short-legged, steady little horse that can jump a bit – short-legged to enable the rider to get on and off quickly, and steady enough to stand quiet while the falconer takes up the hawk. To assist this the saddle should have a holster carrying a long weight like a clock weight. This, fastened by a cord from the pommel through the ring of the bit, may then be thrown on the ground to tether the horse when the falconer dismounts.'

In English rook-hawking with falcons, when considerable distances may be covered while following a flight:

> 'A good horse that can gallop, but that is quiet enough to carry a hawk, is indispensable. . . . We have always found thoroughbred horses (especially young ones) more fearless and better suited to this work than others. A good deal may be done with a very nervous horse by keeping him in a loose box with three or four live pigeons till he is thoroughly used to them . . .' – 1892[47].

In hunting with the goshawk, involving shorter flights, the horse was more simply a mode of transport to, from and in the field.

HOT   (obs.) Of meat, warm or freshly-killed:
'. . . Fede hir with an olde hote colver [culver, pigeon or dove]. . . .' – 1486[5].

This writer's phrase 'hote of it selfe' appears to mean rich, very nourishing. Hot (hote or whote), meaning rich, is met with in other old texts and has also been used to describe meat which has been re-warmed. Writing in the 13th century, Emperor Frederick[35] advises that if meat has cooled it should be immersed in fresh warm water and fed to the hawk when it has reached body temperature. A hot gorge (obs.) is a meal of freshly-killed food given to or taken by a hawk. Cool (obs.) usually means bland, less rich, not rich.

HOT GORGE, A   See preceding entry.

HUNGER STREAKS   See FRET MARKS.

HUNGER TRACES   See FRET MARKS.

HYE   See CONDITION, High or low.

I

ICELAND FALCON; ICELANDER   See GYRFALCON.

IGNOBLE   See under FALCONS, Noble.

IMMEW (unv., obs.); **EMMEW** (unv., obs.)   Apparently to put (a hawk) into the mews.

IMP; YMP(E) (obs.) (Latin *impono* = to put, place, or set in. Cf. Medieval Latin (Brit.–Ir.[48]) *impo* = imp, plant (beans).) To repair a hawk's tail- or primary wing-feather when the shaft is cracked or broken. In simple terms, imping involves inserting an imping needle into the shaft of a broken feather and reuniting the two parts, or adding part of a similar feather using the same technique, or attaching a near-complete similar feather to the existing cropped-off stump by plugging or sewing in. An imping needle (or imping-needle) is often triangular in section but sometimes oval or square, filed to that shape from iron or steel wire of such temper that it is neither easily bent nor brittle; bicycle spokes are suggested in Woodford (1987[84]) and

74 IMPING

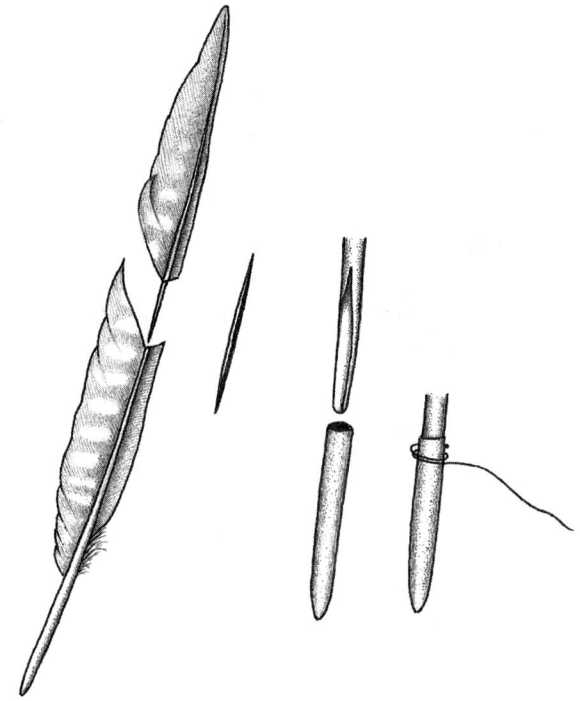

Left: A broken feather being imped, using an imping needle. To its right, an imping needle; these are often triangular in section. Right: An alternative method of repairing a feather, known as sewing in.

fine piano wire is used by Fox (1995[34]). Harting (1898[40]) notes that in his day a Suffolk whitesmith (worker in metals) supplied imping needles ready-made. Both ends of a needle are sharpened for easy insertion into the shaft of the feather where it can be glued into place, although traditionally it is simply dipped in strong brine before insertion, the repair becoming firm as the metal rusts:

> '... Take a square ymping needle, like unto a Glovers needle, laye it in Vineager and salte water ...' – 1575[81].

'Diamond cement', white of egg, heated cobbler's wax, and pine resin have been mentioned in old texts as fixing agents. A slightly modified technique is recorded by Stonehenge (1856[76]):

> 'The broken feather is to be obliquely cut off, and the artificial one exactly shaped to fit it; then, by inserting two needles, and using a little solution of isinglass in spirit of wine, the two may be strongly spliced together.'

A method in use today and sometimes referred to as plugging employs a plug of bamboo or carbon fibre inserted into the cropped-off hollow barrels of the old feather and the matching new portion; all is secured with a quick-setting adhesive. Michell (1900[59]) records a process which he calls 'plugging', but which is not the same as the foregoing. It involves glueing 'a chunk of some feather which is not hollow, but has a solid pith' into the hollow ends of the broken feather and the new portion, and joining the two halves with a needle. In a traditional method, neither needle nor plug is used, the shaft of the new portion of feather being inserted into the hollow barrel of the old, then sewn and bound into place ('sewing in' – 1892[47]). Splinting the shaft of a damaged feather with bamboo is traditional to Japanese falconry; a similar technique may have seen some limited use in the West. Falconers collect and store moulted tail- and primary wing-feathers for future imping.

Note: If the shaft is bent or slightly creased, the feather can simply be dipped in hot water; the softening of the shaft and air expanding inside often bring about an instantaneous return to the original form.

IMPING (Obsolete spelling: 'empynge' (c.1600).) The procedure or art of repairing a hawk's broken or damaged feathers; see preceding entry.

IMPING NEEDLE; IMPING-NEEDLE See IMP.

IMPRINT (n., recent) Broadly and in simple terms in falconry: a hawk which, while young, has become imprinted (fully or to some degree) on Man. Such a hawk has learned to identify Man as her own kind and is certain to have some behavioural abnormalities. If an EYASS is handled too early or her training begun too soon, she might continue with behaviours that in her wild counterparts will moderate or stop after they leave the eyrie. She might never grow out of being over-possessive of her food and mantling heavily over it in the presence of Man, to protect it from theft by a perceived competitor. She might scream (falconer's term) as she would when a parent approached the eyrie. The screaming, which begins as baby food- or recognition-calls, might continue for some time or for ever; a hawk which screams (rather than vocalises normally) is known to falconers as a screamer. Due to her confidence and lack of fear, there is a likelihood of her being aggressive towards the falconer and his dogs. These long-recognized exaggerated behaviours are often annoying and obstructive, but are accepted by some as tolerable when set against the hawk's tameness and the reduced likelihood of losing her in the field.

More than three centuries before the appearance

of the term 'imprint' in falconry, Latham (1615[49]) expresses his dislike of the behaviour of eyasses:

> 'But leaving to speake any more of these kind of scratching Hawkes, that I did never love should come too neere my fingers, and to returne unto the curteous and faire conditioned *Haggard Faulcon*, whose gallent disposition I know not how to extoll, or praise so sufficiently as shee deserves.'

IMPRINT   (vb, recent) In the term's common understanding in falconry: of a falconer, to cause (a young hawk) to become an imprint, that is, in simple terms, to take her as an EYASS and rear her in the company of humans. It is thought by some to be desirable to imprint a small accipiter such as a sparrowhawk which, being naturally highly strung, is less unstable and more biddable when imprinted. She will doubtless scream, but the sound is less penetrating (therefore less irritating to the human ear) than that of larger hawks, and she may be located in the field by the sound of her voice.

IMPRINTING   (lay) In a young animal at a critical time, in a particular context, or as a result of particular stimuli: an example of 'programmed learning' whereby (among other requirements for survival) it acquires its biologically correct identity. Austrian ethologist Konrad Lorenz (1903–1989) coined the term imprinting (*Prägung* in German) for this phenomenon in the 1930s.

INDEW   Spelling of ENDUE.

INEW; INEAWE Spellings of ENEW.

INK(E)   (obs.) The neck of quarry, on which a hawk might TIRE.

> '*Inke*, whether it be of Partridge, fowle, doves, or any other pray, is the necke from the head to the body.' – 1615[49].

INSEAM   Spelling of ENSEAM.

INSEAMED   Spelling of ENSEAMED.

INTERMEW   (Taken to be formed on French *entre-* = between + French *muer* = to moult; cf. Old French *entremué* = half-moulted.) Of a falconer, to keep (a hawk) inactive in the mews for the duration of her moult.

INTERMEWED   (Obs. spellings: ENTERMEWED, ENTERMURED ('entermured *goshawke*' – 1619[6]).) In the common understanding, the term describes a hawk which has completed her moult in captivity. In Mavrogordato (1973 gl.[58]), the term is applied to

> 'A hawk (in particular an eyass) moulted in captivity.'

It can be used in combinations: an example is intermewed eyass, which strictly is a wild-caught EYASS that has gone on to complete her first moult, but today can describe a captive-bred eyass that has completed her first moult. But to Latham:

> '*Intermew'd* is from the first exchaunge of a *Hawkes* coat, or from her first mewing [moult], till shee come to bee a white *Hawke*.' – 1615 gl.[49],

which seems to be from her first moult (in her second year) until after her second moult (in her third year). Later that century, Cox (1677 gl.[25]) was obviously paraphrasing this information when he wrote:

> '*Intermewing*, is from the first exchange of the *Hawks* Coat, till she turn white: and this is so called from the first Mewing.'

See HAWK, White.

Intermewed is sometimes met with today in such as 'once-' 'twice-' or 'five times intermewed', indicating the number of moults in captivity a hawk has had. Other combinations: 'Entermewed Jass [eyass] Falcon' (1679[53]), intermewed passager, intermewed haggard, each having moulted in captivity, although Blome (1686 [1929][9]) says of a wild hawk taken after her first moult:

> '... When she hath preyed for herself a year, and hath mewed most of her Feathers, she is called an *Intermewed Haggard*.'

INTERMEWER   (obs.) (Also spelt ENTERMEWER. INTERVIEW and ENTERVIEW are apparently the same.) Commonly understood to be a hawk in her second year, having moulted once in captivity.

> 'ENTERMEWERS – A falconer's term for Hawks of the second year, after they have moulted their immature-plumage.' – 1913[79].

The Turbervile (1575[81]) definition is:

> '... They are called Entermewers or Hawkes of the first cote*, that is from the middle of May, till June, July, August, September, October, November, December. Those Hawkes are called Entermewers, for that they cast the old, and have new feathers ...';

the same writer also notes:

> 'That Sacre [saker] that is taken [from the wild as] an entermewer, is the best hawke.'

It is assumed that both Turbervile passages refer to a hawk moulting for the first time.

*For another interpretation of 'hawk of the first coat', see qus. in HAWK, White.

INTERVIEW   See ENTERVIEW.

INWARD; INWARDS See HOLD IN THE HEAD.

J

JACK The male MERLIN.

JACKET, Hawking A sleeveless jacket or waistcoat (sometimes worn by contemporary falconers) with pockets for accommodating most or all of the equipment normally held in a hawking bag (see BAG, Hawking). It has a large pocket for game.

JACK-HAWK (obs.) A male hawk, probably exclusively lay.

JACK HOBBY Uncommon, obsolete name for the male HOBBY.

JACK KESTREL; JACK CASTRELL Uncommon, obsolete names for the male KESTREL.

JACK MERLIN; JACK-MERLIN (probably obs.) The male MERLIN.

JANGAOLI See HALSBAND.

JASHAWK; JASS-HAWK See next entry.

JASS (unc., obs.) Spelling of EYASS, so far only found in adjectival use:
> 'Lost of his Majesties . . . an Entermewed Jass Falcon, having newly Mewed her long Feathers, with the Kings Varvels*.' – 1679[53].

Also met with in other obsolete combinations: 'jass-hawk' (1706[67]), 'jashawk' (1755).
*See VARVELS.

JEOUKE Spelling of JOUK (vb).

JER Shortening of jerfalcon; see GYRFALCON.

JERFALCON Obsolete spelling of GYRFALCON.

JERKIN (In (?)early use, c.1500. Formed on jer (shortening of jerfalcon) + diminutive -kin, indicating male smaller than female.) The male GYRFALCON.

JERKYN Obsolete spelling of jerkin, the male GYRFALCON.

JESS (n.) See JESSES.

JESS (vb) See JESSES.

JESSEBUITES See JESSES.

JESSED See JESSES.

JESSES For idioms and combination terms which include 'jesses', see next entry.

JESSES; singular **JESS** (Latin *jacio, jacto* = to throw, cast; Medieval Latin (Brit.–Ir.[48]) *jactus, jectus, gessus, gescia* = jess. Obs. English spellings and forms: GESSES (1486[5]), CHESSES and GESTS (both 17th C., OED), GESSE (singular, 1486[5]), JESSE (singular, 1856[76]). Latham (1618[50]) has 'jessebuites' (unc. and obs.), which clearly combines the terms jess and BEWIT, but means jesses.) A pair of straps, one attached to each of a hawk's tarsi. Part of the equipment for restraining her, they remain on the hawk until the need for replacement through wear and tear. Historically in the West, they are usually made of leather.

> 'Hawkys have aboute ther legges Gesse[s] made of leder most commynly. som of silke. . . .' – 1486[5].

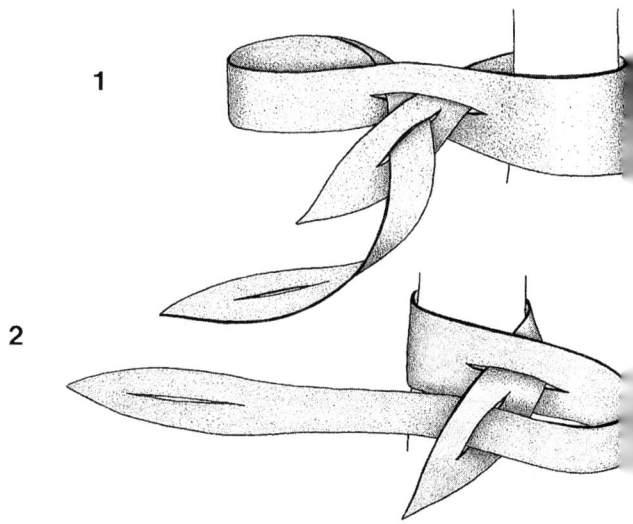

Ways of fitting the traditional jess to a hawk's tarsus; both have seen use up to modern times. 2 is the method shown in Emperor Frederick II of Hohenstaufen's 13th century treatise.

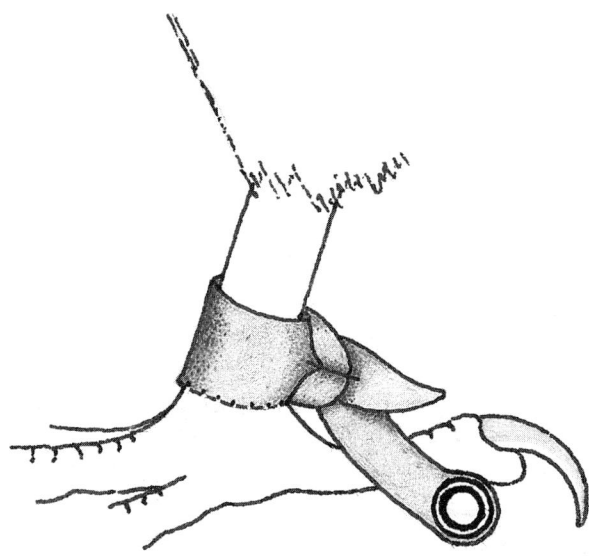

The modified traditional jess, fitted here (correctly) to the hawk's left tarsus. The eyelet is for a removable mews jess. Dimensions vary according to the falconer's views: the extension to the eyelet may be shorter than shown, and the anklet broader particularly with the slender-legged accipiters.

To fit jesses to a hawk is to jess her, after which she is said to be jessed; the procedure is known as jessing. In the case of the traditional pattern used in the West, the free, slitted ends of the two jesses are attached to one ring of the SWIVEL, the LEASH threaded through the other. While the hawk is being carried, the leash might be 'halved' at the swivel and the two free lengths wound in loops round the fingers of the fist. Leash and swivel are removed when the hawk flies. In the field, with swivel and leash removed, the jesses are used to restrain a hawk on the fist; they are gripped in the falconer's gloved hand and released when he casts her off or slips her. An obsolete alternative arrangement to the swivel is a pair of small metal rings known as varvels. These and the swivel (also see TYRRIT) have been employed concurrently in falconry for centuries, and there is evidence that varvels were still in minor use as recently as the turn of the 19th and 20th centuries; see 1898 qu. in VARVELS. One varvel was sewn or knotted on to the free end of each jess, and the leash threaded through both. The hawk was flown with the leash removed and customarily the varvels in place.

> '*Jesses*, are those short straps of leather, which are fastned to the *Hawks* legs, & so to the lease [leash] by varvels, anlets [small rings], or such like.' – 1615 gl.[49]

In recent times in the West, there have been two common designs of jess: the traditional pattern and aylmeri. The history of a certain obsolete, little-used design of leather jess is uncertain: a mid-19th century English source[76] describes it as a 'running noose' which is opened to slip over the hawk's foot then closed on her tarsus. Dogskin is one hide known to have been used in the past: in the early 16th century, King James IV of Scotland was supplied with dog skins for jess-making. Harting (1898[40]) writes of making jesses for a merlin out of an old dogskin glove. Turbervile (1575[81]) mentions 'Shameuse leather, or soft Calves leather'. Other materials have been 'white leather' (horse hide tanned in alum and salt) and a strong calf leather called 'shoemaker's kip' (1855[73]). Kangaroo hide and calf-skin are among those favoured today.

TRADITIONAL JESSES. Of ancient design, each of these is one piece of pre-stretched leather, cut to a pattern for an individual hawk. When knotted onto the hawk's tarsus by passing the ends through slits in order, it neither tightens nor slackens but maintains a nice tolerance between leather and tarsus. The free ends are slitted for fitting to a swivel. In the West today, traditional jesses are obsolescent, largely because of the danger of a slit becoming hooked up on such as a twig in a tree or a thorn in a hedge. To reduce risk, the falconer might make the slits less exposed by rolling or twisting the ends of the jesses between a wetted finger and thumb before a flight. A modification to the traditional jess, apparently dating from the mid-19th century, is an attempt to reduce the risk of hooking up. It is fitted to the hawk's tarsus in the same way, but its shortened free end has a brass eyelet for a mews jess (a leather strap with a BUTTON at one end and a slit for the swivel at the other) which is removed when the hawk flies. This system (sometimes referred to as 'false' aylmeri) is distrusted by some falconers, as a hind talon sometimes catches in an eyelet.

AYLMERI (taken to be a quasi-plural, sometimes incorrectly named aylmeris; sometimes called aylmeri anklets). The successor to traditional jesses and in common use today. They are named for the deviser, the late Major Guy Aylmer. They are a pair of pre-stretched leather anklets, one looped round each of the hawk's tarsi; the two ends of each are clamped together by a brass eyelet. Mews jesses (leather straps with a BUTTON at one end and a slit for the swivel at the other) are worn in the eyelets; with swivel and

78 JESSING

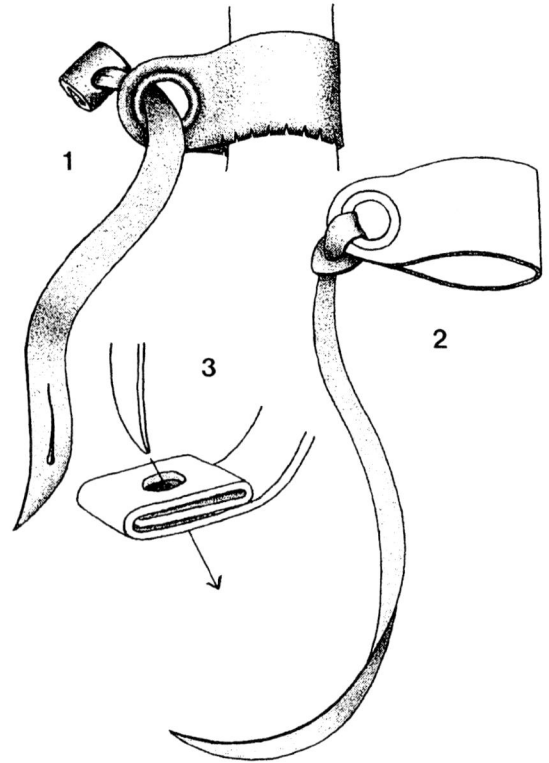

1: An aylmeri anklet fitted to the hawk's tarsus, the two ends conjoined at a brass eyelet. The little slits at the lower edge (sometimes also on the upper) are to allow the leather to roll outwards and help prevent chafing. The mews jess threaded through the eyelet has a button at one end, a swivel-slit at the other. 2: A type of field or hunting jess. One is knotted semi-permanently to each aylmeri anklet at the eyelet and has no swivel-slit. 3: The usual method of forming a button.

leash in place, the hawk is held on the fist or tethered to her perch. When the hawk is flown, leash, swivel and mews jesses are removed. Or the latter may be replaced with field or hunting jesses (the same as the mews jesses but unslitted to minimize the danger of hooking up) which remain in the eyelets during a flight; these enable the falconer to restrain the hawk on the fist as needed. Another pattern of field jesses is a pair of narrow strips of leather with no slit for a swivel, one knotted semi-permanently to each anklet at the eyelet, the mews jesses being removed before a flight. Lengths of cord through the eyelets have been used as an alternative arrangement; these, held on to by the falconer, slide free of the eyelets when the hawk is slipped.

'FALSE' AYLMERI. See TRADITIONAL JESSES (above) and AYLMERI (preceding).
FIELD JESSES. See AYLMERI (above).
HUNTING JESSES. See AYLMERI (above).
MEWS JESSES. See AYLMERI (above).
HACK JESSES (inf.). For a hawk at hack, jesses which have no slits at the free ends, therefore unlikely to become hooked up. See HACKING.
FALSE JESSES (now unc.). A section of cord arranged into loops attached to the legs of a live or dead lure and tied to a creance. Michell (1900[59]) calls the arrangement the 'double-ring knot'.

JESSING   See preceding entry.

JET (obs.) (Latin *jacio, jacto* = to throw, cast.) Not taken to be a falconer's term, but used by Latham (1618[50]): after having fed on a kill, a goshawk shows her satisfaction

'... with feaking, jetting, rowsing, and such like joyous shews and signes also of inward pleasure and contentment.'

In OED, to jet is 'Of a bird: To move the tail up and down jerkily'; in the Latham context, it is conceivable that jetting is applied to the characteristic side-to-side 'wagging' of a short-winged hawk's tail. In Bert (1619[6]), the meaning of the phrase 'jet up and downe' (of a goshawk having taken stand in a tree) is different and may mean to move from branch to branch:

'... When she doth remove and jet up and downe, then I give her my voyce, which shee is glad to heare; having taken her downe, I sup her ...';

compare this from English poet Francis Quarles (*Emblems*, 1635):

'Like as the Hagard, cloyster'd in her Mue ...
Jets oft from Perch to Perch ...'.

JILL   The female ferret; more commonly, gill. See FERRETING under HAWKING, Categories of.

JOIN   Of the least experienced of two hawks flown together (in a cast): to become a co-pursuer of the quarry. Or according to Michell (1900[59]):

'When she seizes her quarry in the air she "binds" to it; and when her companion in the flight comes up and also takes hold, she or he is said to "join.".'

JOKIN   (obs.) Sleep, sleeping. See next entry.

JOUK(E)   (vb, obs.) (Other spellings and forms: JEOUKE (1575[81]), JOYKE, JOWK, JUKE, also JUG; all obs.) To sleep, to roost, to sleep upon the perch. From Berners (1486[5]) are:

'... Youre hauke Joukith. and not slepith.'
'She Joykith when she slepith.'

To confirm the presence of 'Lyce or Mightes' in a hawk, *A Perfect Booke* (c.1575[38]) recommends:
> '... Sodenly awake her from jokin and then abowght her sere* they wilbe.'

*See CERE.

JOUKE (n.) Spelling of JUCK.

JOWK Spelling of JOUK (vb).

JOYKE Form of JOUK (vb).

JUCK(E) (obs.) (Alternative spellings: JUK and JOUKE (both 1575[81]), JUKE (1619[6]); all obs.) Part of a wing given to a hawk as TIRING.
> '... You maye give hir plumage [feathers as casting] and a Juk of a joynt.' – 1575[81];

and (ibid.),
> '... Joukes of wings of small birdes, & Quailes.'

JUG Form of JOUK (vb).

JUGGER; JUGGER FALCON See FALCON, Lugger.

JUK Spelling of JUCK.

JUKE (vb) Form of JOUK (vb).

JUKE (n.) Spelling of JUCK.

JUKE, At (unv., obs.) At roost (OED). See JOUK (vb).

JUMP TO THE FIST See FIST, Jump to the.

JUTTY (obs.) (Taken to be form of 'jetty'.) Apparently river-bank. This passage is from Berners (1486[5]):
> 'Iff youre hawke nym the fowle at the fer side of the Ryver or of the pitt from yow. Then she sleeth the fowle at the fer Jutty. and if she slee it uppon that side that ye ben on. as it may hape dyverse times. Then ye shall say she hath sleen the fowle at the Jutty ferry.' This might be paraphrased: 'If your hawk takes the bird at the far side of the river or pond, she kills it at the "far jutty", and if she kills it on the side that you are on, as may happen at times, you shall say she has killed it at the "jutty ferry".'

The terms 'fer Jutty' and 'Jutty ferry' appear to mean (or signify) far river-bank and near river-bank respectively. Although it is assumed that in the 15th century both idioms were acknowledged as authentic to falconry, it seems likely that they were already archaic and their precise significance was unclear.

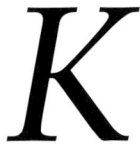

KASTREL Obsolete spelling of KESTREL.

KEEL Sometimes, to falconers, a hawk's sternum or its outer rim. More in BREASTBONE.

KEEN Of a hawk, hungry and responsive in training, or hungry and eager to hunt. Also see SHARP SET, and compare YARAK.

KEEP HER MARK See MARK, Fly at.

KEEP THE AIR Of quarry, to make an escape by out-flying a hawk.

KESTREL (common) *Falco tinnunculus* (Old French *cresserelle*, *crécerelle*, *quercerelle*.) Alternative names and forms (all obsolete):
  KESTRIL
  KISTRELL
  KASTREL
  CASTREL
  KISTRESS (-ess suggests the female.)

  JACK KESTREL (unc.); JACK CASTRELL (1686 [1929][9]; unc.). The male.
  KESTRILET. The male; diminutive -et suggests male smaller than female.
  There also exists a long list of largely obsolete English vernacular names.

The commonest British falcon, preying mainly on voles, mice and invertebrates, therefore unsuitable for falconry. However, being relatively easily obtainable and easy to tame, it is looked on by some as suitable as a first bird for a novice falconer. It is generally agreed that such a small hawk should be taken on only under the supervision of an experienced falconer: the smaller the bird, the smaller the margin for error in feeding her and cutting down her weight. An alternative use for a kestrel was noted in 1726[51]:
> 'If in one corner ... you enclose a Kastrel, it will secure your Dove-house from birds of prey.'

80 KESTRIL

Female kestrel. (John Hawkins).

KESTRIL Obsolete spelling of KESTREL.

KESTRILET Obsolete name for the male KESTREL.

KEY; KEY OF THE FOOT See FOOT (n.).

KILL Quarry caught and killed. According to Bert (1619[6]), a catch (obsolete) is quarry caught by a hawk.

KILL, The The action or moment of a hawk taking or killing quarry.

KISTRELL Obsolete form of KESTREL.

KISTRESS Obsolete name for the KESTREL (perhaps the female).

KITCHEN HAWK See FALCON, Lanner.

KITE, Fork-tailed Obsolete name for the red kite; see KITE, Royal.

KITE, Red See next entry.

KITE, Royal (obs.); KITE ROYAL (1575[81], obs.) Old names in England for the red kite (*Milvus milvus*, formerly *Milvus regalis*), the quarry in kite-hawking. Swann (1913[79]) suggests that

'The term Royal Kite originated in the fact that only the King's falcons could take it, its powers of flight being beyond those of the lesser kinds of falcons.'

Otherwise, simply that in former times the kite was considered to be 'royal game'. Fork-tailed kite is an obsolete alternative name. Also see MILAN.

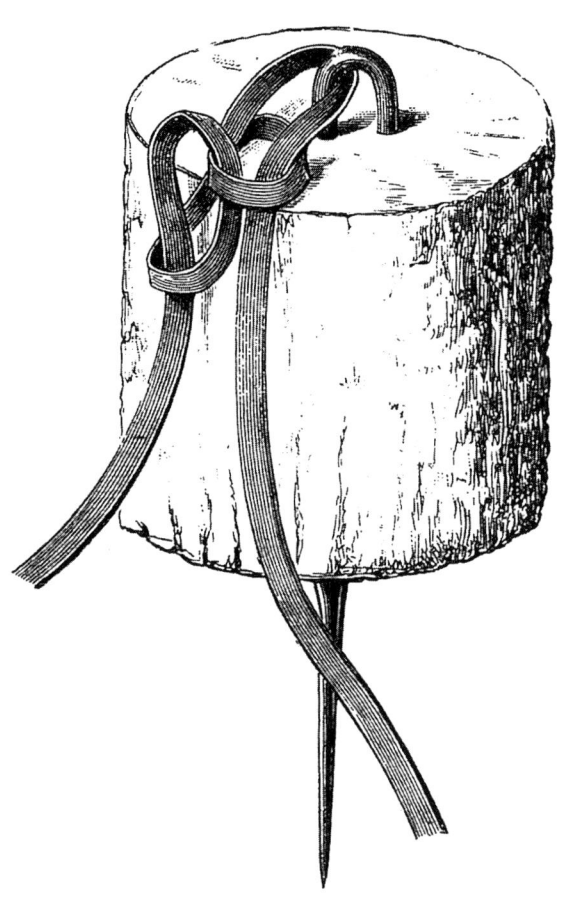

Block of basic design and the falconer's knot. (From a late 19th century drawing).

KITE-HAWKING See HAWKING, Categories of.

KNOCK THE FIST See FIST, Knock the.

KNOT, Cadge For description, see SCREEN PERCH under PERCHES.

KNOT, Double ring- See FALSE JESSES under JESSES.

KNOT, Falconer's The knot used to tie the hawk's LEASH to her perch, or the CREANCE to the SWIVEL or SWIVEL-SLITS of the JESSES. It is a locked slip knot, made and unmade with one hand, the hawk being upon the other. Often two knots are tied for greater security.

KNOT, Figure-of-eight Under LEASH.

KNOT, Screen perch See SCREEN PERCH under PERCHES.

44: *Henry VIII's falconer, Robert Cheseman, by Hans Holbein (1497–1543). (Courtesy Sotheby's)*

45: *Daring small birds with a hooded hawk. Engraving after Jan Stradanus (Flemish, 1525–1603). (Courtesy Sotheby's)*

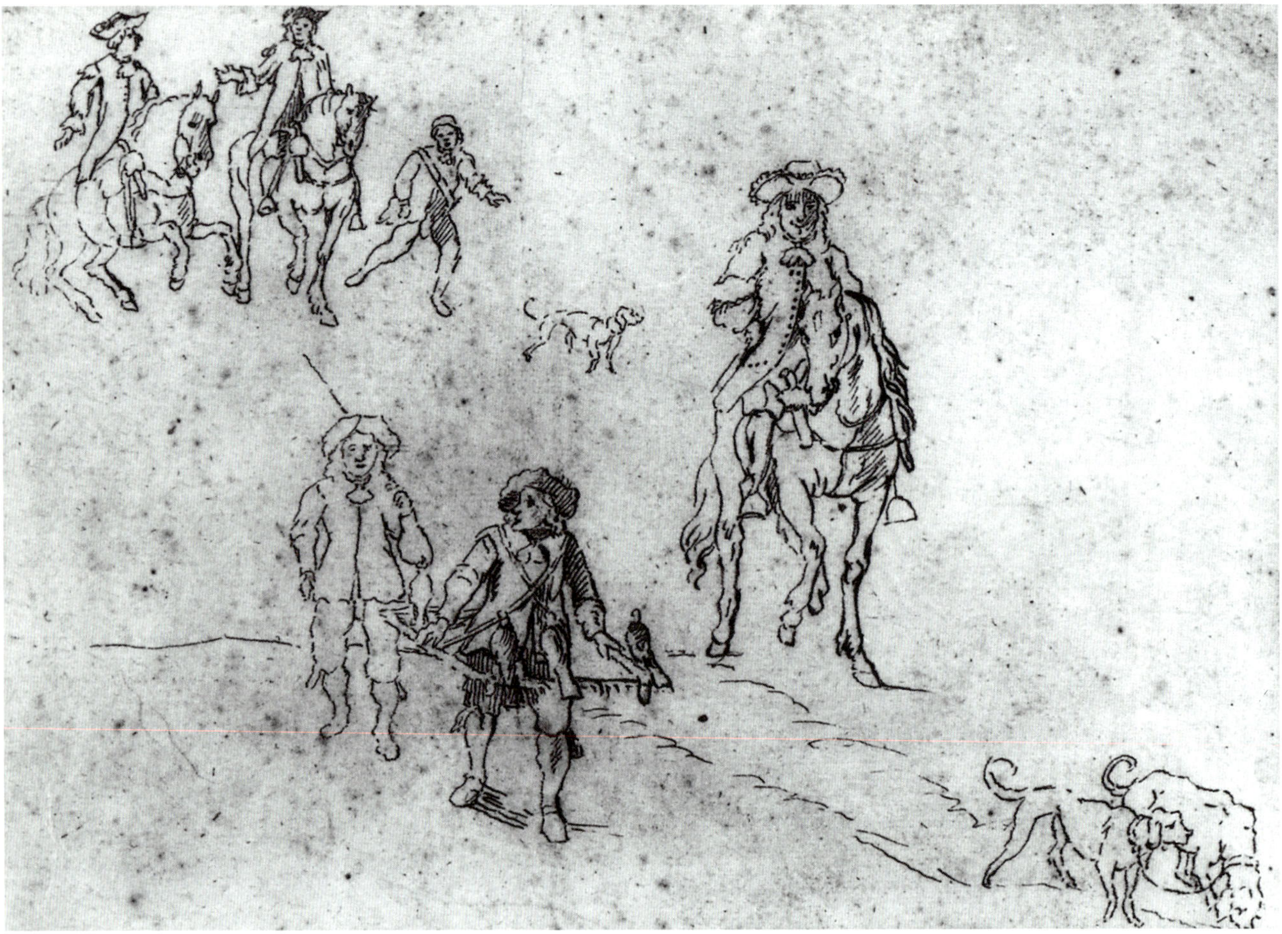

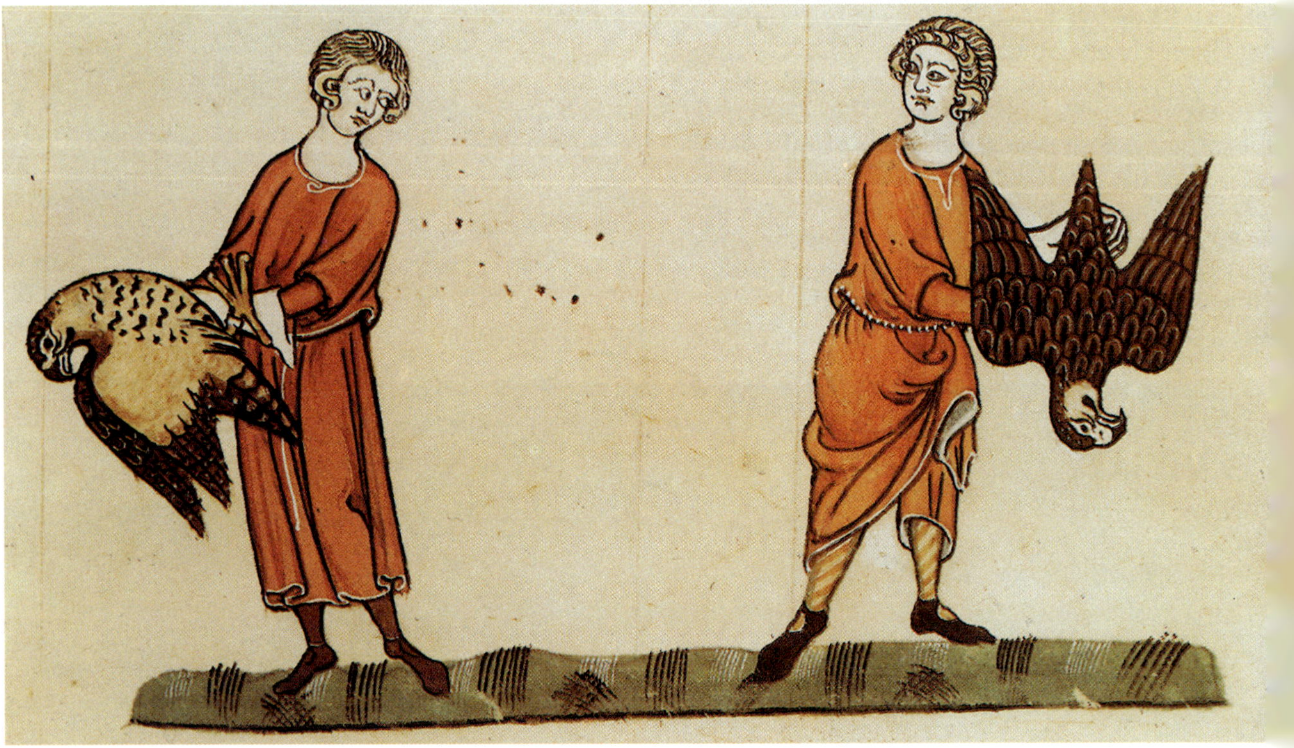

46: *Opposite above: Falconers, cadger and dogs. Pen drawing by F.D. Leard (18th century). (Courtesy Sotheby's)*

47-48: *Opposite below and this page above: Two illustrations from Emperor Frederick II's* De Arte Venandi cum Avibus *(early 14th century copy). Falconers dealing with bating hawks (opposite). Wetting a hawk by spraying her with water from a well-rinsed mouth (above). (Courtesy Sotheby's)*

49: *The 4th Earl of Bedford (1593–1641) as a boy, attributed to Robert Peake, c.1600. The inclusion of the hobby recalls 'Ther is an Hoby. And that hauke is for a yong man' in the old list of 'all maner of hawkys & to whom they belong', first appearing in print in 1486. The portrait is on display at Woburn Abbey, Bedfordshire.*

50: Opposite above: *Pheasant hawking, from an etching Wenceslaus Hollar, 1671.*

51: Opposite below: *Le Vo du Héron. A heron-hawking party close to the royal chateau at Loo in th province of Gelderland Netherlands. Among thos present is William III, King o the Low Countries 1849-9 (mounted, centre). Falcone Jan Bots (right foregroun makes in to the falcon an heron. (By permission of th British Library, from the copy of Schlegel and d Wulverhorst's Traité d Fauconnerie, 1844-5 (Cup652c9)*

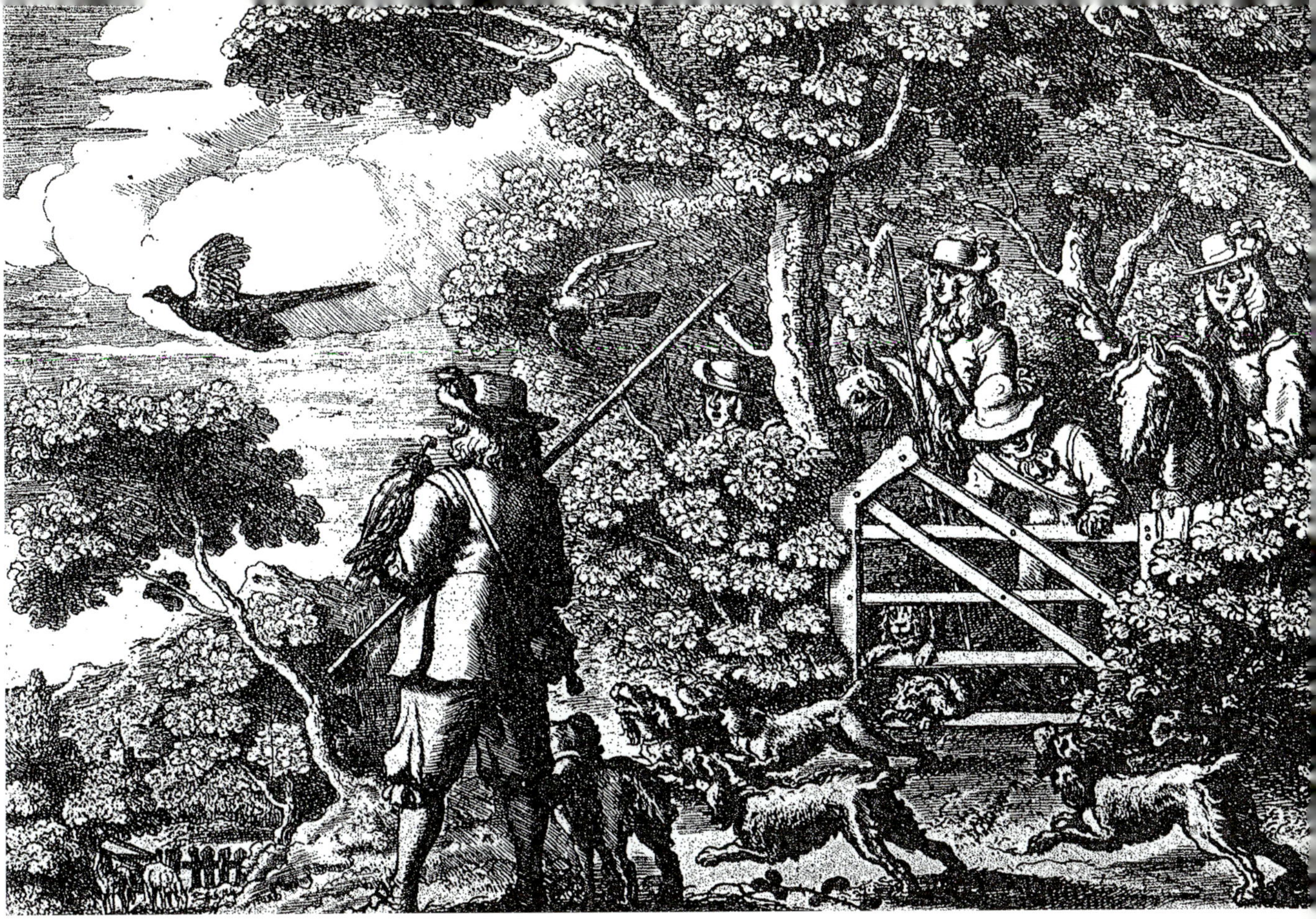
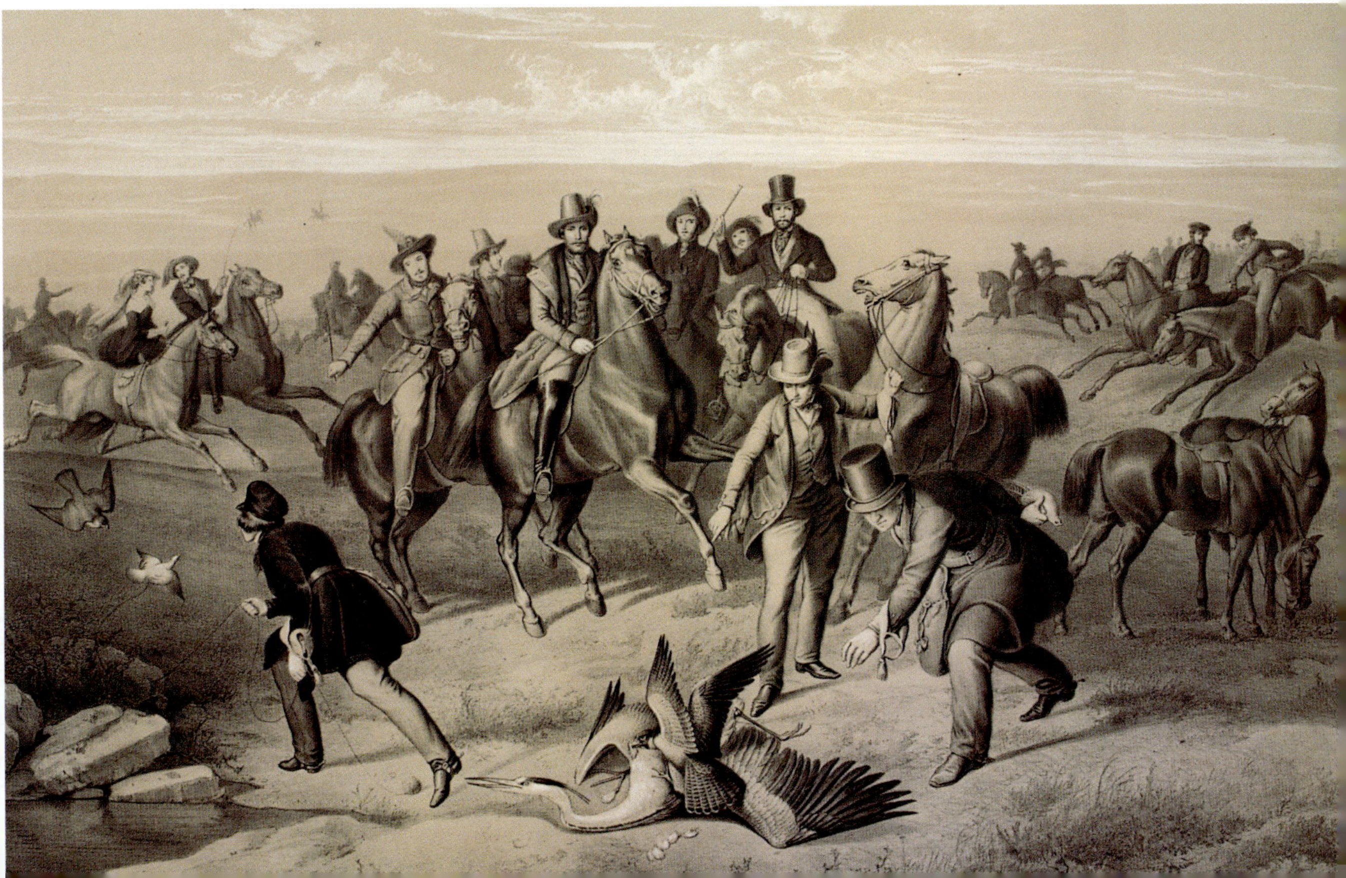

52: *Exercising a falcon with the swung lure at the National Birds of Prey Centre in Gloucestershire. The dramatic final moment: Philip Jones setting up a perfect high catch. (A. Walker)*

53-54: *Adrian Walker at Whipsnade Wild Animal Park exercising a falcon to the swung lure. (M. Lyster / © Z.S.L.)*

55: Adrian Walker giving early lessons to a male red-tailed hawk, still on the creance. (B.E. & K.L. Yull)

56: Falconer Phillip Glasier, founder in 1967 of the Falconry Centre (now the National Birds of Prey Centre), Newent, calling his female Harris' hawk 'Islay' to the fist. (A. Walker)

57: Above left: *Generations apart. In the foreground is falconer and author Lorant de Bastyai. (A. Walker)*

58: Above: *Hawking in the late evening. (A. Walker)*

59: *Adrian Walker and European eagle owl. Owls were once used as decoys in certain categories of hawking. (B.E. & K.L. Yull)*

L

LABRADOR FALCON See GYRFALCON.

LADDER (probably modern adoption; inf.) Of a hawk having taken stand in a tree, to progress upwards branch by branch.

LADY'S HAWK See MERLIN.

LAGGAR FALCON Alternative form of lugger falcon; see FALCON, Lugger.

LAID IN See PUT IN 2.

LAMPING Under HAWKING, Categories of.

LANARE (obs.) In Berners (1486[5]), the female lanner falcon, with (ibid.) lanrett for the male; see FALCON, Lanner.

LAND (1575[81], [?]obs.) Of dogs or beaters, to drive waterfowl out of the water for a hawk to fly at.

LANER(E) Obsolete spelling of lanner; see FALCON, Lanner.

LANNARD Uncommon, obsolete form of lanner; see FALCON, Lanner.

LANNERET; LANRETT (obs.) The male lanner falcon; see FALCON, Lanner.

LANNER FALCON See FALCON, Lanner.

LANTINER (obs.) (Usually occurs with capital L. Form of Lenten + -er. Alternative spelling: LENTINER.) A hawk taken from the wild in Lent, or Spring, before her moult. The term may also be used adjectivally, as in:

> 'A Lentiner Faulcon of the Kings lost from Chelsey the 24 of this instant July, with the Kings Vervells* on.' – 1677[53]

*See VARVELS. Other obsolete combinations are Lent-hawk and Lenten hawk. Turbervile (1575[81]) writes of 'March Hawks' or 'Lentiners', so named
> '. . . bycause they are taken in Lent with lime**, or suche like meanes.'

**Bird-lime; see also under TRAPS AND TRAPPING.

LARK In Britain, in the context of falconry, the skylark (*Alauda arvensis*). See LARK-HAWKING under HAWKING, Categories of.

LARK, Ground See RINGER.

LARK, Mounting See RINGER.

LARK, Ringing See RING UP.

LARK-CATCHER (obs.); **LARKER** (obs.) One who traps or catches skylarks. Both are perhaps exclusively lay terms; more in DARING.

LARK-HAWKING Under HAWKING, Categories of.

LAY IN (1677, probably obs.) Of a hawk during a chase, to drive quarry into cover. Put in, an old but surviving term, is synonymous.

LAYNES Perhaps form of LINES.

LAY OUT (obs.) To drive (quarry) out of cover; more in PUT OUT.

LAY UP Of a ferret, to remain in the burrow after killing and feeding on a rabbit, when it is said to be laid up.

LEAN See 1677 qu. in HOLD IN THE HEAD.

LEAN OUT See RAKE AWAY.

LEAPING-POLE See POLE, Hawking.

LEASE; LEASSE Obsolete forms of LEASH.

LEASH; LEASE (1575[81], obs.); **LEASSE** (1575[81], obs.) The thong or cord with which a hawk is restrained. The free ends of the JESSES are attached to one ring of the SWIVEL, the leash threaded through the other ring. Formerly, a varvel (a metal ring) was sewn or knotted on to the free end of each jess, and the leash threaded through both VARVELS.

Traditionally in the West, the leash is a flat hide thong, usually no more than 4'6" (137.16cm.) in length. One end is tapered to allow it to be slipped easily through one ring of the swivel; a BUTTON at the other end abuts the ring and acts as a stop when the free end is tied to the ring of the perch.

82 Leash, A

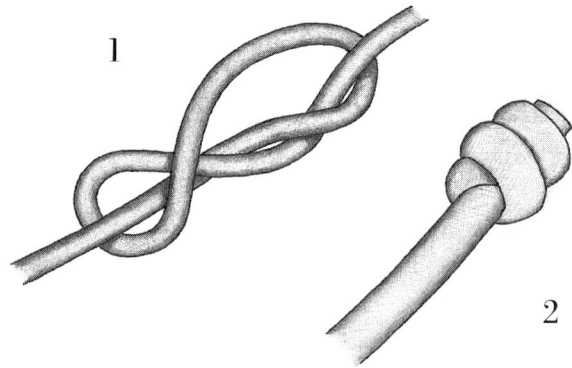

1: Forming the figure-of-eight knot for the modern man-made fibre leash. 2: The finished knot pulled tight.

When carrying a hawk on the fist, the leash might be 'halved' at the swivel and the two free lengths wound loosely in loops round the fingers of the gloved hand.

'*Lease* or leashe is a small long thong of leather, by which the Faulconer holdeth his *Hawke* fast, folding it many times about their fingers.' – 1615 gl.[49]

Or with the jesses gripped between the fingers of the fist in a SAFETY POSITION, the leash might be tied to the ring of the glove for added insurance against the hawk flying away should she bate off. The leash and swivel are removed when the hawk flies. Whale skin ('nothing is better . . . than 'porpoise' hide or the leather of the white whale' – 1892[47]) has been mentioned among various leathers for leashes in the past, while today rawhide and latigo are used. Although hide leashes are still in use currently, falconers often prefer those in man-made fibres because of the leather's tendency to de-nature and break unexpectedly, especially at the button. For traditionalists today, a flat woven Terylene leash (with a resemblance to a rawhide leash) can be bought; otherwise, a modern leash is a 'round' cord of braided man-made fibres, with a figure-of-eight knot at one end and sometimes a leather washer threaded on to abut it. The end protruding from the knot is heated and flattened (to prevent the knot undoing) and the unknotted end is heat-sealed to avoid fraying. For small accipiters and merlins, a leather bootlace was once thought adequate as a leash but is prone to breakage and is little used today; instead, a lightweight braided man-made fibre cord is usual.

See also LINES.

LEASH, A (obs.); A LECE (obs.) Three, as in 'a leash of hawks'. The Berners (1486[5]) list of collective terms includes 'a cast of haukis of ye tour.ii'* and 'a lece of thessame haukis.iii'. Turbervile (1575[81]) reports that lanners

'. . . are highly esteemed in Fraunce, and (as they say) there made to the river, and there do they use to flee with a caste or leashe of Laners to the brooke [at waterfowl] . . .'.

*See HAWK OF THE TOWER.

LEASH, Short (unc., obs.) An extension to the JESSES in the form of a slip of leather, one end attached to VARVELS knotted on to the free ends of the jesses, the other end to one ring of the SWIVEL. This obsolete item of furniture, described (and named *courtrier*) in Schlegel's 19th century French-language treatise[74], gave more freedom of movement to (in this case) a goshawk on the screen perch. Lascelles (1892[47]) was aware of such an extension for sparrowhawks and may have used it, although he is not precise about how it was arranged. What was perhaps a similar system was employed in the 13th century by Emperor Frederick, using (in transl.[35]) bits of leather. The translators' footnote suggests (contrary to common understanding) that these bits of leather are known to falconers as bewits.

LECE, A   See LEASH, A.

LEG-BELL   See BELL (n.).

LENT-HAWK; LENTEN HAWK   See LANTINER.

LENTINER   Spelling of LANTINER.

LESSEN HERSELF   See SHUT IN.

LEWER(S); LEWRE   Obsolete spellings of lure; see LURE (n. and vb).

LEWNES   Form of LINES.

LIE   Of quarry, to remain immobile on the ground or in cover.

LIE TO THE POINT; LIE TO THE DOG   See DOGS IN HAWKING.

LIME   Shortening of BIRD-LIME, found under TRAPS AND TRAPPING.

LIME-BUSH; LIME-RODS   See BIRD-LIME under TRAPS AND TRAPPING.

LINES   (obs.) (Singular, but of plural form. French *longe* = a hawk's leash[74]. Medieval Latin (Brit.–Ir.[48]) *longia, longa, loignia* = 'loyn', 'lune' [(?)a hawk's leash]. Other forms: LUNES,

LEWNES (1486[5]), LOYNES, perhaps LAYNES; all obs.)
An old term for the hawk's LEASH. It occurs in singular form ('loyne') in Turbervile (1575[81]). Bert (1619[6]) writes of allowing his goshawk to bathe in a brook,
> '... holding my fist to the water, and the end of my lines in my right hand...'.

Harting, in one of his glossaries (1891[39]), quotes from earlier writers in considering the definition of 'lunes' or 'lines'. In the pertinent extract, the Phillips[67] and Strutt[77] definitions are ambiguous, or not wholly accurate; however, Harting comes to what seems to be the logical conclusion. The entry (the square brackets are Harting's) reads:
> '"Lunes for hawks, leashes or long lines to call them." – Phillips, "New World of Words," 1696. "The jesses were made sufficiently long for the knots [ends] to appear between the middle and the little fingers of the hand that held them, so that the *lunes*, or small thongs of leather, might be fastened to them with tyrrits or rings, and the *lunes* were loosely wound round the little finger." – Strutt, "Sports and Pastimes,"... Hence it would appear that the lunes took the place of the modern leash, which is attached to the jesses with a swivel or varvels. Bert terms them "lines," thus:- "until he hath with her *lines* fastened her *calling-cranes* unto her." – "Treatise of Hawkes," 1619...'.

'Lunes' is clearly plural in Phillips, which makes his definition misleading; furthermore, his phrase 'long lines to call them' suggests confusion with a CREANCE. Strutt is misled into thinking that more than one thong of leather is involved. In reviewing the fuller passage in Bert's treatise[6], it is clear that 'untill he that hath her, hath with her lines fastened her calling-cranes unto her' means in effect: 'until he that has the hawk on the fist has attached her leash to the creance'.

Also see TYRRIT, SWIVEL, and VARVELS.

'Loynes' are assigned a different use in *A Perfect Booke* (c.1575[38]); this is the suggestion for 'Entering w^t the order therof', that is, how the hawk should be given her first kill:
> '... Let yor hawke stande loose upon a lowe pearche in a light chamber, and secretly convaye a prety bygge chiken or pygeon into the chamber (or fasten one w^t loynes to som flatt thinge in the chamber...) And wache w^tought the doore untill she take & kill it...'.

LIVE GORGE, A   See GORGE, A.

LONG-OPEN (unv., obs.) Apparently the longest primary feather in a hawk's wing. For comparison, Schlegel's mid-19th century French-language treatise has *la longue* as the name for the longest of the primary feathers (*pennes*), in a falcon the second counted from the wing-tip, the fourth in a goshawk or sparrowhawk[74].

LONG SINGLE; **LONG SENGLE** Under FOOT (n.).

LONG-WINGED HAWK; **LONGWINGED HAWK**; **LONGWING** See HAWK, Long-winged.

LORE   (Perhaps adapt. Latin *lorum* = a strap, a narrow strip of leather. Medieval Latin (Brit.–Ir.[48]) *lora* = (?)a narrow strip.) The region between a hawk's eye and the upper beak, on which small hair-like feathers grow. See FEATHERS, Crine.

LOW   See CONDITION, High or low.

LOW IN FLESH   See FLESH, Raised in.

LOYNE   See LINES.

LOYNES   Form of LINES.

LUER   Obsolete spelling of lure; see LURE (n. and vb).

LUGGER FALCON   See FALCON, Lugger.

LUNES   Form of LINES.

LURE   For idioms and combination terms which include 'lure', see next entry.

LURE   (n. and vb)
> **LURE** (n.) (Obs. spellings: LEWRE (1575[81]), LUER (1615), LEWER and LEWERS (both 1619[6]), the latter singular). Historically, the lure is an imitation (sometimes dead, sometimes live) bird or animal attached to a line and used in training before entering a hawk at wild quarry, to teach her some flight techniques and to rehearse her for taking quarry, footing it properly (plate 77), and resisting the temptation to carry it. The whole procedure is known as making (a hawk) to the lure; she is said to be made to the lure when this stage is complete (these idioms are now uncommon or obsolete). Later, in the field, having been made thoroughly 'fond of the lewre' (1575[81]) by the reward of food it provides, she is called to it after an unsuccessful flight. Additionally, the swung lure and to some extent the dragged lure are employed for exercising hawks in the training ground or exercise field.
> '*Luer* is that whereto Faulconers call their young *Hawkes* by casting it up in the aire, being made of feathers and leather in such wise that in the motion it lookes not unlike a fowle.' – 1615 gl.[49]

The lure, in rough imitation of quarry a hawk is (or will be) flown at, has a long history. The complete equipment is made up of the lure itself, a swivel, a line, and sometimes a stick.

LURE SWIVEL. The lure is fastened to one ring, the lure-line to the other. It prevents the line twisting and kinking when the lure is swung or dragged.

LURE-LINE; LURE STRING[40]. A length of line, one end fastened to the swivel, the other to the lure-stick (if used). Today it is usually of soft braided cotton and is wound onto the lure-stick when the equipment is not in use. On some surviving antique lures, the braided line has at the end a substantial knot or tassel for gripping in the hand when swinging. Otherwise, a leather line with a BUTTON for gripping or a slit for fingers was not unusual.

LURE-STICK. It is suspected that this was not widely employed until recent times. When used, it is of wood and gripped in the hand; the lure-line is wound onto it when the equipment is not in use. An arrangement to discourage a hawk from carrying the lure (particularly the swung bird-wing type) has been to drill out and weight the stick with melted-in lead, or, instead of using a stick, to thread on a lump of lead to act as a dragweight.

LURE-POLE. The pole to which a lure on a line is attached; this arrangement is used in pole luring, described below.

A falcon of whatever species is almost invariably flown at birds, therefore she is first made to a bird-wing lure. A digression from this usual custom is noted in a 19th century French-language treatise[74], where a gyrfalcon which is to be flown at hares or rabbits might be made to a hare-skin stuffed with hay before being entered at a live captive animal. A similar arrangement is described in the 13th century by Emperor Frederick[35], where the skin of a hare, stuffed with chopped straw and garnished with meat, is used for the early training of gyrfalcons which will subsequently be flown at large avian quarry.

BIRD-WING LURE; SWUNG LURE (recent idioms); formerly simply LURE. Historically, this device has been for use (chiefly but not exclusively) with falcons, swung and thrown up to be caught in the air by the hawk or thrown out to be taken on the ground. The basic ancient design (pairs of birds' wings tied together or attached to a pad, garnished with meat and attached to a line) has not altered, but there have been a host of variations on it and modifications to it, some of which, particularly in modern times, make an attempt at mimicking the appearance and behaviour of a real bird. The lure which Emperor Frederick[35] used in the 13th century in crane-hawking with gyrfalcons was made from a pair of crane's wings. The bones of the two wings were bound together with strips of deerskin, two free ends of which were left protruding from the upper and lower sides for tying on meat. A long leather strap corresponded to the modern lure-line; a slit was cut into its extreme end for the falconer's fingers. To carry the lure when not in use, the falconer tucked under his belt a wooden walnut-sized ball attached to the strap. The Emperor recommended that a lure for sakers in heron-hawking should be made from four herons' wings to achieve a weight which discouraged carrying. Remarkably, he suggested, for duck-hawking with peregrines, a lure made from the wings of 11 mallard or other duck (that is 22 wings), making it heavy enough to discourage carrying. Pictorial evidence from the Middle Ages up to recent times confirms that in the West the lure was often slung over the falconer's shoulder when not in use, the lure-line doubled to form a large loop. Numerous references are made in older hawking literature to wings secured to a pad of leather; leather pads, in horseshoe and other shapes, are homemade or bought today, ready for usually four wings to be attached and meat tied on. Occasionally, a real horseshoe was used:

'A very good lure is made of a horseshoe, well padded with tow, and bound and covered with leather. It should be covered over with two pairs of wings, of which wild duck's will be found to be the best . . .' – 1892[47];

this was likely to injure the hawk if it accidentally struck her. While admitting the dangers in using a heavy lure, Harting (1898[40]) writes:

'Some falconers . . . approve of a heavy lure, as they consider that it prevents a hawk from attempting to carry the meat away, a fault which, when once acquired, is very troublesome to cure.'

Another design is described thus:

'The ORDINARY LURE is a bunch of gaudy feathers, with a cord and tassel . . . In the middle of the feathers is a forked piece of wood, to which is tied a piece of raw meat.' – 1856[76];

the significance of the word 'ordinary' is not elaborated upon, nor is another design of lure discussed. For a merlin, Harting (1898[40]) recommends a small bag of wash-leather partly filled with lead shot, tied tightly round the middle with a bootlace and garnished with feathers at each end. Sometimes, perhaps particularly with a merlin, the lure is used to call the falcon to the fist; it is swung to attract her, then caught in the gloved hand.

Beebe[4] (N.Am.) describes a contemporary pattern of lure for falcons which has a body made of dyed sheared sheepskin and calf-skin wings with thin metal inserts which give it realism when swung. Modern falconers use and commend a variety of different materials and constructions as well as methods of operation for both swung and dragged lures. Clockwork automata (birds with flapping wings) are sometimes used.

RABBIT LURE; GROUND LURE (recent idioms); DRAGGED LURE (modern, inf.); formerly simply LURE. A lure constructed in rough imitation of furred ground-quarry. With meat tied on, it is thrown out on a line or dragged along the ground to be caught by the hawk and fed from. With a goshawk which is to be flown at fur, she may first be made to a lure of this type. The buteos and hawk-eagles used in Western falconry in recent and modern times may be made to the same kind of lure. There is no evidence to suggest that historically this pattern was used widely for the goshawk; rather, she might first be tempted to fly to and feed on a dead rabbit or game-bird, then flown at bagged quarry, and quite soon afterwards entered at wild quarry, although there are indications that the use of a lure in imitation of a bird was not uncommon.

LURE-SWINGING (modern idiom). The practice or art of exercising a falcon to the swung lure. Employing the lure in the field is known as luring, but this term is obsolescent. In the exercise field, a falconer is said to stoop her to the lure, or stoop her, or lure fly her (the latter modern). Michell (1900[59]) writes of 'flying hawks to the lure', and of hawks making 'stoops at the lure'. Certain modern treatises minutely describe techniques of lure-swinging in the training ground or exercise field, and these vary from writer to writer (FR[36], FR[4]). In the most basic of terms, the free end of the lure-line (or the lure-stick if used) is gripped in the fist; the lure-line is held along its length by the fingers of the free hand and the lure swung in circles in the vertical plane. When stooping a falcon for exercise, the circling motion is interrupted to present the lure to the approaching bird; it is then pulled out of her reach, and the falconer resumes swinging and prepares for another 'pass'. At the end of a session, the lure is thrown out onto the ground or up in the air for her to catch (plates 52–4). Beebe[4] (N.Am.) uses the term hand-luring for this technique, which differentiates it from

POLE LURING described by him. For this, Beebe suggests using a fibreglass fishing-rod 'blank' (a rod with no fitments) as a lure-pole; to one end of this is attached the lure on a line. The falconer swings the rod in a near-horizontal plane, pulling the lure through the air at speed and in wide circles for the falcon to chase. A similar system has seen use by native falconers in India, and the following method of entering a merlin at larks, in a 19th century Persian text, is reminiscent:

> 'If you want to train a "cast" of [two] merlins to fly larks, train them quickly, luring them three times or four times a day to a lure made of pigeons' wings. Now get a live lark, and for three days, – after the merlin has been made hot and excited by being called to the lure – tie the lark to the end of a long stick, and fly the hawk at that, making it stoop four or five times. Then let the hawk take, and eat half of the lark.' – 1908, in transl.[68]

LURE-BAG ([?]recent). A bag (worn at the waist) of sufficient size to carry only the lure. Otherwise, the term is an occasional synonym for hawking bag (see BAG, Hawking).

ENTER TO THE LURE. Of a falconer, to introduce (a hawk) to the lure.

MAKE TO THE LURE (now unc. or obs.). Of a falconer, to encourage (a hawk) to chase, come to, take and foot the lure reliably over the longer period.

MADE TO THE LURE (now unc. or obs.). The state in a hawk when the above lessons are satisfactorily concluded.

DRY LURE (unc., obs.). According to Turbervile (1575[81]), a lure with no food upon it:

> '. . . Call hir to the drye lewre, without a Pullette, or any thing uppon it.'

DEAD LURE (obs.). To Harting (1898[40]), a dead bird or animal used as a lure. The term is used by Michell (1900[59]) for a bird-wing lure for stooping a merlin.

LIVE LURE (obs.). A live bird or animal used as a lure. The use of live lures is now illegal in Britain and some European countries. Formerly, it was not unusual for the falconer or austringer to carry a live bird into the field in his bag for use as a lure; it might be thrown out on a creance, or tied to what Turbervile (1575[81]) calls his 'drye lewre', a lure with no food upon it.

LURE (vb, obsolescent). Of a falconer, to employ a lure; to swing the lure in the field to attract a hawk's attention, to call her back, or to call her in.

'The falconer . . . should always halloo when he is luring.' – 1826[75].

In the case of a bird-wing lure, the idiom 'swing the lure' is preferred today. Turbervile (1575[81]) refers to luring with the voice ('hearing the keeper lewre': an obsolete application) as well as with the lure in the field; fuller qu. in HOLD IN THE HEAD.

LURING (obsolescent). The procedure or act of swinging a lure.

MAKE UP A LURE ([?]modern). To prepare or tie meat to a lure.

BAIT THE LURE. To tie meat to the lure.

LURED (obs.). The same as 'made to the lure' and applied to a hawk whose lessons in coming to, taking and footing the lure are concluded. Turbervile (1575[81]) has the obsolete idioms 'well lewred' and 'throughly lewred', which mean thoroughly made to the lure.

LURE-BOUND. Often applied to a falcon in the field: over-keen on the lure, ignoring quarry and obsessively circling overhead at a low level waiting for the lure to be offered. An uncommon and obsolete equivalent ('wedded to the lure') occurs in Lascelles (1892[47]):

'It is a very bad plan to keep hawks that are fit to be entered [at quarry] flying on at the lure day after day, for weeks together. Such hawks will become very tame and very handy, but they will lose all that dash which is the special charm of the passage hawk, and will become so wedded to the lure that they will fly at nothing else.'

WEDDED TO THE LURE. See preceding.
TAKE THE LURE. Of a hawk, to catch the lure.
COME TO THE LURE. Of a hawk when summoned, to come and take the lure.
CHECK AT THE LURE. Of a hawk coming to the lure, to shy away.
LURE OFF (unc.). To tempt (a hawk) from a perch using the lure. A lost hawk, having taken stand in a tree,

'. . . may be lured off, down wind, with a live pigeon in a string.' – 1898[40].

LURE-HACKED. See HACKED under HACKING.

LURED See preceding entry.

LURING See LURE (n. and vb).

LYING OUT Of quarry (perhaps particularly rabbits), at rest in the open.

MADE See MAKE.

MADE HAWK See MAKE.

MAGPIE *Pica pica*, the quarry in British magpie-hawking.

MAGPIE-HAWKING Under HAWKING, Categories of.

MAIL (n., obs.) (Also MAILS (obsolescent). Obs. spellings: MAILL, MAYLL (both 1486), MAYLE.) Collectively, a grown hawk's breast feathers. Berners (1486[5]) lists names for different colourations:

'Hawkes have White maill. Canvasmaill or Rede maill. And som call Rede maill Iren mayll. White maill is soone knawe. Canvasmaill is betwene white maill and Iron maill. And Iron maill is varri Rede.'

In the same text is 'mayles', presumably plural because both the female and the male goshawk are named:

'A Goshawke nor a tercell in thare sore aage [sore age, first year] have nott thair mayles named. bot it is calde their plumage. and after the cote*. it is calde theyr Maill.'

*The phrase 'and after the cote' may mean 'until after this coat [of feathers]'; the suggestion here appears to be that the breast feathers are not referred to as mail (or their colouration specified) until after the first moult. Also see PLUMAGE 1. According to Turbervile (1575[81]),

> 'They [haggard peregrines] are ordinarily of foure mayles, eyther blancke [(?)pale], russet, browne, or turtle maylde, and some pure white maylde, without any jote or spotte of any other colour, but those a man shall very seldome see.'

On the perceived significance of colour, see PLUME 1 (n.). Also see FEATHERS, Breast.

MAIL (vb, obs.); **MAYLE** (obs.); **MAIL UP** (obs.); **MALE** (obs.); **MALE UP** (obs.) Of a hawk trapper, to wrap up (a trapped wild hawk) in a sock or cloth. Of a falconer, to make (a hawk) manageable by wrapping (her) in a cloth during procedures such as COPING or IMPING. Other idioms (all obsolete): mailed and mailed up (also spelt 'maled', 'maled up', both 1619[6]) mean wrapped up; 'unmale' (1619[6]) and 'un-male' (1908, in transl.[68]) mean to unwrap (a mailed hawk); 'unmaled' (1619[6]) means unwrapped. Spellings 'unmail' and 'unmailed' are hypothetical, not having been found so far. Bert (1619[6]) writes of mailing a hawk to keep her warm:

> '... I would keepe her still maled up, lest she should catch colde until I had made her pills ready ...'.

In his chapter headed 'Wherein the Austringer is taught to reclaime his Hawke from any ill-condition', this writer sets down a procedure he has used for making a HOOD-SHY goshawk good to the hood. First, she is watched (see WATCH) for one night and in the morning wrapped in a handkerchief; then:

> 'My hawke thus maled up, I lay her upon a cushion, and carry her up and down under my arme...';

presently, he hoods and unhoods her and continues to do so for the rest of the day.

Uncommon and obsolete 'truss' is an alternative. Also see SOCK.

MAILED 1 See MAIL (vb).

MAILED 2 (obs.) Provided with breast feathers. A hawk might be

> '... blancke, russet, browne, or turtle maylde...' – 1575[81];

fuller qu. in MAIL (n.).

MAILS (obsolescent); **MAIL** (obs.) Collectively, a grown hawk's breast feathers. See MAIL (n.), and FEATHERS, Breast.

MAIL UP; MAILED UP; MAILED 1 See MAIL (vb).

MAKE (now unc. or obs.) By itself, the term means (of a falconer) to educate or train (a hawk):

> 'Me thinkes I heare some man say, I have taken a very painefull course in making my hawke.' – 1619[6].

She is said to be made (or described as a made hawk) when her overall training is complete; these idioms are probably obsolete. According to Harting (1898[40]), she is made at her (in this case a goshawk's) entering; this is an obsolete application:

> 'The critical stage was now passed. The hawk had killed wild quarry, and was "made."'

Compare HAWK, Make. Unmade (obs.) means untrained or not fully trained. To make to the hood is to accustom (a hawk) to accepting and wearing the hood, and to make to the lure is to encourage (her) to come to, take and foot the lure reliably. When these lessons are satisfactorily concluded, a hawk is said to be made to the hood and – to the lure. These idioms are in uncommon use or obsolete.

There are further combinations. Berners (1486[5]) uses the obsolete 'make an hawke to the querre' for a procedure involving releasing a live bird ('a tame Malarde') for a goshawk to take; therefore the phrase is presumed to be synonymous with 'enter a hawk at (in this case captive) quarry' (see ENTER); then, once the quarry is taken:

> '... Let hir slee [kill] it. and plymme well upon hir. and serve her so.ii.or.iii.tymes and then she is made to the quarre.'

Note: In this passage, the implication is that the austringer allows the hawk to feed well upon the kill as a memorable reward; obsolete 'plymme' may be related to 'plume', meaning to pluck (she will naturally plume before feeding), but in this instance means to feed. To make a hawk to the river means to train her for flying at waterfowl ('And if you be disposed to frame and make this bird to the river...' – 1615[49]). To make her to the brook is the same, and to make her to the field means to train her for hunting in open country ('... For of your other flights, as to the brooke, or to the field, which you may also make her unto...' – 1615[49]). These three idioms are obsolete.

MAKE-FALCON See HAWK, Make.

MAKE-HAWK See HAWK, Make.

88 Make In

MAKE IN (Alternatives: GO IN (now unc.) and GET IN (unc., obs.).) Used by itself: of a falconer, to approach a hawk when she is on a kill or the lure in order to pick her up. Also, he might make into her, and the hawk might be made into.

MAKE INTO See preceding entry.

MAKE OUT See CHECK 1 (vb), and RAKE AWAY.

MAKE POINT; MAKE HER POINT See POINT, Make.

MALAR STRIPE See MOUSTACHIAL STRIPE.

MALE; MALE UP; MALED; MALED UP See MAIL (vb).

MAN Of a falconer, to tame (a hawk) by carrying her on the fist, a process which precedes and is concurrent with training. Broadly, it is accustoming a hawk to the presence of Man and is a basis for procedures such as the now obsolete practice of watching (see WATCH), encouraging her to feed on the fist, introducing her to strange sights and sounds, and making her to the hood (if applicable). The process is known as manning. Bert (1619[6]) uses the uncommon and obsolete idiom 'in manning':

> 'Bee not negligent towards your Hawke at no time, but especially whilest she is in manning, if you be, shee will pay you for it in her flying.'

Manned and well-manned, spelt 'well mand' (1618[50]), describe a hawk when the process of manning is satisfactorily concluded and she is tame and tractable. Unmanned describes a hawk whose manning has not started.

MANAGING (unv., obs.) In the context of falconry, perhaps equates to manning; see preceding entry. In his glossary, Latham (1615[49]) offers a broad definition:

> '*Managing*, is to handle any thing with cunning according to the true nature thereof.'

MANGALA Under GLOVE, Hawking.

MANNED See MAN.

MANNING See MAN.

MANNING, In See MAN.

MANNY (rare, obs.) Of a hawk, manned or tame.

MANTELL; MANTILL; MANTYLL Obsolete spellings of MANTLE (vb 2).

MANTLE (vbs) (Cf. Latin *mantellum* = a cloak,

From George Turbervile's 16th century treatise, a falconer apparently adjusting the position of the feet of his hawk with a little stick. Note how this tool is inaccurately depicted in the later Cox version (right).

a means of covering or hiding something.) 1. In the common understanding today, used by itself: of a hawk, to spread and arch her wings and fan her tail in order to hide food held in her feet. The fuller idiom 'mantle over' (a kill etc.) is also current and correct. (Plate 78).

2. An obsolescent application (also spelt 'mantill', 'mantell', 'mantyll'; all 1486[5] and obs.) is: of a perching hawk, to spread and stretch one wing and the corresponding leg at the same time, sometimes slewing her tail towards that side, often then repeating the action with the opposite wing and leg. 'Stretch' is probably used most commonly today. The Berners (1486[5]) description, is:

> '... She mantellith and not stretchith when she puttith her leges from hir oon after an other: and hir

Frontispiece from the hawking section of Nicholas Cox's The Gentleman's Recreation, 1677.

wynges folow after hier legg[s]. then she dooth mantill hir. . . .'.

To Cox (1674[25]), mantling is:

'. . . When she stretcheth one of her wings after her leg, and so the other.'

A more recent description is from Michell (1900[59]):

'. . . To "mantle" is to stretch out the leg in a sideways and backward direction, and afterwards stretch the wing over it . . .'.

3. A rare and obsolete application is: to spread the wings and fan the tail in a show of aggression. To Lascelles (1892 gl.[47]), it is:

'To sit on the perch with wings and tail fully spread – a sign of an ill-tempered hawk.'

Compare DECK.

MANTLE (n.) The area of back between a hawk's wings.

MANTLE OVER See MANTLE (vb 1).

MARCH HAWK See LANTINER.

MAR-HAWK (obs.); MARHAWK (obs.) (Other spellings; all obs.) One who spoils (mars) a hawk by inept management.

'. . . He whiche taketh not that delyght in his Hawke, but doeth rather exercise it for a pompe and boast, than upon a naturall instinct: or beeyng a poore manne, doeth use it to get hys lyving, such a man in mine opinion shall seldome prove a perfecte Falconer, but a marrehawke, and shall beare the bagge after a right Falconer.' – 1575[81].

MARK 1 (vb) Of a falconer in the field, to watch where the hawk and the quarry go. Members of the field (markers) may be appointed to act as observers and mark the flight, that is, watch a flight from a vantage point and note where hawk and quarry go. A hawk, having killed, might be marked down, that is, her location noted. If quarry is marked down, it has been observed to fall or go into cover and its location is known.

MARK 2 (vb, now unc.) Of a short-winged hawk during a chase, to mark where quarry has gone into cover by alighting on a suitable perch close by, or, of a falcon, by waiting on over the spot.

MARK 1 (n.) The spot or elevated perch from where a short- or broad-winged hawk marks her quarry. Of a goshawk having taken stand close to where the austringer's dogs have reached a pheasant first, Latham (1618[50]) writes:

> '... Shee was not wont to remove or stirre from the mark or the man, but diligently to attend and waite his leisure; and when he thought fit time to have her, shee would come downe most willingly to his fist.'

MARK 2 (n., unv., obs.) A hawk's quarry.

MARK! (inf.) The cry of a falconer to the hawking party at the instant of a promising slip or stoop, bidding them note where the hawk and (or) her quarry go. Members of the field may be formally appointed by the falconer to mark the hawk and the quarry; these are known as markers.

MARK, At Of a short-winged hawk (and now correct for a broad-winged hawk) during a chase: marking where quarry has gone into cover, ideally by taking stand on an elevated perch nearby. Bert (1619 chap.hdg[6]) uses the term in the context of a goshawk positioning herself incorrectly and offers advice on

> 'What course is to be taken with a Hawke that hath flowne a Partridge, and will continually sit upon the ground at marke, and thereby is likely to beate out her selfe from her true flying, by missing of many flights.'

Compare next entry.

MARK, Fall at (probably obs.) Of a short-winged hawk during a chase, to alight on the ground, marking the spot where quarry has gone into cover. This is condemned as a vice by those who prefer the hawk to take stand in a nearby tree straightaway so that she is in a good position for a flight when the quarry is reflushed. The author of a Persian treatise (1908, in transl.[68]), writing on the training of a goshawk, suggests encouraging the hawk to fall before taking stand in a tree:

> '... Cast her on the ground and play with her so as to teach her to run round and round you ... The object of this instruction on the ground is to teach her to run round the bush and block the quarry after she has "put it in," and then to rise and take up a commanding position on a tree to watch the bush from thence, so that the partridge escape her not.'

In reclaiming a short-winged hawk, there is this advice in *A Perfect Booke* (c.1575[38]):

> '*Note*, use to call her from the grounde furste, and that will make her fall at marke in the plaine felde, otherwyse she will to a tree.'

MARK, Fly at (probably obs.) Of a short-winged hawk during a chase, to take stand in a tree, marking the place where quarry has gone into cover:

> '... Generally said of a Goshawk when, having "put in" a covey of partridges, she takes stand, marking the spot where they disappeared from view until the falconer arrives to put them out to her.' – 1891 gl.[39]

Cox (1677 gl.[25]) uses an uncommon, probably obsolete idiom, which is merely an extension of the foregoing:

> '*Hawk keeps her mark*, is when she waits at the place where she lays in *Partridge*, or the like, until it be retrived [retrieved, reflushed].'

MARK, Fly to (probably obs.) Of a falcon, to mount and then mark the spot where the quarry lies or has gone into cover by waiting on over it (see WAIT ON). In the same context, the uncommon and probably obsolete 'keep her mark' appears to mean to remain waiting on over the spot until the falconer flushes the quarry; compare 1677 qu. in preceding entry. Latham (1618[50]) uses the obsolete idiom 'mount aloft upon the mark' in the context of the ideal hunting behaviour of a long-winged hawk; she

> '... is taught by nature, and also enforced further by nurture, to clime and mount aloft upon the marke, for her better advantage, and after that manner kill it [quarry] at the downecome [by stooping and striking] ...'.

MARK, Fly to the (obs.) Of a goshawk, according to Turbervile (1575[81]), to pursue (quarry) until it has gone into cover and then (in this case) alight upon the ground:

> '... And if she flee it to the marke agayne, you must put hir to a tree, and retryve [retrieve, reflush] it the second time, crying when it springeth ...'.

Compare MARK, Fall at.

MARK, Keep her See MARK, Fly at, and MARK, Fly to.

MARK, Mount aloft upon the See MARK, Fly to.

MARK DOWN See MARK 1 (vb).

MARKER A member of the field posted by the falconer as an observer to watch where hawk and quarry go. For an early use, see 1486 qu. in PUT UP 2 (vb).

MARK THE FLIGHT See MARK 1 (vb).

MARLIN(E); MARLYN Obsolete forms of MERLIN.

MARROW (Obs. form: MARY.) Bone marrow, once given to hawks for remedial or restorative purposes or to envelope medicine. More in MARROW (Appendix).

MARY Obsolete form of MARROW.

MATAGASSE See SHRIKE.

MAYLDE See MAILED 2.

MAYLE 1 See MAIL (n.)

MAYLE 2 See MAIL (vb).

MEAT, Hard-washed See MEAT, Washed.

MEAT, Hawk; HAWK'S MEAT; HAWK FOOD
Ideal food for falconers' hawks (the same as or similar to the natural prey of their wild counterparts) is not always available in sufficient quantities, therefore a number of supplements have been used over the centuries. Favoured among these has been well-chosen beef,
  '... neyther slymey nor fylmey, clene pared and pyked from all dryth fatt and strings.' – c.1575[38].
Other meats have been sheep's heart (for small hawks), mutton, and pork, although these last two are now reckoned to be unsuitable. In feeding, the dietetic demands and predisposition of a species are considered. Today, in addition to her share of any kill, a hawk might be given day-old cockerels, captive-bred rats, mice and quail, and so-called 'butcher's meat', usually lean (shin of) beef. To compensate for any mineral and vitamin deficiencies in her food, dietary additives are given. Historically, pigeon or dove has been a staple hawk meat. From the Estate accounts of the Cecils at Theobalds, Hertfordshire (c.1600[63]), comes a reference to this and some other noteworthy entries:
  'Paid for 2 dozen pidgeons for hawks, 4s.6d.; meate for pidgeons, 4s.6d.; yeard of flannell*, 1s.2d.; for empynge [imping] ould Haggard**, 2s.; my expenses when Jerkin [male gyrfalcon] was lost, 1s.5d.; my horse shoeing, 1s.4d.; two mallards, 1s.1d.; two sheeps heartes, 2d.; crossing the river, 2d.; charges for horse and self when Haggard was lost, 1s.; paid unto one for taking up Haggard, 14d.; meate for Spanyells, 12s.; bells, jesses, buetts§, hoods, etc., 6s.8d.'

*Perhaps for casting; see CASTING 2.
**See HAGGARD (n.).
§Obsolete spelling of bewits; see BEWIT.
Various meats to assist the moult, put flesh on a thin hawk, and as ingredients in remedies, are recommended in the 15th century in Berners[5]; these range from frog to peacock, swan to hedgehog. Substitute or emergency rations (apparently mainly for eyasses) recommended in the 13th century by Emperor Frederick[35] are unsalted fresh or cooked cheese (the latter the translators compare to cottage cheese) and hens' eggs cooked in milk.

MEAT, Unwashed See second 1486 qu. in next entry.

MEAT, Washed (Spelt 'wash-' and 'washe meete' in Berners (1486[5]).) Meat soaked in water and squeezed of its goodness. While giving a meal in bulk, it has little nutritive value and will result in weight-loss in a hawk. Hard-washed meat is cut up small, soaked for a long time and wrung out hard, becoming almost white in colour. Washed meat was associated with the process of enseaming:
  '... Whan she hath cast hir sercellis [sarcels, outer primary feathers] in mew. then and not erst it is tyme for to fede hir with wash meete and to begynne to ensayme hire.' – 1486[5].
See ENSEAM.
  'Wash'd meat and stones* maketh a hawk to flie, But great casting and long fasting maketh her to die.' – Proverb (1615[49]).
*See RANGLE. Washed meat is considered unsafe for the delicate constitution of a small hawk:
  'If yowre hawke be a spare hawke [sparrowhawk]: ever fede hir with unwassh meet ...' – 1486[5].
Harting (1898[40]) makes this observation:
  'It was long supposed that it [washed meat] also made them more keen to fly at a quarry such as rooks, of which they do not much like the taste, because the pleasure of feeding on warm, fresh killed flesh would be so great by comparison with their ordinary tasteless food.'
The use of washed meat is obsolescent in the West today.

MEAT BOX; FOOD BOX See BAG, Hawking.

MERLIN *Falco columbarius* (Anglo-French *merilun*; Old French *esmerillon*; Modern French *émerillon*; Medieval Latin (Brit.–Ir.[48]) *esmerillunus* and others.)
'Merlin' has sometimes been reserved for the female; 'jack' is customary for the male. Alternative names and forms:

Merlin. (E.&D. Hosking; FLPA, Images of Nature).

MERLYON (1486[5], obs.)
MARLYN and **MARLIN(E)** (1575[81], obs.)
JACK MERLIN. The male.
JACK-MERLIN (1900[59], probably obsolete). The male.
PIGEON HAWK; PIGEON-HAWK. Former vernacular English name. North America, vernacular.

A small mostly migratory falcon with races in Europe, Asia and North America. Resident in the British Isles, it is a hawk of open country, moorland, hills and fells. Its prey is small birds such as larks and pipits, sometimes insects, lizards and small mammals. As a falconer's bird, it is relatively easy to tame and train but is delicate and considered unsuitable for a beginner. In Britain, there is a long history of flying it singly or in a cast at the skylark (*Alauda arvensis*):

'The quarry which . . . affords the finest flight for the Merlin is the sky-lark . . .' – 1855[73];

but (ibid.),

'The strongest female Merlins may be trained to fly pigeons admirably . . .'.

Also see 1892 qu. in CAST, A. It has been a tradition to release merlins after a season's flying, as they may not survive the winter in captivity and do not perform as well the following year. The sobriquet 'lady's hawk' for the merlin appears to be inspired by a line in the old list of the 'hierarchy' of hawks and their owners, a version of which was first seen in print in the late 15th century in *The Boke of St Albans*[5] ('Ther is a Merlyon. And that hawke is for a lady'). The merlin was probably assigned condescendingly to a lady because of the hawk's small size, docility and tractability. See NAMES 3. (Plates 10, 11 and 72).

MERLYON   Obsolete form of MERLIN.

METESE   Perhaps obsolete form of MUTE.

MEW   (n., obs.) (French *muer* = to moult, from Latin *muto* = to alter, change.) A place or building to house hawks, especially at the time of their moult.

'*Mew*, is that place, whether it be abroad or in the house where you set downe your Hawke, during the time that shee raseth her feathers.' – 1615 gl.[49]

MEWS is the form used today. Hawk house or hawk-house is an alternative and is sometimes met with currently.

MEW   (vb, now unc.) Of a hawk, to moult; of a falconer, to moult (a hawk). Mewed means moulted, or having been moulted by the falconer. A mewed hawk (probably obs.) is one which has completed her moult or is in her second year, having moulted once; more in HAWK, Mewed. Mewing is moulting; occasionally, as an obsolete verbal noun, it indicates the moult itself, as in 'her first mewing' (1615[49]); fuller qu. in INTERMEWED.

MEW, Draw from the   (obs.) To withdraw (a hawk) from the MEWS at the end of her moult. Berners (1486[5]) has the obsolete idioms 'drawe owte of mewe' and 'take . . . owte of mewe' in which 'mewe' might be taken to mean the hawk's moult as much as the building. This writer also uses the shortened 'draw', which is synonymous:

'Som folkys usen when an hawke has cast hir sarcell* to begynne and wash hir meete. and fede hir so in mew with wash meete a monyth or.vi.weekys or ever [before] thay drawe thaym.'

*In a normal moult, the SARCEL is the last primary feather in a hawk's wing to be dropped. Also, a hawk might be drawn:

'And if yowre hawke be harde pennyd*: she may be drawne to be reclaymed.' – 1486[5].

*See PENNED, Hard. Latham (1615[49]) has the verbal noun 'drawing', meaning 'drawing from the mew':

'. . . It is necessarie that you take of her old jessis, and put her on a paire both new and strong that they may if it be possible continue and last untill the time of her drawing . . .'.

MEW, In   (obs.) In the MEWS to moult, in:

'Iff ye love wele yowre hawke. kepe her wele. and put hir nott late in mewe....' – 1486[5].

Otherwise (depending on context), simply 'in the mews'.

MEW A HAWK   See MOULT A HAWK.

MEW AT THE GRATE   See MOULT A HAWK.

MEW AT THE STOCK   (or **THE STONE**) See MOULT A HAWK.

MEWED   See MEW (vb).

MEWED, Clean   See MOULTED, Clean.

MEWED HAWK   See HAWK, Mewed.

MEWER   (unc., obs.) A moulting hawk, or one ready for the moult.

MEWING   See MEW (vb).

MEWS   (French *muer* = to moult, from Latin *muto* = to alter, change. Singular, of plural form, as in quarters.) Historically, quarters where hawks are kept during the moult, or a complex of rooms, one or more being set aside for hawks during their moult. Today, in the context of falconry, mews is usually applied loosely to indoor quarters for housing hawks. An obsolete form is MEW. Hawk house or hawk-house is an alternative and is sometimes met with currently.

MEWS, King's   The King's Mews was for centuries located near Charing Cross in London. Until Henry VIII's reign it housed the royal hawks, but the birds were removed to make way for King Henry's stud of horses when the Royal Stables in Bloomsbury were destroyed by fire. The present Royal Mews at Buckingham Palace is a mews in one of its altered senses: in this case, a complex of buildings grouped round a quadrangle. Described as some of the finest stabling in existence, it houses most of the State carriage horses, the Gold State Coach and other ceremonial coaches, and old and modern wheeled transport. FR[69].

MEWS, Royal   See preceding entry.

MEWTE   Obsolete spelling of MUTE.

MEWTING; MEWTINGS   See MUTES.

MEWTS   Obsolete spelling of MUTES.

MILAN   (obs.) (French *milan*. Old French *milan royal* = the red kite. Other obs. forms in OED: MYL(L)AN (15th C.), MYLLAINE (16th C.).) The kite.

MILION; MILLION   See MYLION.

MOLLEN   A notable family of Dutch falconers and hawk-trappers from Valkenswaard near Eindhoven in Holland. Valkenswaard was famous for its falconers and the hawks on passage they trapped and sold on to European and British falconers and hawking clubs.

'The village of Falconswaerd ... has for many years furnished falconers to the rest of Europe. I have known many falconers in England, and in the service of different princes on the Continent; but I never met with one who was not a native of Falconswaerd.' – 1826[75].

MONEL   An alloy used in bell-making. More in BELL (n.).

MOOR-BIRD   The red grouse; see GROUSE, Red.

MOOR-COCK   The blackcock; see BLACK-GAME.

MOOR-FOWL; MOOR-GAME   See GROUSE, Red.

MOOR-HEN; MOORHEN; WATER-HEN; WATERHEN (Moor perhaps form of *mere* = a pool or stretch of standing water.) *Gallinula chloropus*, a fresh waterfowl sometimes hunted by British austringers. Moorhen is also an occasional vernacular name for the female red grouse.

MOULT   (vb) (From Latin *muto* = to alter, change.) To shed and replace feathers. Moulting is (with the hawks in falconry) annual and lasts usually no more than six months, from spring through to late summer or autumn. There are sequences in which major and minor feathers are shed. The major feathers of the wings and the tail-feathers are usually dropped in matching pairs. A primary on the left wing, for example, is dropped within a short time of the corresponding feather on the right wing; the two central tail-feathers, known as the deck feathers, are shed within a short time of one another, as often are a pair of primaries and a pair of tail-feathers. More will not be shed until the new feathers are part-grown. The timing and length of the moult (as well as the order in which the feathers are dropped) vary somewhat from species to species and from moult to moult. The moult can even be manipulated with diet, altered light patterns (day-lengths, photoperiods) ambient temperature, and with modern drugs. Most falconers' birds will complete or almost complete their moult (that is, shed and replace all or most of their feathers) in one season.

MOULT (n.) See MOULTS.

MOULT, Fly through the See MOULT A HAWK.

MOULT, The A hawk's yearly cycle of feather replacement, or the period during which a hawk moults.

MOULT A HAWK; MEW A HAWK (now unc.) Of a falconer, to put a hawk into the mews for the duration of her moult. Historically and usually during this period, hawks have been kept loose in a spacious, airy room in semi-isolation from Man, neither manned nor flown and only visited to give them food and water to bathe in. In old texts, a loft is sometimes specified as a suitable site.

> 'Who so puttyth his hawke in mewe in the begynnyng of Lentyn [Lent]. if she be kepit as she awth to be. she shall be mewed. in the begynnyng of Auguste.' – 1486[5];

and (ibid.), summarizing a discourse on the hawk's condition at the time of her moult, and on feeding:

> 'Bot who so will that an hawke endure and mew kyndli. myn councell is that she be not to high noder to low. noder in grete destresse of hungre. bot like as she wolde flee best....'.

This might be paraphrased: 'He who wishes a hawk to [?]fare and moult well, my counsel is that she is neither too high nor too low in condition, nor very hungry, rather that she is in the condition in which she would fly best....'

However:

> 'With care ... hawks can be flown at all stages of the moult, especially at quarry, such as game, which they are very fond of, and at which they can be used when in very high condition.' – 1892[47].

This is known as flying a hawk through the moult; the high condition encourages a satisfactory moult. Turbervile (1575[81]) writes of 'mewing [a falcon] at the stock, or the stone'. According to his description, this is moulting her indoors tethered to a stone block which tapers from bottom to top and is 'a Cubite high'; a cubit is usually 18–22 inches (45.72–55.88cm.), a measurement derived from the length of the human forearm. The perch is set on a table with a tray top filled with sand among which are pebbles suitable as RANGLE. In the Blome version of mewing at the stock (1686 [1929][9]), the hawk is tethered short to a mound of turfs. In Turbervile, an alternative is to 'mewe [her] at the Grate', when she is taken on the fist every day to check on her health, carried in the fresh air, and called to the lure. The definition of grate is as yet uncertain but may be an arrangement of horizontal slats or laths on which the hawk perches or on which her perch is set.

MOULTED Describes a hawk which has moulted or has completed her first moult; more in MOULTS. Unmoulted (now unc. or obs.) is usually applied to a hawk in her first year, before her first moult.

MOULTED, Clean; MOULTED CLEAN (unv.) The state in a hawk which has finished her moult.

> 'The whole process [of the moult] takes six months to complete, or even longer, before a hawk has become clean moulted.' – 1936 [1970][8].

In Cox (1677[25]), the obsolete 'clean mewed' means the same. To Michell (1900[59]), clean moulted describes a hawk which has not only finished her moult but has replaced every feather, the latter case not necessarily being the outcome of the former:

> '... Most falconers consider it rather a feather in their cap to have their hawks "clean moulted," that is to say, with a complete suit of new feathers on their bodies.'

Harting (1898[40]) remarks that, as quarry, larks are '... good fliers, especially if clean moulted ...'.

MOULTS The number of moults a hawk has had is sometimes used to indicate her age or the period of her captivity. As well as simply being a hawk which has completed her moult, a moulted or mewed hawk can be a hawk in her second year, having moulted once; a hawk of one, two or three moults is in her second, third or fourth year. 'Mews' has occasionally been met with instead of 'moults' in this context, but is obsolete. This formula is rarely if ever used today.

MOUNT; MOUNT UP Of a falcon, to ascend in flight towards her PITCH, or to pursue quarry in an upward direction. Sometimes to mount is (of quarry) to ascend in flight, as with a skylark in lark-hawking.

MOUNT, At the (obs.); **AT THE SOUCE** (1486, obs.); **AT (THE) SOUSE** (obs.); **AT THE SOWCE** (1618, obs.); **AT SOURCE** (1575, obs.) (Souce, its forms, and source all imply rising; cf. Old and Modern French *sourdre* = to rise, spring, etc.) These idioms appear to be applied particularly in the context of flying a hawk at rising quarry. Quarry 'at souse' or 'at the souse' is in the act of rising from the ground. Of the (in this case short-winged) hawk herself:

> 'Iff yowre hawke nym [takes] the fowle a lofte: ye shall say she toke it at the mounte or at the souce.' – 1486[5].

Latham (1618[50]), rebuking himself for having encouraged his goshawk to make so many short slips at partridge that she refuses this quarry when it is at a distance, writes:

> '... I began to call to minde and consider of her ill nature, and also of my owne foolish and former error, how that I had too long at first taught her to snatch and catch them up at the sowce, and nuzled her too much therein* ...'.

*These last words might be paraphrased: 'caused her to become wedded to these short slips'; also see NUZZLE. 'The source' (obs.) is used by Turbervile (1575[81]) in the context of flying falcons from the fist at rising or mounting quarry:

> 'There is yet another kynde of flight to the field which is called the great flight, as to the Cranes, wilde Geese ... Hearons, and many other suche lyke, and these you maye flee from the fiste, whiche is properly tearmed the Source.'

Turbervile also uses the obsolete term 'at source' (apparently meaning 'as they rise') when writing of flying a goshawk at wild geese:

> '... The Falconer shall ryde after [the hawk] apace, and strike upon his Tabarde [tabor, drum], untill hee rayse the Wildegeese. And if his hawke seaze any of them at Source, he shall quickely succoure hir, and rewarde hir, &c.'

Note: In OED, noun 'source' is (in an obsolete sense) the act of rising on the wing, on the part of a hawk or other bird (1612); also in OED, verb 'source' is (in an obsolete sense), of a bird of prey, to rise *after* seizing its quarry. The second of these is as yet unverified as authentic to falconry.

MOUNT, On the ([?]obs.) Of a falcon, ascending in flight.

MOUNT ALOFT UPON THE MARK See MARK, Fly to.

MOUNTEE; MOUNTEE, At the See MOUNTY.

MOUNTEE, Hawk of the See MOUNTY.

MOUNTIE See MOUNTY.

MOUNT UP See MOUNT.

MOUNTY (obs); **MOUNTIE** (obs.); **MOUNTEE** (obs.) The mounting flight of (usually) a falcon, or the action of her rising in flight; also occasionally the pitch itself, that is, the height attained and kept by her.

> '... As I take it the *Hearne* [heron], and the stately flight, and mountie thereunto is the thing for the which these *Hawkes* [gyrfalcons] are most accounted off, and desired in these daies ...' – 1615[49].

This writer also uses the phrase 'clime to the mounty', which in effect means mount to her pitch. Basing his comments on hearsay, Turbervile (1575[81]) reports ('if it bee trewe') that 'the great Turke' flew eagles in a cast, and describes the highest-flying of the two as being 'at the mountee, a very stately pitche'. Michell (1900[59]) has 'hawks of the mountee' as a name for long-winged game- or duck-hawks; this is obsolete.

MOUSTACHE(S) See next entry.

MOUSTACHIAL STRIPE; MALAR STRIPE (Malar = pertaining to the cheek. Also MOUSTACHE(S) (lay and inf.).) The stripe, more or less pronounced, of darkly marked feathers which tapers downwards from the region of the eye in many species of falcon.

MURZALET See CARRY-FIST.

MUSKET The male SPARROWHAWK.

MUSKET-HAWK Obsolete name for the male SPARROWHAWK.

MUSKYTE Obsolete spelling of musket, the male SPARROWHAWK.

MUTE (Old French *meutir*. Obs. spelling: MEWTE (1575[81]). Obs. forms: MUTESS(E), MUTISE, others, also METESE, which may be an error (all 1486[5]).) Historically, of hawks in general: to expel droppings; today usually said of falcons in particular. Berners, writing on short-winged hawks in the 15th century[5], states:

> '... Ye shall say yowre hawke mutessith or mutith and not sklysith*.'

*In OED, sklice is a form of slice; therefore the Berners statement contradicts the traditional understanding that to slice is an idiom applied solely to short-winged hawks. See MUTES, and SLICE. In the Latham glossary (1615[49]):

> 'Dropping is when a *Hawke* muteth directly downeward**, in severall drops, and jerketh it not longwaies from her§.'

**As does a falcon;
§as does a short-winged hawk. Neither 'dropping' nor 'droppings' is used by falconers today. 'Muting', also from the Latham glossary, appears to be a noun in:

> '*Muting* is the excrements or order [ordure] which comes from *Hawkes*, and containeth both dunge and urine.'

MUTE, A See next entry.

MUTES (Obs. spelling: MEWTS (1686 [1929])[9]. Obs. forms: MUTINGS (1898[40]), MEWTINGS (1856[76]), probably MUTING and MEWTING.) The droppings (faeces and concentrated urine) of a hawk, historically both long- and short-winged. For the forcefully and almost horizontally discharged excrement of a short-winged hawk, SLICINGS is an alternative.

'It is an Indian saying that "When carried instead of two mutings it makes three".' – 1908 ft.⁶⁸,

suggesting that a hawk defecates more frequently when carried. 'A mute' ('two mutes', etc.) may be either the product (1619⁶) or the action of verb MUTE, and is correct currently in both senses.

MUTESS(E)   Obsolete form of MUTE.

MUTING; MUTINGS See MUTES.

MUTISE   Obsolete form of MUTE.

MYLION (1575⁸¹, obs.) (Also spelt MYL(L)YON, MILION and MILLION; all 1575⁸¹, all obs. Cf. Latin *millio* = a kind of hawk.) An unidentified kind of hawk, but according to Turbervile (1575⁸¹) it is a falcon which (like the gyrfalcon) is flown at such as herons and kites; compare MILAN (obsolete name for the kite).

MYLYON; MYLLYON See preceding entry.

NAMES   1 This is a simplified list of the most frequently occurring names for hawks taken from the wild for use in falconry, according to their age and development. As will be seen from the expanded entries in their alphabetical places in *The Encyclopedia*, definitions may vary according to the views of different authorities. The list, chronologically arranged, precludes shades of meaning and concentrates on basic and broadly-accepted definitions.

   EYASS. A nestling hawk, unable to fly; a young wild hawk taken from the eyrie.
   BOWER (obs.) A young short-winged hawk when she first leaves the eyrie and clambers onto boughs.
   BRANCHER. A young short-winged (later also broad-winged) hawk which is able to hop or make experimental flights from branch to branch, perhaps venturing from tree to tree, but has not yet left the immediate vicinity of the eyrie.
   RAMAGE HAWK (obs.). A young hawk, either about to leave or having left the vicinity of the eyrie.
   SORE HAWK (now unc.). A hawk in immature plumage; a hawk of the first year, hunting for herself and yet to have her first moult.
   PASSAGE HAWK; PASSAGER. A wild hawk, strictly the peregrine falcon, still in her immature plumage, trapped on her first southward migration.
   HAGGARD. A wild-caught hawk taken in full adult plumage or after she has moulted once in the wild state.

Note: In the United Kingdom, 1988 saw the general end to the taking of wild hawks under licence for the purposes of falconry. The current official view is that there is sufficient supply of captive-bred hawks to meet the demands of falconers. It might be said therefore that in the U.K. the terms brancher, passage hawk, sore hawk, and haggard should be considered obsolescent. However it is almost certain that falconers there will perpetuate some or all of these names when referring to wild hawks. The term eyass is already used for a captive-bred nestling, and brancher might well survive as the name for a captive-bred short- or broad-winged hawk at the next stage of her development.

NAMES   2 For the purposes of comparison with English terms, this is a list of French names for wild hawks according to the season in which they are caught; it is recorded by Charles d'Arcussia in his French treatise *Fauconnerie* (1605). Translated, simplified, and with new annotations in square brackets, it is:

   Niais. A hawk taken in May.
   Gentil. Taken in June, July or August.
   Pelerin or *passager*. Taken from September to December.
   Antenere, *antannaire*, or *antevere* [(?)misspelling]. Taken in January, February, or March. [Clearly a hawk of the previous year: cf. French *antan* = (in an obs. sense) last year. The slight

similarity to LANTINER is probably coincidental.]

Agar. After her first moult. [Note similarity to HAGGARD.]

NAMES 3 The most famous version of the list of 'all manner of hawks and to whom they belong' (allocating particular hawks to different ranks or classes of people) is appended to the hawking section of *The Boke of St Albans*[5], first published in 1486. It is the view of Hands[37] that the list (which in similar form pre-dates *The Boke of St Albans*) was probably never intended to be taken seriously and that its 'impractical artificial hierarchy'[37] was not observed. It may well be fruitless, therefore, to look for much of significance in it, while acknowledging that it was compiled by someone at some time for some purpose. FR.[37] This is the list, somewhat edited, with new annotations in square brackets:

'And now foloys the naamys of all maner of hawkys & to whom they belong.

Theys haukes belong to an Emproure.
Theys be the names of all maner of hawkes. First an Egle. a Bawtere. a Melowne.... And theis be not enlured. ne reclaymed. by cause that thay be so ponderowse to the perch portatiff*. And theis.iii.by ther nature belong to an Emprowre.'

[This passage is puzzling. *It is tempting to wonder if the hidden concept here might be: '. . . Eagles are not called to or carried on the fist because of their weight but are transported on a portable perch such as a crutch.' 'Bawtere' may be an error for vawtere = vulture, '. . . or by transposition of letters for BAWRET' (OED); this last seems improbable, but see BAWREL. The vulture has no connection with falconry. 'Melowne' is uncertain, but Hands[37] suggests it is probably kite: cf. French *milan* = the kite; Old French *milan royal* = the red kite. Historically, the kite has been quarry, not a falconer's bird.]

'**Theis hawkes belong to a kyng.**
Ther is a Gerfawken. a Tercell of a gerfauken. And theys belong to a kyng.'

[These are gyrfalcon and jerkin, female and male gyrfalcon.]

'**For a prynce.**
Ther is a Fawken gentill. and a Tercell gentill. and theys be for a prynce.'

[See FALCON GENTLE.]

'**For a duke.**
Ther is a Fawken of the rock. And that is for a duke.'

[As a prince (preceding) is assigned peregrines, and an earl (following) a peregrine, 'Fawken of the rock' is doubtless also peregrine, but the significance of the name, therefore the hawk's precise

'The naamys of all maner of hawkys & to whom they belong.' Part of the famous list from the hawking section of The Boke of St Albans (1486).

identity, is unknown. Compare 'I know her spirits are as coy and wild as haggards of the rock' (William Shakespeare, *Much Ado About Nothing*).]

'**For an Erle.**
Ther is a Fawken peregryne. And that is for an Erle.'

[See FALCON, Peregrine.]

'**For a Baron.**
Also ther is a Bastarde and that hauke is for a Baron.'

[The significance of 'Bastarde' is uncertain, although (in this context) it has been taken to mean cross-bred hawk. It is worth noting that odd colouration in a hawk was often interpreted by medieval falconers to be the result of wild hybridization.]

'**Hawkes for a knyght.**
Ther is a Sacre and a Sacret. And theis be for a knyght.'

[These are saker and sakret, female and male saker falcon.]

'**Hawkis for a Squyer.**
Ther is a Lanare and a Lanrell. And theys belong to a Squyer.'
['Lanrell' is clearly a misspelling of lanrett; these are lanner and lanneret, female and male lanner falcon.]
'**For a lady.**
Ther is a Merlyon. And that hawke is for a lady.'
[This is merlin.]
'**An hawke for a yong man.**
Ther is an Hoby. And that hauke is for a yong man. And theys be hawkes of the towre . . .'
[This is hobby. Where met with in other instances, a hawk of the tower is a falcon, which when hunting habitually mounts or rings up and waits on. It seems that here the term is to apply to hobby as well as the other falcons in the list.]
'**And yit ther be moo kyndis** [more kinds] **of hawkes.**
Ther is a Goshawke. and that hauke is for a yeman. Ther is a Tercell. And that is for a powere man.'
['Goshawke' = female goshawk; 'yemen' = yeoman; 'Tercell' = tiercel (male) goshawk. It is misleading that the goshawk, with which much of the Berners treatise deals, has been relegated to the yeoman and the tiercel goshawk to the poor man; there is evidence that, in Tudor and pre-Tudor times, this most capable of hunters (the female at least) saw much broader use across the classes than the list suggests.]
'Ther is a Spare hawke. and he is an hawke for a prest. Ther is a Muskyte. And he is for an holiwater clerke.'
['Spare hawke' = sparrowhawk (despite being 'he', this is taken to be the female); 'prest' = priest; 'Muskyte' = musket (male sparrowhawk); 'holiwater clerke' = holy-water clerk, a lowly attendant in church ritual who carried the vessel containing holy water.]
Note: 'A kestrel for a knave' appears in a list in a Harleian MS in the British Library.

NAMES, Scientific   In the binomial system of classification, employing the generic and specific names (example *Accipiter gentilis*, the goshawk), the first indicates the genus; the second identifies the species and distinguishes one living thing from another within the genus. Correctly, these should be followed by the originator of the name and the date of naming; this is now often ignored. In the trinomial system, employing generic, specific and subspecific names (example *Accipiter gentilis atricapillus*, the American goshawk), the subspecific name identifies a subspecies or race. A rule is that the subspecific name of the species upon which a particular group of living things is founded must be a repeat of the specific name (an example is *Accipiter gentilis gentilis*, the European goshawk), whereby it is readily discernible as the nominate subspecies.

Tautonyms (same names), as in *Buteo buteo*, the common buzzard, come about as a result of a change at some time in the generic name: an obsolete scientific name for this hawk is *Falco buteo*. The nominate subspecies (Eurasia) is *Buteo buteo buteo*. A scientific name is not necessarily appropriate or relevant and the original intended significance is sometimes obscure or lost; but each complete name is unique, thereby identifying precisely a particular living thing. A scientific (sometimes called a Latin) name may contain words formed from both the Latin and the Greek.

NAME-TAG; NAME-PLATE   A lightweight identity plate, slotted onto one jess, bearing name, address and telephone number of the hawk's owner. Less cumbersome methods of identification are preferred today, such as engraving the bell or marking the radio transmitter. VARVELS (no longer in use) often bore the name or coat of arms of the hawk's owner.

NAPE   The back of a hawk's neck.

NAREL; NARELL   See next entry.

NARES   (Latin *naris*, Old French *narel* = a nostril. From a French and English dictionary (1611[23]): '*Nareau*, a narell, or nosethrill'. Obs. English (singular) form: NAREL; plural 'narellis' (1486[5]).) A hawk's nostrils or nasal passages.
'The Hoolis in the hawkes beke bene callede the Nares.' – 1486[5].

NIAISE   (obs.) Form of nyas:
'A Niaise is a young Hawke, tane crying out of the nest.' – 1616 marginal note[46].
See EYASS.

NIARD   Form of nyas; see EYASS.

NIAS(E)   Spelling of nyas; see EYASS.

NICTITATING MEMBRANE   (Sci. *membrana nictitans*.) The opaque third or inner eyelid in birds which cleans and moistens the cornea. It usually closes to protect the eye at the moment a hawk strikes her quarry.

NIDE   See EYE.

NOBLE   See under FALCONS, Noble.

NOBLE FALCONS   See FALCONS, Noble.

NOMME   (obs.) (Taken to be related to old lay verb nim (nym, nymme) = to take, steal, filch.) Of a hawk, to take or BIND TO (quarry).

'And if yowre hawke Nomme a fowle. and the fowle breke a way fro hir. she hath discomfet many federes of the fowle. and is brokyn a way. for in kyndeli spech ye shall say youre hawke hath Nomme or seesid a fowle and not take it.' – 1486[5].

Note: In this difficult passage, it may be that a negative is lacking in both 'the fowle breke a way' and 'is brokyn a way'[37]. This would seem to be so, on consideration of the next passage in the same text; for that, see RIFLER. The above might tentatively be adjusted to:

'And if yowre hawke Nomme a fowle. and the fowle breke not a way fro hir. she hath discomfet [disordered] many federes of the fowle. and is not brokyn a way. for in kyndeli [kindly, proper] spech ye shall say youre hawke hath Nomme or seesid [seized] a fowle and not take it.'

NOOK   See TOOTH.

NORWAY FALCON; NORWEGIAN See GYRFALCON.

NOTCH   See TOOTH.

NOTCHED   See EMARGINATION.

NOTE; NUT See PREEN GLAND.

NOUSEL(L); NOUSLE Forms of NUZZLE.

NOUSLED   See NUZZLE.

NOWSEL(L)   Form of NUZZLE.

NUT   See PREEN GLAND.

NUZZELL; NUZLE Spellings of NUZZLE.

NUZZLE (obs.) (Alternative spellings and forms: NUZZELL and NUZLE (both 1618[50]), NOWSEL (1575[81]), NOWSELL (1688), NOUSEL(L), NOUSLE; all obs.) Of a falconer or of the circumstances arranged by him, to accustom (a hawk) to taking quarry with enthusiasm, in the following instance towards the end of her reclamation:

'. . . Let her kill some two or three more [live trains*], it will so nuzzell her, as that shee wil not after misse the wilde Rooke or any other thing you shall after this manner make her unto.' – 1618[50].

*See TRAIN 2 (n.).

'Nowsell, to entize or inure the Hawk to love to fly at her Prey.' – 1688[43].

Turbervile (1575[81]) uses the phrase 'perfectlye nousled and in bloud' to mean in effect (of the hawk) full of vigour and thoroughly accustomed to taking quarry. Also see 1618 qu. in MOUNT, At the.

NYAS (obs.); **NYESS** (obs.) (For etymology and alternative spellings and forms, see EYASS.) A nestling hawk; an eyass. Used adjectivally (also obsolete) in such as 'Nyasse Hawke' (1575[81]) and in:

'How to keepe Nyasse Sparowhawkes.' – 1575 chap.hdg[81].

NYASSE (adj.) See preceding entry.

NYE   See EYE.

NYESS   Form of NYAS.

OIL The secretion from a hawk's PREEN GLAND.

OIL GLAND   See PREEN GLAND.

OIL HERSELF (unc.); **ENOIL HERSELF** (obs.) (Enoil = (in an obs. lay sense) to anoint.) Of a hawk while preening, to transfer oil from her PREEN GLAND to her feathers, using her beak. Having offered a hawk a bath:

'. . . If she did jumpe to the water, I would have something in my fist ready to shew her, when she made shew of comming from the water; which should make her ever after, when shee had done, looke for the fist, where she should dry, prune [preen], and oyle her selfe . . .' – 1619[6].

The hawk, having bathed, might

'. . . rejoyce* by enoyling hir after the water, before she flee againe.' – 1575[81].

*Show her contentment.

OSTRAGER; OSTREGER; OSTREGIER Obsolete forms of AUSTRINGER.

OSTRINGER Obsolete spelling of AUSTRINGER.

OVERHAWKED (obs.); **OVER-HAWKED** (obs.) Of a falconer, in the position of keeping or attempting to keep too many hawks:
> 'Probably the commonest fault in young falconers of the modern school is that of keeping too many hawks. Almost every writer on the subject has warned them over and over again against this rage for being "over-hawked"; and yet it is still the cause of endless failures, disappointments, and disasters.' – 1900[59].

OWLS   See EAGLE OWL.

P

PACK   (n.) A gathering or family of grouse.

PACK   (vb) To collect together, said of grouse, partridges, etc.

PANEL(L)   See next entry.

PANNEL (obs.); **PANELL** (c.1575[38], obs.); **PANEL** (1678[67], obs.) (Origin obscure.) A hawk's stomach, or the lower bowel. The fundament or lower part of the alimentary canal of a hawk (OED).
> '*Pannel*, is the Pipe next the Fundament of a *Hawk* where she digesteth her meat from her body.' – 1677 gl.[25]

In one instance, apparently the VENT (or that region) of a long-winged hawk, corresponding to the brayle of a short-winged hawk; see 1611 qu. in FEATHERS, Brail.

PARABUTEO   (Prefix para- = (among other senses) alongside, close by, here apparently indicating a resemblance to genus *Buteo*.) A genus containing one species, *Parabuteo unicintus*; see HAWK, Harris'.

PARTRIDGE   (Latin *perdix*.) Common or Hungarian (*Perdix perdix*) and red-legged or French (*Alectoris rufa*), quarry in British partridge-hawking.

PARTRIDGE-HAWK   In North America, a vernacular name for the American goshawk. Also loosely in Britain, a hawk for flying partridge, as are the obsolete 'partridger' (1575[81]) and 'partringer' (1619[6]).

PARTRIDGE-HAWKING   See GAME-HAWKING under HAWKING, Categories of.

PARTRIDGER   See PARTRIDGE-HAWK.

PARTRINGER   See PARTRIDGE-HAWK.

PASSAGE   1 (n.) The migratory flight of wild hawks, on which they might be trapped. See HAWK, Passage.

PASSAGE   2 (n.) The regular flight or movement of wild birds (or quarry) to or from their feeding ground; or according to Salvin & Brodrick (1855[73]), it is:
> 'The flight of Herons to and from the Heronry during the breeding season.'

Wild birds (or potential quarry) moving thus might be described as, for example, passaging rooks.

PASSAGE   (adj.) See HAWK, Passage.

PASSAGE, On   Of a wild hawk, migrating. Sometimes of any wild bird, moving from point to point in the field.

PASSAGE-HAWK; **PASSAGEHAWK**   See HAWK, Passage.

PASSAGER   See HAWK, Passage.

PASSAGING   See PASSAGE 2 (n.).

PASSENGER   See HAWK, Passage.

PEARCH   Obsolete spelling of perch; see PERCHES.

PEG (obs.); **RING PEG** (1900[59], obs.) A peg of metal or wood, an eye at one end, sharp at the other. It is driven into the ground close to a hawk's perch outdoors, the leash tied to the eye. Hence 'pegging out' (see WEATHER). This arrangement seldom used today.

PEG, Ring   See preceding entry.

PEG OUT   See WEATHER.

PELF   (obs.) The remains of a kill after a hawk has fed upon it. See 1615 qu. in PILL (n.).

PELT   (obs.) A hawk's dead quarry; a kill. Or:

'*Pelt*, is the dead body of any fowle howsoever dismembered.' – 1615 gl.⁴⁹

Compare preceding entry and PILL (n.).

PEN (n., obs.); **PENNE** (obs.) (Latin *penna* = a feather.) Where met with in old hawking treatises, usually a primary feather in a hawk's wing, but may occasionally be any major feather of the wing or tail.

PEN (vb, obs.) Of a hawk of any age, to grow feathers; or of an eyass, to grow her first true feathers after the downy stage. In a discourse on 'How a man shall take an hawke fro the Eyrer [female parent]', the advice in Berners (1486⁵) is:

'... After when she begynnyth to penne. and plumyth. and spalchith. and pikith her selfe. putt hir in a cloose warme place. ...'.

The obsolete verbs plume, spalch and pike are all terms related to preening; see PREEN, SPALCH, and PICK.

PENNED (obs.) Feathered, as in tender penned, hard penned, and penned hard.

PENNED, Hard; HARD-PENNED; PENNED HARD (obs.) (Penned = feathered; Latin *penna* = a feather.) Traditional terms for the state (in an EYASS) of having her first true feathers (after the downy stage) fully grown and hard, and in a hawk at a later stage, having her feathers full-grown and hard after the moult. An alternative (current) idiom is HARD DOWN or hard-down.

PENNED, Tender (probably obs.) Literally means having delicate feathers and describes a hawk while her feathers are still developing and growing: feathers 'in the blood' (developing and supplied with blood) are soft, fragile and prone to damage. Traditionally a hawk is not manned or flown until her moult is finished; the manning of an EYASS does not begin until her first true feathers (after the downy stage) are full-grown and hard.

'And if yowre hawke be harde pennyd: she may be drawne [from the mews] to be reclaymed. For all the while that she is tender pennyd: she is not habull to be reclaymed.' – 1486⁵.

See preceding entry. Also see notes on flying a hawk through the moult in MOULT A HAWK.

PENNES See FEATHERS, Primary.

PENS See FEATHERS, Primary.

PERCH; PEARCH (obs.)

'*Pearch*, is any thing whereon you set your *Hawke*, when shee is from your fist.' – 1615 gl.⁴⁹

For the various designs and arrangements, see PERCHES.

PERCH, Go to (obs.) Of a hawk in the field, to find an elevated perch; also see STAND, Take. Bert (1619⁶) applies the term to quarry; in this case, it is a pheasant which 'goeth to pearch' while being chased by a goshawk. This author also uses the phrase 'take from perch', which means (of the hawk) to take perching quarry. He writes of

'The discommodities that I have met with in having my hawke take a Phesant from pearch ...'; for example, '... Many times shee hangeth of one side of the bough, having fast holde upon the Pheasant, and the Pheasant upon the other ...'.

PERCH, Take from See preceding entry.

PERCHES In broad terms, a design of perch is chosen bearing in mind the natural perching habits of a particular bird: an open-spaces wild peregrine or golden eagle might most frequently stand more or less flat-footed while at rest, whereas a woodland accipiter would have varying sizes of rounded boughs on which to perch. Inappropriate perching often leads to foot disorders in falconers' birds.

LAWN PERCH (probably recent). An unspecific term for a perch used outdoors.

BLOCK; BLOCK PERCH (rare); **BLOCK-PERCH** (rare). A perch chiefly but not exclusively for falcons. Traditionally, with some variations on the basic theme, it is cylindrical or conical with a flat top and usually made of wood, sometimes sandstone. If conical, it almost invariably tapers downwards, although some old texts mention the reverse; the downward taper allows a falcon's dropped (rather than squirted) mutes to fall to the floor rather than dribble down the sides and soil her brail feathers and train. It is sufficiently high at the top where she perches for her train to be clear of the ground. Materials for the top have been cork, sometimes fashioned into a low dome, and leather, but these are difficult to keep free of bacteria which may cause disease in hawks' feet. Sometimes the perch is left uncovered or, today, covered with synthetic turf, which is easily cleaned. The block is used outdoors and fixed into the ground with an integral steel spike. When used today, it may have a removable spike so that the perch can be screwed to a floor or onto a flat base and is therefore suitable for indoors and outdoors. The simplest arrangement for tethering the hawk has been to tie the leash with the falconer's knot to a staple driven

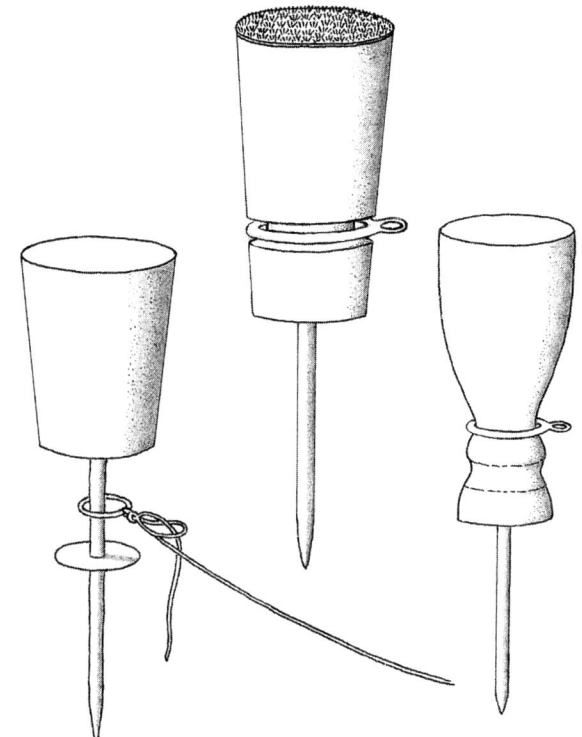

Types of falcon block in use today.

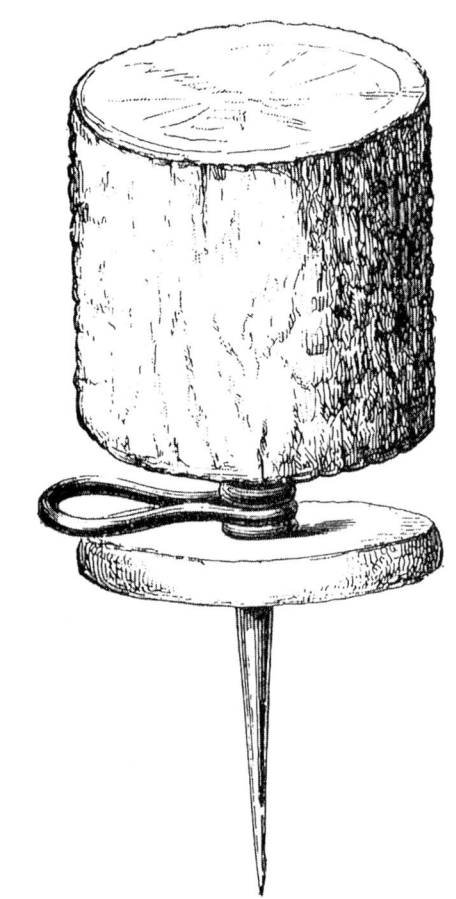

Described by J.E. Harting in his Hints on the Management of Hawks *(1898) as 'Studley's Patent Block'.*

A block with grooves cut into its top to allow rainwater to drain away. (From a late 19th century drawing).

into the top; invariably today, the falcon's block incorporates a free-moving ring of continuous steel to which the leash is tied. The downward tapering design was known to Emperor Frederick in 13th century Italy and used outdoors (sometimes indoors) for falcons (plate 25). It is termed (in transl.[35]) a block or stool; the latter is not authentic to the English language of falconry. It was made of wood or stone with a short iron spike for fixing into the ground. The ring (to which the leash was tied) was a separate component; it was a hoop of wood or metal, held loosely in place when the spike was driven through it and into the ground. Sometimes, with a stone block, the leash was tied to a peg in the ground. The Emperor notes that there were in use at that time stone stools which were quadrangular rather than conical; he dismisses these because of the likelihood of the leash becoming snagged on the sharp corners. Turbervile (1575[81]) writes of 'mewing [a falcon] at the stock, or the stone'. This is moulting her indoors tethered to a block 'a Cubite high', tapering upwards; it is set on a table with a tray top filled with sand. The description of how she was tethered to it is set down thus:

> 'Then take a small corde of the bignesse of a bowstring, or little more, put it through a ring, and binde it about the stone, in suche sorte that the ring or swyvle may go rounde about the stone, without any stoppe or lette . . .'.

Michell (1900[59]) uses the term 'field block' (ibid. also written 'field-block') for a block which is carried with the falconer into the field. For more idioms associated with the block, see WEATHER.

ARAB (or **ARABIAN**) **PERCH.** Used by Arab falconers for a falcon, sometimes seen in the West, and functionally similar to the block. It has a flat circular padded top for perching set on a slender turned pedestal shod with a spike for driving into the ground. Traditionally it has no ring, the leash being tied to the pedestal; when used by Western falconers, a metal ring may be fitted to the pedestal. Arab perches (as used by Arab falconers) are often ornate (plate 35).

BOW PERCH; BOW-PERCH. An upright arch-shaped perch mainly for short-winged hawks. It is sufficiently high at the apex where the hawk perches for her train to be clear of the ground. In a simple (but obsolete) form it is a curved or bent bough, its sharpened ends pushed into the ground. It might be

> '. . . a sapling of ash or hazel, steeped in hot water, and bent into the form of a bow, being held securely in position by a piece of strong wire, fixed across the tangent of the bow. The two ends of the wood should be shod with iron spikes, for fixing it into the ground.' – 1936 [1970][8].

Alternatively, it can be a naturally or artificially curved bough (or now a length of plastic piping) fitted into sockets on a steel frame which incorporates two steel spikes; or it may be metal throughout. A modern bow perch might have, instead of spikes, heavy feet, or interchangeable spikes and feet, making it suitable for outdoors or indoors. A continuous metal ring (to which the hawk's leash is tied) slides freely from one side of the bow to the other as the bird moves. The apex of the bow, once wrapped with

Male goshawk on bow perch (G.E. Lodge). *The perch has modifications said to be by F.H. Salvin. It is of iron, and has three spikes, the one in the centre twice as long as the others. The padded top is covered with leather. The fan-like cross-struts are to prevent the hawk passing through the hoop and tangling her leash. But because the ring (attached to a strut) cannot slide from one side of the perch to the other, the leash may still foul. The design is obsolete.* (Courtesy the Tryon and Swan Gallery).

(among other materials) linen, cotton or canvas, now may be wound with cord or padded with synthetic turf. In a modification rarely if ever seen today, the space beneath the bow is almost entirely filled with a textile screen held taut on a bow-shaped frame, leaving only a gap to allow the ring to slide unhindered. The system reduces the risk of the hawk tangling her leash by passing through the bow (plate 21). Falconer and author F.H.Salvin is said to have devised another modification to the bow perch. It has three spikes, the one in the centre twice as long as the others, the top lightly padded and covered with saddler's leather. Four cross-struts arranged in a fan prevent the hawk passing through the bow and tangling herself. There is no provision for the free movement of a ring[40]. The design is obsolete.

104 PERCHES

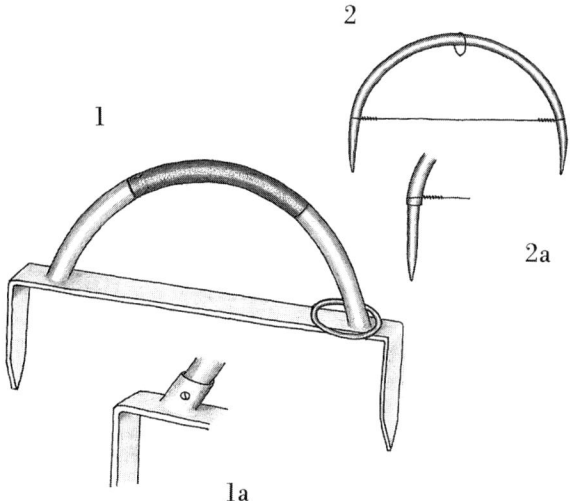

1: A version of the one-piece steel bow perch used in the modern pursuit; it is padded at the apex. 1a: An alternative design with sockets to accommodate a bent bough or a length of plastic piping. 2: A traditional bow perch, often made from a bent ash sapling or bough sharpened at the ends and braced with wire. 2a: A modification, using plastic piping and glued-in steel spikes for driving into the ground.

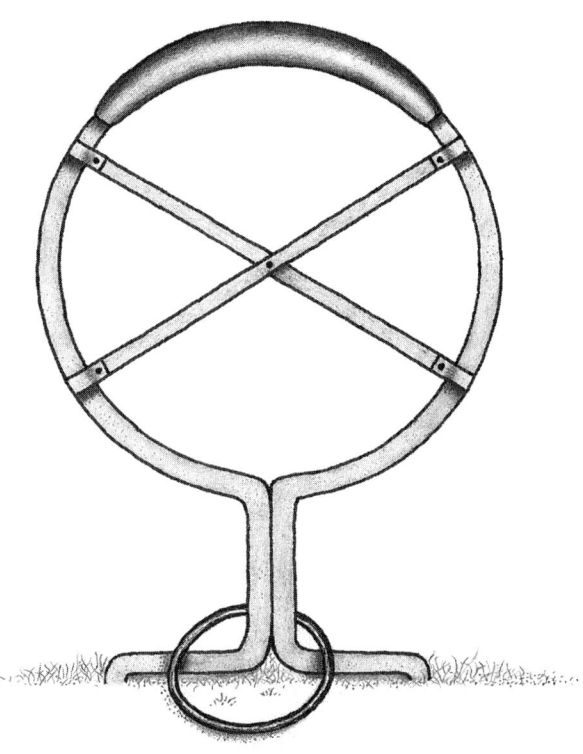

A ring perch, the two spikes driven into the ground.

RING PERCH. A circular steel perch (the circle in the vertical plane), padded at the top for comfortable perching. It has integral steel spikes for driving into the ground and a free-moving steel ring to which the leash is tied. To prevent the hawk passing through the circle and tangling her leash, strips (often of leather) are fastened across it. It is used mainly for short-winged hawks. Its origins are uncertain, but it appears to be an attempted improvement on the bow perch.

D-PERCH. A D-shaped (the curve uppermost) or elliptical perch, sometimes used for short-winged hawks, not dissimilar to the ring perch. It is built round a central steel pin which is driven into the ground. The perch itself is sometimes designed to rotate on the pin, theoretically preventing the leash from fouling.

ROUNDPERCH. A recent innovation of German falconer and animal painter Renz Waller (died 1979)[58]. It resembles a small drum when its outer sleeve of cloth or other material is fitted; perching for the hawk is on the top rim. It seems that the design never caught on.

T-PERCH (obs.). Presumed to be invariably made of wood, a simple upright with a horizontal cross-piece on which the hawk perches. This design (resembling a gardener's dibber, having a sharpened end for driving into the ground) is sometimes shown in the older printed English treatises. A similar pattern appears in old Oriental and sometimes European art. The painting *The Hawk* by Englishman Sir Edwin Landseer (1802–1873) depicts a falcon on a T-perch with a padded cross-piece; this is taken to be on a stand. Although so far unverified, a falconer may once have carried a small T-perch into the field in his hawking bag. Michell (1900[59]) names this pattern the 'crutch-perch' and illustrates it with a ring (to which the leash is tied) slipped loosely onto the upright. This writer suggests that

'Probably for an eagle it is the best resting-place that could be provided.'

SCREEN PERCH. For use indoors, a stand supporting a horizontal beam or pole, usually waist to breast height to the falconer; alternatively, the ends of the beam may be fixed to opposite walls. On it a hawk (or more than one hawk) is tethered short, her movements limited by the length of her jesses; the swivel is held at the top of the beam by the tightly tied leash. The screen perch knot is made by halving the leash at the

A design for a screen perch with various innovations, such as its collapsibility and the 'guyrope' for stability. (From J.E. Harting's Hints on the Management of Hawks, *1898).*

swivel, passing the two ends round the beam, tying a half bow underneath, and finally passing the two free ends through the loop of the bow to lock the knot. (The same kind of knot may be used for tethering a hawk to a cadge.) The knot cannot be tied with one hand, therefore the hawk is put on the perch first. From the beam hangs a screen (sometimes double) of such as hessian, weighted so that it is taut, or its lower corners attached to the stand. The screen allows the hawk to climb back up should she bate off and prevents her from attempting to recover the perch from the wrong side. A flat beam supporting the whole of the foot suits a falcon; for short-winged hawks, a beam or pole rounded in section is usual. Some falconers may vary the surface of the perch (in places smooth, uneven, hard, and padded), believing that a choice of surfaces is likely to keep a hawk's feet healthy. The screen perch is mistrusted by some latter-day falconers for reasons of welfare: should a

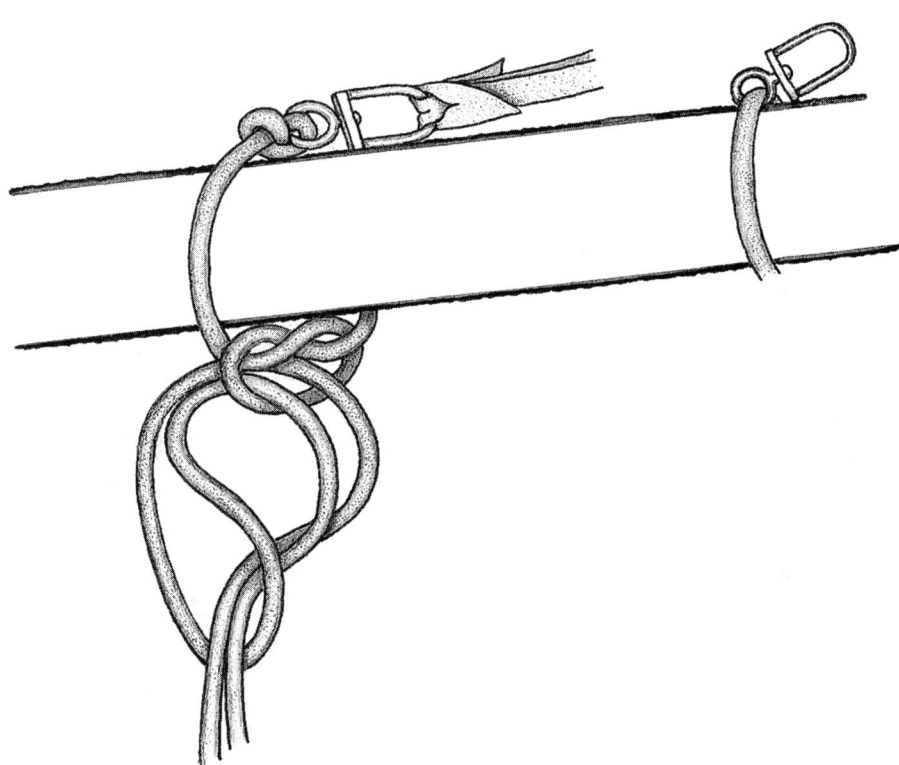

The usual screen perch knot; optional methods of holding the swivel to the top of the beam are shown.

hawk bate along the perch, she may break tail-feathers as they are forced either side of the beam, and the tips of primary feathers can be knocked off as she (a falcon) strikes her wing-tips on the beam while fanning. Hawks have been known to die by hanging upside-down from their jesses, not having found a way of climbing back up after bating off.

Mavrogordato[58] devised a modification to the screen perch to reduce the risk of tail and primary feather damage. A half-hoop or bow of round iron is fastened to the pole, raising the level of the perch in one place. The hawk is tethered as already described to the padded apex of the bow. The screen is extended to fill the space between the bow and the beam. Hawks choose to perch on the highest point and, he points out, dislike bating downwards.

HIGH AND LOW PERCHES (in transl.[35]; not English-language falconer's terms) are indoor perches, described in the 13th century by Emperor Frederick and shown in illustrations in his treatise. They are also termed (in transl.) racks, which again is not an authentic term. These were stands wide enough to accommodate a number of hawks. The high perch was a horizontal board 12 inches (30.48cm.) broad, laid flat and supported at eye-level on two pairs of legs (plate 26). The birds were tethered to the board, the varvels held tight to its top by the tied leash as is the swivel on the screen perch. The textile screen was apparently unknown to the Emperor. The cross-piece on a low perch was of round or squared wood and was of sufficient height that the hawk's tail was clear of the floor; a leash-length of 18 inches (45.72cm.) was allowed. The Emperor also used individual low perches of T-perch type.

SHELF PERCH. Used indoors for falcons, it is a flat shelf fixed to a wall and set just high enough for the hawk's train to be clear of the floor. It may be padded at a raised outer rim or covered on the whole upper surface with synthetic turf. The bird's leash is tied to a ring or eye under the shelf. A falcon will contentedly perch facing the wall, her tail out of harm's way over the rim. The shelf perch is used today, but not widely.

CAR-SEAT PERCH. A perch to slip over a car seat, with easily gripped perching at the top, a ring or eye to which to tie the leash, and perhaps a material such as hessian hanging down for the hawk to climb up and recover herself should she bate off. There are others arrangements for transporting a hawk in a vehicle such as the box cadge, or a scaled-down screen perch in the load-space of a van, or a travelling box.

MAKESHIFT PERCHES. Among those mentioned in old texts as temporary blocks are a stone, a turf mound, and an upturned flowerpot with the leash threaded through the hole and tied to a spike driven into the ground underneath it.

Also see TROLLEY.

PEREGRINE FALCON See FALCON, Peregrine.

PETTY SINGLE; PETTY SENGLE Under FOOT (n.).

PICK (obs.) (Other forms: PIKE, PYKE, perhaps PRICK; all obs.) Related to PREEN; perhaps form of peck. The phrase 'proine [preen] and picke' is used by Turbervile (1575[81]); 'picke' may refer to the boring action of a bird's beak while she is preening, or be related to the human application, as in:

'. . . And them that were lowsy and ful of vermyne he hym self wold pyke and make them clene.' – 1483[18].

Also see 1486 qu. in FEATHERS, Reform the.

PICK UP; TAKE UP To encourage (a hawk) to step willingly onto the fist from the perch, the lure or a kill. The terms may also be applied when an unmanned hawk is taken from her perch onto the fist against her will. Take up is sometimes used to mean to withdraw (a hawk) from the mews or from hack with a view to preparing her for hunting; this is probably obsolete.

PICK-UP PIECE (probably modern) A piece of meat with which to pick up a hawk; a piece of meat, held in the fist, used to tempt a hawk to step off a kill or the lure and onto the fist.

PIE (obs.) The magpie (*Pica pica*). More in MAGPIE-HAWKING under HAWKING, Categories of.

PIGEON HARNESS Under TRAPS AND TRAPPING.

PIGEON-HAWK See HAWK, Pigeon.

PIKE; PYKE Forms of PICK.

PILL (n., obs.) (Cf. peel = the skin of various things. Also PELF (obs.).) The remains of a kill (skin and inedible remnants) after a hawk has fed upon it:

> '*Pill*, and pelfe of a fowle, is that refuse and broken remaines which are left after the *Hawke* hath beene releived [relieved, fed].' – 1615 gl.⁴⁹

PILL   (vb, unv., obs.) To make prey of; or to pluck, pull at or tear (a kill, perhaps especially furred).

PINCHED FEATHER   See FEATHER, Pinched.

PINCHING OFF   See FEATHER, Pinched.

PINCH OUT   See FEATHER, Pinched.

PITCH   (n.); GATE (1575, obs.) The height which a falcon seeks then keeps while waiting on above the falconer, a POINT, or the spot where quarry lies.

> '*Stooping*, is when a *Hawke* being upon her wings at the height of her pitch, bendeth violentlie downe to strike the fowle or any other pray.' – 1615 gl.⁴⁹

The quality is often specified in the old treatises, such as in 'a lofty pitch' or 'a very stately pitche' (the latter, 1575⁸¹); today it might be a high or a low pitch. To fly at pitch ([?]obs.) is, of a falcon, to WAIT ON at the height from which she will stoop. The idiom 'pitch and stoop' has been met with describing the falcon's hunting technique of waiting on and stooping.

Pitch and the less common (now obs.) 'gate' are synonymous. The latter occurs in Turbervile (1575⁸¹; see qu. in RAKE AWAY), also in Latham (1618⁵⁰):

> 'It is not unknowne but that the best metled *Hawke* [falcon], and highest flier of any kinde, may bee abused and drawne downe farre from her wonted gate, as eyther with too much flying, or too hard feeding, as to be wearied . . .'.

The term 'place' is used to mean 'pitch' in scattered instances but is of doubtful authenticity as a falconer's term. A suggestion is that it was taken from William Shakespeare's line 'A falcon, tow'ring in her pride of place' in *Macbeth*. Note: Berners (1486⁵) uses 'pride' in the context of a hawk's tendency to soar, and it appears in this case to mean wildness or independence; the recommendation is to feed her on meat washed in the juice of fennel:

> '. . . and that shall take away that pride from hir and make hir to leve her sowryng whether she be lene or fatte.'

This last phrase might be taken to imply 'whatever her CONDITION in the future'.

PITCH   (vb) Of a short-winged hawk in the field, to fly up to (an elevated perch). Occasionally, the phrase 'pitch on (or onto) the ground' is met with.

PITCH, Fly at   See PITCH (n.).

PITCH AND STOOP   See PITCH (n.).

PITH   See FEATHER, Parts of a.

PLACE   See PITCH (n.).

PLOONGE, The   See PLUNGE, The.

PLUCK   Of a hawk, to tear off feathers or fur from a kill with her beak. The obsolete verb PILL may be to pull off fur in particular, but this is so far unverified. To plume is (of a hawk) to pluck feathers from a kill; more in PLUME 1 (vb).

PLUGGING   See IMP.

PLUMAGE   1 (obs.) (From Latin *pluma* = a small or downy feather.) The lay collective name for any bird's feathers; but see second 1486 qu. in MAIL (n.). Also, acccording to Berners (1486⁵),

> '. . . The feederis und[er] the wynges are plumage.'

PLUMAGE   2 (obs.) Casting (or roughage) in the form of small feathers with a hawk's food. An alternative spelling is in:

> '*Plummage* are small downie feather[s] which the Hawke takes, or are given her for casting.' – 1615 gl.⁴⁹

See CASTING 2.

PLUME   1 (n., obs.) (From Latin *pluma* = a small or downy feather.) According to Latham (1615 gl.⁴⁹), a hawk's plumage as a whole, with particular regard to the colouration and its perceived significance:

> '*Plume* is the generall colour or mixtures of feathers in a *Hawke*, which sheweth her constitution.'

In the text, this writer comments that in his view '. . . blanke Hawks . . .' are '. . . the kindest and lovingst hawkes of all others . . .';

'blanke' (French *blanc*) means white and is taken to signify paleness here; white in 'white hawk' is not the same (see HAWK, White). To Latham, certain

> '. . . kindes of aukeward quallities are for the most part found in your black* and swarthie plumed Hawkes . . .';

*taken to mean dark; and (ibid.):

> 'There is another kinde of *plumed Hawks*, between a blacke & a tawnie, as it were of a suddie [(?)muddy] colour, which be as great mettelled *Hawks* & as sprightfull [full of spirit] as can flie.'

Turbervile (1575⁸¹), quoting in translation from a French treatise (taken to be by Arthelouche de

Alagona[28]), records that colouration is a consideration when prescribing medicines, and that:
> '...The blancke Falcons are flegmaticke...',
> '...The blacke Falcons are melancholicke...', and 'The russet Falcons be of sanguine & chollericke complexion...'.

PLUME 2 (n.) The decorative tuft of small feathers and coloured wools on the top of the Dutch hood. More in PLUME under HOODS AND HOODING.

PLUME 1 (vb) Of a hawk, to pluck feathers from a kill. A less common, obsolete synonym is deplume (1856 gl.[76], 1900[59]). An obsolete spelling (for the act) occurs in the Latham glossary (1615[49]):
> '*Plumming*, is when a *Hawke* ceaseth [seizes] a fowle, and pulleth the feathers from the body.'

Berners (1486[5]) uses a verbal variant (which means feeds on as much as plucks) in 'the fowle that she plumyth on'. Note: The obsolete verb PILL may also mean to pluck, but perhaps especially furred quarry.

PLUME 2 (vb, obs.) To PREEN.

PLUME, Fly at See FLY AT FEATHER.

PLUMED Feathered, as in 'swarthie plumed *Hawkes*' – 1615[49]; fuller quote in PLUME 1 (n.)

PLUME ON See PLUME 1 (vb).

PLUMMAGE See PLUMAGE 2.

PLUMMING Obsolete spelling of pluming. See PLUME 1 (vb).

PLUNGE, The (obs.); THE PLOONGE (1575, obs.) Of waterfowl, the action of seeking refuge in water or, according to Turbervile (1575[81]), diving:
> '...For if it happen that a fowle beeing often stouped*, will not spring agayne, but will rather fall to diving (which Falconers call the ploonge) then must you take hir with dogges...'.

*Attacked by a stooping falcon.

PLY (obs., rare); PLIE (1575[81], obs., rare) A bend or crook, or the wrist joint, in a hawk's wing.
> 'The Ply, or bent of the Wing, is the middle joynt in the pinion.' – 1688[43].

PLYMME (unv., obs.) Perhaps related to the verb plume (in the sense of to pluck), but obliquely meaning to feed in:
> '...Let hir slee it [kill the quarry]. and plymme well uppon hir.' – 1486[5].

POINT (vb and n.) For these and all dog-related idioms and combination terms which include 'point', see DOGS IN HAWKING.

POINT, Make (probably obs.); **MAKE HER POINT** (obs.) Of a short- or long-winged hawk, to rise in the air, marking where quarry has gone into cover. Of a goshawk, Sebright (1826[75]) says:
> '...After having made his point, by rising perpendicularly in the air, he takes his stand upon a neighbouring tree.'

Writing on partridge-hawking with a falcon, Michell (1900[59]) notes:
> 'The hawk will mark it [the spot where quarry has put in]...by making her point, *i.e.* throwing up into the air over the spot, and she will wait on while you beat.'

POLE, Hawking (obs.); **POLE** (obs.) A pole, once used for vaulting ditches and brooks whilst out hawking. The lay equivalent may be 'leaping-pole'. There is an oft-told story of Henry VIII's pole snapping while vaulting a water-filled ditch. It is said that the hawking monarch would have drowned but for the quick action of the attendant, one Edmund Moody, who pulled him to safety.

POLE HAWK (obs.) A live hawk used as a decoy by trappers. More in DUTCH METHOD under TRAPS AND TRAPPING.

POLE LURING Under LURE (n. and vb).

POLE PIGEON (obs.) A live pigeon used as a lure by trappers. More in DUTCH METHOD under TRAPS AND TRAPPING.

POUCH See BAG, Hawking.

POULT (obs.) Of a hawk in the field, to seek out and catch domestic poultry.

POUNCE (unc., obs.) To take (quarry) with the talons or pounces; more in FOOT (n.).

POUNCES; POWNCES Under FOOT (n.).

POWDER-DOWN (Adopt. German *Puderdunen* (1840).) A particular kind of small feathers (down-plumules) which lie among the contour feathers of the grown bird and continually disintegrate to produce a fine grey or bluish powder which permeates the plumage, giving, it is presumed, some waterproofing. It is noticeable as a dusting on the outer surfaces of feathers; this effect is sometimes known as bloom.

PRAIRIE Popular shortening of prairie falcon; see FALCON, Prairie.

PRAIRIE FALCON See FALCON, Prairie.

PREEN (Apparently variant of prune = to trim (vines, etc.). Obs. spelling: PRENE, written 'preue', n inverted (1486[5]). Obs. forms: PROWNE (c.1450[10]), PROYNE (1486), PROINE (1575[81]), PREYNE (c.1575[38]), PRUNE. Also PLUME (obs.).) To tidy, dress and oil the feathers with the beak. Berners (1486[5]) says:

> '... Youre hawke proynith. and not pikith. and she pro[y]nyth not bot [preens only] whan she begynnyth at hir leggys. and fetcheth moystour like oyle. at hir taill. and bawmeth [(?)anoints] hir fete. & strikyth the federis of hir Wynges thorow her beke....'.

It is notable that early observers used different terms to describe the various ways they perceived a hawk cared for her feathers. PICK (variants pike, pyke and perhaps prick), reform the feathers (FEATHERS, Reform the) and SPALCH are associated with preening and are considered in their alphabetical places. Of them all, only preen survives, conceivably because it refers to the one act which correctly includes oiling the feathers with the secretion from the PREEN GLAND. The precise differences in sense in the obsolete terms are obscure, which makes the sentence which includes the phrase 'plumyth and spalchith and pikith her selfe' (1486[5]) difficult to interpret exactly.

PREEN AND PICK   See PICK.

PREEN GLAND; **OIL GLAND** (unc.); **NOTE** (obs.); **NUT** (unc., obs.) (Note and nut appear to derive from nut (the fruit), probably a reference to the preen gland's shape and size.) The uropygial gland (scientific term not used by falconers) at the upper base of the tail, lying roughly over the last vertebra. It produces an oily substance which a hawk transfers to her feathers with her beak whilst preening, for conditioning and waterproofing.

> '... And it is calde the note. than as she fetchis the oyle.' – 1486[5].

PRENE   Obsolete spelling of PREEN.

PREY   That which a wild hawk catches and feeds on. Correctly, a falconer's hawk takes quarry. Latham (1615[49]) enters both prey and quarry in his glossary of terms:

> 'Pray, is any thing that a *Hawke* killeth, and feedeth her selfe thereupon.'
> 'Quarrie, is taken for the fowle which is flowne at, and slaine at any time, especially when young *Hawkes** are flowne thereunto.'

*To particularize young hawks in this context is not usual.

PREYNE   Obsolete form of PREEN.

PRICK   Perhaps the same as PICK.

PRIDE   See note in PITCH (n.).

PRIMARIES   See FEATHERS, Primary.

PRINCIPALS; PRINCIPAL FEATHERS; PRINCIPAL-FEATHERS   See FEATHERS, Principal.

PROPORTIONS   Certain adjectives have been used to convey the proportions of a hawk. This archaic listing is in Berners (1486[5]):

> 'First ye shall say This is a fayr hawke. an hudge hauke. a longe hawke. a short thike hawke. & say not this is a grete hawke. also ye shall say this hauke has a large beke Or a shortt beke. and call it not bille. an hudge hede or a small hede fayre sesoned. ...'

Also (ibid.):

> 'This hawke has an hudge legge or a flat leg. or a rownde legge. or a faire enserid legge*.'

*This last phrase is considered in CERE.

PROINE; PROYNE   Obsolete forms of PREEN.

PROWNE   Obsolete form of PREEN.

PRUNE   Obsolete form of PREEN.

PULER   (obs.) (Apparently from vb pule = (in one sense) 'To pipe plaintively, as a chicken, or the young of any animal; also said of the cry of a kite.' – OED.) A fledgeling bird (lay). A rare falconry term, although used by Latham (1618[50]) in his treatise as a name for a young hawk ('*Eyas, Brancher,* and *Puler*'); he does not elaborate.

PULL   By itself: to feed. A growing eyass might be said to be old enough to pull for herself. It is used in 'pull through the hood', meaning to feed whilst hooded, and in 'pull at', which means to feed on (meat, tiring, etc.).

PULL AT   See preceding entry.

PULL THROUGH THE HOOD   See FEED THROUGH THE HOOD.

PURGES (obs.); **SCOURINGS** (obs.) Falconers of the past, much preoccupied with the cleanliness of their hawks' 'inward passages' (1618[50]), were keen on purges. These were often associated with the process of enseaming; see ENSEAM.

> 'Scouringes be good for mewed hawkes, or otherwyse for some foule lusty hawke for spede in thensayminge [the enseaming] ...' – c.1575[38].

The best scouring the anonymous writer of this text knew was a concoction of butter, beef marrow, sugar candy, saffron and chive.

PURSE   See BAG, Hawking.

PUT AWAY THE CROP   See CROP, Put over the.

PUT DOWN   (inf.) Of a falconer, to put (a hawk) on the perch. Also see SET DOWN.

PUT IN   1; **LAY IN** (1677 gl.[25], probably obs.) Of a hawk during a chase, to drive (quarry) into cover.

PUT IN   2 Of quarry during a chase, to go into cover, when it is said to be or have been put in or laid in (latter probably obsolete).

PUT-IN, The   (unc.) A development during a chase where quarry has been driven into cover.

PUT IN HER HEAD   See HOLD IN THE HEAD.

PUT OUT   Of falconer or his dogs, to drive (quarry) out of cover; of a member or members of the hawking party, to flush quarry by beating, driving, shouting, or (formerly) with the sound of drums. Members of the field or the dogs would put quarry out to (rather than for) the hawk. Turbervile (1575[81]) uses the obsolete 'lay out', which means the same.

PUT OVER   See CROP, Put over the.

PUT OVER THE CROP   See CROP, Put over the.

PUT UP   1 (vb) Of a falconer, to CAST OFF (a falcon) so that she might mount. Of an austringer, to throw off (a short-winged hawk) into a tree or to another elevated perch.

PUT UP   2 (vb) Of a falconer or his dogs, physically to flush, drive or startle (quarry) into flight; of members of the hawking party, to flush (avian quarry) by beating, driving, shouting, or (formerly) with the sound of drums.
'. . . Ye shall say put up a partriche.' – 1486[5].
Also (ibid.), the quarry might be put up:
'. . . Goo in to the felde. and let yowre spanyellis fynde a Covy of partrichys. and when thay be putt upp. and begynne to scatre. ye most have markeris to marke som of thaym. and then cowple up yowre houndys.'

PYKE; PIKE Forms of PICK.

QUARRE; QUERRE Obsolete spellings of QUARRY (n.).

QUARRE, Make   (and **Made**) **to the** See 1486 qus and notes in MAKE.

QUARRED   Spelling of QUARRIED.

QUARRIE   Obsolete spelling of QUARRY 1 (vb).

QUARRIED   (obs.); **QUARRED** (obs.) Of a hawk, successfully taught to take quarry, or her state after her first few kills. Of a recently reclaimed hawk, Turbervile (1575[81]) uses the phrases 'well in bloude, and well quarried' and 'well entred and quarred', which mean in effect hunting vigorously and successfully.

QUARRY   (n.) (Adopt. Old French *cuirée*, *curée*. Obsolete spellings: QUARRE and QUERRE.) That which a falconer and hawk hunt; any fur or feather at which a hawk is flown. Plural 'quarries' is met with in certain contexts, as is singular 'a quarry'.
Also see 1615 qus in PREY.

QUARRY   1 (vb, obs.); **QUARRIE** (1618, obs.) Of a falconer, to teach or encourage (an inexperienced hawk) to take quarry, or arrange the circumstances whereby she is able to make a kill or regular kills.
'. . . And having a good make-*Hawke**, you shall wel quarrie her [the inexperienced hawk], and then she will be worthy the accounting of . . .' – 1618[50].
After which she is said to be quarried (obs.).
*See HAWK, Make.

QUARRY   2 (vb, obs.) Of a hawk, to take, or hunt and kill, or catch and feed on quarry; this is so far unverified as a falconer's term.

QUARRY, Bagged; BAGGED GAME Literally,

live quarry kept in a bag until needed. In the common understanding in falconry, a captive live bird or animal which a hawk might be offered as her first kill, or a bird or animal carried to the field in the hawking bag for use as a lure. The terms appear to be of recent adoption by falconers. 'Hand-fowle' is the Latham (1618[50]) equivalent, with 'hand Partridge' in the same text; both of these are obsolete. Once, the use of bagged quarry was almost invariably the method of rehearsing a hawk for chasing, taking and footing wild quarry; the practice is now illegal in Britain and some European countries. Historically, disabling or disadvantaging bagged quarry to make it relatively easy for an inexperienced hawk to catch has been widely practised in the East and the West. One method has been to stitch close its eyelids (or SEEL it), another to crop flight-feathers; furthermore, it would usually be attached to a line.

QUARRY-BOOK   See QUARRY LIST.

QUARRY HAWK   See HAWK, Make.

QUARRY LIST   A written record of named quarry taken by a hawk. 'Various' (or 'sundries') are quarries not intended to be taken or not intentionally flown at. In lark-hawking with merlins:

> 'Of the total bag, "Jack" killed 13 larks, while "Jill" is credited with 29 larks, 1 various.' – 1898[40].

The quarry-book that Michell (1900[59]) kept contained such additional information as hawks' performances, details of flights and weather, in other words (his) '... a summary of the day's sport'.

QUERRE, Fly to the, and **Slain at the**   See FLY TO THE QUERRE.

QUERRE, Make to the   See 1486 qus and notes in MAKE.

QUICK   (adj., obs.) Alive. Of a hawk recently entered:

> '*Note*: yf you gorge not yor hawke w^t the taken praye or elles w^t some quick byrd* closely theron sometymes, she will never flye lustely: for lack of good servin spoyles all.' – c.1575[38].

*The quick bird is, in this case, bagged.

QUICK   (n., unc.) The living part of beak and talons to be avoided when coping a hawk; see COPE.

QUILL   See FEATHER, Parts of a.

QUILL, In the   See BLOOD, In the.

RABBIT   See HARES and RABBITS.

RAISED IN FLESH   See FLESH, Raised in.

RAKE   1 (unc., obs.) Of a hawk, to strike quarry in the air with the feet. Perhaps also to strike quarry and detach only some feathers or fur. Or of a short-winged hawk, to strike or slash at flying quarry in passing. Compare RUFF.

RAKE   2 (unv. and obs. in all senses.) Of such as a goshawk, to take prey (?)or quarry close to the ground. Or (broadly of a hawk) to take prey (?)or quarry in a manner other than by stooping. Or (of a falcon) to fly close to the ground.

> 'To "rake" is to fly low like an owl.' – 1852[16].

RAKE AWAY; RAKE OFF; RAKE OUT (1575) Usually said of a falcon waiting on: to drift off too far from the falconer; to fly wide of or away from a good position for a flight; to give up the pursuit of quarry and drift off down-wind; to pursue quarry far away and leave the falconer altogether. Of a game-hawk, as her flying season progresses:

> 'After about twenty successful flights, the danger of raking away or settling on a rick passes because the peregrine loves game and knows that if it waits on it will eventually be served.' – 1987[84].

Drastic corrective measures are set down by Turbervile (1575[81]):

> 'And when she [falcon] is at hir gate*, if percase she gadde out after some checke§, and kill it, then take the pray from hir angerly, and beat hir therewith about the head, and hoode hir up without any rewarde: and hereby she will the lesse delyght to rake out after a checke.'

*Her PITCH.

§Quarry not intended to be flown at; see CHECK

1 (vb). The same writer also applies 'rake out' to quarry which flies a great distance away from where it has been put up; see his first qu. in HOLD IN THE HEAD. 'Lean out' is an obsolete, so far unverified alternative. 'Make out' (also unverified and obsolete) may have a similar meaning, or be related to CHECK 1 (vb).

RAKEE (unv., obs.) A hawk which flies wide of a good position for a flight; a hawk which rakes away. See preceding entry.

RAKE OFF See RAKE AWAY.

RAKE OUT See RAKE AWAY.

RAMAGE (adj., obs.); RAMMAGE (obs.) (Etymology in HAWK, Ramage.) Wild, in the sense of untame.

> 'Yea and it shall be rather better to let hir [goshawk] bee a little rammage still, than to man hir over much.' – 1575[81].

> '*Ramage* is when a *Hawke* is wild, coy, or disdainfull to [t]he man, and contrary to be reclaimed.' – 1615 gl.[49]

The same writer says of lanners:

> '... In my observation they are very Ramage and coy Hawkes ...' – 1618[50].

> 'RAMAGE. – Wild and stubborn' – 1892 gl.[47]

RAMAGE (n.) See HAWK, Ramage.

RAMAGE-HAWK See HAWK, Ramage.

RAMAGENESS (obs.) (Spelt 'ramagenes' (1575[81]).) Untameness in a hawk. Latham (1615[49]) associates 'ramagenes' with a hawk's 'fretting angrie humors' when she is first drawn from the mews.

RAMAGER See HAWK, Ramage.

RAMISH (adj., obs.); RAMMISH (1619[6], obs.) Untame; the same as RAMAGE (adj.).

RAMISH (n.); **RAMMISH** See HAWK, Ramish.

RAMISH HAWK; RAMMISH HAWK See HAWK, Ramish.

RAMISHNESS (obs.) ('Rammishnesse' – 1619[6].) Untameness or unmanageable behaviour in a hawk.

RANDOM (**RAUNDON** or **RANDON**), **At (the)** (obs.) (Cf. Old French *randir* = to run quickly, gallop. At random = (among other lay senses) headlong, at great speed.) Apparently (in the context of falconry), at speed and from behind.

> 'And if the fowle spryng not* bot flee a long after the Rev[er] and the hawke [goshawk] nym [takes] it then. ye shall say she slew it at the Raundon.' – 1486[5].

*This phrase suggests that the quarry is encountered already in flight, or that it is making off in level flight; the river is not a defining factor but is included here as an example of where such a chase might take place. Referring to short-winged hawks, Turbervile (1575[81]) writes:

> 'Nowe that other sort which I speake of, do slay their praye and game by mayne force of wing, at randon and before head ...'.

RANGLE; STONES (1615[49], obs.) Small rounded pebbles put within reach of a hawk on her perch, or given to her by opening her beak and pushing them down into her crop. Alternatively, the falconer can encourage her

> '... to swallow them one after another concealed in small pieces of meat.' – 1898[40].

To Latham (1618[50]), to give stones is 'stoning' or 'stoaning'; the term is obsolete. Persian Taymer Mirza (fl. mid-19th century), in a chapter on the management of hawks during the moult, writes (in transl.[68]):

> 'In front of each long-winged hawk there should be a handful of pebbles ranging from a size smaller than a pea to a size larger than a bean; for it is the habit of all falcons in the mew [not, in his view, of short-winged hawks] to swallow small stones on most afternoons before they are fed, and to cast them up again with a great deal of "bile".'

Swallowing stones has long been thought to aid a hawk's digestion and is linked with the process of enseaming, particularly with the loosening of fat lining the stomach and the dispersal of mucus or bile; see ENSEAM. To offer or administer rangle appear to be obsolescent in Western falconry, despite the belief that wild hawks swallow small stones. Burton (1852[16]), writing on falconry in the Sindh (delta of the Indus) reports that the bazdar (falconer)

> '... gives his falcons bits of rangle the size of a pea in order to prevent their laying eggs.'

RAPE (unv., obs.) Of a hawk, to claw or scratch ([?]quarry).

RAPTOR (semi-scientific) (Latin = one that seizes or drags away, a robber, etc.) Any bird of prey, including vulture and owl. A term not authentic to falconry but sometimes used by falconers today as a broad term.

RAPTORES (obs.) Formerly, the name of the order containing all the birds of prey.

> 'The term *Raptatores* of that naturalist [Illiger] I have ventured to alter to *Raptores*, which appears to me more classical. The former I believe is not in use.' – 1823[52].

60-62: *Peregrine falcon flying a rook by K.W.F. Bauerle (1831–1912). (Courtesy Sotheby's)*

63-64: *Above and left: Dramatic scenes of hunting with the goshawk by K.W.F. Bauerle (1831–1912).*
(Courtesy Sotheby's)

65: *Opposite: Shaheen and wild duck.*
(Archibald Thorburn, d. 1935)
(Courtesy the Tryon & Swann Gallery)

66: *Heron-hawking.*
(G.E. Lodge, d. 1954)
(Courtesy the Tryon & Swann Gallery)

67: *Greenland falcon and ptarmigan.* (G.E. Lodge) (Courtesy the Tryon & Swann Gallery)

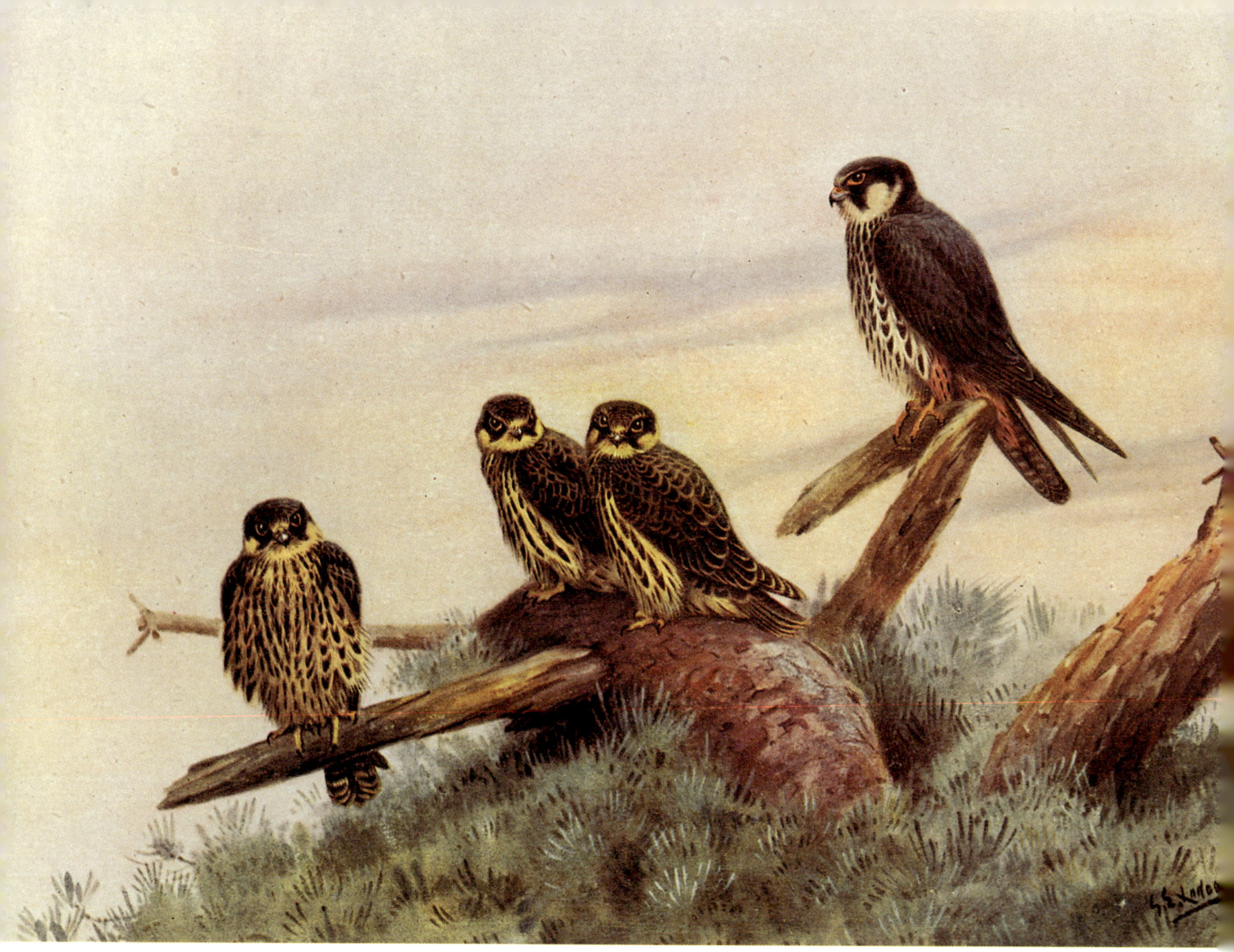

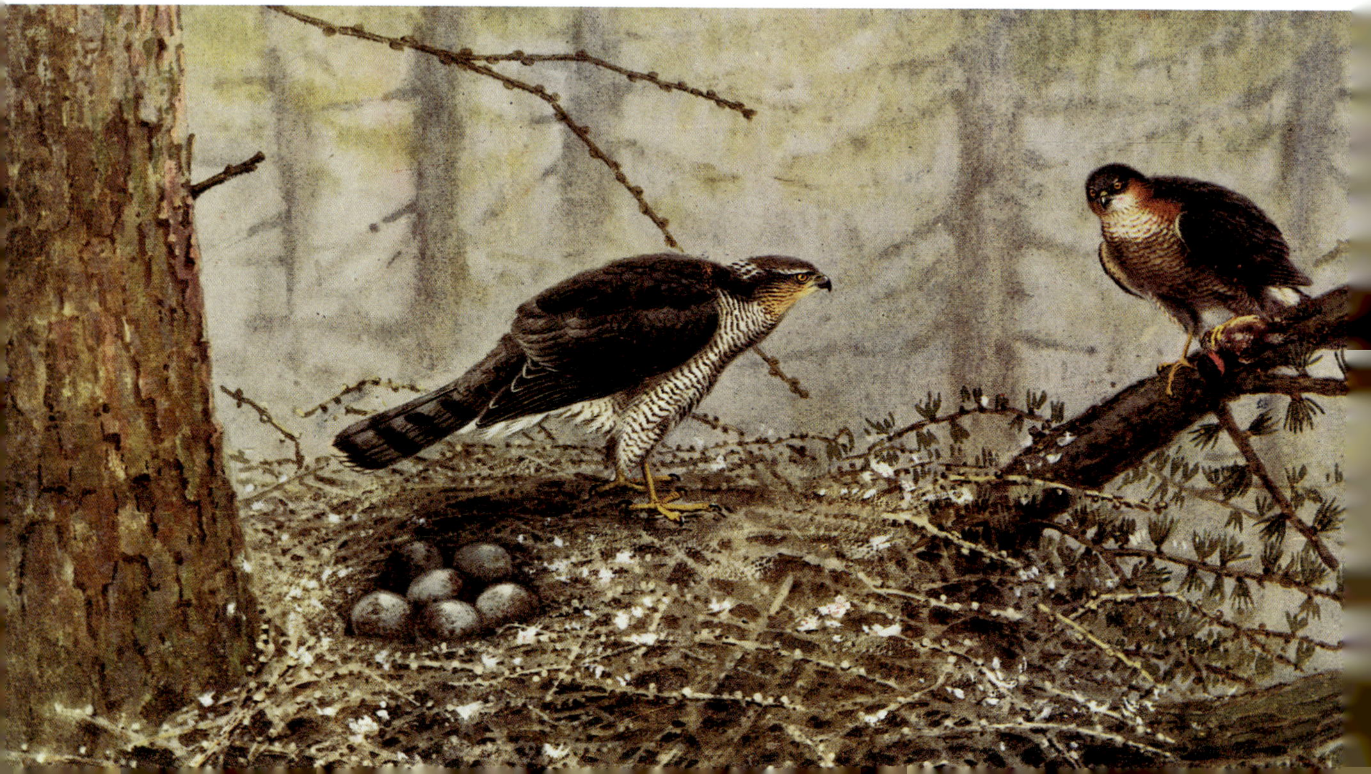

70: *Golden eagle.* (G.E. Lodge)
(Courtesy the Tryon & Swann Gallery)

68: **Opposite above**: *Hobby and young.* (G.E. Lodge)
(Courtesy the Tryon & Swann Gallery)

69: **Opposite below**: *Sparrowhawks.* (G.E. Lodge)
(Courtesy the Tryon & Swann Gallery)

71: *Peregrine and red-legged partridge.* (G.E. Lodge) (Courtesy the Tryon & Swann Gallery)

72: *Jack snipe missed by a merlin.* (G.E. Lodge) (Courtesy the Tryon & Swann Gallery)

73: Above: *An engraving from Francis Barlow's* Sixty-seven Excellent and Useful Prints *(1755).*

74: *Opposite below: Lanneret being flown through the moult (note the incomplete tail). He is riding a thermal to gain lift on a windless summer day.* (B.E. & K.L. Yull)

75: *Right: The chase moments before the kill. The bird is a changeable hawk-eagle, flown by Briton David Dawson Wood in India in the 1960s.*

76: *Female Harris' hawk breaking into a kill.* (A. Walker)

77: Above: Footing the rabbit lure. (B.E. & K.L. Yull)

78: Left: Mantling, in the current understanding. The bird (and that in the picture above) is a male tawny eagle (Aquila rapax). (B.E. & K.L. Yull)

79: Below: Male Harris' hawk coo[ls] himself on a warm day. (K. Taylor)

RAPTORIAL BIRDS (semi-scientific) The birds of prey, a term not used by falconers.

REBATE TO THE FIST (obs.) In Berners (1486[5]): of a falconer, to encourage (a bating hawk) to recover the fist:
> 'The secunde [after bating in a list of terms] is rebate youre hawke: to yowre fyst. & thatt is whan yowre hawke batith. the leest mevyng [moving] that ye can make with yowre fyst she will rebate ayen [again] uppon yowre fyst.'

The implication appears to be that the fist should be held as still as possible and the bating hawk will flutter up to it once more. Today, a bating hawk might get back up, 'to the fist' being implied (inf.). Compare RECOVER THE FIST or – PERCH.

RE-BLOCK A HOOD See HOOD-BLOCK 1 under HOODS AND HOODING.

RECLAIM (obsolescent); RECLAYME (obs.) Of a falconer, to MAN and tame (a hawk), or to man and train (her). The Harting (1891 gl.[39]) definition 'to make a hawk tame, gentle, and familiar' corresponds with that of Latham (1615 gl.[49]), who phrases it thus:
> '*Reclaiming* is to tame, make gentle, or to bring a *Hawke* to familiaritie with the man.'

In the text, this writer's phrase 'reclaiming and making' means manning and training. He also uses the verb reclaim to mean (of the hawk herself) to come to a state of tameness and familiarity with Man; this application is obsolete. To Lascelles (1892 gl.[47]), to reclaim a hawk is, of the falconer,
> 'To tame a hawk, or bring her from her wild condition to such a point that she is fit to enter at quarry.'

This agrees most closely with the various Berners (1486[5]) references which, in sum, suggest that reclaiming is the falconer's preparation of a hawk from first taking her up, to entering her at quarry. The same writer's phrases 'come to the Reclame' and 'come to Reclayme' appear to mean, of the hawk herself, to come to the state of readiness for entering at quarry. In the same text, 'wele Reclaymed' favours 'well-manned and -trained'. These three idioms are obsolete.

RECLAIM, The (obs.) (Spelt 'the Reclame'[5].) According to Berners (1486[5]), the state in a hawk of readiness for entering at quarry; more in preceding entry.

RECLAIMED (obsolescent) Describes a hawk which has been prepared and trained to the point of readiness for entering at quarry. Unreclaimed (probably obsolete) describes a hawk which is unmanned and untrained, or can occasionally mean untame.

RECLAMATION (obsolescent) The preparation which a hawk undergos to ready her for hunting. More in RECLAIM.

RECOVER HERSELF See next entry.

RECOVER THE FIST or – PERCH Of a hawk, to get back up onto the fist or her perch after bating off. 'Recover herself' (inf.) has occasionally been met with and means to get back up in either situation.

RED See MAIL (n.), and HAWK, Red.

RED-TAIL; REDTAIL Popular shortenings of red-tailed hawk; see HAWK, Red-tailed.

RED-TAILED HAWK See HAWK, Red-tailed.

REFLUSH See FLUSH.

REFLUSH, The See FLUSH, The.

REFORM THE FEATHERS See FEATHERS, Reform the.

REFUSE By itself: of a hawk, to give up a flight, or to decline to fly quarry. It also occurs with the quarry in question named:
> 'Goshawks are capricious creatures; they will refuse a leveret, and half an hour later fly well at a full-grown hare.' – 1900[59]

Compare FLY TAIL TO TAIL.

REFUSER (unv., obs.) A hawk which declines to fly quarry.

REJOICE (obs.) (Spelt 'rejoyse' (1486), 'rejoyce' (1575[81]).) Of a hawk, to display signs of contentment, such as rousing or feaking; see ROUSE, and FEAK.
> 'And whan yowre hawke hath slayne a fowle. and is rewarded as I have sayde. let hir not flie in no whise tyll y[t] she have rejo[y]sed hir. that is to say. tyll she have sewed. or snyded her beke [feaked]. or ellys rowsed her....' – 1486[5].

RELIEVE (obs.) Of a hawk, to feed; of a falconer, to feed (a hawk). To be relieved (obs.) is, of a hawk, to be fed by the falconer. Example of use in 1615 qu. in PILL (n.).

RELIEVED See preceding entry.

RETERIVE, The See RETRIEVE, The.

RETRIEVE (probably obs.); RETRIVE (1486, obs.); RETRYVE (1575[81], obs.) (French *retrouver* = (in one sense) to find again.) Of a falconer or of dogs working with hawks, to flush (quarry) for a second time, that is, when it has fallen or gone into cover again after the initial flush. Berners (1486[5]) notes that after a short-winged hawk has killed, been fed a little and allowed to FEAK and ROUSE, the austringer should

> '. . . go and retrieve moo [more (quarry)] and she will nym [take] plente.'

In the same text, a dog for retrieving in this sense is named 'a Retriver'; on entering a short-winged hawk at her first wild quarry:

> 'Iff ye have a chastised hounde: that will be rebuket: and is a Retriver: uncouple him and no moo of yowre houndis. and goo to a sengler [solitary] partrich: of the covy so sparplid [dispersed, scattered]. and be as nygh as ye can to the Risyng therof and if yowre hawke desire cast hir to it. and if she take it. then is yowre hawke made for that yere. . . .'.

The first part of this passage might be paraphrased: 'If you have an obedient dog which will retrieve . . .'. Also, the quarry might be retrieved, that is, found and flushed for a second time. This idiom is probably obsolete; for example of use, see 1677 qu. in MARK, Fly at. Compare REFLUSH under FLUSH.

RETRIEVE, The (probably obs.) (Spelt 'the retrive' (1616), 'the reterive' (1618[50]), 'the retrove' (1619[6]).) The rediscovery and second springing of quarry when it has fallen or gone into cover again.

> 'The long-winged hawke . . . gathereth up againe to her first pitch, and there expecteth the retrive.' – 1616[78].

Compare THE REFLUSH under FLUSH, The.

RETRIEVED; **RETRIVED** See RETRIEVE.

RETRIVER See RETRIEVE.

RETRIVE; **RETRYVE** See RETRIEVE.

RETRIVE, The; **THE RETROVE** See RETRIEVE, The.

RICK-HAWK (obs.) A hawk which carries a kill onto a rick of hay rather than remaining on it, on the ground, until the falconer makes in to her. Similarly, a tree-hawk (obs.) is a hawk which carries a kill into a tree. Both terms may have been coined by Michell (1900[59]).

RIDGE, Supra-orbital See BROW.

RIDGE-SOARER (recent or modern) A hawk which relies on updraughts from hillsides to reach her pitch. Writing of falcons in game-hawking, Upton, in Woodford (1987[84]), believes that

> 'Too much use of hillsides can spoil a hawk. She will become a ridge-soarer rather than a waiting-on hawk. She will get into the habit of going away to find an updraught rather than flying upwards to her pitch. While she is away the grouse or partridge may well take the opportunity to slip away to safer country.'

RIFELER Spelling of RIFLER.

RIFLE (obs.) (Old French *rifler*, *riffler* = to graze or scratch.) Of a hawk, to grab the feathers of her quarry and fail to BIND TO its body.

RIFLER (obs.); **RIFELER** (obs.) A hawk that habitually grabs the feathers of her quarry instead of taking a firm grip on its body. From Berners (1486[5]):

> 'And oft tyme it happith mony an hawke for egernesse when he shulde Nomme [take] a fowle he seesith bot the federis. and as ofte as he doos so he Riflith. therfore such hawkys been called Rifeleres if they doo ofte so.'

RING Part of some types of perch: a free-moving hoop of continuous steel to which the hawk's leash is tied. See PERCHES.

RING (vb) See RING UP.

RINGER Quarry which ascends in circling flight, such as the skylark in lark-hawking:

> 'The third sort of lark*, is the veritable "ringer". With the start he has, he keeps ahead of the hawk, climbing up in spiral circles. Why not in a straight line?** . . . Possibly he finds that he can get on more pace by having the wind now in front, now at the back, and between whiles at the side.' – 1900[59].

*The first two described by this writer are 'ground larks', those which are deep in the moult and do not mount, and 'mounting larks', those which may be hampered by the moult but (as he puts it) 'go up and try to keep the air'. The authenticity as falconers' terms of ground lark and mounting lark is unverified.

**'Straight line' means vertical, as is the skylark's characteristic song-flight.

RING UP; **RING** ([?]obs.) Of a falcon, to ascend in circling flight to reach her PITCH, or in pursuit of her quarry; such a flight is known as a ringing flight. The pursued quarry might also be said to ring up. Michell (1900[59]) writes of 'flying ringing larks late in the season' with a merlin.

RISE Of quarry, to fly up from the ground.

RIVER, Fly (to) the See FLY TO THE RIVER.

RIVER, Make to the See MAKE.

RIVER-HAWK (unc., obs.) A term used by Latham (1618[50]) for a hawk chiefly for flying at duck.

ROIL (obs.); **ROYLE** (obs.) Of a hawk in the field, to wander, be independent. Bert (1619 chap.hdg[6]) offers advice on
> 'How to bring a Hawke that will royle and seeke for Poultry at a house, to good perfection and staidnesse, and how to get that Hawkes love in whom an ill Keeper hath bred such carelesnes.'

ROBIN The male HOBBY.

ROOK *Corvus frugilegus*, the quarry in ROOK-HAWKING, found under HAWKING, Categories of.

ROOK-HAWK A falcon for ROOK-HAWKING, found under HAWKING, Categories of.

ROOK-HAWKING See under HAWKING, Categories of.

ROUNDPERCH See under PERCHES.

ROUND WINGED HAWK See under HAWK, Short-winged.

ROUSE (Obs. spellings: ROWSE (1486[5]), ROWZE and ROWSE (both 1575[81]).) Of a hawk, to raise her feathers, shake them vigorously, then allow them to settle again.
> 'She Rousith when she shakith all hir federis and hir body to gedre [together].' – 1486[5]

To rouse in the company of Man is a sign of relaxation and tameness in a hawk and is traditionally looked on as one of the outward signs of a hawk's contentment. Also she is sometimes unwilling to fly until she has roused.

> '... Suffer hir until she rowse or mewte, and when she hath done either of them, unhoode hir, and let hir flee ...' – 1575[81]

Also see 1486 qu. in REJOICE.

ROWSE; ROWZE Obsolete spellings of ROUSE.

ROYLE Spelling of ROIL.

RUFF (obs.) Of a hawk, to strike (quarry) without binding to it, making (its) feathers or fur fly. Turbervile (1575[81]) claims that, after his recommended treatment for a broken talon,
> '... If she be a falcon, she shall strike or ruffe a Ducke as before hir hurt.'

Compare RAKE 1.

RUFTER See RUFTER HOOD under HOODS AND HOODING

RUN 1 Of avian quarry such as partridges, to leave cover, or the spot where they lie, on foot.

RUN 2 Under DOGS IN HAWKING.

RUN CUNNING (unv., obs.) A term used by Michell (1900[59]): of a hawk in the field, to indulge in laziness and a particular kind of opportunism, described by this writer as 'an abominable vice'. Using as an example merlins ('... which seem to me the most prone of any hawks ...'), he notes:
> 'The line adopted by the offender is to fly lazily after the quarry, waiting for it to put in, when he marks the place, and going straight to it jumps (if he can) upon the fugitive. Sometimes the offence originates in double flights [flights with a cast of hawks], when an inferior hawk, having allowed her partner to do all or most of the work, cuts in at the finish, and secures the quarry.'

RUN IN See under DOGS IN HAWKING.

S

SACRE Obsolete spelling of saker; see FALCON, Saker.

SACRET Obsolete spelling of sakret, the male saker falcon; see FALCON, Saker.

SAFETY POSITION (recent or modern) The falconer's hold on the jesses of a hawk on the fist, often when leash and swivel have been removed before a flight, or while they are being removed, or while the falconer is tying the leash to the perch. The jesses are gripped between the fingers of the fist as a precaution against the hawk escaping if she bates off. Commonly, the free ends of the jesses are passed down between thumb and fore-finger into the palm, then out towards the back of the fist between the two upper and two lower fingers. See comments in VARVELS.

SAGER Obsolete form of saker; see FALCON, Saker.

SAHARA LANNER See ALPHANET.

SAILS (obs.) The wings of a hawk.

SAKER, American Uncommon, obsolete, probably exclusively lay name for the prairie falcon; see FALCON, Prairie.

SAKERET; SACKERET Obsolete spellings of sakret, the male saker falcon; see FALCON, Saker.

SAKER FALCON See FALCON, Saker.

SAKRET The male saker falcon; see FALCON, Saker.

SARCEL (obs.) (French *cerceau*[74]. Cf. circ-, the first element of certain words, denoting or suggesting circle, circular motion, etc.; the moulting of this feather might be said to complete a cycle. Other English spellings and forms (all obs.): SERCELL, SARCELL and CERCELL (all 1486[5]), SARCILL, others; also SARCEL FEATHER; CESSEL may be the same. Medieval Latin *saxellus* of 13th century Emperor Frederick is the same (swing feather in transl.[35], so far unverified as authentic to the English language of falconry).) The outermost (or first) primary feather in a hawk's wing. For comparison: in a 19th century French-language treatise, a falcon is said to have one *cerceau* on each wing, goshawks and sparrowhawks, three; in each case, the *cerceaux* are those outward of the longest feather of the wing[74].

In a normal moult, the sarcels are the last primaries to be moulted in short-, long- and broad-winged hawks. Berners (1486[5]) says:
> 'And the federis that sum call the pynyon feder. of a noder fowle. of an hawke: it is calde the Sercell.'

This writer adds:
> '. . . Yit it has bene seen: that hawkes have cast that same first. as I have herde say. bot that other Rewle [casting it last] is gendrall. . . .'.

SARCILL Spelling of SARCEL.

SCALES See WEIGHING MACHINE.

SCIENTIFIC NAMES See NAMES, Scientific.

SCLISE Obsolete form of SLICE.

SCOURINGS See PURGES.

SCRAPE A shallow depression excavated into the ground by some birds of prey for use as a nest.

SCREAM Of a falconer's bird, to vocalise persistently in the presence of Man, indicating that she is to some degree an imprint. See IMPRINT (n.).

SCREAMER A hawk which screams. See IMPRINT (n.).

SCREAMING YARAK, In See YARAK.

SCREEN Part of the SCREEN PERCH, found under PERCHES.

SCUTES (occ.) The scales on a hawk's legs.

SEAGULL The common gull (*Larus canus*) and black-headed gull (*L.ridibundus*), quarry in SEAGULL-HAWKING, found under HAWKING, Categories of.

SEAGULL-HAWKING See HAWKING, Categories of.

SEAL Spelling of SEEL.

SEAMED See ENSEAMED.

SEAR(E) Obsolete spelling of CERE.

SEAR OF THE FOOT See CERE.

SEAZE Spelling of SEIZE.

SECONDARIES See FEATHERS, Secondary.

SEDGE See SIEGE.

SEDGE, At; AT SEIDGE See SIEGE.

SEEL (obs.); ENSILE (obs.) (Perhaps from Latin *cilium* = an eyelid, also particularly its edge. Cf. Medieval Latin (Brit.–Ir.[48]) *cilio* = to hood [a hawk]; this perhaps should instead be to seel. Other spellings: SEAL, SELE, SILE (1398 – OED); all obs., as are all idioms connected with seeling below.) To close the eyelids (usually of a newly caught hawk) by suturing them with thread (both silk and linen have been mentioned); she is then said to be or have been seeled or ensiled, or described as a seeled or ensiled hawk. This operation has the same effect as hooding her, that is, depriving her of sight to keep her calm until the proper process of manning is started. It is a practice which pre-dates the hood in the West but which has also been concurrent with hooding. Latham (1615[49]) recommends:
> '. . . It is best after her taking [from the wild] (assoone as you may) to set her downe, and let her sit where she may rest quietly for the first night, either seeled, or in a rufter hood . . .'.

The seeling of falcons is described in detail in the

13th century by Emperor Frederick[35] who also used the hood, recently introduced into Europe. Using a needle, a linen thread is passed through one lower eyelid, led over the bird's head, and through the other lower lid. The thread is tightened, pulling up the eyelids to cover the eyes, tied off, and hidden beneath the feathers of the hawk's crown so that the possibility of hooking it with a talon is reduced. Later, by slackening the thread until the lids half-cover the eyes, sight is partially restored; in translation[35], 'half-seeled' and 'half-sighted' describe a hawk in this state (these idioms appear not to be part of the English language of falconry). Ultimately the thread is dispensed with altogether. The reasoning was that to restore her sight gradually and accustom her to strange sights by degrees was less stressful than to reopen the eyes (correctly unseel the hawk) in one step. This gradual reversal is advocated by Persian falconer Taymur Mirza[68] in the 19th century. In the 15th century, Berners[5] records a method of seeling hawks which recommends drawing the upper eyelids downwards:

> 'Take the needell and threde: and put it thorow the over igh lid and so of that other. and make hem fast under the beke: . . .'.

This writer then dismisses the alternative method:

> 'Sum usen to ensile hem with the needer igh lidde a bone the beke on the hede almost: bot that is the wors way For of reeson the over igh lidde closith more justly then the nether be cause of the largenesse.'

This might be paraphrased: 'Some are wont to seel them with the lower eyelids tied above the beak, on top of the head almost, but that is the worse way, for the upper eyelid closes better than the lower because of its size.'

This last statement is of doubtful accuracy. When a wild goshawk is taken, Taymur Mirza (in transl.[68]) suggests:

> 'On the spot, "seel" her eyes with blue thread . . .';

the translator's footnote adds:

> 'That is with thread dyed with indigo: indigo is good for wounds.'

Although it has been chiefly practised with newly caught hawks, Turbervile (1575[81]) writes of seeling hawks as they are drawn from the mews after moulting:

> 'And when you have seeled hir, keepe hir so seeled twoo or three dayes, untill she will be gently hooded.'

Seeling hawks is long-obsolete in the West (as is seeling bagged quarry to disadvantage it), but a similar procedure to that described by Emperor Frederick is still practised by hawk-trappers in the Middle East[1].

SEELED   See preceding entry.

SEESE   Spelling of SEIZE.

SEIDGE, At   See SIEGE.

SEIZE   (obs.) (Other spellings: SEESE (1486[5]), SEAZE (1575[81]), CEASE; all obs.) Of a hawk, to BIND TO (quarry). The act is recorded in the Latham glossary (1615[49]):

> '*Ceasing* is when a Hawke taketh any thing into her foot, and gripeth or holdeth it fast.'

SELE   Spelling of SEEL.

SELF-HUNT   (probably recent) Of a trained hawk, to go off hunting for herself, independent of the falconer.

SENGLE   See FOOT (n.).

SERCELL   Spelling of SARCEL.

SERE   Obsolete spelling of CERE.

SERES OF THE LEGS AND FEET   See CERE.

SERVE   Of a falconer or his dogs, to provide (a hawk) with quarry by flushing it: 'serve her with the Spaniels' (1619[6]). Or for a newly reclaimed hawk: 'serve her so [with bagged quarry].ii. or.iii. tymes' (1486[5]). Fuller qus in (respectively) DRAW AFTER, and MAKE.

SET   1 (unc., obs.) Of a falconer, to bring (a hawk) to a state of hunger and keenness to hunt:

> 'The next day "set" her [falcon] by giving her washed meat* . . .' – 1908, in transl.[68]

Also (ibid.), the hawk might be set by the falconer:

> '. . . She must be keenly "set" by being given well-washed meat.'

Compare SHARP SET.
*See MEAT, Washed.

SET   2 See DOGS IN HAWKING.

SET DOWN   (now unc.); PUT DOWN (inf.) Of a falconer, to put (a hawk) on the perch. Berners[5], in the 15th century, uses 'cast to the perch'. According to Latham (1615 gl.[49]),

> '*Setting downe*, is when a *Hawke* is put into the Mew.'

SEW; SEW THE BEAK   Obsolete alternatives to FEAK.

SEWING IN   See IMP.

SHAFT   See FEATHER, Parts of a.

SHAHEEN   (Urdu, adopt. Persian *shahin* = (literally) royal (bird) – OED. Also occasionally spelt 'shahin' in English-language texts.) A long used group-name for two Asian falcons. Notes below presuppose that, despite some uncertainty, they are different species and that one (the red-naped shaheen), together with the Barbary falcon, should be regarded as a distinct species. See FALCON, Barbary.

Among the smaller races of peregrine, the Indian black shaheen (*Falco peregrinus peregrinator*) has seen some use in the West as a falconer's bird.

Note: An uncommon and obsolete alternative name is sultan falcon (1871[70]). The still smaller peregrine-like Asian red-naped shaheen (*F.pelegrinoides babylonicus*) has been used to some extent in Western falconry. An entry in a late 19th century encyclopedia of sport[32] records current scientific names for the two shaheens:

> 'In India there are used ... the black shaheen, *Falco peregrinator*; the red-naped shaheen, *Falco babylonicus* ...'.

Shaheens were also flown in traditional Persian falconry; falconers appeared to identify three varieties, each from a different region (1908 ft.[68]), although it is not possible from this source exactly to identify the birds in question. (Plate 65).

SHAHIN   See preceding entry.

SHARP   See SHARP SET.

SHARPIE; SHARPY   Popular shortenings of sharp-shinned hawk; see HAWK, Sharp-shinned.

SHARP SET; SHARP   Of a hawk, hungry, in flying condition and keen to hunt. Bert (1619[6]), writing on short-winged hawks, uses the phrase 'very hungry and sharpe'. Compare SET 1. 'In yarak' means in keen hunting condition, but is specifically applied to short-winged hawks; see YARAK.

SHARP-SHIN   Popular shortening of sharp-shinned hawk; see HAWK, Sharp-shinned.

SHARP-SHINNED HAWK   See HAWK, Sharp-shinned.

SHEATH   The protective covering in which a new feather is furled while developing.

SHED A FEATHER   See FEATHER, Drop a.

SHIFT   Of quarry attacked by a hawk, to swerve or dodge, to take sudden evasive action. Michell (1900[59]) writes:

> 'It has been said that the rook in full plumage is no mean flier. He has also a good head on his glossy shoulders, and he shifts cleverly enough while his lungs and muscles hold out.'

The idiom 'shift from the stoop' means (of quarry) to evade the hawk's stoop. Michell also notes:

> 'Larks and other birds often dash themselves hard against the ground in shifting downwards from the stoop, and bound up again like balls.'

'The shift' used by the same writer is the quarry's action in shifting; this idiom is uncommon and probably obsolete.

SHIFT, The   See preceding entry.

SHIFT FROM THE STOOP   See SHIFT.

SHIKRA   *Accipiter badius* (Cf. Urdu *shikari* = native hunter.) A very small accipiter of Asia and Africa south of the Sahara. The nominate *A.b.badius*, from Sri Lanka and the southern tip of India, is the subspecies most associated with falconry. It is roughly intermediate in size between the sharp-shinned hawk and the European sparrowhawk but of more robust build, somewhat like a goshawk in miniature: its former generic name is *Micrastur* (formed on Greek *mikros* = small + Latin *astur* = the goshawk). As an austringer's bird, it is hardier and temperamentally more placid than the European sparrowhawk but has less dash as a hunter.

The wild shikra takes lizards, small mammals and some birds, often using the STILL-HUNTING technique. Radcliffe (1871[70]) writes of Indian falconers using it in great numbers, finding it suitable for flying at certain avian quarries but only when thrown; see THROWING A HAWK. It has been used in the West, but not widely. In his English treatise, Mavrogordato (1973[58]) writes of training

Shikra. (E.&D. Hosking; FLPA, Images of Nature).

a haggard female for throwing at sparrows and small rats.

SHOCK-MARKS   See FRET MARKS.

SHORT LEASH   See LEASH, Short.

SHORT-WINGED HAWK; SHORTWING; SHORT-WING   See HAWK, Short-winged.

SHOUT, The   See CALLS.

SHRIKE; MATAGASSE (1575[81], obs.) (Cf. mattagess in OED: Provençal *mata-r* = to kill + *agassa* = magpie; the last element (-agess) taken to be a reference to the bird's pied plumage.) A bird of the family *Laniidae*, having a hooked beak and certain behaviour not dissimilar to that of a hawk. Not a bird of prey in the common understanding but there are records of it having been trained, famously by King Louis XIII of France. Little information is to be found about training methods and quarry caught, but in a mid-19th century Persian treatise on hawking[68] the writer notes that when trained a shrike will take sparrows and a species of lark or warbler and also 'comes well to the lure from a distance'. There are numerous written records of a tethered shrike being used as a look-out, warning the trapper by calling when a wild hawk approaches; more in DUTCH METHOD under TRAPS AND TRAPPING. In Sebright's notes (1826[75]), the bird is described as:

'A Butcher Bird, called by Linnæus, *Lanius Excubitor**; that is, the Warder Butcher Bird, from the look-out that he keeps for the falcon . . .'.

*The great grey shrike; Latin *excubitor* = sentinel. Hence the 'sentinel shrike' in Swann (1913[79]), which

'. . . is in fact still so employed [as a look-out in trapping] in Holland.'

SHRIKE, Sentinel   See preceding entry.

SHUT IN   Of a falcon, to close or partially close her wings for the stoop, making herself both more aerodynamic and less visible to her quarry. The obsolete 'lessen herself' is an alternative idiom.

SIEGE (obs.); **SEDGE** (obs.) (From Latin *sedes* = a seat.) The heron's station by water. According to Harting (1891 gl.[39]), 'at sedge' is

'. . . A corruption of "at siege;" said of a heron when at the water-side, in contradistinction to being "on passage."'

'*Hern at seidge*, is when you finde a *Hern* standing by the water-side watching for Prey, or the like.' – 1677 gl.[25]

The term for a number of herons is a siege or sedge.

SIEGE, At   See preceding entry.

SILE   Spelling of SEEL.

SINGLE; SENGLE   See FOOT (n.).

SIT DOWN   Said of a falcon while hunting, during training, or while being exercised: to perch in a tree or on a fence or roof top when she should be flying. In the field, sitting down may be brought about by discouragement through having been kept waiting on too long with no quarry served. In the training ground or exercise field, it may be due to fatigue or boredom, or she may have been upset in some other way. Sitting down is a fault in falcons; it is habit-forming and difficult to correct. In the older texts, take stand (see STAND, Take) can mean the same.

A somewhat different application is in:

'. . . We have known Eyess Falcons compel a Sea Eagle to sit down.' – 1855[73];

the falcons were trained, the sea eagle wild.

SKLYCE   Obsolete form of SLICE.

SKYLARK   *Alauda arvensis*, the quarry in LARK-HAWKING, found under HAWKING, Categories of.

SLEIGHT FALCON   See FALCON, Slight.

SLICE   (Adapt. Old French *esclicier*, *esclisser* = to squirt. Obs. forms: SCLISE ('sclisith', c.1450[10] = slices), SKLYSE ('sklysith', 1486 = slices), SLYSE (1575).) Usually said only of a short-winged hawk: to discharge excrement, which is squirted rather than dropped as is a falcon's. However Berners (1486[5]), writing on short-winged hawks, says:

'. . . Ye shall say yowre hawke mutessith or mutith and not sklysith.'

Turbervile (1575[81]) observes that a sign of 'goodnesse and excellencie' in a short-winged hawk is when she is

'. . . able to slyse farre from hir when she meweth.'

Slice is also correct (or has come to be correct) when applied to a broad-winged hawk or eagle. 'Sliming' is either the same as or an error for slicing in:

'*Sliming*, is when a *Hawke* muteth from her longwaies in one intire substance, and doth not drop any part thereof.' – 1615 gl.[49]

The same term occurs in another glossary, the definition perhaps inspired by the foregoing:

'*Sliming*, is when a *Hawk* muteth without dropping.' – 1677[25];

but in the same glossary is:
> '*Slice*, is when a *Hawk* muteth a great distance from her.'

SLICE, A   See next entry.

SLICINGS; SLICING   The excrement, squirted forcibly and lengthways, of a short-winged hawk; also considered correct today for that of a broad-winged hawk or eagle. 'A slice' is as much the act as the product. More in SLICE.

SLIGHT FALCON; SLEIGHT FALCON   See FALCON, Slight.

SLIGHT TERCEL   See FALCON, Slight.

SLIME   See GLEAM (n.), and GLEET.

SLIMING   See SLICE.

SLIP   (n.) A flight at quarry by a hawk released from the fist. The kind of slip might be indicated, as in:
> 'A young and inexperienced [rook-] hawk may have a short slip to begin with, say sixty or seventy yards.' – 1898[40];

and (ibid.):
> '...Rooks that year were not very plentiful, and we had many a long slip without a kill.'

It might be 'a close slip', 'an up-wind slip', etc.

SLIP   (vb) Of a falconer, to release (a hawk) from the fist at quarry.

SLYSE   Obsolete form of SLICE.

SMALL-BIRD HAWK   See HAWK, Small-bird.

SMITE THE BEAK   Perhaps an obsolete alternative to FEAK.

SNITE   (obs.) (Apparently adopted from the lay verb meaning (in one sense) to clear or blow the nose.) Of a hawk, to sneeze.

SNURT   (n., obs.) In a hawk, a 'cold in the head'; for more, see SNURT (Appendix).

SNURT   (vb, obs.) Of a hawk, to sneeze.

SNYDE THE BEAK; SNYTE THE BEAK   Obsolete alternatives to FEAK.

SOAR   (adj.) Obsolete spelling of SORE.

SOAR   (vb) 1. (Spelt 'sowre' (1486); the action spelt 'soring' (1575[81]).). In the lay sense: of a wild hawk, to glide or circle at a height, perhaps for a sustained period, often as a prey-search technique. If used of a falconer's hawk, soaring may be applied to a falcon which has ceased to WAIT ON in the strict sense and, although remaining aloft, has abandoned the flight. It is also sometimes applied to any hawk which goes up and stays up against the falconer's wishes. Michell (1900[59]) says:
> 'Soaring and waiting on are analogous things, or rather they are the same with a difference. The best game-hawks, which wait on mountains high, are soaring as they do so; that is, the movement of the wings is the same, but the difference is that the waiter-on is, as it were, anchored to a fixed point below – the man or the dog, whereas the soarer is merely floating about like a yacht which has no particular destination.'

Towards the end of a short-winged hawk's reclamation, the Berners (1486[5]) instruction is to
> '... encrece her melis [meals] every day better and better. And or [before] she come to the Reclame* make her that she sowre not. For thogh she be wele Reclaymed hit may happyn that she will sowre: so hegh in to the Eyre. that ye shall Nether se hir nor fynde hir.'

*In this writer's definition, to the point where she is ready to be entered at quarry.

2. Formerly and occasionally in the context of falconry, to wait on; compare HAWK OF THE SOAR. Also see Turbervile's comments in HAWK, Sore.

SOAR, From the   See comments in WAIT ON.

SOAR, On the   (occ., inf.) Soaring as opposed to waiting on, and perhaps particularly applicable to wild hawks; compare SORE (vb), and WAIT ON. Michell (1900[59]) uses the uncommon, probably obsolete idiom 'take to the soar' in:
> '... A peregrine which has taken to the soar often seems so engrossed in the pleasant occupation as to forget all about mundane affairs, and, sailing along in ever-widening circles, drifts farther and farther downwind, until the falconer, if unmounted, can keep her in view no longer.'

SOAR, Take to the   See preceding entry.

SOARAGE   1 See HAWK, Sore.

SOARAGE   2 See SORE AGE.

SOAR-HAWK; SOARHAWK   See HAWK, Sore.

SOCK   A jacket or simply a toeless light sock for wrapping up a hawk, used by hawk-trappers for wild-caught birds and by falconers to immobilize an untame or sick hawk for a short period. In the 13th century, Emperor Frederick[35] describes a linen cover or sack for restraining a hawk; it is open at both ends and fitted with drawstrings. A similar pattern is sometimes seen today. Also see MAIL (vb).

SORE (now unc.) (Cf. sorrel = a horse of reddish-brown colour; French *saure* = (of horses) sorrel. Obsolete spelling: SOAR.) Red or, obliquely, immature: describes a hawk in her first year, before her first moult, still in her reddish-brown (referred to as red) plumage. It is found in combinations such as sore hawk, sore goshawk, sore falcon, sorefalcon (obs.), 'Sore Tassel Gentle' (1677[53], obs.), etc. This note on another (uncommon, obsolete) use is from Turbervile (1575[81]):

> '. . . That kind of feather [immature] is called the Sore feather.'

Also see HAWK, Sore, and HAWK, Red.

SORE AGE (obs.); **SORE-AGE** (obs.); **SOAR-AGE** (obs.) A hawk's first year; the period before her first moult when she is in her 'red' plumage.

> 'Ye shall understonde that the first yere of an hawke whether she be calde Brawncher or Eyesh*. that first yere is calde hir sore aage. and all that yere she is calde a sore hawke. . . .' – 1486[5].

*These are brancher and eyass; this form of eyass has not been met with elsewhere, the usual spelling in this text being 'eyes', plural 'eyeses'. See BRANCHER (n.), and EYASS.

Another use for SOARAGE, see HAWK, Sore.

SORE FEATHER See SORE.

SORE-HAWK; **SOREHAWK** See HAWK, Sore.

SOUCE (or **SOWCE**), **At the** See MOUNT, At the.

SOURCE; **AT SOURCE**; **THE SOURCE** See MOUNT, At the.

SOUSE, At (the) See MOUNT, At the.

SOWRE Obsolete spelling of SOAR (vb 1).

SPALCH (obs.) (Old French *esp(e)lucher*; Modern French *éplucher* = (in one sense) to go through (something) 'with a fine tooth-comb'.) Related to PREEN.

> 'Of a hawk: To clean (itself) with the beak.' – OED. 'Put her oute a-gayn to prowne [preen] and spalch herself.' – c.1450[10].

SPAR Popular shortening of SPARROWHAWK.

SPARHAWK; **SPAR-HAWK**; **SPARE HAWK** Obsolete forms of SPARROWHAWK.

SPARROWHAWK *Accipiter nisus* (Old English spearhafoc, formed on spearwa = sparrow, and hafoc = hawk.) Formerly, 'sparrowhawk' (and its variants) was often reserved for the female, with 'musket' (and its variants) customary for the male. Most commonly today she is 'female sparrowhawk', the male customarily 'musket'.
Alternative names and forms:

SPARROW-HAWK. Variation, formerly and currently.
SPARHAWK or **SPAR-HAWK** (obs.)
SPERHAWKE (c.1450[10], obs.)
*****SPERE HAWK** (obs.)
*****ASPARE HAWK** (obs.)
*****SPARE HAWK** (obs.)

*Berners (1486[5]) offers lengthy explanations for these differences in form. Summarized, they are:

> SPERE HAWK: 'She may be callid a Spere hawke for of all the hawkys that ther be she is moost spere. that is to say moost tendre to kepe. for the leest mysdyetyng and mysentendyng sleth [kills] her.'
> ASPARE HAWK: 'Also she may be calde an aspare hawke of sharpenesse of hir corage. and of hir lokyng quicly. and also of hir fleyng For she is moost asper and sharpe in all thyng that belong unto hir of any other hawkys.' Definitions of the obsolete lay 'asper' or 'aspre' are cruel, hardy, savage, etc.
> SPARE HAWK: 'She may be also callid a spare hawke for.ii.Resones. oon is she sparith goshawkys and tercellys both. . . .' Taken to signify that the sparrowhawk may be used for hawking while the goshawks are being reclaimed, that is, to fill the gap until the goshawks are ready for hunting. Less clear is: 'Also as I sayde ye may call hir a spare hawk: for an oder cause. for and ther weer a shippe fraght full of hawkis. and no thyng ellis. and ther were a spare hawke among thaym ther shuld no custom be payd be cause of hir [(?)no duty should be paid on her].'

ASPERE HAWK (obs.); **ASPERE-HAWK** (obs.)
SPERVER (Old French *esperver*, others, Modern French *épervier* = sparrowhawk. Obs.)
SPAR. Popular shortening.
PIGEON HAWK (obs.); **PIGEON-HAWK** (obs.). Chiefly vernacular.
SMALL-BIRD HAWK ([?]Lay, obs.)
MUSKET. (Perhaps [indicative of its small size] from Latin *musca* = a fly + diminutive -et. French (1853[74]) *mouchet*.) Traditionally and currently, the male. Numerous obsolete spellings.
MUSKYTE (obs.) and extant form (musket) occur in Berners (1486[5]). The male.
MUSKET-HAWK (obs.). The male.

The nominate European sparrowhawk, *Accipiter nisus nisus*, breeds throughout the British Isles and much of Europe, east to Iran. It preys almost exclusively on birds in flight, the musket taking small birds, the much larger female those up to the size of a woodpigeon (or ring dove, *Columba palumbus*). Its wild hunting techniques vary somewhat. It is extremely manoeuvrable in flight, therefore rapid chases in woodland are usual, as are more opportunistic flights in the open where it will fly along a hedgerow, and vault it to take prey by surprise on the opposite side. It will fly into the centre of a flock of small birds and take one out. Also, with a rapid dash from a concealed perch, it will take unsuspecting prey such as garden birds. As an austringer's (formerly, strictly sperviter's) bird, it has a long history of use in Britain. It is generally considered unsuitable for the inexperienced, especially the musket because of his small size and extreme fragility. The sparrowhawk is usually flown from the fist, or out of trees or from a lower perch. In the West, it is occasionally either thrown (see THROWING A HAWK) or slipped with the aid of a HALSBAND. Traditionally in Britain, quarries are sparrows, starlings, blackbirds, and thrushes; among larger quarry flown at with the female are partridge, the moorhen (*Gallinula chloropus*), also formerly the corncrake or land rail (*Crex crex*) and the little owl (*Athene noctua*). On training sparrowhawks, FR[58]. (Plates 19, 20, 21, 22 and 69).

SPARROWHAWK, Black   *Accipiter melanoleucus*
Alternative names and forms:
   BLACK SPAR. Shortening heard currently.
   GREAT SPARROWHAWK. Lay.
   MUSKET. The male, when the subject is this species.
This, the largest of the so-called sparrowhawks, is found in forested regions of Africa south of the Sahara, preying on birds and small mammals. It is roughly intermediate in size between the Cooper's hawk and the goshawk but lacks their sturdiness of build. It has a short history of use in falconry and is not used widely as an austringer's bird outside Africa where it is flown today with success at certain game-birds.

SPARROWHAWKS   There are numerous species of so-called sparrowhawks world-wide, a group which includes the tiny sharp-shinned hawk (*Accipiter striatus*) of the Americas and the medium-sized black sparrowhawk (*A.melanoleucus*) of Africa, both of which have been used as austringers' birds in recent and modern times. As a rule they are finer in build than the goshawk type, with long slender legs. Their prey is predominantly birds, usually taken in flight. The European sparrowhawk (*A.nisus nisus*), resident in Britain, has long been (and is) used in Western falconry; other subspecies of *A.nisus* have a long history of use elsewhere in the world.

SPARVITER   Spelling of SPERVITER.

SPERHAWKE; SPERE HAWK   Obsolete forms of SPARROWHAWK.

SPERVER   Obsolete name for the SPARROWHAWK.

SPERVITER   (1486, obs.); **SPARVITER** (obs.) (Old French *espreveteur*. Alternative English spelling: SPERVYTER (obs.). SPEVITER (unc., obs.) is perhaps a misspelling.) One who keeps and flies sparrowhawks specifically. Example of use, see 1486 qu. in AUSTRINGER.

SPEVITER   Perhaps misspelling of SPERVITER.

SPIZAETUS   (Greek *spizias* = the sparrowhawk + Greek *aetos* = an eagle.) The genus from which certain hawk-eagles have been drawn for use in falconry. See HAWK-EAGLES.

SPOIL THE CROP   See CROP, Spoil the.

SPRING   Of a falconer or his dogs, to flush (quarry). They might spring a partridge, or spring it to (rather than for) a hawk; also, quarry might be sprung. The quarry itself might spring, but this application is less common; for example of this use, see 1575 qu. in MARK, Fly to the.

SPRING TO THE FIST   See FIST, Jump to the.

STAGE   Obsolete alternative to CADGE.

STALE   See TRAPS AND TRAPPING.

STALK   See FOOT (n.).

STAND   (n., [?]obs.) An elevated perch taken by a short-winged hawk in the field in a tactical hunting manoeuvre. According to Latham (1618[50]), an 'ill propertie' in goshawks is:
   '... when they have flone a Partridge hard to any covart, and takes it not at the first flight, there will they sit still on the ground, and will not get up to any stand for their better vantage; which is a most vilde [vile], foolish, and dull condition.'
More in STAND, Take.

STAND   (vb, obs.) Of a hawk, to remain in idleness on the perch.

STAND, Go to   See next entry.

STAND, Take   Of a short-winged hawk in the field (and now considered correct also for a broad-winged hawk or hawk-eagle): to go to an elevated perch where she waits to be served quarry. Also, broadly, of any hawk in the field: to find a perch, not necessarily as a hunting manoeuvre. Where taking stand might be thought to be a fault is considered by falconer F.H.Salvin in an article in the magazine *The Field*, reprinted in Harting (1898[40]); this is an extract:

> 'Whether the Goshawk should be trained to come "to the fist" or "to the lure" seems at the present day [1889] to be a disputed question. According to tradition, and to the teaching of the old masters of falconry, "a hawk should know no perch but her master's fist," and upon being flown, should be taught to return to it after an unsuccessful flight'; that is, not to take stand in a tree; should she take stand, '... It has been found in practice that a swing of the lure (a small dead rabbit on a line answers very well) will bring a Goshawk out of a tree quicker than anything else.'

According to Turbervile (1575[81]), an imperfect falcon will, after one or two stoops at the quarry, 'take stand on a tree'; in a falcon, this is invariably regarded as a fault. Occasional obsolete alternatives to take stand are 'take a (the, her) stand' and 'go to stand'. According to Latham (1618[50]), falcons flown in too low condition or for too long are spoiled

> '... and drawne cleane from their wings, and forced to flye about the mans head, and goe to stand ...'.

To 'take a bough' (1619[6], obs.) or 'take a tree' (1575[81], obs.) are self-explanatory. Compare PERCH, Go to. Less commonly, to take stand is (of a short-winged hawk) to alight upon the ground; this application is obsolete and perhaps incorrect, but for comparison with French terms, see BLOCK (vb). Compare MARK, Fall at.

STANDING Of avian quarry, at rest on the ground as opposed to having risen.

STAND TO THE HOOD See HOODS AND HOODING.

STAUNCH (obs.) Of a hawk as a hunter, reliable, resolute, experienced, as in 'an old staunche flying Hawke' (1615[49]); fuller qu. in HAWK, Make. Also, of a dog, dependable:

> 'Let such as you cast off at first be old staunch-Hounds, which are sure.' – 1677[25].

It is also used in the idiom 'a staunch point'; see DOGS IN HAWKING.

STERNUM The BREASTBONE or (sometimes to falconers) keel.

STICKY-FOOTED (probably modern) Of a hawk, unable to release her grip on (for example) the glove. A hawk flown from the fist will often reflexively grip the glove when she sights quarry; if her talons are over-sharp, they may become embedded in the leather, probably delaying the slip slightly. She might also be sticky-footed for a few moments after feeding on the fist; until she has relaxed her feet she cannot leave the fist smoothly. She may also be so termed when she cannot relax her grip on the lure or a kill, brought about by excitement or anxiety. The state or behaviour is known as sticky-footedness (correct currently).

STILL-HUNTING In a lay sense: of a wild hawk, a technique in which she waits immobile on a high or concealed perch to ambush prey, or in which she moves from perch to perch, pausing to look and listen for prey. Historically, the term is not authentic to falconry, but it may now occasionally be met with applied to flying such as a short- or broad-winged hawk out of a tree or off a pole and exploiting this behaviour.

STOANING Form of STONING.

STOCK, Feeding See FEEDING STOCK.

STOCK, Mew at the See MOULT A HAWK.

STOMACH (obs.) In old hawking texts: variously, a hawk's hunger, appetite, relish for food, disposition or constitution; but most commonly it is (or relates to) her digestive system or its state and how the latter influences her general health and keenness to hunt. In the context of enseaming, it is used in such obsolete phrases as 'come to a stomach' and 'bring her to a stomach' to signify that the hawk's digestive system has come to or is being brought to robust health and efficiency. As Bert (1619[6]) says:

> '... You must labour to get her a good stomake.'

Conversely, through poor management a falconer might 'take her stomake awaye' (c.1575[38]). See ENSEAM.

STONE, Mew at the See MOULT A HAWK.

STONES See RANGLE.

STONING (1618[50], obs.) (Also spelt 'stoaning'[50].) The giving of RANGLE to a hawk.

STOOP (n.) (Taken to be akin to 'steep'. Swoop (n.) is met with as a falconer's synonym for stoop, but rarely; otherwise, it is lay or poetic.) A hawk's gravity-assisted head-first attacking dive at quarry, most commonly that of a falcon. Its style or quality may be specified, examples being false, vertical, hard, good, bad, downwind. The term may also be applied to the fast downward attacking flight of any hawk. Recounting an incident in blackbird-hawking with a sparrowhawk, Michell (1900[59]) writes:

> 'One of these [blackbirds] is driven out, and Ruby makes a fine stoop at him out of the tree, but fails to hit him, and he puts in.'

STOOP 1 (vb) (Swoop (vb) has been met with as a falconer's synonym for stoop, but rarely; otherwise, it is lay or poetic.) Most commonly said of a falcon: to execute a head-first attacking dive at quarry beneath her. Less commonly of other hawks: to execute a fast downward attack on quarry. Michell (1900[59]), writing of a sparrowhawk flying a partridge, notes:

> '. . . She makes a sort of half-turn in the air, comes down in a slanting course, half stooping and half flying, and before the partridge has gone forty yards, strikes him full on the back with both feet.'

STOOP 2 (vb); **STOOP TO THE LURE** Of a falconer, to exercise (a falcon), using the swung lure. More in LURE (n. and vb).

STOOP 3 (vb) See STOOP AT.

STOOP, Dummy See next entry.

STOOP, False (unc.) 1. Apparently a hesitation or change of course by a stooping falcon in the pursuit of one quarry because she has seen another. In OED, noun 'check' is (in one sense) 'A false stoop, when a hawk forsakes her quarry for baser game'. See CHECK 1 (vb).
2. In a passage in Upton (1987[82]), a false stoop is a feint; of a famous English rook-hawk (peregrine) in the 1890s:

> 'She could race up over rooks with hardly any effort, but when there would never make a bad stoop, but frequently make false ones, missing the rook by a yard or more, and terrifying it most ably, but often not meaning to kill it until her sixth or seventh stoop.'

According to Upton (inf.), a 'dummy stoop' is when the hawk appears to start a stoop but immediately swings upwards again. Good rook-hawks do this to shepherd a flock of rooks away from potential cover or perhaps to attempt to force one rook (usually an inferior one) into a vulnerable position.

STOOP AT; **STOOP** (obs.) Of a falcon, to attack (quarry) by stooping. Turbervile (1575[81]) uses the phrase 'stoupe a fowle'. Also, a falcon might stoop at the lure.

STOOPED AT; **STOOPED** (obs.) Of quarry, attacked by a stooping falcon. Turbervile (1575[81]) writes of 'a fowle beeing often stouped'; fuller quote in PLUNGE, The.

STOOP TO THE LURE See STOOP 2 (vb).

STRADDLE THE BLOCK Of a hawk, to step off the block and have her jesses slip down either side of it, due to either the jesses being too long or the perch too narrow. Being then unable to move away from the perch, she may injure herself or damage feathers in an effort to recover herself. To straddle the perch can be, of such as a short-winged hawk on a bow perch, to have her legs slip down either side of the bow, perhaps resulting in tail-feather damage.

STRADDLE THE PERCH See preceding entry.

STRAIN (obs.) (Also spelt STREYN(E) and STRENE ('streynith' and 'strenyth', both 1486[5] and obs.).) Of a hawk, to grip. Of a hawk in an attack, to grip (quarry) with the feet.

> '. . . She streynith and not Clithith nor Cratchith.' – 1486[5];

this qu. is considered in CLUTCH.

STRENE Spelling of STRAIN.

STRETCH See MANTLE (vb 2), and WARBLE.

STRETCH, At the ([?]obs.) Of a hawk, flying at full speed. On the stretch ([?]obs.) and on her stretches (obs.) appear to mean the same.

STRETCH, On the See preceding entry.

STRETCHER Under FOOT (n.).

STRETCHES, On her See STRETCH, At the.

STREYN(E) Spelling of STRAIN.

STRIKE (n.) The moment of contact between a hawk's feet and quarry.

STRIKE (vb) Of a hawk, to hit, CUT or grip (quarry) with the feet.

STROKE See next entry.

STROKING (obs.) The traditional practice of accustoming an unreclaimed hawk to being touched, using fingers, a feather or such as a pigeon's wing. A 'switch' (or 'wand') for the same purpose is mentioned in some old texts, and such a device is depicted in medieval and later art. Michell (1900[59]) suggests using 'an uncut pencil or a short stick'. Latham (1615[49]) recommends:

> '. . . Take her upon your fist gently, and cease not to carry her the whole day continually, using a feather

in steede of your hand to touch and stroake her withall, and when you finde her gentle and willing to be toucht without starting: then may you alone by your selfe pull off her hood, and quicly, and gently put it on againe . . .'.

For 'A Falcon lately taken', Turbervile (1575[81]) suggests:

'Then muste you have a little rownde stycke hanging in a little string, with the whiche you shall oftentymes stroke and handle your Falcon.'

Today, a falconer touches his hawk as little as possible, therefore stroking as such is inapplicable in the modern pursuit.

STUD   (unv., obs.) An establishment of hawks.

STUMP(E)   Apparently part of a wing given to a hawk as TIRING. Clearer is 'a stumpe of a Partridge wing' in Bert (1619[6]).

SULTAN FALCON   See SHAHEEN.

SUMMED   See FULL-SUMMED.

SUNDRIES   See QUARRY LIST.

SUP   (obs.) Of a falconer, to give the last meal of the day to (a hawk).

SWEEP   Perhaps an obsolete alternative to FEAK.

SWITCH   See STROKING.

SWIVEL; SWYVLE (1575[81], obs.); **TYRRIT** (obs.)   A metal device of ancient design consisting of two rings which are conjoined with a pin or rivet (a separate component) and revolve independently of one another; otherwise, the pin is part of one ring, and this is usual today. Of a size to suit a particular hawk, it is used between LEASH and JESSES to help prevent the leash twisting and kinking and the jesses becoming intertwined. The old, widely used flat brass figure-of-eight swivel (two rings or D-rings riveted together) is now considered unsafe. Those often favoured today are stoutly made of stainless steel, phosphor-bronze or brass, with one ring invariably D-shaped; the free, slitted ends of the jesses are attached to the D-ring, the leash threaded through the other. However, some contemporary (particularly American) falconers prefer a ball-bearing game-fishing swivel.

A type having seen sporadic use is the spring or spring-clip swivel; this pattern is unsafe, but where

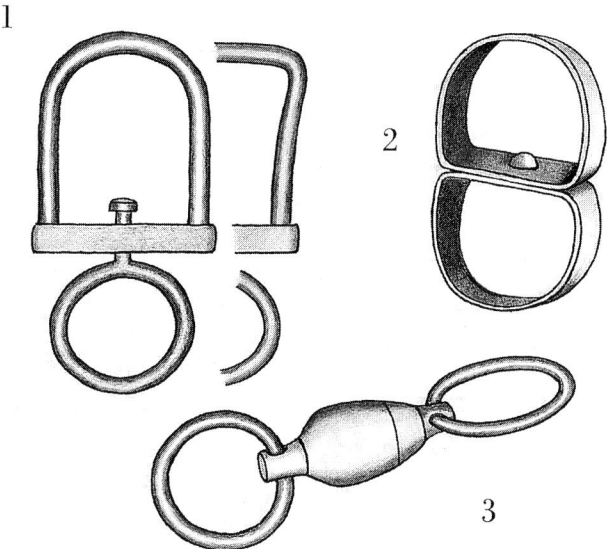

Swivels. 1: Two versions of the D pattern swivel, widely used today. 2: A pattern of traditional flat brass swivel, now considered unsafe. 3. Ball-bearing game-fishing swivel, favoured by some contemporary falconers.

one might be useful is noted by Michell (1900[59]). He writes of taking up a hawk at the end of her hack (see HACKING); she has been 'hacked to the fist' and is wearing unslitted jesses:

'As she stands complacently breakfasting on the fist, the jesses are grasped in the fingers of the left hand. A couple of snips with a sharp pair of strong nail-scissors make a slit in the two jesses. And through these a spring swivel is deftly slipped.'

In the 13th century, Emperor Frederick[35] writes of swivels being made of iron, brass or silver. The Berners (1486[5]) recommendation of 'a payre of tyrettis' is considered in TYRRIT. Other uses for a swivel, see BAG, Hawking, and LURE (n. and vb).

SWIVEL, Ball-bearing   See preceding entry.

SWIVEL, Spring   or **Spring-clip** See SWIVEL.

SWIVEL-SLITS   Slits in the free ends of JESSES to accommodate the SWIVEL.

SWOOP   Usually lay or poetic alternative to STOOP (n. and vb).

SWYVLE   Obsolete spelling of SWIVEL.

T

TABOR (obs.) (Old French *tabur*. Cf. tambour.) A small drum. Sometimes in Western medieval and later falconry, drums were beaten to put up quarry. Berners (1486[5]) refers to the so-spelt tabur; more in next entry. Turbervile (1575[81]) uses the form 'tabarde'; see this writer's second qu. in MOUNT, At the.

TABUR STYKE (obs.); **TABUR-STYCKE** (1856, obs.) (Lay tabor-stick = drumstick.) An early misinterpretation of a Berners (1486[5]) passage may have led 'tabur styke' to persist as a term for a kind of lure. It has been seemingly misdescribed as a rod surmounted by a carved bird, used to lure a hawk; and:
> 'THE TABUR-STYCKE and DRAWER* are modifications of the same [a feathery lure], merely using a stick instead of a cord.' – 1856[76].

The Berners passage in question reads:
> '... Looke backewarde towarde the hawke. and with yowre hande or with yowre tabur styke: becke [beckon] yowre hawk. to come to you. and when she is on the wyng. and comyth low bi the grounde. and is almost at yow. then smyte youre tabur ...';

the noise of the beaten tabur (tabor, drum) puts up the quarry. Most plausibly here, the tabur styke is simply a drum stick and its use for summoning the hawk is incidental. Fuller qu. in FLY TO THE VIEW.

*Note: The unverified 'drawer' has been met with only rarely elsewhere and appears simply to be an obsolete synonym for lure; it is probable that the word literally means a device for drawing (or luring) a hawk.

TACKLER (unv., obs.) A hawk at hack, or hack hawk.
> '*Hack Hawk*, that is, a *Tackler*.' – 1686 [1929] gl.[9]

See HACKING.

TAIL A hawk's train. Berners (1486[5]) uses tail, spelt 'tayll' and 'tayle'. Both terms tail and train are used by contemporary falconers. More in TRAIN 1 (n.).

TAIL, Bind (or **Tie**) **the** To wrap up or tie a hawk's tail. This is done when there is the highest risk of feather-damage, for example during her manning and early training or for her transportation by box or hamper. One method is to bind the closed tail roughly half-way along its length with paper and water-soluble glue or with old-style gummed parcel tape. Another has been to wrap the whole of the folded tail in cloth. In the case of a sparrowhawk, whose tail-feathers are extremely fragile, Michell (1900[59]) recommends that
> '... While the business of reclamation lasts it is a good plan to tie the tail [using an unspecified kind of thread]. This is done by making a half-knot round the shaft of the outer feather, nearly half-way down, passing the ends over and under the tail, and making a double knot of them on the shaft of the outer feather on the other side.'

An alternative arrangement in use today, is a sheath made of card or plastic, sometimes referred to as a tail guard. It slips on and off easily and is often kept in place with a simple loop over the tail-bell.

TAIL, Tie the See preceding entry.

TAIL-BELL (n.) See BELL (n.).

TAIL-BELL (vb) To equip (a hawk) with a tail-bell. More in BELL (n.).

TAIL-BELLED Of a hawk, wearing a tail-bell. More in BELL (n.).

TAIL-BELLING The procedure of equipping a hawk with a tail-bell. More in BELL (n.)

TAIL-CHASE See CHASE, Stern.

TAIL-COVERTS See FEATHERS, Covert.

TAIL-FEATHERS See TRAIN 1 (n.).

TAIL GUARD See TAIL, Bind (or Tie) the.

TAINT (vb) See FRET MARKS.

TAINTS; TAYNTS See FRET MARKS.

TAKE Of a hawk, to catch (quarry or lure); in current use, but a 15th century directive is that
> '... in kyndeli spech ye shall say youre hawke hath Nomme or seesid [seized] a fowle and not take it.' – 1486[5].

Fuller qu. in NOMME.

TAKE A BOUGH; -TREE See STAND, Take.

TAKE DOWN By itself: to call (a hawk in flight or perching) to the lure or to the fist. When calling a goshawk out of a tree to the fist, Bert (1619[6]) writes:

'. . . Having taken her downe, I sup her . . .'.

Also met with have been 'take down to the lure' and 'take down with the lure'. The hawk might be taken down; Harting (1898[40]) writes:

'. . . The partridges may be found, flushed and flown at, but may "put in" to some copse or thick covert, from which they cannot easily be dislodged in time to serve the hawk [peregrine tiercel], which must then be taken down.'

TAKE (or DRAW) OUT OF MEW See MEW, Draw from the.

TAKE STAND; TAKE A STAND See STAND, Take.

TAKE THE AIR; TAKE TO THE AIR (unc.) Of quarry, to climb into the air.

'When rooks take the air at the sight of an approaching hawk, an indescribable scene of confusion ensues.' – 1898[40].

Less commonly, of a falcon, to mount; this application is obsolete.

TAKE UP See PICK UP.

TALLENTS; TALLANTES Obsolete forms of TALONS, found under FOOT (n.).

TALONS See FOOT (n.).

TAP THE FIST See FIST, Knock the.

TARCEL; TARSEL(L) Obsolete forms of TIERCEL.

TARSUS; plural TARSI Under FOOT (n.).

TARTARET; TARTARET FALCON See FALCON, Barbary.

TASSEL 1; TASSELL Obsolete forms of TIERCEL.

TASSEL 2 See PLUME under HOODS AND HOODING; also see GLOVE, Hawking.

TASSEL GENTLE Form of tiercel gentle; see FALCON GENTLE, and FALCON, Peregrine.

TELEMETRY A radio transmitting-receiving system for tracking a lost hawk or a hawk at hack, or for locating a hawk quickly in the field if she has killed out of sight or in cover. The lightweight transmitter is often clipped to a mount fixed to the barrels of the central two tail-feathers (deck feathers); the mount remains in place until the feathers are moulted. Or the transmitter may be fastened to the tarsus with a BEWIT. A multidirectional antenna may be used with the receiver for rough location while travelling by car; a hand-held directional antenna gives a more precise bearing. The system is considered to be indispensable by falconers who fly hawks of all kinds. (Plate 43).

TENDER PENNED See PENNED, Tender.

TERCEL (now unc. or obs.) An alternative form of TIERCEL, used into the 20th century, but considered archaic today.

TERCEL, Slight See FALCON, Slight.

TERCELET Obsolete alternative to TIERCEL.

TERCEL- (or **TARCEL-**) **GENTLE** Forms of tiercel gentle; see FALCON GENTLE, and FALCON, Peregrine.

TERRET; TERRIT Forms of TYRRIT.

TEWEL (obs.) (Adopt. Old French *tuel*, *tuele* = a tube or pipe. Other spellings: TEWELL, TUEL, TUELL (1575[81]); all obs.) The lower bowel of a hawk, or the VENT. Compare PANNEL, and BRAYLE 2.

TEYNTE, The See FRET MARKS.

THIEF (unc., obs.) (Spelt 'thefe' and 'theef' (both 1486[5]).) A term which occurs in Berners (1486[5]), applied to a goshawk wearing no bells, apparently for reasons of stealth:

'Understonde ye that a Goshawke shulde not flie to any fowle of the Ryver with bellis in no wise. and therfore a goshawke is calde a theef.'

The practice of flying a hawk without bells is uncommon; see Michell's comments in BELL (n.).

THROATLASH See HOODS AND HOODING.

THROWING A HAWK A method (of Eastern, probably Indian origin) of slipping a small accipiter. She is taught to accept being held in the hand, which may be gloved (or 'A careful [Indian] falconer uses a small pad . . .' – 1908 ft.[68]) to avoid soiling or damaging her feathers. With the palm upwards, she is gripped gently, her wings held closed, head facing forward, feet back. Radcliffe (1871[70]), writing on falconry in India, notes how she is transferred to the throwing hand:

'Eastern falconers always carry a hawk on the right hand, the left is passed gently over the head down the back till the thumb and fingers reach her thighs; the hawk is then grasped, lifted, and transferred to

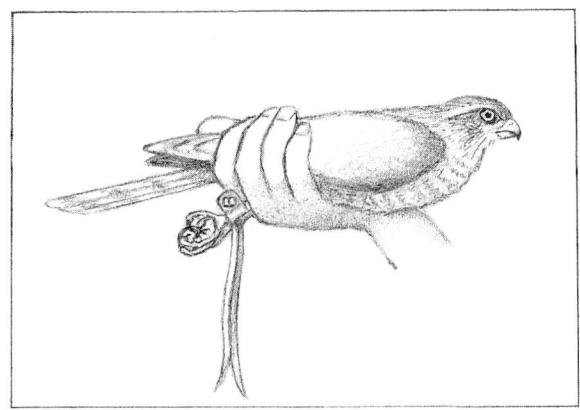

Throwing a hawk, a procedure restricted to small short-winged hawks.

the right, her breast resting on the palm, legs extended along the tail.'

When quarry is sighted or rises, the austringer throws her towards it overarm, as he might a javelin.

'The moment I saw the quarry hastening away . . . I "shied" my bird after it as Lilly does a cricket ball.' – 1852[16].

THROW OFF   See CAST OFF.

THROW-OFF, The   (unc., obs.) The action of a falconer casting off his hawk; see CAST OFF.

THROW UP   Of a hawk, to ascend quickly. The term is often applied in the case of a falcon whose downward speed in a stoop provides the impetus for her to pull out and rise again effortlessly. Example of use in POINT, Make.

THROW UP, The; THE THROW-UP (both unc. and [?]obs.) The action of a hawk throwing up.

THRUMS (1619[6], obs.); **THRUMMES** (1615 gl.[49], obs.) Short pieces of waste coarse yarn once given as casting to hawks. See CASTING 2.

TIERCEL   (Comes via Old French *tiers* or *tierce* from Latin *tertius* = a third part. TERCEL was used into the 20th century but today is considered archaic and customarily replaced by tiercel. Obsolete spellings, forms and alternatives: TARCEL, TARSEL(L), TASSEL(L), TYERCEL, TYERCLE, TIERCELET, TERCELET, TYERCLET, others.) A male hawk, the name signifying that roughly estimated he is one third smaller than the female. Traditionally and currently, the tiercel is the male peregrine falcon and the male goshawk when the subject is these species in particular; in other contexts, peregrine tiercel or tiercel peregrine and tiercel goshawk are usual. Obsolete forms such as 'Tarsell of a Goshawke' (1619[6]) sometimes occur. Tiercel has been (and is) used if the subject is another male hawk, whether or not it has its own traditional name, but not the sparrowhawk, merlin or hobby. Otherwise it might be combined with the species name: an obsolete example is 'Tercell of a gerfauken' (1486[5]), also 'ger-tiercel' (1900[59]), notwithstanding jerkin (or variant) having been the name for the male gyrfalcon from at latest the turn of the 15th and 16th centuries. A modern example is 'tiercel prairie' (inf.), the male prairie falcon having no name of its own. A general comment from Turbervile (1575[81]) is:

'You must note, that all these kynde of Hawkes [long- and short-winged, and eagle], have their Tyercelles, whiche are the male byrdes and cockes of everie sorte and gender [kind] . . .'.

There is a less plausible alternative to the traditional explanation that tiercel signifies size difference between the sexes:

'. . . Some authorities state . . . that of the three young birds usually found in the nest two are females and the third a male, hence the term *tercel*.' – 1913[79].

Perhaps one of these authorities is Turbervile (1575[81]), who writes:

'He [in this case a male goshawk] is termed a Tyerclet, for that there are most commonly disclosed [hatched] three byrdes in one selfe eyree, two Hawkes, and one Tiercell.'

Note that 'Hawkes' here means female hawks. This passage might suggest (though so far there is no supporting evidence) that 'Tyerclet' (tyercl- + diminutive -et, literally meaning little tiercel) was once reserved for the male EYASS. It has also been said that the third egg was the smaller and produced a male[37].

Blome (1686 [1929][9]), himself not a falconer nor always reliable, obtained his information from antecedent texts and certain experts of his day; the source of the terms in the following obsolete formula is not known:

'The *Male* of an *Eyess*, is an *Eyess Tassel*; of a *Brancher*, a *Brancher Tassel*; of a *Lentiner*, a *Lentiner Tassel*; of the *Soar* or *Ramage-Hawk*, the *Soar Tassel*; and of a *Haggard* the *Haggard Tassel*.'

TIERCELET   Obsolete alternative to TIERCEL.

TIERCEL   (or TERCEL) **GENTLE**; TERCEL- or TARCEL-GENTLE See FALCON GENTLE, and FALCON, Peregrine.

TIE THE TAIL   See TAIL, Bind (or Tie) the.

TIMBER (occ., obs.) (In one lay sense, to construct (such as a house) from wood.) Of a hawk (or other bird), to build a nest.

TIMBERING (unv., obs.) (In one lay sense, building material, especially wood.) Nest material. See 1486 qu. in DRAW 2.

TIRE; **TYRE** (obs.) (French *tirer* = to draw or pull; Medieval Latin (Brit.–Ir.[48]) *tiro* = to tug, wrench. Among lay meanings of vb tire is 'To exercise oneself *upon* (in thought or action)' – OED.) Of a hawk, to pull at tough or bony food, which is known as TIRING or tirings; of a falconer, to feed (a hawk) with tiring. Phillott (1908 ft.[68]) notes:

> 'A tame hawk's nostrils get choked up with blood and dust. Eastern falconers are generally particular about keeping the nostrils clean. One of the advantages of "tiring" is that it induces a flow of water that keeps the nostrils clean.'

> 'Loke that thy hawke tire every other day while she is fleyng, for nothyng ... woll clense a hawkes hedde as tyryng.' – c.1450[10].

To tire is also simply (of a hawk) to feed or to tear flesh, but this application is obsolete.

TIRE THROUGH THE HOOD See FEED THROUGH THE HOOD.

TIRING; **TYRING** (obs.); **TIRINGS** Tiring, a tiring, or tirings is tough, sinewy or bony food such as a wing, a leg or a neck with little meat on it. Pulling at it exercises a hawk's neck-, back- and leg-muscles; picking at it keeps her occupied, prolongs her meal, and helps to keep her beak in good order. Also see TIRE.

> 'A tiring may consist of anything tough which is appetising enough for a hawk to keep pulling and picking at it to satisfy her hunger.' – 1900[59];

also it

> '... provides them with "casting" in the shape of feathers, which are unavoidably swallowed with almost every mouthful.' – 1898[40].

> 'With tirings there will often be a small quantity of castings which will be swallowed with the pickings of meat.' – 1900[59].

Although pork is unsuitable for a hawk,

> 'The swetteste tyryng that is to goshawke and sperhawke is a pigge is tayle.' – c.1450[10].

> '... I would tend her many times with tyring and plumage ...' – 1619[6].

The terms 'stumpe' and 'stumpe of a wing' used by Latham (1618[50] and 1615[49]) appear to be part of a bird's limb fed as tiring. Bert (1619[6]) writes of 'a stumpe of a Partridge wing' being used to feed a hawk during hooding lessons.

TOE Under FOOT (n.).

TOLL, Fly to the See FLY TO THE VIEW.

TOMIUM (sci.); plural **TOMIA** See next entry.

TOOTH; **NOTCH**; **NOOK** (obs.) (Middle English nok(e) = corner, angle.) The notching on each cutting edge (tomium) of the upper beak, peculiar to falcons and a few other raptors not associated with falconry, giving the appearance of a tooth-like projection: 'the true dentated beak' (1855[73]). In falcons, this serration (in conjunction with a corresponding configuration on the lower beak) is believed to be an aid to breaking the spinal cord of prey by biting. In other hawks, in the absence of a tooth, a 'lobe' or downward curving cutting edge, more or less pronounced, is sometimes present; this is known as a festoon (not a falconer's term). Note: In a mid-19th century French-language treatise[74], 'Le feston du bec des faucons' ('the festoon on the beak of falcons') refers to the falcon's tooth.

TOWER (obs.) (From Latin *turris* = a tower. Cf. lay vb tower = to mount to a great height, rise aloft.) Of a falcon, to seek height as a hunting manoeuvre.

> 'My lord protector's hawks do tower so well ...' – William Shakespeare (*Henry VI Part 2*).

See RING UP, and WAIT ON. Obsolete HAWK OF THE TOWER is a general name for a falcon, apparently signifying that in hunting she characteristically seeks height.

TOWER HAWK (In plural, spelt 'Towre Hawkes' – 1575[81].) See HAWK OF THE TOWER.

T-PERCH Under PERCHES.

TRAIN 1 (n.); **TRAYNE** (obs.) ([?]From Latin *traho* = (among other senses) to draw or drag along.) The traditional and surviving term for a hawk's tail. It contains 12 major feathers. The two in the centre are the deck feathers or decks; the remaining 10 have no English name(s) that can so far be traced. Instead, they are often simply numbered or counted (one to five left and right) from the deck feathers outwards. According to Berners (1486[5]), the 'Beme feder of the tayle' is the upper, most-visible of the two deck feathers when the tail is folded; more in FEATHERS, Deck. Note: The term train is applied to the tails of birds other than hawks, especially the peacock. Applied to hawks, it makes what seems to be an early appearance in print in the last quarter of the 16th century[81]. Both terms tail and train are used by contemporary falconers.

TRAIN 2 (n., obs.); TRAYNE (obs.) (Perhaps from Old French *traïne* = guile, (?)suggesting the use of artifice in using this device to lure a hawk. But perhaps from Latin *traho* = (among other senses) to attract, allure, or to draw or drag along. Medieval Latin *trahina* (Emperor Frederick[35]) = a lure (live or dead); Medieval Latin (Brit.–Ir.[48]) *traina* = lure [for a hawk]. Compare TRAIN under TRAPS AND TRAPPING.) Captive or bagged quarry, often on a line, which a hawk is given for her first kill or her first few kills.

> 'When a Sparowhawke is manned and reclaymed, then give her nine or ten traynes at the least, and when she killeth, feede hir up alwayes ...' – 1575[81].

'Train' has occasionally been met with meaning dead or imitation quarry used for the purposes of training hawks, hence a blurring of distinction between the train and the lure. The terms themselves may be interchangeable, but it seems that correctly the train is always live. See LURE (n. and vb).

TRAIN 3 (n.) See TRAPS AND TRAPPING.

TRAIN (vb) Of a falconer, to educate (a hawk). Sometimes, of the hawk herself, to undergo her education, as in 'a merlin trains quickly'.

TRAPS AND TRAPPING

  ACCIPITRARY (rare, obs. Cf. Medieval Latin (Brit.–Ir.[48]) *accipitrarius* = a falconer). A keeper of hawks; a falconer; one who catches birds of prey (1847 – OED). No firm evidence can be found to suggest that this term is authentic to falconry.

Below are listed some traditional contrivances and procedures for trapping hawks.

  BOWNET; BOW-NET. An oval or circular net, half of which is secured to a wooden or metal bow or half-hoop; the remainder is spread and pegged to the ground. When set, the bow lies upon the pegged-down net. The wild hawk binds to a tethered live lure, and the bow is pulled over her with a long line operated by the trapper hidden at a distance.

  DUTCH METHOD. Named after a method once used in Holland, chiefly for trapping falcons on their autumnal migration. An elaborate arrangement of live decoys, live lures and bownets was developed, all moved and operated by lines leading to the trapper's sod hut some distance away. A pole hawk is a hawk employed

The bownet. (G.E. Lodge; courtesy the Tryon and Swann Gallery).

as a decoy and raised and lowered by a line attached to the top of a tall pole; a pole pigeon, also a decoy, is raised and lowered in the same way. A pigeon (the lure) is drawn out of a shelter close to a bownet in order to invite a committed attack from the wild hawk; the pigeon, once gripped firmly by the hawk, is pulled to the bownet which is then sprung. A tethered shrike, which called in alarm at the approach of a wild hawk, was employed as a sentinel. More in SHRIKE. FR[74].

  GERMAN TRAP. A spring-operated automatic trap for taking short-winged hawks. Twin bows holding the nets snap together from horizontal (when set) to vertical (when sprung). It has a compartment below for a live lure.

  SWEDISH GOSHAWK TRAP. A trap which is sprung by the hawk. It is wood-framed, its apertures covered with net. When set, two doors at the top (like the slopes of a house roof) are held open by a hinged bar against the tension of powerful elastic. The hawk, tempted in by a live lure in a compartment at the bottom, dislodges the bar and the doors snap shut.

  BIRD-LIME (obs.); **LIME** (obs.)

> 'With the barkes of Holme [holly] they make Bird-lyme.' – 1578[54].

A simple interpretation of the Dutch method of trapping hawks on passage. At the top, the trapper's sod hut with turfs removed to provide a peephole. The lines to manipulate the birds and spring the trap are operated from here. Below it, the shrike; its hollow mound provides a look-out point and refuge. Below the pole hawk are (left) the pole pigeon and its hollow mound, and (right) the pigeon lure, drawn out of its mound towards the bownet which is camouflaged with a sprinkling of grass or leaves. More elaborate arrangements on this theme were employed with additional decoys and traps.

A sticky substance often smeared on branches of trees, once used to take (usually) small birds. Historically in the West, bird-lime seems to have been used to some extent for taking wild hawks, despite the difficulty in removing it from feathers and the fact that nets have been employed from ancient times. Blome (1686 [1929][9]) goes into detail about the taking of hawks with a 'Lime-bush', an artificial bush with twigs smeared with bird-lime, and 'Lime-rods', limed sticks arranged so that the hawk cannot avoid them when she comes to an accustomed perch. A 19th century French-language treatise[74] describes a method of taking a wild hawk with a pigeon to which is attached a cord, weighted at its free end and smeared with bird-lime. On taking the pigeon in flight, the hawk becomes entangled in the cord and falls to the ground. In the East and Far East, bird-lime has been used to trap hawks. In Japan, according to Jameson[45], passage falcons were once trapped with a pigeon as a lure. On the approach of the hawk (the hidden trapper having been alerted by a tethered golden plover acting as sentinel), the pigeon was dragged on a line close to a sandbag covered with bird-lime. When the hawk had bound to the pigeon, both were pulled up to the limed sandbag. Later, the hawk's feathers were cleaned with a mustard solution. Note certain similarities to the Dutch method above.

STALE (obs. Perhaps from Anglo-French *estale* = (?)a live decoy). A live (also perhaps stuffed) decoy bird. A live bird used to entice a hawk into a snare or a net (1686 [1929][9]).

PIGEON HARNESS. A lightweight leather harness fitted to a live pigeon; nooses on the outside close onto the feet of the hawk when she takes the bird.

URINES; GRINS; GRINES (all obs. Perhaps formed on Medieval English arains (Old French *araignes*) = spiders, the net reminiscent of a spider's web. Also spelt URIVES and URVES (both 1686 [1929][9], perhaps misspellings; both obs.). Nets with which to catch hawks. Berners (1486[5]) says:

'Who so will take hawkes he must have nettis wich ben called urines and tho must be made of good small threde. and it hade need to be died other green or blwe for espieng of thee hawke. . . .'. This might be paraphrased: 'He who wishes to take hawks must have nets known as urines. They must be made of good fine thread dyed either green or blue so that hawk cannot see them ...'.

Not specifically in a falconry context, OED has a grin as

'... a snare for catching birds or animals, made of cord, hair, wire, or the like, with a running noose.'

Not in a falconry context:

'*Grinning hares*, the devilish art of setting grins ... to hang hares.' – 1824[56].

WINDING UP. A method of ensnaring a nervous hawk which cannot be approached and picked up in the normal way. When she is on the ground feeding on the lure or a kill, the falconer walks round her at a distance and winds a CREANCE (one end attached to a peg in the ground or held by a companion) around her legs.

ESCAPED HAWKS. The Berners (1486[5]) method of recapturing a hawk at night is described as:

'A praty [pretty, artful] craft to take an hawke that is brokyn owt of mew....';

the advice is to

'Looke where an hawke perchith for all nyght: in any maner place. and softe and layserly [leisurely, without haste] clymbe to her with a sconce or a lanterne that hath bot oon light. in yowre hande and let the light be towarde the hawke so that she se not yowre face and ye may take hir by the leggys or oder wise as ye lyst....'.

In a 19th century Persian treatise[68], light is recommended in the capture of a wild short-winged hawk in a tree at night. The falconer reaches up with a long pole, at the end of which is a horsehair noose and, a little below it, a lighted candle. The light keeps the hawk quiescent and allows the falconer to see to slip the noose over her head. An updated version (for lost hawks) is noted by Glasier (1986[36]), using battery-generated light and a nylon noose.

TRAIN (obs.). A trap or snare for catching wild animals, or a decoy or lure to entice a hawk into a trap. Compare suggested etymology in TRAIN 2 (n.). The term is so far unverified as authentic to falconry.

SNARES. Historically, there have been numerous primitive mechanical or automatic devices for snaring hawks. A method set down in the late 19th century is described as a 'self-acting

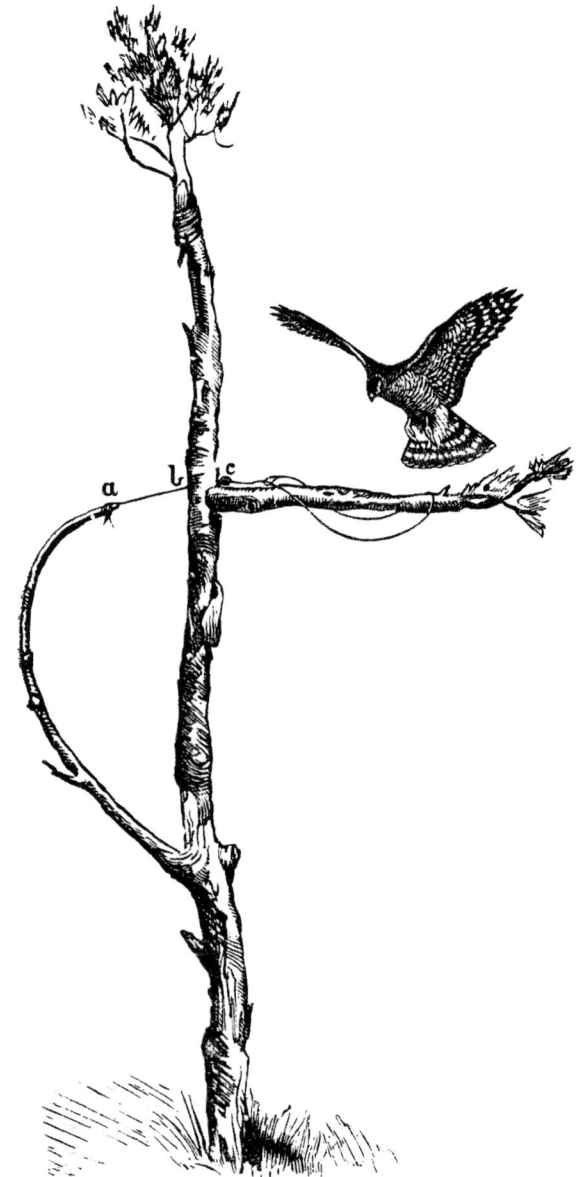

Above and opposite: Self-acting snare.

snare for merlin or sparrowhawk'[40]. The hawk dislodges a cut-through branch on which the snare is laid, at the same time releasing a whippy branch which acts as a spring to close the noose on the hawk's legs.

Other methods of trapping, traditionally employed in the East and Far East, have sometimes been used or adapted in the West.

BAL-CHATRI (India). Considered suitable for trapping small hawks, a hemispherical cage

placed like an upturned bowl, with a live lure inside. The construction might be of split bamboo covered with net or wholly of wire. The upper, outer surface is furnished with nooses for ensnaring the hawk's feet when she attempts to take the lure. It might either be pegged to the ground or fitted with a dragweight and line.

BARAK (India, Pakistan, North Africa and the Middle East). For trapping falcons. A light feathery ball incorporating many nooses is attached to the jesses of a slow-flying hawk (the barak), which is then released. The wild falcon, believing the barak to be carrying prey, gives chase and seizes the ball, her feet becoming trapped by the nooses. Writing of hawk-trapping in Pakistan, Cox (1985[24]) describes a small bundle of nooses of horsehair, cat-gut or nylon fishing-line fitted to the jesses of a lugger falcon. The barak, with its eyes stitched closed (seeled), is turned loose to attract a piratical attack from a saker or peregrine. A note in a 19th century Persian treatise[68] outlines a similar arrangement which employs a sparrow's skin and nooses made from the hair of a horse's tail.

DHO-GAZA; DO-GAZA; DO-GUZ. (Middle East, India. The *kiri-ami* of Japan is similar[45]). A fine net strung vertically between two poles to take a wild hawk in flight. Coloured to blend in with the surroundings, it is not noticed by the approaching hawk which attempts to take a live lure tethered on the opposite side. On being struck, the net collapses and closes like a purse. In a 19th century Persian treatise (in transl.[68]), an eagle owl, previously made to the lure, is used to attract the wild hawk:

'The owl, in accordance with its previous training, flies straight for the lure [positioned on the ground in the centre of the net], and is soon closely mobbed by all the birds of the neighbourhood.... If you are near the hills, perhaps a goshawk ... or else a saker falcon will come down and join the crowd. The owl, however, having no other object but to reach its goal, ignores the clamouring presence of its pursuers and continues on its straight course. The first bird to buffet the owl, on its alighting on the lure, is a fast prisoner in the net.'

There are descriptions in old and recent Western hawking literature of two vertical nets, strung between poles and set at right-angles to one another, with a live lure or decoy in the angle between, and variations on the same theme.

TRAYNE Spelling of TRAIN 1 and 2 (ns).

TREAD (obs.) Of hawks (and birds in general) to copulate. Of wild migrants:
'I my Self have seen both Swallowes and Hobbies build and tread upon their first Appearance.' – 1673[61].

TREE, Take a See STAND, Take.

TREE-HAWK (obs.) A hawk which carries a kill into a tree rather than remaining on it, on the ground, until the falconer makes in to her. Simi-

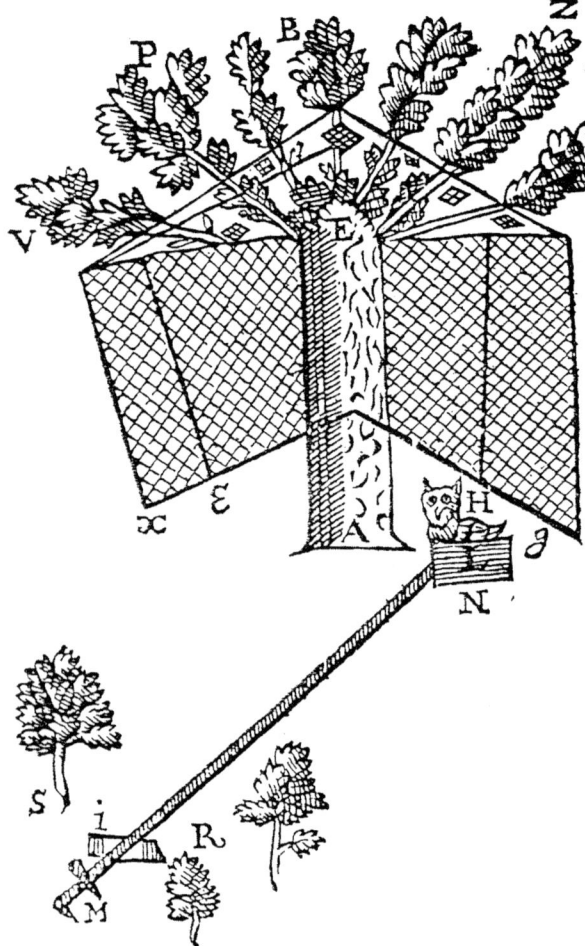

Diagram in Richard Blome's late 17th century English treatise showing nets set up around a tree. The trapper manipulates the decoy owl (described as a 'Horn-Coot') with the long line.

larly, a rick-hawk (obs.) is a hawk which carries a kill onto a rick of hay. Both terms may have been coined by Michell (1900[59]).

TROLLEY (unc., obs.) A system of two tall T-perches set some distance apart with a taut line between. The hawk's leash is tied to a free-running metal ring threaded onto the line, allowing her to fly from perch to perch. With no need for a CREANCE, it appears to have been a hands-free method of calling a hawk to the fist during her training, or an arrangement which gave her freedom of movement not allowed by other perches. Mavrogordato (1973[58]) describes (but does not name) a similar system for calling off a hawk in training, but in this case the line is close to the ground, stretched taut between two pegs. A pole at one end serves as a perch, and the hawk is tied with a long leash to a ring threaded onto the line. When she is called to the lure, her flight is restricted, which in theory discourages her from carrying; see CARRY 2 (vb). These and similar arrangements allow a hawk to reach sufficient speed in flight to injure herself when stopped abruptly at the end of the line; they are not commonly used today and are unsuitable for an unattended hawk.

TRUSS 1 (obs.) Of a hawk, to take or BIND TO (quarry). The Harting (1891 gl.[39]) definition, perhaps influenced by notes in Latham[49], is more specific:

'TRUSS . . . to clutch the quarry in the air instead of striking it to the ground.'

A passage in Latham (1615[49]) advises the austringer to

'. . . Throw the [bagged] Fesant up aloft unto her [goshawk], using your voyce withall, and there let her trusse it and fall with it to the ground . . .'.

In the Latham glossary[49], a definition of the action is given:

'*Trussing* is when a *Hawke* raseth* a fowle aloft, and so descendeth downe with it to the ground.'

*'Raseth' here clearly means rases (that is, strikes or similar), not raises; compare lay verb to rase, meaning (in an obsolete sense) to scratch or slash. An inexact interpretation of the foregoing is set down later in the 17th century by Cox[25] in his glossary:

'*Trussing*, is when she raiseth any Fowl aloft, and soaring with it, at length descendeth with it to the ground.'

In the same century, an almost identical definition appears in Blome's glossary[9]. A misinterpretation can have a long life, as the following mid-19th century version by Burton[16] confirms:

'The short-winged hawk "trusses" her prey, raising it aloft and descending rapidly with it to the ground.'

TRUSS 2 See MAIL (vb).

TRUSSING See TRUSS 1.

TUEL; TUELL Spellings of TEWEL.

TUNICIAN See ALPHANET.

TUNISIAN LANNER See ALPHANET.

TURN HEAD See HOLD IN THE HEAD.

TURN OVER Of a falcon at a height or waiting on: to change from the level to the downward with a rapid twist or flip onto her side or back, at which point she begins her stoop. She might 'turn over for the stoop'.

> 'She [merlin] had taken the lark with that very last stoop for which I had seen her turn over ...' – 1900[59].

TURN TAIL; TURN TAIL TO TAIL (1575, unc., obs.) Of a hawk, to give up the pursuit of quarry in mid-flight. A Turbervile (1575[81]) chapter heading is:

> 'Howe to helpe a Hawke that turneth tayle to tayle, and giveth over hir game.'

This writer also uses the more common turn tail ('turne tayle'). Compare FLY TAIL TO TAIL.

TYERCEL; TYERCLE Obsolete spellings of TIERCEL.

TYERCLET Obsolete alternative to TIERCEL.

TYRE; TYRING Obsolete forms of TIRE and TIRING.

TYRET(T); TYRRETT Spellings of TYRRIT.

TYRRIT (obs.) (Apparently from Old French *touret*; de Noirmont (1867–8[29]), writing on hawking in France, uses the term and says:

> 'Pour empêcher les jets et la longe de s'enrouler, on interposait entre eux un *touret*, composé de deux anneaux de métal, tournant l'un sur l'autre.' In translation: 'To prevent jesses and leash twisting up, a tyrrit is put between them, made up of two metal rings turning one upon the other.'

For comparison, Schlegel (1853[74]) in his French-language treatise has *vervelles* as two rings joined by a pin around which they turn:

> 'On appelle vervelles deux anneaux attachés l'un à l'autre par une cheville, autour de laquelle ils se tournent ...',

adding in a footnote:

> 'En anglais, swivel ...';

in the English language of falconry, VARVELS is not the same. Other spellings and forms: TYRET, TYRETT, TYRRETT, TERRET, TERRIT; all obs.) In the English language of falconry, the old name for the SWIVEL. But note that a tyrrit (surviving as terret or territ) is a non-swivelling metal ring for a variety of purposes (for example as a guide for reins on horse harness); also it is sometimes met with in older falconry texts as the simple ring attached to the free end of each jess; see VARVELS. Also note the contradiction in this 15th century passage:

> '... The lewnes [LINES, leash] shulde be fastened to theym [the jesses]. with a payre of tyretts. wich tyrettis shuld rest upon the lewnes. and not upon the gesses. for hyngyng and fastynyng upon trees when she flyeth. and tho saame lewnes. yow shall fastyn than abowte yowre lyttyll fyngre slackely. in compaysyng [encompassing] the saame in.iiii.or.v.folde. as a bowstryng unocupyede and the terettys serve to kepe hir from wyndyng whan she [indistinct; taken to be (or to be an error for) bates].' – 1486[5];

a pair of simple rings would not prevent the leash and jesses from twisting up when the hawk bates, whereas a swivel (onto one ring of which both jesses are knotted) might. For clarification, a liberty might be taken with the above passage and the concept updated to:

> 'The leash should be fastened to the jesses via a swivel. The leash and swivel are removed when the hawk flies, the swivel threaded onto the leash to prevent its loss. If the swivel is left on the hawk, her jesses might get caught up in a tree. When she is on the fist with swivel and leash attached, the spare leash should be wound in loops round the fingers of the fist. The swivel helps stop her jesses twisting up when she bates, most importantly when she is tied to her perch.'

UNCLOSED See DISCLOSED.

UNDERWEIGHT (probably recent) Heard today, it may signify that a hawk is suffering from malnutrition through having had her weight cut down too hard; see CUT DOWN 2.

UNHACKED See HACKING.

UNHOODED Of a hawk, not wearing a HOOD. Obsolete equivalents are BARE FACED and bare-headed.

UNMADE See MAKE.

UNMALE; UN-MALE; UNMALED See MAIL (vb).

136 Unmanned

UNMANNED   See MAN.

UNMOULTED   See MOULTED.

UNRECLAIMED   See RECLAIMED.

UNSEEL   See SEEL.

UNSUMMED   See FULL-SUMMED.

UNWASHED MEAT   See MEAT, Washed.

UPLAND GAME   ([?]N.Am. only) Certain gallinaceous birds taken with hawks.

URINES   See TRAPS AND TRAPPING.

URIVES; URVES   Perhaps misspellings of URINES, found under TRAPS AND TRAPPING.

UROPYGIAL GLAND   See PREEN GLAND.

VALKENSWAARD   See DUTCH HOOD under HOODS AND HOODING, BELL (n.), and MOLLEN.

VANE   See FEATHERS, Parts of a.

VARIOUS   See QUARRY LIST.

VARVELS (obs.) (Medieval Latin (Brit.–Ir.[48]) *varvella* = 'varvel', ring linking jess to leash. Alternative spellings: VERVELLS (1677), VERVELLES (1575), VERVAILES (1675), singular VERVEL (1686), others; all obs.) Small, usually flat washer-like rings (often of silver, even gold[47]), one attached to the free end of each jess. Another pattern is in the form of a very short tube. While the hawk is being carried, the LEASH is passed through the holes in both varvels and might be 'halved' and gripped in loops by the fingers of the fist, or it may be knotted to hold the varvels together, or the unbuttoned end threaded through a slit in the leather to bring about the same result.

> 'At the ende thereof [of the jesses] it shall not bee amisse to sette two Vervelles of Sylver, the one thereof maye have the armes of the King, or Queene whom you serve, and the other a Scutcheon of your owne armes. For as much as when they flee out, if they chaunce to be taken up, they may the sooner be returned againe and restored to their owners, the which must then remember to rewarde the taker up of his Hawke liberally.' – 1575[81].

'A Soare Faulcon with the Vervailes of Sir William Godbold of Gillingham.' – 1675[53].

Harting (1898[40]) notes:

> 'It was formerly the practice to use "varvels" instead of a swivel, and some falconers still prefer them for a goshawk. These are little flattened silver rings of the diameter of a threepenny piece, which are sewn

Silver varvels, c.1600. Left: Flat washer-like pattern, inscribed 'Couronell Huchinson'; outside diameter 12mm (Victoria and Albert Museum). Right: Tube type varvel, with (in this case) shield and crest, the ring inscribed 'Spensor'; outside diameter of ring 9mm (Victoria and Albert Museum). In both cases, the thickness of the metal is less than 1mm. Centre: Tube type, inscribed 'Sr Henry Lee K^t Baroñt', with his crest on the shield (from Illustrated Catalogue of the Heraldic Exhibition, Burlington House, *1894).*

How a varvel is knotted onto the free end of a jess.

on*, one at the end of each jess. They have this to recommend them, that they need not be removed, as a swivel must be, when the hawk is flown; the leash is easily slipped through them; and, being flat, the owner's name may be engraved on one side, his address on the other**, which is useful in case a hawk gets lost. On the other hand, if a hawk be tied on the perch with varvels on, it is apt to get the jesses twisted up tightly in turning round and round, whereas a swivel prevents this.'

*Varvels were also knotted onto the free ends of

the jesses, which were slit to accommodate them. **In the case of the tube pattern, inscriptions are found on the outer side.

In the 13th century, Emperor Frederick[35] writes of a pair of rings of iron, bronze or horn, one attached to the free end of each jess. To prevent the hawk flying away should she bate off the fist, his recommendation is that the free ends of the varvelled jesses be passed from the back of the fist between the two upper and two lower fingers into the palm, where they are gripped. This he appears to contradict later, describing what is the usual current SAFETY POSITION, achieved by passing the jesses down between thumb and fore-finger into the palm, and out towards the back of the fist between the two upper and two lower fingers. Also see notes in TYRRIT.

VARVELLED (obs.) Of a hawk (also of her jesses), furnished with VARVELS.

VENT The excretory opening in birds. The term is used currently by falconers; also, occasionally, it is applied to the general area round a hawk's vent. Also see BRAYLE 2, PANNEL, and TEWEL.

VERVEL Spelling of varvel; see VARVELS.

VERVELLS; VERVELLES; VERVAILES Spellings of VARVELS.

VIEW, Fly to the (Spelt 'flee to the vew'.) See FLY TO THE VIEW.

WAITING-ON (adj.) See next entry.

WAIT ON; HANG ON (obs.) Of a falcon, to circle at a high elevation (her PITCH) above the falconer, a POINT, or the place where quarry lies; she is then said to be waiting on. From this position, she will stoop at quarry flushed beneath her. Strictly, only falcons are said to wait on, although height may be involved in flights with certain other hawks. In the absence of an alternative, falconers today may use the term in the context of flying a broad-winged hawk, even an eagle, when a high soaring or waiting flight is involved. The idiom 'flying quarry from the soar' has been met with (inf.), used in the context of a waiting flight by a broad-winged hawk. 'Waiting-on' is sometimes used adjectivally with 'flight' and less commonly in such as 'a waiting-on falcon', '-peregrine', etc. Also see 1900 qu. in SOAR (vb).

WAKE See WATCH.

WAND See STROKING.

WARBEL Spelling of WARBLE.

WARBILE Spelling of WARBLE.

WARBLE (probably obs.); **WARBLE HER WINGS** (obs.) (Origin obscure. Among other obs. spellings: WARBEL (1486[5]), WARBILE.) Of a hawk, to execute a distinctive stretching movement in which she brings her wings up over her back until they almost touch and spreads her tail at the same time. 'Stretch' is probably used most commonly today. Berners (1486[5]) says:

'She warbbelyth when she drawith booth her wyngys over the myddys of her backe. and ther they mete both and softely shakyth them. and let hem fall ayen.'

And (ibid.):

'... Moost comynly she doth that [mantles*] affore or she warbelyth hir.'

'... Rousing** themselves, "mantling"* and "warbling" (crossing the wings over the back, after stretching the legs), as though they had escaped a prison.' – 1852[16].

*See MANTLE (vb 2).

**See ROUSE.

WARDER BUTCHER BIRD See SHRIKE.

WASHED MEAT See MEAT, Washed.

WATCH (obs.); **WAKE** (obs.) To keep (a recently taken hawk) awake, sometimes for a few nights and days at a stretch. The hawk is kept on the fist continuously, seeled or hooded at first or in a darkened room, the task often shared between the falconer and his assistant(s). Or she might be carried during the day, then set on a perch beside the falconer's bed at night and frequently roused. Her resistance is lowered through being deprived of sleep, and her manning hastened. Watching a hawk is actually 'breaking' her and is now considered inhumane.

> '... Wake her all nyght and the morow all day.' – 1486[5].

> '... One may safely say that a hawk which is waked well directly after it is captured will be reclaimed three or four times as soon as one which is not.' – 1900[59].

A hawk might be watched:

> 'First, let your hawke be taken on the fiste, and hoodded, then let hir be watched three dayes and nightes, before you unhoode hir, and feede hir alwayes hooded in an easie rufter hoode.' – 1575[81].

Historically, watching has been an acceptable and fundamental procedure in the reclamation of a hawk; it is now obsolete as such, although a contemporary falconer might favour protracted periods of non-stop manning (some hours at a stretch), and he might at first man a hawk in a dimly-lit room where her surroundings and the falconer himself appear less alarming.

WATER-HEN; WATERHEN See MOOR-HEN.

WEATHER Of a falconer, to allow (a hawk) to take the air outdoors; to put down (a hawk) unhooded on a perch outdoors. From 'The Fawkner's Glasse' in *A Perfect Booke* (c.1575[38]):

> 'Wether her morninge & nonetyme if you flye or call her.'

Also of the hawk herself, to be outdoors on her perch; she might 'weather on the lawn until mid-day'.

> 'He muste remember every evening to tye out his hawke a weathering ...' – 1575[81].

> '*Weathering* is when you set your *Hawke* abroad to take the aire, either by day or night, in the frost, or in the sunne, or at any other season.' – 1615 gl.[49]

> '*Weathering*, is when you air your *Hawk* in Frost, Sun, or by the Fire-side.' – 1677 gl.[25]

Barbary falcon and two hobbies by Archibald Thorburn

Obsolete 'pegging out' is met with occasionally, meaning setting down (a hawk) on a perch outdoors. Despite the idiom's form, the way the hawk is tethered is not necessarily a factor (that is, whether the leash is tied to a PEG in the ground or to the perch).

Michell (1900[59]) uses 'pegged out' under different circumstances. He writes of carrying with him a 'field block' (portable perch) while hunting with a falcon; in the field she (in this case, a merlin) will sit on it

> '... more comfortably than if merely pegged out on the prickly grass ...'.

According to this writer, a falconer might 'peg a hawk out at the block', or 'weather her at the block', and hawks might be 'at blocks on the lawn'; these idioms are obsolete. Today, a hawk might be put on her block (or perch), or put out on her block (or perch), or simply put down, and then be on her block (or perch), with hawks being on blocks (or perches). Also see GARDEN A HAWK.

WEATHERED (probably obs.) In a hawk, her state after having spent time on her perch in the open air. When she is wet following a treatment for 'lice, mites or other vermine', Turbervile (1575[81]) recommends:

> '... set hir by a fire, or in the Sunne, till she be throughly wetherd.'

WEATHERING See WEATHER.

WEATHERING GROUND ([?]recent) A place outdoors, usually providing some shelter, where hawks are put down unhooded on their perches (plate 41).

WEATHERING LAWN (recent) A place outdoors where hawks are put to WEATHER.

WEB (Spelt 'webbe' (1575[81]).) See FEATHER, Parts of a.

WEDDED TO Broadly, of a hawk, to have a consistent preference for. It is often applied in the context of an especially strong interest in and an eagerness to fly at a particular kind of quarry. It may also be applied in the context of a hawk having a strong preference for a routine, a mode of hunting, or a particular food. Or as Latham (1618[50]) notes:

> '... If wee will bestow on her [the falcon gentle] but one three weekes, or a moneths well luring and training with Doves* to cause her to love us, shee will be wholly wedded to us, and will not [fly] away.'

*Bagged or captive quarry; see TRAIN 2 (n.). Above application is obsolete. Lascelles (1892[47]) writes of a falcon being 'wedded to the lure'; see this writer's qu. in LURE-BOUND, found under LURE (n. and vb).

WEIGHING MACHINE; SCALES For weighing a hawk, conventional mechanical (plate 42) or electronic, modified to incorporate a perch. Weighing a hawk is thought by modern Western falconers to be indispensable, although her weight does not in itself determine her condition. More in CONDITION, High or low.

WEIGHT, Flying (recent) The weight at which a hawk flies best, or her mean weight which might be adjusted up or down when other factors are taken into account. It is not decided upon and then fixed but is a short-term value, constantly reviewed. See CONDITION, High or low.

WELL-HACKED See HACKING.

WELL-MANNED See MAN.

WETTING A HAWK The practice (now little if ever used in the West) of sprinkling or spraying a hawk with cold water to make her manageable if, for example, she persistently bates off the fist. Sebright (1826[75]) notes that, after wetting a hawk which will not stand to the hood,

'... he should be carried on the fist until he is dry, with his wing *brailed**, be stroked with a feather, and hooded and unhooded very frequently.'

*See BRAIL (vb). A method described in the 13th century by Emperor Frederick[35] (who suggests it also be used to cool a hawk while travelling in hot weather) is to squirt water from a well-rinsed mouth (plate 48). In a 19th century Persian treatise[68], wetting a hawk (in this case a passage saker on the third or fourth day of her manning) under her wings is advised, although its exact purpose is not explained; the translator's footnote says:

'Presumably as in India, water would be blown in a spray out of the mouth and with force, the falconer's hand [the fist] being raised and lowered to make the falcon expand her wings and expose the soft feathers underneath.'

According to Harting, writing in the late 19th century[40], squirting water from the mouth was still being practised by Dutch falconers in his time. He notes that

'This causes the feathers, by a sudden muscular contraction, to be pressed close to the body, and the bird then remains still for some little time.'

Also see 1855 qu. in HOOD-SHY, found under HOODS AND HOODING.

WHISTLE (the article)

'... A loud-toned whistle, either for recalling the Hawks, or communicating with an assistant at a distance.' – 1855[73].

A whistle (such as a shepherd's call or football referee's whistle) is used by some contemporary falconers for calling a hawk.

WHISTLE (vb) To call or call off (a hawk) by whistling. The phrase 'whistle a hawk' is correct.

WHISTLE OFF To call off (a hawk) by whistling, or to whistle in encouragement when slipping (her).

'When you have thus manned, reclaymed, and lewred your Falcon, go out with hir into the fieldes and whistle hir of your fyst, standing still to see what she will do, and whether she will rake out or not.' – 1575[81].

'... Where finding of a Mallard he whistled off his Faulcon...' – 1633[60].

Also see CALL 1.

WHITE HAWK See HAWK, White.

WHOTE; HOTE Spellings of HOT.

WHUR (obs.) (Apparently form of whirr.) According to Cox (1677 gl.[25]):

'*Whur*, is the rising and fluttering of Partridge or Pheasant.'

WHURRE (unv., obs.) (Or *the* whurre.) Perhaps the same as WHUR.

WILD-CAUGHT Of a hawk, taken from the wild. More specifically, according to Michell (1900[59]):

'Wild-caught is a more inclusive term [than passage*]; and it is often used in the case of sparrow-hawks, merlins, and hobbies, when casually caught by bird-catchers or gamekeepers, and not killed in the process.'

*As in passage hawk; see HAWK, Passage. Mavrogordato (1973[58]), writing on the sparrowhawk, applies wild-caught specifically to a hawk trapped before it has acquired its adult plumage.

WINDING UP See TRAPS AND TRAPPING.

WING-COVERTS See FEATHERS, Covert.

WING-FANNING See FANNING.

WINNOWING See FANNING.

WORK See DOGS IN HAWKING.

WRIST 1 Usually a lay or poetic form of FIST.

WRIST 2 The outer major joint of a hawk's wing; the CARPUS.

Y

YARAK (Perhaps from Persian *yaraki* = strength. An idiom apparently introduced into the English language of falconry in the 19th century.) The state in a short-winged hawk which is hungry, in flying condition and keen to hunt, when she is said to be in yarak. Compare SHARP SET. Of a goshawk in yarak:

> 'This happy condition may be known by the erect crest, eager look, and puffed-up plumage, together with the peculiar cry of hunger. If . . . it sits perfectly still upon the fist, moving only its head about, in watch for the expected game, there is little fear of the result.' – 1855[73].

An austringer might

> '. . . bring her into "yarak"; that is, into a state of eagerness for killing quarry.' – 1900[59].
>
> 'It requires about ten days to get this Hawk into '*yarak*'.' – 1855[73].

The idiom 'in screaming yarak' occurs in Michell (1900[59]). In the same text is 'out of yarak':

> 'Goshawks will thrive upon rats, weasels, squirrels, rooks, and, in short, almost any kind of bird or animal, except water-hens, which are indigestible and apt to bring them out of yarak.'

YMP(E) Obsolete spelling of IMP.

Saker falcon by Archibald Thorburn

A brefe Rule to keep a hawke by for him that hath knowledge.
    Tyringe after fedinge
    Water & wether at her nedinge
    After every gorge fastinge
    With twise a week castinge
    Makes her sounde & longe lastinge
Anon; from *A Perfect Booke for Kepinge of Sparhawkes or Goshawkes*, c.1575.

APPENDIX
Diseases and Ailments

It is not surprising that, before the era of modern veterinary medicine, falconers were much preoccupied with preserving the good health of their hawks and with ways of treating illness. In many old treatises, Western and Eastern, considerable space is devoted to methods of treating sick hawks, which from a modern perspective may often appear utterly bizarre or 'kill or cure'. It is of course impossible to know in how many cases patients recovered from illness as a result of treatment; but it can be said with some certainty that, for whatever reasons, large numbers of hawks met an untimely end.

This section restricts itself to long-recognized ailments with traditional names and some associated terms occurring in English-language texts. With those old terms which have survived into contemporary use, the definite article, once frequently present (in such as 'the blain'), is obsolete.

AGGRESTEYNE (obs.) Perhaps a kind of irritation of the skin in a hawk which induces self-mutilation. Berners (1486[5]) notes:
 'Whan ye se yowre hawke hurte his fete with his Beke. and pullyth her tayll*. then she hath the aggresteyne.'
*This means 'pull out her tail-feathers'.

AGRUM (obs.) (Cf. agrom = an affliction of the human tongue.) In Berners (1486[5]), there is
 'A medecyne for the Reume clepid [called] Agrum.'
This line (ibid.) describes the symptoms:
 'When thou seeth thy hauke upon his mouth and his chekis blobbed*. then she hath thys sekenes calde Agrum.'
*Apparently swollen or affected by swellings. The remedy here is to cauterize the nares (nostrils) with a hot needle.

ANGUILLE (obs.); **ANGUELLE** (obs.) (From Latin *anguilla* = an eel. Cf. Medieval Latin [Brit.–Ir.[48]] *anguillula* = little worm.) A worm which infests hawks.
 '... Wormys called anguilles ...' – c.1450[10].
In Berners (1486[5]), there is
 'A medecyne for wormys called anguellis.'

APOPLEXY See FIT (below).

ARTETIKE (obs.) An unidentified condition in hawks. Berners (1486[5]) notes the symptom thus:
 'When ye se yowre hawke fat abowte the hert trust it for trouth she hath the artetike.'
Note: OED has 'artetik' as an obsolete form of arthritic (Old French *artetique*).

ASMA See PANTAS (below).

BACK-WORM See FILANDERS (below).

BLAIN (Blain (lay) = blister.) A condition in the wings of captive hawks, long known to falconers and historically difficult to treat and cure. It appears as a fluid-filled blister at the wrist (the outer major joint or carpus). The first outward signs may be a drooping wing and damp feathers round the joint caused by the blister weeping. The cause is uncertain, although repeated striking of the wing on some hard object while bating has been suggested.

BLOW FOR LICE See c.1575 qu. in PEPPER (below).

BOTCHES (obs.); **BOOCHES** (obs.) (Berners (1486[5]) has both spellings.) Abscesses, swellings, etc. Berners (1486[5]) has a treatment
 'For booches that growe in an hawkis Jowe [jaw].'
This involves initially cutting them and letting out the matter.

BUMBLEFOOT; BUMBLE-FOOT (Apparently adopted from the foot complaint of the same name in domestic poultry.) A condition or conditions of the foot (rarely found in wild hawks) usually in the form of 'corns' or ulcerated lesions on the underside. Known contributing causes in falconers' hawks are unsuitable perching, injuries including piercing of the sole of the foot by an over-sharp talon (particularly that on a hind toe), and poor hygiene. Old treatments included simple home surgery to open the affected part and release any contents. The condition (but not the name) has long been known to falconers; obsolete names which probably describe the same condition are pinne in (or of) the foot, pin, and pinne. Phillott (1908 ft.[68]) notes:
 '"Podager" is said to be gout in the feet (from pod "a foot"), but the name was probably applied to the initial stage of the "pinne in the feet" of other writers.'
Turbervile (1575[81]), in his 'diseases and cures of Hawkes', uses the spellings pin, pinne and pynne, and appears to give a clue to the origin of the term:
 'The Pynne is a swelling disease, that doth resemble sharpe nayles, rysing up in the bottome or palme of the Hawkes foote ...';
this is probably what would now be called bumblefoot. The same writer has a chapter headed:
 'Of the swelling in a Hawkes foote, which we tearme the pin, or pin Goute.'
In this last instance, 'knubbes' (lumps) erupt on the foot, but Turbervile does not say where. Compare GOUT (below).

CAUTERIZING IRONS See next entry.

CAUTERY; CAUTERIZATION The searing of external tissue with a hot iron in the treatment of illness,

The booke of Falconrie.

Of the cauterising instruments and tooles, vvherevvith Falconers do seare their Havvkes in desperate cures, when nothing else vvill serue the turne but fire, the last refuge of all others.

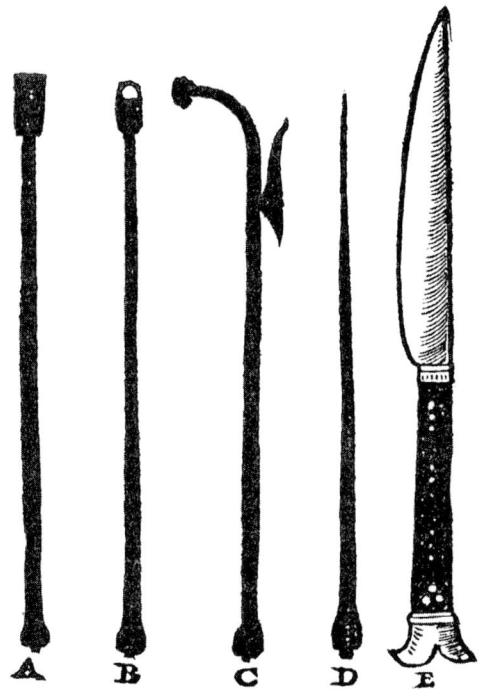

Hauing sundrie times in my collection of Falconrie, spoken of cauterie, to be bestowed vpon Hawkes, according to the diuersitie of their diseases and hurts, it shall be very needefull for me here in the later ende of my third booke, to set down the proportion and shape of the yrons, which are proper to ye matter, and maner of cure, being a very necessary thing for euery good Falconer to haue those yrons about him continually to serue his turne. Wherefore

A to D are cauterizing irons, shown in George Turbervile's treatise (1575). A: to cauterize the head; B: the nares (note the hole to help avoid the frelon); C: the head (the blade on the back is to 'cut the skin under the nares if need be'); D: to cauterize or enlarge the nares. E is a knife for other purposes.

once practised by falconers on their hawks. The pertinent chapter in Turbervile (1575[81]) is headed:

>'Of the cauterising instruments and tooles, wherewith Falconers do seare their Hawkes in desperate cures, when nothing else will serve the turne but fire, the last refuge of all others.'

In Cox (1677 gl.[25]),

>'*Cauterizing-Irons*, are Irons to sear with.'

CORN   A swelling or induration on a hawk's foot, usually on the underside. See BUMBLEFOOT (above).

CRAMP   (Perhaps also CROCK (obs.).) Historically, an untreatable disease of hawks, described as affecting (variously or inclusively) the muscles, joints, and bones. If heard today, the term may relate to osteodystrophy (bone disease resulting from mineral imbalance) in young hawks. In a sparrowhawk, according to Salvin & Brodrick (1855[73]), cramp

>'... paralyses the lower extremities without breaking the bones.'

And ibid.:

>'The wing-bones are the parts first affected in the young Peregrine ...'.

In Berners (1486[5]) 'croampe' in the wings appears to be different:

>'The Croampe commyth to an hawke with takyng of colode [cold] in hir yowthe. Therfore it is goode for an hawke to kepe hir warme: yonge and hoold [young and old]. ...';

the treatment (placing the wing between two halves of a warm loaf) might suggest a rheumatic or arthritic condition. Elsewhere, this writer offers

>'A medecyne for the crampe in the thigh in the legge and in the fote of an hawke.'

A symptom is described thus:

>'When ye se youre hauke lay hir oon fote uppo[n] her oder fote. she is take with the crampe.'

According to the text, the condition is treated by drawing blood from the affected foot and the leg. Latham (1618[50]) says that cramp, as well as RYE (below),

>'... followeth after the *Hawke* hath beene hard flone and laboured, especially in the winter time, in wet and drye, when as afterward they bee set up or downe to rest the night time, in some moist or dampe place, low, neere unto some earthen floore ...'; these conditions have '... oft times caused the *Crampe* to lay hold upon every joynt and limme of the whole body ...'.

CRAMPGOUT   See GOUT (below).

CRAY   A disorder affecting the lower bowel (or tewel) in which excrement is hard and difficult to pass; a type of constipation. In *A Perfect Booke* (c.1575[38]):

>'Craye is a stoppinge or drynes in the tewell so that she cannot mute, wch cometh by long contynued feding w^t stinkinge, olde, slymy or stryngy meates, as the strings in beefe & in rumpes of mutton wch are dylygently to be pycked oute, or elles if the hawke be lowe will stick in the tewell & stope her mutes.'

Latham (1618[50]) writes that 'craye' can occur as a result of cold, but is also

>'... taken by a continuance of grosse [(?)coarse, inferior, unwholesome] and cold washt meat that is given the Hawke to feede upon ...'.

Turbervile (1575[81]) writes of a form of the affliction which he calls 'stone Craye', named from the formation of what was perceived to be a stone in the tewel:

>'... When ye see that hir tuell is chafed, & but little droppes from hyr, and that the feathers of hir trayne are much filed [filled] with hir muting, and that she is evermore picking with hyr beake about hir tuell, be ye sure she hath ye stone in hir tuell, which we cal the stone Craye.'

Berners (1486[5]) may be referring to a similar complaint (not described) when she offers

>'A medecyne for an hauke that has the stoon.'

Elsewhere, this writer has a different treatment for 'The stoone in the fundement', a symptom of which is described thus:

>'When yowre hawke may not metese [mute] then she hathe thatt sekenes calde the stoon.'

CROAKS; KECKS (obs.) A disease or one of a variety of infections of the respiratory system in hawks, the signs of which (hence its echoic names) may include noisy or croaking breathing particularly after any exertion, and a change in the voice. The term croaks survives into modern usage and still implies any respiratory condition which displays the above symptoms. Compare PINNE IN THE THROAT (below).

CROAMPE   See CRAMP (above).

CROCK   See CRAMP (above).

CROP, Inflammation of the.   See INFLAMMATION OF THE CROP (below).

DRYING   (obs.) Dehydration.

>'Drynge cometh many wayes (and no disease so daungerous or comith so unawares upon them as this doth) vizt by to many castinges of lynnen or other after she is clene [taken to mean enseamed]; lack of water; abaytinge her fleshe to hastely in tymes of reclayminge and entering; by over muche batinge or flyinge in the heate; by to muche fedinge w^t unblody meates or by to muche fedinge w^t whote [hot = (in this case) rich] meates, as pygeons or swallowes contynually.' – c.1575[38].

In the same text is the recommendation to feed her marrow to 'moysten her'; fuller qu. in MARROW (below).

FALLERA   (obs.) A condition in hawks which causes the talons to become white.

>'When ye se that yowre hawkes clees [claws] wax white: then she has the fallera.' – 1486[5].

FALLING EVIL   See FIT (below).

FELLANDERS; FELLENDEN Forms of FILANDERS (below).

FILANDER Form of FILANDERS (next entry).

FILANDERS ([?]obs.) (Latin *filum* = a thread; Latin *filans* = thread-like. *Filaria* is a genus of parasitic worm. Alternative spellings and forms (all obs.): FILANDER (c.1680, unc.), FILLANDERS, FELLANDERS, FYLANDERS (1575[81]), FYLAUNDRES ('fylaundris' – 1486), also FELLENDEN (unv.).) Disease caused by intestinal worms, and (sometimes, in certain spellings) the worms themselves. According to Turbervile (1575[81]):

'These Filanders (as the very name doth import,) are smal as threedes, & one quarter of an ynche long, and more proper and peculiar to Falcons, than to any other hawke or fowle.'

This writer adds that the worms 'lye in the raynes [taken to be the same as reins (Latin *renes*) = kidneys]', and he offers a treatment. They may also, he notes, infest 'the guts, or pannell of a hawke', and are 'in their gorge', even in 'hawkes legges and thighes', and for these there are different treatments. In Berners (1486[5]) is

'A medecyne for wormys in an hawke wiche sekenesse is called the Fylaundris.'

In a c.1680 text[14], the affliction is described as

'... That obstinate Disease of the Filander or back-worm.'

In Blome (1686 [1929][9]), filander and back-worm are also given as synonymous.

FILLANDERS Spelling of FILANDERS (above).

FILM IN THE EYE See PINNE AND WEBBE (below).

FIT A broad term for any convulsion or seizure in a hawk. Apoplexy and the falling evil are terms used by the earlier writers.

FORMICA (obs.) (Latin *formica* = an ant. '... A sodayn bytyng as it were of an ante wherof it [the disease] hath hys name.' – 1543[80].) An ulcer, abscess or excrescence affecting a hawk's beak.

'This is a Distemper which commonly seizeth on the Horn of *Hawks* Beaks, which will eat the Beak away, and this is occasioned by a Worm, as most men are of opinion.' – 1677[25].

FROUNCE; FROWNCE (obs.) Long recognized by falconers, a disease of a hawk's mouth, later affecting the throat, respiratory tract and other organs. Turbervile (1575[81]) writes:

'The Frownce proceedeth of moyst & colde humors, which descend from the hawkes head to their palate, and yᵉ roote of yᵉ tongue.' Affected hawks '... loose their appetite, & cannot close their clap [lower beak], whereof they oftentimes dye: & that disease is named yᵉ Eagles bane. For ... the Eagle seldome when dyeth of age, but onely by meane hir beake doth overgrowe, so as she cannot feede & gorge hir selfe.'

In *A Perfect Booke* (c.1575[38]):

'Frounce is a canker or soore in the mouth growin of heate by to muche flying &c . . .'.

It is now known that the flesh of pigeon can harbour *Trichomonas gallinae*, the organism which causes the disease. To avoid any risk, falconers today may avoid using pigeon altogether, or freeze and thaw it before feeding. In Berners (1486[5]), other meats are said to be responsible:

'The frounce commyth whan a man fedith his hawke withe Porke or cattisflesh*.iiii.days to geyder [together].'

*Taken to be the flesh of cats, although 'cats-flesh' is also horse-meat, once sold as food for domestic cats. Elsewhere in this text is 'A medecyne for the dry Frounce' with no description of the disease. This writer's 'frounches' (obs.) are also dealt with separately; a medicine is prescribed

'For blaynis i haukes mouthes cald frounches*.'

*Taken to be the name for the 'blaynis' (blains, blisters, pustules) themselves rather than for the disease.

FROUNCE, Dry See preceding entry.

FROUNCHES See FROUNCE (above).

FROWNCE Obsolete spelling of FROUNCE (above).

FYLANDERS; FYLAUNDRES Spellings of FILANDERS (above).

GALBANUM (obs.) (Latin; also Anglicized to galbane.) A gum resin derived from certain species of umbelliferous plant, genus *Ferula*, especially *F.galbaniflua*. In *A Perfect Booke* (c.1575[38]), in a chapter dealing with 'Swellinge or Gowte', is this remedy:

'... To drawe ought any swellinge, take a lytle galbanum twise as much venice turpentine & a good quantytye of red or yellow wax: melt all theise & make a paster* therof, and bynde it fynely therto & change it every xxiiii owres.'

*Taken to be the same as or an error for plaister (dressing).

'It is regarded as an internal remedy in chronic mucous catarrh and rheumatism, and is applied externally in the form of a galbanum plaister as a mild stimulant to relieve tumours and chronic pulmonary affections.' – 1891 gl.[39]

GOUT (Also spelt GOWTE (obs.). PODAGRE and PODAGER (both obs.) are the same: Latin *podagra* = gout in the feet (of Man).) In simple terms, a condition (or conditions) brought about by the kidney's inability to excrete uric acid adequately. Uric acid crystals are deposited on body organs or in joints, causing, respectively, visceral and articular gout. The earlier writers were aware of different forms of gout, that is, one which affected the hawk's internal organs and one her joints. What is now known as articular gout is a disabling condition of the feet which falconers have recognized in their hawks for centuries. An unhelpfully broad diagnosis is in Berners (1486[5]):

'When yowre hawkes fete be swollyn she hath the podagre. . . .'.

According to Turbervile (1575[81]), gout is

'. . . none other thing than a hard tumor and swelling, full of corruption aboute the joyntes of a Hawkes foote and stretchers [toes], which disease is verie painefull and offensive, by meane whereof the Hawke cannot pray. Truly the Gowte is an incurable evill . . .'.

GOUT IN THE HEAD AND KIDNEYS (tentatively rendered from the spelling in the qu. below). Perhaps the same as visceral gout. According to Berners:

'When ye se yowre hawke may not endew [digest] her meete nor remou[n]te her astate*. she hath the gowte in the hede and in the Raynes§.'

*Perhaps 'regain her (former) condition'.

§Kidneys, or that region; the fact that the head and kidneys are anatomically distant makes the symptoms perplexing. A misunderstanding of another text is suspected.

GOUT IN THE THROAT. According to Berners:

'When ye se yowre hawke blaw [blow, pant] oftyn tymes: and that it commys of no batyng. ye may be sure she hath the gowte in the throte.'

CRAMPGOUT is mentioned by Turbervile but not elaborated upon beyond implying that, when suffering from it, the hawk has discomfort in her feet.

PIN GOUT. See BUMBLEFOOT (above).

GOWTE Obsolete spelling of GOUT (above).

HAWE (obs.) (Cf. haw = the nictitating membrane (third eyelid).) An affliction of a hawk's eye which, according to Turbervile (1575[81]),

'. . . commeth after the same manner that it commeth in horses: namely, sometyme by a blowe, or a stripe, sometyme by a disease in the heade, & moste commonly by hurting of the eye with the streyghtnesse of the hoode . . . And you shall discerne the comming of this disease, by seeing a little filme growing up from the bending of hir beake, and covering hir eye by little and little.'

HIPPOBOSCIDAE Under PARASITES, External (below).

INFLAMMATION OF THE CROP An old term, still in occasional use, for a condition (or a symptom of more than one condition) characterized by a hawk regurgitating the contents of her crop. Berners (1486[5]) offers

'A medicine for an hauke that castis hir flesh.'

And (ibid.) there is

'A Medecyne for hawkys that have payne in theyr croupes.'

Croupe is taken to be anatomically the same as crop, despite 'goorge' being used elsewhere in the text.

JESS SORE; JESS-SORE (probably both recent) A sore on a hawk's tarsus caused by chafing from an ill-fitting jess, or one made of unsuitable leather or which has dried out through insufficient greasing.

KECKS See CROAKS (above).

KIRNELLS (obs.) (Perhaps derives from the same source as kernel = (in one lay sense) a gland, a fatty mass, etc.) A disease only of short-winged hawks, according to Bert (1619[6]). This writer says:

'The kirnells beginne and breede under the eye, betweene the eye and chap*, outwardly appearing, and will very soone shew it selfe as bigge & long as the halfe of an ordinary Beane, and will soone grow greater and swell up the eye, and kill her if it be not prevented.'

*'Chap' here is taken to mean beak in the current sense rather than, as formerly, the lower part of the beak.

MAROW Obsolete spelling of MARROW (next entry).

MARROW (Obs. form: MARY (c.1575); obs. spelling: MAROW (1486).)

Bone marrow, once given to hawks for remedial or restorative purposes, or to envelope medicine. In *A Perfect Booke* (c.1575[38]), 'mary of beefe' is an ingredient in a scouring (purge) and 'mary of a goose' in a medicine for treating CRAY (above); and:

'. . . The mary in a partryche, chiken, or pygeon's wynge bone is veary good to moysten her, & make her lustye, beinge gyven w[t] her meate when she hath kylled.'

In the case of a hawk afflicted with RYE (below):

'. . . And ye yeve [if you give] yowre hawke fresh butter or the marow of hogges that is in the bone of the butte of porke. it shall make hir to cast water wele at the nares [nostrils]. and it will kepe the nares opyn. bot it will make hir hawtyn [(?)hautain, haughty] and prowde*.' – 1486[5].

*'Haughty and proud' taken to mean wild or less tame.

MARY Obsolete form of MARROW (above).

MEGRIM (obs.) (Cf. hemicrania = headache confined to one side of the head, and French *migraine*.) A condition in hawks, a symptom of which is the continual shaking of the head. Compare the megrims or vertigo in domestic pigeons, and the megrims or 'giddiness' in poultry.

MOMEY Form of MUMMY (below).

MOMYAN Form of MUMMY (below).

MUMMEY; MUMMIE Spellings of MUMMY (next entry).

MUMMY (obs.) (From Arabic *mumiya* = bitumen, or an embalmed body or mummy. Alternative spellings and forms: MOMYAN (1486[5]), MUMMIE, MUMMEY (c.1575), MOMEY; all obs.) A bituminous substance derived from mummies, once used medicinally by Man for himself and his animals; or less specifically, a sovereign (very effective) remedy. In *A Perfect Booke* (c.1575[38]), in a chapter on 'Swelling or Gowte', is this advice:

> '... Yf inwardly she be brosed [bruised], gyve her mummey or pyche [pitch] wt her meate.'
> 'He muste alwayes be assured to have mummy in powder in his bagge in a readinesse ... for that it may so fall out, as his hawke may receyve a broose at the encounter of a fowle.' – 1575[81].
> '*Mumiya*, "mummy," is a name in Eastern bazaars now applied to several forms of asphalte, mineral pitch, Jew's pitch, and maltha. Formerly the name was applied to Egyptian mummy; and by the vulgar at the present day this mysterious medicine is supposed to be the extract of negro-boy boiled in oil. "Mummy-oil" is made by mixing equal parts of mummy and clarified butter over the fire.' – 1908 ft.[68]

MUMMY-OIL See 1908 qu. in preceding entry.

NESYNG (unv., obs.) (Perhaps connected to archaic nese = nose.) Apparently sneezing. See 1486 qu. in REFREYNED (below).

PANTAIS Spelling of PANTAS (next entry).

PANTAS (obs.) (Apparently from Old French *pantoisier* = to pant. Alternative spellings: PANTAIS, PANTISE.) In the common understanding, a pulmonary disease in hawks. Writing of pantas, Turbervile (1575[81]) says:

> 'This mischeefe proceedes, when the lungs and those breathing members by excessive heate are overdried, and baked, in such sort, as they cannot by any meanes freely drawe the ayre to them ...';

this writer notes that the condition

> '... is commonly tearmed *Asma* [asthma].'

He also identifies 'Pantas of the gorge [probably crop, otherwise throat]', 'an other Pantas that commeth of colde', and 'Pantas that is in the reynes [(?)in this case, internal organs other than the kidneys] and kidneys'. Michell (1900[59]) believes that pantas is

> '... an old name given to a malady of the liver, when it becomes hot and dried up. The hawk is costive, and opens her beak often, as if gasping for more air.'

PANTISE Spelling of PANTAS (above).

PARASITES, External Among the antique methods of ridding a hawk of external parasites are sprinkling powdered sulphur at the bases of the feathers, fumigation with burning tobacco, and the wet application of a decoction of tobacco with brandy. In an admonition to irresponsible falconers, Latham (1615[49]) refers to tobacco for hawk husbandry in passing:

> 'And let me further advise all yong men, that eyther are, or would be Faulconers, that they doe not dedicate or dispose themselves awry to other exercises, or variety of pleasures: for if they doe, they shall never bee expert in this curious art of Faulconry: therefore they must be no Table or Card players, or other kinde of gamesters, they must be no excessive drinkers or Tobacco takers, but when their Hawkes be lowsie.'

A species of mite

> '... makes its first appearance in the nares [nostrils] of the Hawk, burrowing into these parts as also into the eyelids.' – 1855[73];

the advice here is:

> '... at the first appearance of any soreness about the nares or eyelids ... the parts be well washed out with a fine camel's-hair pencil dipped in a decoction of tobacco followed by the application of a small amount of the precipitate of mercury.'

Hippoboscidae are parasitic blood-sucking flies (deer flies, keds and louse flies[62], flat flies); one, sometimes known as the swallow fly, is found in the nests of swallows and others in the British Isles, as well as on hawks. Although similar at a glance to the house fly, it is flatter and is difficult to kill by crushing.

> 'I have known members of staff here*, strip off in front of the visitors if they spot a flat fly landing on them!' – 1995[64].

*The National Birds of Prey Centre, Gloucestershire.

> 'Swifts are much infested with those pests to the genus called *Hippoboscæ hirundinis*; and often wriggle and scratch themselves in their flight to get rid of that clinging annoyance.' – 1789 [1905][83].
> 'Young Merlins are always infested with a large flying parasite, similar to those upon swallows or young black game; these insects disappear soon after the young Hawks can fly.' – 1855[73].

In Berners (1486[5]), after the general subject of ridding the hawk of external parasites, is this note:

> 'After the opynyon of many Ostregiers: and ye fede yowre hawke contynually with Porke. with Jayes. with Pyes. Or especially bere hir moch in Rayeny weder. thay shall be lowse.' This might be paraphrased: 'In the opinion of many austringers, if you feed your hawk continually with pork, jays or magpies, or especially take her out often in rainy weather, she will be lousy [perhaps means affected with internal parasites].'

PEPPER (obs.) To apply powdered pepper to a hawk's feathers, or to wash a hawk with water and pepper, obsolete methods of ridding feathers of parasites. Bert (1619[6]) notes that in the latter method the pepper must be soaked in water then carefully strained so that no fragments of the seeds remain in her feathers, avoiding the danger of her swallowing them when she preens. In his chapter headed 'Of Hawkes that have lice, mites or other vermine', Turbervile (1575[81]) recommends that a dry mixture of powdered pepper and orpiment (yellow arsenic, trisulphide of arsenic) should be applied to the hawk's feathers; then:

> '... bespoute hir, and squirt a little water on hir with your mouth, and set hir by a fire, or in the Sunne, till she be throughly wetherd.'

A Perfect Booke (c.1575[38]) uses the obsolete phrase 'blow her for lyce'; the recommendation is

'. . . to blowe her w^t fyne pouder of pepper ought [out] of a quill when she is emptye* at nyght late, but furst hode [hood] her to save her eyes.'

*When she has put over her crop; see CROP, Put over the, in main *Encyclopedia*.

PIN   See BUMBLEFOOT (above).

PIN GOUT   See BUMBLEFOOT (above).

PINNE   See BUMBLEFOOT (above).

PINNE AND WEBBE (1575, obs.); **PYN & WEB** (c.1575, obs.) An affliction of the eye in hawks; a spot like a pinhead on the eye and a film over the eye's surface.

'Of the Filme in the eye, which some call the Veroll, or the Pinne and webbe.' – 1575 chap.hdg[81];

in the text, this writer notes that it

'. . . commeth sometimes of disease in the head, & of Rhewmes that distill into the eyes, and sometimes of standing too long, or too close hooded . . .'.

In *A Perfect Booke* (c.1575[38]), a chapter heading is 'Pyn & Web, or stroke.' The text says:

'Pyn or Web or other dymnes [dimness] by strokes* &c. must be spedely loked unto . . .'.

*'By strokes' is taken to mean caused by (the eye) being struck, scratched, or similar.

PINNE IN (or **OF**) **THE FOOT**   See BUMBLEFOOT (above).

PINNE IN THE THROAT (obs.) A disease of short-winged hawks, according to Bert (1619[6]); the pertinent chapter is headed:

'The Pinne in the throat a most desperate and uncurable disease, I have never heard of a long-winged hawke troubled therewith, but I have knowne many short-winged hawkes killed with it.'

In the text, this writer notes:

'This disease is plainely discovered, for upon any bate she wil heave & blow, and rattle in the throat.'

Harting, in his 1886 glossary appended to *A Perfect Booke*[38] (under the heading of PYN AND WEB), refers to Bert and ventures that

'. . . "pinne in the throat" . . . from his description resembles what modern falconers call "croaks".'

Compare CROAKS (above).

PIP (obs.) A disease of the mouth, throat and tongue in hawks.

'The Symptoms of this Distemper are the *Hawk's* frequent Sniting [sneezing], and making a noise twice or thrice in her Sniting.' – 1677[25].

Pip has long been associated with poultry.

PODAGRE; PODAGER   See GOUT (above).

POOSE (unv., obs.) A cough.

PRYNNE (obs.) An ailment affecting a hawk's eyes.

PYN & WEB   See PINNE AND WEBBE (above).

PYNNE   See BUMBLEFOOT (above).

REFREYNED (obs.); **REFRANED** (obs.) (Berners (1486[5]) has both spellings. Cf. obs. lay refreid = affected with a cold (OED).) A state or condition in a hawk which exhibits cold-like symptoms:

'When ye se yowre hawke Nesyng* and Castyng wat[er] thorogh her Nostrellis§ or hir nares then dowteles she is Refraned.' – 1486[5].

*Taken to be sneezing;
§nostrils and nares are the same.

REUME   See 1486 qu. in RYE (below).

RHEUM (obs.) (Other spellings.) An old term for a discharge of moisture, mucus etc., also for a cold.

RY   Spelling of RYE (next entry).

RYE (obs.); **RY** (1486[5], obs.) Latham (1618[50]) has 'Rye or stuffing in the head'. A condition showing itself by a swelling of the hawk's head; Cooper (1985[22]) suggests sinusitis as a possible modern equivalent. Historically, perceived causes vary from blocked nares (nostrils), preventing the escape of corruption in the head (1614[57]), to poor diet.

'Rye is a stuffinge or swellinge of the heade growinge by colde or evell dyet. When she hath it her heade wilbe bygg, & she will shake it ofte . . .' – c.1575[38].

The following Berners (1486[5]) passage perhaps describes the same condition:

'When ye se yowre hauke cloose her Eyghen [eyes]. and shakith hir hede. then hath she the Reume* in the hede.'

*Taken to be the same as RHEUM (above), which is (in one sense) a cold.

SNURT (obs.) Formerly often described as a cold or a cold in the head; Cooper (1985[22]) suggests rhinitis as a possible modern equivalent. Symptoms are nasal discharge and sneezing. Obsolete verb snurt means (of a hawk) to sneeze.

SOUR CROP, Having a   An old term still in occasional use: of a hawk in ill-health, unable to put over the contents of her crop, which begin to putrefy. Without intervention, the result is toxaemia and death. See CROP, Put over the, in main *Encyclopedia*.

SPRAIN   See STRAIN (below).

STONE; STONE IN THE FUNDAMENT   See 1486 qus in CRAY (above).

STONE CRAY   See 1575 qu. in CRAY (above).

STOON   See 1486 qus in CRAY (above).

STRAIN (unv., obs.); **SPRAIN** (unv., obs.) An affliction (so far unidentified) affecting the feet and legs of hawks; perhaps simply an injury sustained during a tussle with quarry.

STUFFING IN THE HEAD   See RYE (above).

TEYNE (Obs.) A respiratory disease in hawks, when, according to Berners (1486[5]),

'She will pante more for oon batyng then an other [hawk] for.iiii.& if she shulde flie a littyll wile she shuld almost lese hir breth. whether she be fatte or lene. and alway she makyth hevy chere. . . .'.

TEYNTE See FRET MARKS in main *Encyclopedia*.

TOBACCO See PARASITES, External (above).

VEROLL (obs.) According to Turbervile (1575[81]), the same as PINNE AND WEBBE (above).

VERTEGO (obs.) (Form of 'vertigo'.) A condition in hawks which causes giddiness; apparently a nervous disorder. The symptoms are described by Bert (1619[6]) as 'a swimming of the braine'.

Source List and Further Reading

1   AL-TIMIMI, Faris. *Falcons and Falconry in Qatar.* 1987.
2   BAILEY, Nathan. *Dictionary.* 1736.
3   BEEBE, F.L., and WEBSTER, H.M. *North American Falconry and Hunting Hawks.* Denver, 1964, 1994.
4   BEEBE, Frank L. *Hawks, Falcons & Falconry.* Hancock House Publishers Ltd, 1976.
5   BERNERS, Dame Juliana (Juliana Barnes, other forms. Attributed to). *The Boke of St Albans containing the Treatises of Hawking, Hunting and Coat-Armour.* First published 1486; various subsequent editions and facsimile reprints. Facsimiles include Elliot Stock, London, 1881; introductory chapters by William Blades. Also see HANDS, Rachel (below).
6   BERT, Edmund. *An Approved Treatise of Hawkes and Hawking.* London, 1619; Quaritch (limited edition of 100), 1891; facsimile reprint, Thames Valley Press, 1972.
7   BEWICK, Thomas. *The History of British Birds.* 1797–1804 [1847].
8   BLAINE, Gilbert. *Falconry.* Philip Allen, 1936; Neville Spearman, 1970.
9   BLOME, Richard. *Hawking or Faulconry.* The Cresset Press, 1929 (first published as part of *The Gentleman's Recreation*, 1686).
10   BOOKE OF HAWKYNG, The. In *Reliquiæ Antiquæ*. Scraps from ancient MSS. Editors T.Wright and J.O.Halliwell, 1841–43.
11   BOURCHIER, John, Lord Berners. *Cronycles of Englande, Fraunce* . . . 1525.
12   BOYLE, Sir Richard. *Lismore Papers.* 1613.
    BROWN, Leslie. *Birds of Prey: their Biology and Ecology.* Hamlyn, 1976.
13   BROWN, Leslie, and AMADON, Dean. *Eagles, Hawks and Falcons of the World.* Country Life Books, 1968.
14   BROWNE, Sir Thomas. *Certain Miscellany Tracts.* Circa 1680.
    BURTON, John A. (editor). *Owls of the World.* Peter Lowe, 1984.
15   BURTON, R. *The English Empire in America.* 1685.
16   BURTON, Richard F. *Falconry in the Valley of the Indus.* John van Voorst, London, 1852; reprint, 1971.
17   CADE, Tom J. *The Falcons of the World.* Collins, 1982.
18   CAXTON, William. *The Golden Legende.* 1483.
19   CENTURY DICTIONARY. *An Encyclopedic Lexicon of the English Language.* 1889–91.
    CERELY, Stanley. *The Gyr Falcon Adventure.* Collins, 1955.
20   CHAMBERS, Ephraim. *Cyclopædia; or an Universal Dictionary of Arts and Sciences.* 1728–1751.
21   Supplement to preceding, 1753.
22   COOPER, J.E. *Veterinary Aspects of Captive Birds of Prey.* The Standfast Press, 1985.
    COOPER, J.E., & GREENWOOD, A.G. (editors). *Recent Advances in the Study of Raptor Diseases.* Chiron Publications Ltd, 1981.
23   COTGRAVE, Randle. *A Dictionarie of the French and English Tongues.* 1611.
24   COX, John. *Observations on Falconry and Pakistan.* 1985.
25   COX, Nicholas. *The Gentleman's Recreation: In Four Parts, viz. Hunting, Hawking, Fowling, Fishing.* 1677 (first published 1674).
    CUDDON, J.A. *The Macmillan Dictionary of Sport and Games.* Macmillan Press Ltd, 1980.
26   CUMMINS, John. *The Hound and the Hawk; the Art of Medieval Hunting.* Weidenfeld and Nicolson, 1988.
    D'ARCUSSIA, Charles. *Fauconnerie.* 1605.
27   DARWIN, Charles. *On the Origin of Species.* First published 1859.
28   DE ALAGONA, Arthelouche. *La Fauconnerie de Messire Arthelouche de Alagona.* 1531.
    DE CHAMERLAT, Christian Antoine. *Falconry and Art.* Sotheby's Publications, 1987.
29   DE NOIRMONT, Baron. *Histoire de la Chasse en France* . . . 1867–8.
30   DYCHE and PARDON. *New General English Dictionary.* Second edition, 1757.
31   ELYOT, Sir Thomas. *The Boke Named the Governor.* London, 1531.
    ENCYCLOPEDIA AMERICANA, The. Grolier Inc., 1990.
32   ENCYCLOPÆDIA OF SPORT. 1897–8.
    FIENNES, Richard and Alice. *The Natural History of the Dog.* Weidenfeld and Nicolson, 1968.
    FITTER, Richard. *The Penguin Dictionary of British Natural History.* Allen Lane (Penguin Books), 1978 (first edition 1967).
    FORD, Emma. *Falconry in Mews and Field.* B.T.Batsford Ltd, 1982.
33   FORD, Emma. *Falconry: Art and Practice.* Blandford, 1992 (revised 1998).
34   FOX, Nick. *Understanding the Bird of Prey.* Hancock House, 1995.
35   FREDERICK II, Emperor. *The Art of Falconry, being the De Arte Venandi cum Avibus of Frederick II of Hohenstaufen.* Circa 1244–1250 MS, translated into English from Medieval Latin and edited by Casey A.Wood & F.Marjorie Fyfe. Stanford University Press, California, 1969 (first edition 1943).
    FREEMAN, Gage Earle, and SALVIN, Francis Henry. *Falconry, Its Claims, History, and Practice.* Longman, Green, Longman, and Roberts, 1859.
36   GLASIER, Phillip. *Falconry and Hawking.* B.T.Batsford Ltd, 1986 (first published 1978).

GOTCH, A.F. *Birds – Their Latin Names Explained.* Blandford Press, 1995.

GREENOAK, Francesca. *All the Birds of the Air. The names, lore and literature of British Birds.* Penguin Books, 1981.

37 HANDS, Rachel. *English Hawking and Hunting in The Boke of St Albans.* Contains a facsimile of the hawking section of the 1486 edition of *The Boke of St Albans.* Oxford University Press, 1975.

HARCOURT, E.S. See SAHABZADAH YAR MUHAMMAD KHAN (below).

38 HARTING, James Edmund. *A Perfect Booke for Kepinge of Sparhawkes or Goshawkes.* Circa 1575 MS transcribed and with introduction and glossary by Harting. Quaritch, London, 1886. Facsimile reprint, Thames Valley Press, 1972.

39 HARTING, James Edmund. *Bibliotheca Accipitraria. A Catalogue of Books Ancient & Modern relating to Falconry.* With glossary of terms. Bernard Quaritch, 1891 (reprinted by The Holland Press, 1964).

40 HARTING, James Edmund. *Hints on the Management of Hawks* to which is added *Practical Falconry, Chapters Historical and Descriptive.* London, Horace Cox, "The Field" Office, 1898 (reprinted by Saiga Publishing, 1981).

HARTING, James Edmund. *A Handbook of British Birds.* New and revised edition, London, 1901.

41 HARTLEY, Ron. Article *Falconry in Zimbabwe.* North American Falconers' Association Journal, vol.22, 1983.

42 HETT, Chas. Louis. *A Glossary of Popular, Local and Old-Fashioned Names of British Birds.* Henry Sotheran & Co., London, 1902.

43 HOLME, Randle. *The Academy of Armory, or a Storehouse of Armory & Blazon.* 1688.

44 HORMAN, William. *Vulgaria.* 1519.

JACKSON, Christine E. *British Names of Birds.* Witherby, 1968.

ILLUSTRATED CATALOGUE of the Heraldic Exhibition, Burlington House. 1894.

45 JAMESON, E.W., Jr. *The Hawking of Japan; the History and Development of Japanese Falconry.* Davis, California, 1962 (reprinted 1972).

46 JONSON, Ben. *The Divell is an Asse.* 1616.

47 LASCELLES, The Hon. Gerald. *Falconry* (from *Coursing and Falconry*). Longmans, Green & Co., the Badminton Library, 1892 (also in large paper, limited to 250 copies. Facsimile reprint, Ashford Press Publishing, 1986).

48 LATHAM, R.E. (prepared by). *Revised Medieval Latin Word-List from British and Irish Sources.* Oxford University Press (for The British Academy), 1994 (first published 1965).

49 LATHAM, Symon. *Lathams Falconry or the Faulcons Lure, and Cure.* London, 1615.

50 LATHAM, Symon. *Lathams New and Second Booke of Faulconry.* London, 1618. This and the preceding title are usually found bound together. Reprinted as one in facsimile, Theatrum Orbis Terrarum Ltd, Amsterdam, and Walter J. Johnson Inc., New Jersey, 1976.

51 LEONI, John. *The Architecture of L.B.Alberti.* 1726.

52 LINNEAN SOCIETY. Transactions. 1823.

53 LONDON GAZETTE. 1675/77/79.

54 LYTE, Henry. *Niewe Herball or Historie of Plantes.* 1578.

55 MACMILLAN'S MAGAZINE. 1881.

56 MACTAGGART, John. *The Scottish Gallovidian Encyclopedia.* 1824.

57 MARKHAM, Gervase. *Cheape and Good Husbandry for the well-ordering of all Beastes and Fowles . . .* London, 1614.

58 MAVROGORDATO, Jack. *A Hawk for the Bush.* Neville Spearman Ltd, 1973 (revised and updated edition. Reprinted, The C.W.Daniel Company, 1985. First published 1960).

59 MICHELL, E.B. *The Art and Practice of Hawking.* London, 1900.

MIKKOLA, Heimo. *Owls of Europe.* T.& A.D.Poyser, 1983.

60 NASH, Thomas. *Quaternio, or the fourefold Way to a happie Life . . .* London, 1633.

61 OSBORNE, Francis. *Works.* 1673 (other dates).

62 O'TOOLE, Christopher (editor). *The Encyclopedia of Insects.* Andromeda Oxford Ltd, 1995.

OXFORD ENGLISH DICTIONARY, The. Oxford University Press, second edition, 1989.

63 PAGE, William (editor). *Victoria History of the Counties of England: Hertfordshire.* Archibald Constable & Co. Ltd, 1902.

64 PARRY-JONES, Jemima. *Falconry: Care, Captive Breeding and Conservation.* David & Charles, 1995 (revised edition; first published 1988).

65 PARRY-JONES, Jemima. *Training Birds of Prey.* David & Charles, 1994.

PARRY-JONES, Jemima. *Understanding Owls.* David & Charles, 1998.

66 PEETERS, Hans J., and JAMESON, E.W., Jr. *American Hawking. A General Account of Falconry in the New World.* Davis, California, 1970.

PERFECT BOOKE FOR KEPINGE OF SPARHAWKES OR GOSHAWKES, A. See HARTING, James Edmund (above).

67 PHILLIPS, Edward. *The New World of English Words; or, a General Dictionary.* Various editions (first published [?]1658).

68 PHILLOTT, Lieut.-Colonel D.C. (translator). *The Baz-nama-yi Nasiri, a Persian Treatise on Falconry* [by Taymur Mirza, fl. mid-19th C.]. English translation. Quaritch, 1908.

69 PITKIN PICTORIALS. *The Royal Mews, Buckingham Palace.* 1994.

70 RADCLIFFE, Lieut-Col.E.Delmé. *Falconry. Notes*

on the Falconidæ Used in India in Falconry. First published, Kent & Co., 1871; facsimile reprint by The Standfast Press, 1971.
71 **RAY, John**. Translation of *Willughby's Ornithology*. 1678.
72 **SAHABZADAH YAR MUHAMMAD KHAN**. *Said Gah-i-shaukati, an Urdu treatise on Falconry in the East*. Translated by Lt.-Colonel E.S.Harcourt, edited by Humphrey ap Evans. Quaritch, 1968.
73 **SALVIN, Francis Henry**, and **BRODRICK, William**. *Falconry in the British Isles*. John van Voorst, Paternoster Row, 1855 (second edition, revised and enlarged, John van Voorst, 1873; facsimile reprints, Thames Valley Press, 1971, and Windward, 1980).
74 **SCHLEGEL, Hermann**, and **DE WULVERHORST, A.H.Verster**. *Traité de Fauconnerie*. 1844–1853. In French (with English translation by Thomas J.Hanlon), Chasse Publications, Denver, 1973.
75 **SEBRIGHT, Sir John**. *Observations upon Hawking*. London, 1826 (facsimile reprint limited to 500 copies, Thames Valley Press, 1973).
76 **STONEHENGE** (pseudonym of J.Walsh, an editor of *The Field*). *Manual of British Rural Sports*. G.Routledge & Co., 1856.
77 **STRUTT, Joseph**. *The Sports and Pastimes of the English People: including the Rural and Domestic Recreations . . . from the earliest period to the present time*. London, 1801.
78 **SURFLET, Richard**. *Maison Rustique, or the Countrie Farm*. 1616 (first published c.1588).
 SWAINSON, Rev. Charles. *Provincial Names and Folk Lore of British Birds*. Published for the English Dialect Society by Trübner and Co., 1885.

79 **SWANN, H.Kirke**. *A Dictionary of English and Folk-Names of British Birds*. Witherby, 1913.
 TAYMUR MIRZA. See PHILLOTT, Lieut.-Colonel D.C. (above).
80 **TRAHERON, Bartholomew**. Translation of *The Most Excellent Works of Chirurgerye* [surgery] *made by J.Vigon*. 1543.
81 **TURBERVILE, George**. *The Booke of Faulconrie or Hauking, for the onely delight and pleasure of all Noblemen and Gentlemen . . .* London, 1575 (facsimile reprint, Da Capo Press, New York, and Theatrum Orbis Terrarum Ltd, Amsterdam, 1969).
 UPTON, Roger. *A Bird in the Hand*. Debretts Peerage Ltd, 1980.
82 **UPTON, Roger**. *O For a Falconer's Voice*. The Crowood Press, 1987.
 WALSH, J. See STONEHENGE (above).
 WEICK, Friedhelm. *Birds of Prey of the World*. Collins, 1980.
83 **WHITE, Rev. Gilbert**. *The Natural History of Selborne* [rearranged]. Elliot Stock, 1905 (first published 1789).
 WILDLIFE AND COUNTRYSIDE ACT 1981. London, HMSO.
 WILDLIFE AND COUNTRYSIDE (**Amendment**) **ACT 1991**. London, HMSO.
 WOOD & FYFE. See FREDERICK II, Emperor (above).
84 **WOODFORD, M.H**. *A Manual of Falconry*. A.& C.Black, 1987 (first published 1960).
85 **WORLIDGE, John**. *Kalendarium Rusticum and Dictionarium*. 1675.